Texas Ranger Lee Hall

Texas Ranger Lee Hall

From the Red River to the Rio Grande

Chuck Parsons

UNT Press
Denton, Texas

10 9 8 7 6 5 4 3 2 1

Permissions:
University of North Texas Press
1155 Union Circle #311336
Denton, TX 76203-5017

The paper used in this book meets the minimum requirements of the American National Standard for Permanence of Paper for Printed Library Materials, z39.48.1984. Binding materials have been chosen for durability.

Library of Congress Cataloging-in-Publication Data

Names: Parsons, Chuck, author.
Title: Texas Ranger Lee Hall : From the Red River to the Rio Grande / Chuck Parsons.
Description: Denton, Texas : University of North Texas Press, [2020] | Includes bibliographical references and index. | Summary: "Book is a biography of Texas Ranger Lee Hall, born in North Carolina in 1849 and died in Texas in 1911. His career ranged all over Texas"-- Provided by publisher.
Identifiers: LCCN 2019044483 | ISBN 9781574417906 (cloth) | ISBN 9781574417999 (ebook)
Subjects: LCSH: Hall, Jesse Lee, 1849-1911. | Texas Rangers--Biography. | Peace officers--Texas--Biography. | Frontier and pioneer life--Texas. | LCGFT: Biographies.
Classification: LCC F391 .P265 2020 | DDC 363.209764 [B]--dc23
LC record available at https://lccn.loc.gov/2019044483

The electronic edition of this book was made possible by the support of the Vick Family Foundation.

Lee Hall is ". . . a man of daring and almost reckless courage, of fine physique and resistless energy, and was thus well fitted to command a body of men intended for peculiarly arduous service against ruthless and cruel Mexican cut-throats, as well as against many desperate criminals of his own race congregated in that section of the State."
—Adjutant General W.H. King. "The Texas Ranger Service and History of the Rangers, with Observations on their value as a police protection."

Table of Contents

List of Illustrations

Preface and Acknowledgments

The topic of Texas Rangers has long been a passion of mine, especially those of the Frontier Battalion period, the 1870s and 1880s. Relentlessly searching the rangers led to a fascination with the "bad guys" they chased; thus my passion and fascination resulted in biographies of those brave men, Charles Brown McKinney, Leander Harvey McNelly, John Reynolds Hughes, John Barklay Armstrong, and ultimately Jesse Lee Hall. Not so strangely, each of those rangers had some association with John Wesley Hardin, another individual who has long held a fascination for me. When I decided to bring Lee Hall "up to date," I had a plan which— if carried out— would provide Wild West fans with an updated biography of "Red" Hall. After all, the only biography on this ranger was written by Dora Neill Raymond and published in 1940 by the University of Oklahoma Press. Granted, it was reprinted in 1982, but not a word was changed. In 2018 Darren L. Ivey provided a chapter on Hall in his impressive three volume series, *The Ranger Ideal: Texas Rangers in the Hall of Fame*, a biography that was based on Raymond's work but also provided a great amount of additional material.

Originally our grand plan to provide an exhaustive biography of Hall was to locate all the source materials that Raymond and Ivey had used plus discover new material that they had somehow missed. Well, not surprisingly the plan quickly disintegrated as many of the sources Raymond had access to are now apparently unobtainable. We never found the "papers" of Mrs. Isham Keith, Hall's eldest daughter, which helped Raymond. But we did discover some new material about characters whom Lee Hall had dealings with, so the following biography is by no means just a rehash of old material.

Another grand idea that had to be shelved was to travel to all the places Hall lived for "grass roots" research, intending to walk on the same ground Hall had walked upon and visit the cemetery where his parents are buried in North Carolina. Explore Sherman and Denison where he first worked as a law officer, and wander over the Indian Territory in which he had served as an Indian Agent. Then there was the Spanish-American War and the Philippine Insurrection. Although Hall and his "Immunes" never got to Cuba (he had intended to be mustered into Roosevelt's "Rough Riders" but was not), we had at one point believed that a visit to Cuba would not be unreasonable. But then Hall was shipped to the Philippines to battle with Aguinaldo during the Philippine Insurrection . . . would a visit to Manila be out of the question? Apparently it was not destined to be, as my "grass roots" research never allowed us out of Texas.

Nevertheless researching the life and career of Lee Hall has been a rewarding experience, making new friends and renewing acquaintances with "old ones" and always learning new information about Texas history as well as that of the United States. We tried to keep track of all those who shared our interest and helped with the research. Hopefully we have not missed anyone; a great thank you is due the following and if we did miss someone our apologies.

Elise Allison, Archivist, Greensboro History Museum, Greensboro, NC; Bob Boze Bell, Executive Editor of *True West* magazine, Cave Creek, AZ; Melleta Bell, Archivist, Sul Ross University, Alpine, TX; Thomas C.

Bicknell, Pensacola, FL; Donaly E. Brice, Lockhart, TX, Senior Reference Archivist, Texas State Archives, retired; Norman Wayne Brown, Independent Historian, Snyder, TX; Jack Caffall, Luling, TX; Tom Caffall, Luling, TX; Jack DeMattos, North Attleboro, MA; Ryan Donnelly, Indianapolis, IN; Tiffany M. Haggard Fink, Houston, TX; Jack Freyer, Victoria, TX; Charles David Grear, New Braunfels, TX; Kurt House, San Antonio, TX; Darren L. Ivey, Manhattan, KS; Dave Johnson, Indianapolis, IN; Roger Kaland, Sun Prairie, WI; Richard E. Lucy, Hermosa Beach, CA; John H. Luckey, Whitehouse, TX; Mike Miller, Director Austin History Center, Austin, TX; Rick Miller, Belton, TX; William Mills, Perry, GA; Jim Mundie, Kenner, LA; Shelley Parks, Goliad Center for Texas History, Goliad, TX; Norman Porter Jr., Pleasanton, TX; Bertha Priddy, Goliad, TX; Ron Priddy, Goliad, TX; The Priddys, Bertha and her son Ron, own the property on which is found the Buzzard Roost Cemetery, now nearly destroyed, but one of the graves is that of John Middleton, victim of Fatheree and Jacobs who entered into the Hall story; Nancy Samuelson, Sacramento, CA; Rick Selcer, Fort Worth, TX; Larry Shaver, Roanoke, VA; Paul N. Spellman, Richmond, TX; Tom Todd, Show Low, AZ; Nora Mae Tyler, Brush Country Museum, Cotulla, TX; Sergio Velasco, Texas State Archives, Austin, TX; Elizabeth "Bess" Whitby, Marketing Manager, University of North Texas Press; Tonia J. Wood, Senior Reference Archivist, Texas State Archives, Austin, TX.

And especially we thank Ron Chrisman, Director of the University of North Texas Press and his editor-in-chief Karen DeVinney who has done such incredible editorial work in making an average manuscript into a winning one.

Illustration 1. Texas Ranger Bicentennial Logo

Texas Ranger Lee Hall

Chapter One

"Lee went to Texas in search of adventure"

—N.A. Jennings, *Charlotte Observer*, January 28, 1900

It was dark behind the counters in that country store in southern Atascosa County, Texas, with the shadows of a late November night closing in. Texas Ranger Captain Lee Hall and his two men had only that day learned that suspicious-looking characters had been hanging around Campbell's store. Hall believed they intended to rob it later that night and devised a plan to capture them in the act, if indeed that was their intent. Store keeper John Campbell was grateful for their presence as he realized he was no match for them without the rangers. So in the darkness they waited.

Sure enough, late that night, the fourth of November 1879, Lee Hall and two of his men waited in the store. In addition there was store clerk John M. Kemper, store proprietor John Campbell, citizen Dave Young and a couple of other concerned citizens who were more than willing to help fight off any would-be robbers. They all waited silently and listened.

Finally they heard the sound of horses approaching. There were five of them. The waiting was soon to bring results.

The bandits entered and believing the store empty they made no effort to move silently. Although surprised that clerk Kemper was there, they quickly subdued him with no effort. They then went about ransacking the store. Only then did Hall stand up from his concealment and shouted for them to surrender. Surprised, the robbers instantly drew their revolvers, but Hall and his men, already with weapons drawn, began the firefight. The flashes of the pistols lit up the room momentarily as gunsmoke filled the air. Those flames and smoke from the robbers' pistols were answered with shots from the rangers and citizens. In less than a minute the gunfight was over. Hall ordered a tentative ceasefire, believing the robbers could no longer resist. The action had ended.

Hall found Charles Westerman, one of the concerned citizens, sprawled on the floor badly wounded, but alive. Crumpled up near him was a Mexican outlaw identified as Louis Varejal— shot to death. Another thief known as John Smith or John Alexander, was gasping his last breaths. Another bandit, Archie Huir (or Hare), was badly wounded but would survive. The other two thieves had somehow managed to escape in the darkness and confusion. They had ridden stolen horses to the store and were now in flight, abandoning their luckless companions. Equally dashed were their hopes of enjoying stolen loot, thanks to Captain Lee Hall.

***

This was certainly not the first gunfight Jesse Lee Hall had experienced in his thirty years. He was born October 9, 1849, in Davidson County, North Carolina, the son of physician James King Hall and Francis Mebane Rankin Hall.[1] If at this juncture of his life he recalled his youth, growing up in an area of the country over a thousand miles back east, he fully understood how different the Lone Star State was from his boyhood home. Just as Texas had its 1836 revolutionary heroes, so did North Carolina. In 1781 Generals Cornwallis and Greene battled there, ultimately forcing the British to surrender at Yorktown, thus ending the American Revolution.

County seat Greensboro (sometimes spelled Greensborough) was situated in the Piedmont Region of Central North Carolina. It was so different there— the gently rolling land, frequently broken up by hills and valleys formed by the many rivers and streams. But here in hot Texas the ground was often arid and cracked from the heat.

Dr. James King Hall had wisely used his profession and lifestyle to become one of the most successful men in that North Carolina area. The physician was indeed a community leader, successful enough to be ranked among the wealthiest men in the county. Then as today it pays to advertise and Dr. Hall was no exception. During the late 1850s he placed the following advertisement in the local newspaper, the *Greensborough Patriot*: "Dr. James K. Hall, having removed to Greensborough, N.C., offers his Professional Services to the public. Office on West Market Street, in the house recently occupied as a residence by Hon. John A. Gilmer. February, 1858."[2] For those who may have read this notice but knew nothing about him, in 1860 he was a forty-three-year-old physician and financially well off. The census record shows his real estate valued at $4,500 and his personal estate at an amazing $22,000. But there was more than medicine and monetary wealth for Dr. Hall. Sometime during the decade of the '40s he met, fell in love, and courted a Miss Francis Mebane Rankin, the daughter of Rev. Jesse Rankin and Polly Paisley Rankin.[3] Although she was ten years his junior, born November 19, 1826, she became— on January 2, 1849— Mrs. J.K. Hall. The marriage record shows both were natives of Davidson County, North Carolina. C.F. Lowe joined the two in holy matrimony; Alfred G. Foster, according to the record, was the only witness.[4] The Halls' first child, and the first of five sons, was born on October 9 of that year. The first official record showing the existence of the future Texas Ranger is that of the 1850 North Carolina census. Enumerator T.L. Tucker recorded that Dr. King was thirty-three, his wife but twenty-three and Jesse L. a mere seven months of age.[5]

There has been a question as to whether the boy's middle name was "Lee" or "Leigh." Biographer Dora Neill Raymond explained that although he signed his name "Leigh Hall" people pronounced it as "Lay Hall" which was confusing. Thus the middle name was "Texanized" to the more common "Lee," which remained with him through the years.[6] Additional verification that he himself changed his middle name is from the *Paris News* editor who wrote a regular column entitled "Backward Glances." In the June 8, 1943, issue editor A.W. Neville wrote how Hall had crossed the Red River north of Sherman, and having been very well educated in North Carolina, obtained a position as teacher of a country school in Grayson County. "Parents seeing his signature on school reports called him Lay Hall, so he changed the spelling to the better understood Lee."[7]

During the 1850s little Jesse L. welcomed siblings into his world. The 1860 census shows the children were brothers Richard M., eight; William P., six; James K. Jr., four, and the youngest child Francis R., a one-year-old boy. Common in that era were members of a previous generation living together: the census record shows Dr. Hall's mother, Martha M. Hall, eighty years of age, living with them. One other individual resided there, "Em" Hall, forty-six, but no relation was shown.

In 1861 Dr. Hall had other concerns, as being a surgeon did not keep him away from the dangers of the battlefields. On the evening of May 7 that year, Guilford County Sheriff C.A. Boon called to order a general meeting at the courthouse to respond to a bill before the Legislature calling for the organization of 10,000 troops, "said troops to be located at different points for the purpose of thorough preparation and drilling." "A very large assemblage" gathered at the courthouse that night and Dr. James K. Hall was called to be the chair; C.C. Cole was appointed secretary. The meeting was intended to determine if there was enough interest on the part of the citizens to extend an invitation to the proper authorities to make Greensboro one of the points of rendezvous. A number of resolutions were passed, essentially informing the authorities that Guilford County and Greensboro would "do their whole duty in this crisis"; that the community felt "complimented" by the idea of making Greensboro "a place for drilling troops for Southern service"; and that these resolutions were to be forwarded to the North Carolina Senator and members of the Legislature. Several in attendance were given the opportunity to make remarks about the resolutions, including Honorable John A. Gilmer,[8] James A. Long, and James R. McLean. "Much enthusiasm was manifested," which showed that Guilford County "was determined to be always right, and never behind in the faithful discharge of every patriotic duty."[9] The report appearing in the *Greensboro Times* of May 8, 1861 [the name of the paper changed through time], was signed by Chairman James K. Hall and Secretary C.C. Cole.

Twenty-five days prior to this meeting, Confederates had fired upon Fort Sumter off the coast of South Carolina. On May 20, thirteen days after the meeting, the state of North Carolina seceded from the United States. The Civil War had begun and Dr. James K. Hall's services as a surgeon were needed. He served in the 12th Regiment of North Carolina Volunteers, headed by Col. James Johnston Pettigrew.

Although few records exist showing the contribution of individual doctors during this conflict, Dr. King occasionally received notice. The *Fayetteville Observer* later in the first year of the war mentions his service: "Letters received from Dr. James K. Hall, principal surgeon of the 12th regiment of N.C. Volunteers— Col. Pettigrew— states that there have been as yet only two deaths in the Regiment. This speaks well for Dr. Hall's skill as a physician, and for his care and attention to those placed under his charge."[10] A decade and a defeated state later, one easily realizes how the war drastically changed not only the Hall family, but most families who survived the war. When the census taker came to enumerate the household members in 1870, Dr. Hall and Frances were there, but eldest son Jesse had gone on—gone to Texas. Now his sibling Richard Moore Hall was the eldest with younger brothers William, James, and Frank, all attending school. It is believed Charles W. had died very young. Grandmother Martha M. Hall had passed on, but "Em" or E.M., Dr. Hall's sister, was there, with no occupation listed. The most drastic change was in the family's economic situation: now Dr. Hall's personal estate was but $100, a reduction from $4,500 in 1860. Perhaps more drastically changed was the amount of his personal estate, now but $3,000; a decade before it was $22,000. The most significant change was that in 1860 he had fourteen slaves to work his land and property, males and females ranging in age from one year to sixty-three years.[11] The war ended all that *peculiar institution* as it was sometimes called and the census after the war of course showed no slaves.

Dr. Hall was now certainly a different man; he had served throughout the war as a surgeon but he was emotionally as well as financially changed. The medical practices of the Civil War were horrendous to the modern mind, amputations without anesthetics, sewing up wounded men, knowing a severe wound would probably result in death no matter the talent of a physician. Dr. Hall had served in Pettigrew's Regiment, the 22nd North Carolina State Line.[12] After the war he returned to his practice, his wife, and sons, with the horrors of the battlefield buried within.

Another doctor from Greensboro was Algernon Sidney Porter, whose wife bore him a son on September 11, 1862, during the second year of the war. The boy was named William Sydney Porter. The boy's mother died when he was three years of age— thus he grew up with only vague memories of his mother, as did all of Greensboro. Young Will Porter "grew up in a town listless under the heel of Reconstruction." The Porter family and the Hall family were friendly, most probably because the heads of household were physicians. Dr. Hall's sons Jesse and Richard found adventure and fame in Texas. The Porter boy, in 1881 or 1882, left for Texas for health reasons and there in Texas renewed acquaintances with the Hall brothers. Porter became famous with his writing skills when he changed his name to O. Henry.[13]

Very little is known about the youngster Lee Hall during his formative years in North Carolina. Dr. Hall years later was interviewed by a reporter from the *Reidsville Times*, the journal from a community less than thirty miles north of Greensboro. One question the reporter asked was: what were Lee and Richard like when boys? "The doctor said he [Lee] was always fond of fun and danger, and could throw himself into more dangerous positions without getting hurt." But it was different with his brother, "while Dick was just the other way, so cautious that he always watched carefully where he stepped, and yet Dick had his arm broken twice while Lee was never hurt." As a lawman Lee continued to "throw himself" into dangerous situations.[14]

Occasional articles in the Greensboro newspaper also suggest Lee was concerned about the habits of his community. Joining a temperance club may have been his expression of concern or learning of the destructive results of imbibing too much from his doctor father. In May of 1869 R.H. Whittaker organized a Friends of Temperance, Greensboro' Council No. 66 with R.P. Troy, who operated a local school for men and boys.[15] Whittaker was elected president with W.P. Hill associate president. The offices of secretary and treasurer were filled but J.L. Hall became the "In Sentinel" with B. Watkins Mebane the "Out Secretary."[16] One must assume Hall and Mebane acted as door-keepers, a position Hall would fill a few years later when he was elected Sergeant-at-Arms in the House of Representatives in Austin. At the meeting of the Friends of Temperance in late June 1869, Troy and Hill remained as president and vice president but J.L. Hall is no longer the In Sentinel, having been replaced by E.R. Jollee.[17] This strongly suggests that Hall was considering a trip west during the latter part of 1869.

Young Lee Hall, yearning for adventure and resenting the evils of Reconstruction, left North Carolina and went to Texas, which, ironically, placed him back into those same "evils." Whether it was just the appeal of adventure or something more dramatic we may never know, but in the late 1860s J.L. Hall left Greensboro; certainly he was in Texas by the end of 1869, settling first in Grayson County. He kept no journal of the trip, nor did any letters he may have sent home survive, so we don't know his route after figuratively placing a "G.T.T." (Gone to Texas) note on his door. From other helpful sources one may reconstruct a reasonable route, however. Fortunately, Oliver Steele Glenn corresponded with his friend J. L. Boardman, a printer operating in Hillsborough, Ohio, as he made a similar trip. Glenn went to Grayson County during the same time and provided a description of his route. His letters were from Denton, Grayson, and Hunt Counties mainly to inform Boardman of the geography and social conditions of the Indian Territory through which he had passed as well as northeast Texas in 1870. Glenn, as did thousands of other travelers, crossed at Colbert's Ferry; he noted in his letter to Boardman the crossing was done on April 21 and then they "were in 'reconstruction' Texas." Hall certainly rode the rails from Greensboro to Richmond, Virginia, on to Chattanooga and Memphis, Tennessee, and then on to Leavenworth, Kansas. Stagecoach lines were available from Leavenworth to Fort Scott and Baxter Springs, Kansas, then on to Fort Gibson, to Perryville, to Boggy Depot, and finally to the Red River, which separated Texas from the Indian Territory, now Oklahoma. Crossing the river at Colbert's Ferry the traveler was about to enter Sherman. The route that O.S. Glenn described in early 1870 could easily have been the same route that J.L. Hall had followed in 1869.[18]

Sherman at this time was a city populated with nearly one thousand people. Correspondent Glenn noted it was the county seat of Grayson County. The town may not have been much different than Macomb, the community from which Lee Hall obtained whatever mail he received, except in the number of inhabitants. Glenn noted the "white frame houses, and neatly kept yards, almost a Paradise after the poverty and wretchedness of the Indian Territory, but . . . we do not find that the white people here live much better than the Indians do. Everything seems neglected and going to decay."[19] At this point in Hall's career he no doubt felt little concern about the quality of life, either among the wretched of the Indian Territory or that of "the white people."

Texas proved to have magnetism then as it does today for many immigrants. The idea of it becoming overcrowded was addressed not long after the end of the war and expressed in some journals. The *Harrison Flag*, a weekly publication in Marshall, Harrison County, edited by J.W. Barrett, expressed his concern in its columns that the "flood of immigration into Texas does not abate in the West. Every steamboat up Red River is crowded with people who are coming to Texas, while the numbers who have taken the overland route cannot be estimated." Editor Barrett concluded his concerns by stating that "in one more year" Texas "will be nearly 'filled up.'"[20]

The young adventurer proved to be one of those immigrants who was causing the state to be "filled up." Jesse Hall was in Grayson County when the 1870 census was conducted, earning his living as a twenty-one-year-old school teacher. What his qualifications were that convinced the school trustees to entrust the young man with educating Grayson County children is unknown. He boarded with the Noah and Amelia Compton family, who had two children, as well as two other boarders: twenty-year-old Napoleon Bonaparte "Nap" Woolsey[21] and E.X. Eavey, forty-five years old. Was it by coincidence that Hall, Woolsey, and Eavey were all natives of North Carolina?[22]

No details of his abilities or effectiveness as a classroom teacher have survived, but one must assume he maintained good discipline among the students. He was young, tall, good-looking, and self-assured. No record exists indicating the number of children he had in that one-room school house, but as there is no information to the contrary we can assume his teaching proved satisfactory to the children and their parents. But he did not choose to remain in that profession, as the occupation did not provide enough excitement for Lee Hall, just as the field of medicine, the profession his father had wished him to pursue, had not been to his liking. Lee Hall needed action in his life.

Presumably he finished out the school term and then looked elsewhere for employment and becoming part of the law enforcement profession appealed to him. He found responsible work as a constable in Grayson County. In July 1871 his duties required him to deliver certain prisoners from Grayson County to the state prison in Huntsville, a journey of well over two hundred miles. Typically the prisoners were all chained together to make it more difficult to escape. While he was en route, tragedy struck the good citizens of Grayson County: acting constable Jack B. Archer was assassinated four miles north of Whitesboro, a small community fifteen miles west of Sherman in Grayson County. Archer, a few days previously, had arrested Harvey Adams for wearing pistols. A man named Corhorne attempted to prevent the arrest but failed. Then on Wednesday, July 12, Constable Archer attempted to arrest Corhorne for the same offense— carrying pistols— and it was then at this point that Adams, released from custody, interfered and shot the constable, wounding him severely. Archer was just going out after dinner when Adams ambushed him. Archer had lost his right arm during the late war; thus he was at a distinct disadvantage, but he managed to mount his horse and ride to a nearby creek where he dismounted, sat down facing the water and there succumbed to his wound. He "was found dead, sitting with his feet in the water."[23] Deputy Sheriff E. P. Caywood[24] gathered a group of angry citizens, numbering nearly thirty, and went in pursuit of Adams. Harvey Adams fled southwest but Caywood and his posse caught up with him near the town of Cleburne in Johnson County, over one hundred miles southwest of Sherman, where Adams, "refusing to surrender, was shot and killed."[25] It was a case of swift and final frontier justice. If Hall had not been delivering prisoners to Huntsville he would have been in the place of Constable J.B. Archer, and perhaps have been ambushed.

During Reconstruction there was considerable lawlessness throughout the state. Following the defeat of the Confederacy many Texans resented the forced societal changes. Federal troops now occupied Texas; there were no more slaves to labor in the fields. Frequently, elected officers were removed from office because they had supported the "Lost Cause" and other non-elected officials were appointed to take their place. Enforcing local and state laws proved difficult in many communities and Grayson County was no exception.

There were also frequent disturbances at the polling places; threats by white ruffians prevented blacks from voting and they even destroyed polling places and voting boxes. Mishandling of the voting boxes became common. The impetus for his presence in Sherman is not recorded, but State Police Lieutenant Ed. W. Brady[26] was at an October 1871 election and reported on what he observed to his superior. His report did not speak well for the election officials of Grayson County. He provided Adjutant General and Police Chief James Davidson a five-page letter in which he recounted his concerns. Brady pointed out that "Although it may not fall under the direct scope of my duties, yet I cannot but believe that you as the Head of my dept. should know exactly the way matters stand and the manner in which they have been conducted by the Registrars and Judges of this Election." His report continued, describing how Mr. Morgan, the Registrar, had failed to follow the basic rules of registering voters in the registration book. He had failed to place the age of the voter opposite the voter's name, so no one could determine the age of the voter if questioned. Secondly, Mr. Morgan had failed to keep the voting box in a safe place; thus they would not be kept secure when the polls were closed. It had not been placed in a safe as directed by law but merely stored in a room in which Mr. Morgan slept, "but during the night no pretense of a guard was kept." Not only was the ballot box itself improperly prepared, but on the next night the box was kept in the post office "where it was taken care of by the Post Masters Rebel Clerks." Finally on the third and fourth nights the box was placed in the safe of "one of the bitterest Rebel Democrats in this section of Country." According to Lieutenant Brady "at no time did the Registrar comply with that portion of the law compelling him to call upon the Sheriff of the County for two guards to assist him in guarding the box." Lieutenant Brady now recommended that the votes in Grayson County be "thrown out" and perhaps the same would be the case for Fannin and Collin Counties, due to the amount of "intimidation."[27] Unfortunately for Lieutenant Brady, apparently no request was made for the sheriff or for Jesse L. Hall to assist during the election to make sure it was properly conducted according to the election laws. Sheriff John W. Hunter was by law under the direction of the Adjutant General and Chief of Police James Davidson, as were his deputies. Section 5 of the State Police bill read, in part: "All sheriffs and their deputies, constables, marshals of cities and towns, and their deputies, and the police of cities and towns, shall be considered as part of the State Police and be subject to the supervisory control of the Governor and chief of State police, and under direction of the Governor or chief of State police, may at any time be called upon to act in concert with the State police in preventing or suppressing crime, or in bringing to justice offenders."[28] Apparently Mr. Morgan merely ignored this direction.

In Grayson County, Sheriff John W. Hunter died while in office. James H. Tuttle was appointed to take his place and took office on November 23, 1872; he served until December 2, 1873.[29] Lee Hall began his career in law enforcement during this time. According to a later report this is how he entered the profession: "When a Deputy Sheriff of Grayson County Captain Hall was then a young man. He was always opposed to hunting down men with posses, preferring to go by himself or with only one other trusted man when a desperate character was to be encountered."[30]

On one occasion Hall was fortunate that he was not a lone lawman as he met up with members of the notorious McDonald family. They had been "released" from the Bonham jail in neighboring Fannin County by friends sometime in 1871 and then found seclusion in the southern part of Texas. Robert Moore, considered the leader of the group, for an unknown reason returned to Grayson County in July of 1872 and joined up with an unknown number of members of the gang. About noon the posse, consisting of Hall and four others named McConnell, Robinson, Copeland, and Cunningham, met up with the Moore party near Farmington, Grayson County, then a small community ten miles south of Sherman, today nearly a ghost town of less than one hundred people. When ordered to surrender they chose to fight; Robert Moore drew his rifle and recklessly charged through the posse firing as he went.

Hall and others fired their weapons as well, and as Moore galloped his horse past posse member McConnell he was hit, receiving wounds in the face and arm. Not wanting Moore to get away, Hall reportedly fired "some fourteen shots at him, and Moore fired nearly as many at Hall." The exchange of gunfire did not end the fight; Moore continued his flight and Hall continued the pursuit for about seven miles in the midst of the heavy rain, making it more dangerous for the footing of the horses. Moore was armed with a breech-loading Henry rifle "and knew how to use it." For Hall to fire fourteen shots at the fleeing man he may have had a breech-loading Henry rifle as well; apparently the hard driving rain affected the accuracy of both hunter and hunted. In spite of the shots fired Moore escaped, but due to his wounds he wisely chose to surrender the next morning in order to obtain needed medical attention. None of the posse was wounded, although Robinson's horse was shot. Hall made out a report in which he pointed out that the citizens of Farmington deserved "great credit" in turning out and assisting the officers. He further explained that "he broke up a camp meeting in drumming up recruits." What was the result of this action? Moore was safely lodged in jail awaiting Grayson County legal action against him. His wounds were not life threatening. The other members of the McDonald-Moore group managed to escape.[31]

Hall was now thinking of entering the world of politics, a decision that would certainly provide excitement but which would depend on the vagaries of the voting public's perception. On November 5, 1872, the election for representative of the Twenty-Seventh Senatorial District was held. The field was made up of eight candidates including Deputy J.L. Hall. The leading candidate was William Henry Trolinger (or Trollinger) who received 733 of the votes cast; J.L. Hall received one vote, which suggests he may have voted for himself.[32] Hall apparently had no ability to politicize and win votes, whereas Trolinger was a man who had considerable political experience, having already served as a representative of St. Clair County, Missouri, to the Twenty-First Missouri General Assembly in 1860. During the war he served as a lieutenant and quartermaster to the

Missouri State Guard; then he and his family located in Texas, settling in the vicinity of Whitesboro, Grayson County.[33] In 1876 Hall would be in Austin working in the State Capitol building as Sergeant-at-Arms.

Meanwhile in Grayson County, in addition to hunting wanted men, there were less dangerous activities to attend to, including being present when officials gathered. Grayson County at this time was far from the heavily settled portions of the state, not too far from what was considered the edge of the frontier. In December 1872 General Philip H. Sheridan, General C.C. Augur, "and other United States notables" were in Denison, just a few miles north of Sherman, on official business. Their purpose was to determine the feasibility of establishing a supply depot for the Texas frontier. This was an opportunity for deputy Hall to make his presence felt, mixing among the notables.[34]

Denison in the early seventies was a wild frontier town, especially once the Missouri, Kansas and Texas Railway crossed the Red River in 1872. In 1873 journalist Edward Smith King visited the area and left a fascinating description of the community: "Every third building in the place was a drinking saloon with gambling appurtenances, filled after night fall with a depraved, adventurous crowd, whose profanity was appalling, whose aspect was hideous. Men drunk and sober danced to rude music in the poorly lighted saloons, and did not lack female partners. In vulgar bestiality of language, in the pure delight of parading profanity and indecency, the ruffian there had no equal." Profanity and indecency were common but there was a greater threat as King noted: "Rough men abounded, and would, without doubt, have knocked anyone upon the head who should find himself alone, unarmed, and late at night, in their clutches."[35] This situation so close to the Texas-Indian Territory border allowed desperadoes to easily escape from Texas lawmen by a short but hurried ride north into "an immense frontier" and enabled "rogues of all grades to commit many crimes with impunity, for, once over the border, a murderer or a horse thief can hide in the hills or in some secluded valley until his pursuers are fatigued, and can then make his way out in another direction."[36]

This was the situation of Grayson County society that Jesse L. Hall found intolerable. The citizens were "enraged" and Hall, "a young man of great courage and unflinching 'nerve,' determined to attempt the capture of some of the desperadoes." According to King, who records his nickname "Red," as a lawman Hall "seemed to bear a charmed life. He moved about tranquilly everyday in a community where there were doubtless an hundred men who would have delighted to shed his blood; was often called to interfere in broils at all hours of the night; yet his life went on." King wrote that even though Hall "had been ambushed and shot at, and threatened times innumerable, yet had always exhibited a scorn for his enemies, which finally ended in forcing them to admire him."[37]

Hall had quickly become a trusted man in a community and the city fathers obviously approved of him wearing a deputy's badge and helping the sheriff enforce the local and state laws. Was it due to Hall's bravery or perhaps there was no one else who would take the job? During these early years some may have thought of Hall as the City Marshal of Sherman, or a deputy. Contemporary sources, however, frequently identify him as a constable.[38]

On December 21, 1872, a tie contractor working for the railroad was robbed and murdered in Denison, part of the lawlessness that accompanied the building of the tracks. Even though the amount of money he had on him was "a small sum," authorities believed the $70 or $80 he had was the motive for the crime. The person he had been seen with became the suspected murderer, and Hall arrested him and delivered him before Justice Shackelford. That man was released and then disappeared but the reporter did not know the reason he had been released. Another report identified the tie contractor as a man named Grover and his assailant was named O'Neil. This report also noted that Grover initially survived the attack but was not expected to live.[39] On or about the thirteenth of December another murder was committed, this time at Red River City, only this time the motive was not so base as robbery. The murderer believed the victim was interfering with his marriage, and deciding to deal with the matter personally he "charged him with being too intimate with his wife." The *Sherman Patriot,* which reported the news from the sister city commented on these two incidents: "They are certainly having lively times out at the future great city, and commercial metropolis of North Texas." [40] It is apparent that the city fathers of Denison envisioned their city to rival Dallas in importance very soon.

By early January 1873 Hall had his office in the building on the corner of Skiddy and Rusk Streets. Deputy Sheriff McDowell had his office there as well as "our efficient constable" Lee Hall. [41] Hall now had earned the respect of the communities of Grayson County and was developing a highly regarded county-wide reputation.

Hall was active in dealing with desperate men not only in Grayson County but also with thieves active in the Indian Territory, that dangerous land north of the Red River. Excitement was everywhere with the railroad increasing its track mileage to Grayson County, with wagons filling the streets with bales of cotton, and with men looking for excitement and perhaps easy wealth. Occasionally there was violence and Hall could only aid in determining the cause and preventing further violence, not only on the streets, but also on the rail line. In early November horse thieves stole several head right there in Sherman. On November 29 a horse thief was killed near Georgetown, only a few miles north of Sherman and close to the Red River. The thief had intended to cross the river and lose himself in the Indian Territory. [42]

On Christmas Eve 1872, only days after this excitement of horse stealing, the rail line reached Denison, inching the "Iron Horse" closer to Sherman. The report from Denison reflected the excitement: "The track-layers on the Missouri, Kansas and Texas Railway reached this city to-day, and the regular passenger train leaves here to-night for the north. Denison, on its third monthly birthday, with its 2,500 inhabitants, 400 buildings, two newspapers, two banks and other business represented in about the same ratio, sends Christmas greetings to the outside world. Five hundred bales of cotton are here awaiting shipment on the first freight train north." [43]

The New Year of 1873 was merrily brought in although no accounts of Lee Hall's particular activities found their way to available newspapers. February, however, proved to be different. A strange incident occurred when lawman Hall was *arrested.* On February 6, 1873, a deputy U.S. marshal named Page actually placed Hall under arrest, charging him with "rescuing" U.S. prisoners. Hall was accused of releasing the prisoners when they were to be held in custody. Deputy Page delivered Hall to Austin where he was "examined" before a commissioner's court. The examination proved Hall was totally innocent and he was discharged. Not so for deputy Page as he was accused of blackmailing; he somehow escaped and Austin authorities were unable to locate him. This was probably Hall's first experience in Austin. Why the Austin authorities did not convince Hall to track down the alleged blackmailer is unknown. [44]

On the fourteenth of February Hall returned from his forced visit to the capital and his return was noted in the Denison paper: "Constable J.L. Hall returned to our city last Friday, and has again resumed his official duties." [45]

Although Hall had superior success as a lawman, apparently the office of constable was not enough. In the spring of 1873, he, as did others, began considering a campaign for the county sheriff of Grayson. By May he was one of several who had announced, with notices such as this: "We are authorized to announce J.L. Hall as a candidate for the office of Sheriff of Grayson [C]ounty, at the ensuing election, subject to the action of the Democratic Convention." [46] A week later another announcement appeared, only this was more complimentary: "We announce in this issue J.L. Hall for Sheriff, subject to the action of the Democratic convention. Mr. Hall is well known to our citizens as a brave and energetic man, and he is well qualified by experience for that office. He will secure a good portion of the votes cast in Denison." [47]

The race for county sheriff was observed closely not only in Grayson County but in adjacent Fannin County as well, most particularly in the county seat of Bonham. The *Sherman Democrat* announced the Democratic candidates for the "shrievalty" were Hall and J.W. Vaden. Commented the editor of the Bonham paper: "'Shrievalty.' What is that? In our county we find it difficult to procure candidates for the officers we already have, let alone introducing new and outlandish positions of state like that."[48] Certainly the editor of the Bonham paper knew what the word meant, even if it may have been misspelled in the *Sherman Democrat*. Was it an intended jab at a rival newspaper, even in a different county?

The candidates by July were Hall, James W. Vaden, Stephen H. Scott, and now E.P. Caywood, who had been deputy sheriff for the previous two years.[49] In August the *Denison News* was ready to further praise Jesse Lee Hall. "Our friend J.L. Hall, Deputy Sheriff," the article began, "was in the city Saturday [August 2]. He is, without question, one of the hardest working deputies in the county. It is well known Hall is a candidate for Sheriff, subject to the action of the Democratic Convention. He is a fearless, energetic officer, and would no doubt fill the position with credit to himself and county." But that was not all that the editor stressed as he continued, "One thing is certain, he would enter upon his duties with much experience, which is of no little importance in a position of this character."[50]

Cooke County's Gainesville also had an interest in the politics of Grayson County. A lengthy article appeared in the *Gainesville Gazette* that praised not only Hall but Mr. G.A. Dickerman, a candidate for the office of District Clerk. He was the current clerk and wished to remain in that office. Hall, the Gainesville editor wrote, "is a young man of intelligence, sociability, shrewdness, good morals and extraordinary qualifications for sheriff – the office he has been repeatedly requested to announce for." The *Gainesville Gazette* had paid a visit to Sherman and had met "our old time friends." Gainesville is the county seat of Cooke County, which is the neighboring county to the immediate west, but when did they become "old time friends"? The editor continued: "Having known him for a long time, and seen him tried, we know the metal of which he is composed." The praise was not only general, but apparently the editor knew personally of one of the successes of the "thief catcher" as he called him casually. Hall had, on one occasion, "followed a desperado to Little Rock, Ark., arrested him and brought him back without the least assistance." And on another occasion, "after Hall had been struck senseless by a pistol that had been handed to a prisoner by some accomplices, he followed his man to New Orleans, captured him and brought him back."[51]

In spite of all the praise Hall received, the Democratic Convention did not choose Hall as the candidate for Grayson County sheriff. On the first ballot Hall received forty votes, Vaden seventy, Shannon fifty-two, and Scott a mere ten. On the second ballot Hall received fifty-five and Vaden eighty with Shannon receiving thirty-two. On the third it was between Hall and Vaden: Hall received sixty-seven with Vaden receiving 104. The result: "Mr. Vaden receiving the highest number of votes cast was declared the unanimous choice of the convention." [52] On Dec. 2, 1872, James W. Vaden would be elected county sheriff by voters.

Lawlessness persisted in northeast Texas and Hall continued the dangerous work of bringing in desperately wanted men. Among the most notorious of desperadoes of this section was one William Andrew Jackson Posey, best known by historians as Bill Posey. He was born in 1846 in Talapoosa, Alabama, to first cousins Benjamin Franklin Posey and Eliza Berryhill. The parents were each half Creek, making son Bill and each of the fifteen children one-half Creek. After several moves westward the family located in the Indian Territory around present-day Tulsa, but for an unknown reason Benjamin F. Posey moved his family to Texas, where Bill became a cowboy and an expert horseman. When the war came the Posey men naturally joined Confederate forces, but Private William Posey, working as a teamster, chose to desert the army in 1864. A year later Posey married Elizabeth Wallace in Limestone

County, Texas, and the couple then settled east of Waco in McLennan County. Elizabeth's brother Matthew Wallace had also married and they settled near the Poseys as neighbors. Being an expert horseman it was perhaps only natural that Bill Posey became a cowboy and along with Matt Wallace drove cattle up the Chisholm Trail. It was not long before neighboring ranchers determined that the cattle Posey and Wallace were driving to Kansas were some of theirs. Accusations were made against Posey while Wallace managed to distance himself for his own safety. Posey was charged with theft; his legal counsel at that time was Richard Coke, the future governor of Texas who obtained an acquittal for his client. Later Posey was charged with theft of two mules, but this time at his trial he was found guilty and sentenced to prison. Posey was lodged in the McLennan County jail until he could be delivered to Huntsville, but his friends delivered him and four other prisoners to liberty. [53]

Posey and his brother-in-law had ostensibly broken up their operation of stealing cattle and horses and mules but Wallace continued attending to Posey's affairs, which, according to one account, "he was fast converting into his own, thinking Posey would hardly dare return to these parts." To his misfortune, however, Wallace "reckoned without his host." Wallace, in an effort to remove himself from the bad crowd associating with Posey, moved to Waco and found lodging for his growing family. Moving closer to the courthouse square did not guarantee safety for Matthew A. Wallace, however. During the night of June 29, 1873, a group of men numbering about thirty rode up to Wallace's house, called him out and made him a prisoner. The mob then took him fifty yards away, found a mesquite tree and administered "lynch law" justice to the man. The limb "being low, they tied a rope to his feet and attached it to another tree near by to prevent him from touching the ground. He died from strangulation." [54] The coroner's jury determined only that Wallace came to his death at the hands of unknown parties. Although some considered the men who lynched Wallace were those he had robbed, others believed the mob was made up of brother-in-law Bill Posey and members of his crowd.

The thievery and murderous actions by Posey and his gang were not limited to McLennan County, but were conducted in a much wider area, including north across the Red River in the Indian Territory, closer to the law enforcement area of Grayson County and Lee Hall. Posey and Hall would meet up later and it would require a lengthy journey with the former as a prisoner. W.A.J. "Bill" Posey would continue creating terror among the citizens but now Hall had less murderous men to deal with.

In September two "bunco men" robbed a man in Denison of some $2,000, having swindled him out of his money on some nonexistent land. The victim of the bunco ploy was able to identify the pair and Hall kept on their trail until he caught up with them in Kansas. On September 30 Hall was back in Sherman having delivered the two into the hands of the county jailer. Hall expected he would be delivering them to Huntsville soon.[55]

Although Hall certainly enjoyed his adventurous life in Texas, he never forgot his friends and family back in North Carolina. And he retained a sense of humor even though his daily work was with the malevolent aspects of society. In addition to being a good horseman and detective he was the secretary of a social club, *Les Cinquante*, of undetermined purpose. Was it a literary club of young men, or young men and ladies of Grayson County? Somehow the publishers of the *Greensboro Patriot* received an invitation to attend a "hop" in Sherman. Perhaps the *Cinquantes* was a dancing club? But the recipient was forced to decline the invitation, noting that the distance— from North Carolina to Texas —"is a most too far."[56] Actually Hall had invited the publishers of his hometown newspaper to the Editorial Convention which was to be held in Sherman. The Texas press was notified in general that "ample preparation" was being made "for the reception and accommodation of as many of the editors as will honor the convention that is to assemble here on the 10th day of September, with their presence." Not only were North Texas newspaper editors welcomed, but so also were editors from the entire state. In addition to the pleasant fellowship of the editors in

Sherman, a free excursion to Chicago and St. Louis "and perhaps other important points" would be made available courtesy of Mr. Stevens of the M., K. & T. Railway.[57] The convention was a total success, but what garnered considerable attention in the Denison paper was the reporting about the Editorial Ball, the event that Hall had described as a "hop" in his invitation to the *Greensboro Patriot* editor. The ball was given under the auspices of Les Cinquante club of Sherman and "the editorial fraternity figured conspicuously in the 'mazy dance.'" The music was the very best that could be secured, and the banquet was a sumptuous one; the community of Sherman "may greatly boast of her fair women and gallant men." Certainly Secretary of the Cinquante Club Lee Hall enjoyed himself as much as anyone else, he being such a "gallant" man.[58]

Being a lawman required travel and sometimes it could be for pleasure. He had not been home for several years and now after delivering the bunco men to the proper authorities he went back to North Carolina for a visit. His presence in Greensboro was for family, but newspaper editor Joseph H. Fetzer noted in his journal how he was "pleased to meet in our city a few days ago" the son of Dr. J.K. Hall. The thirty-five-year-old Fetzer was from Virginia, but his wife Mary and four children were all born in North Carolina. After enumerating the Fetzer family, census taker Thomas C. Starbuck next visited the household of Dr. Algernon Sydney Porter, whose eight-year-old son would later enjoy fame as a short story writer and spend time with Lee Hall down in Texas where he had gone for his health. Fetzer, in his brief journalistic notice, pointed out that Lee "had been residing in Sherman, Texas, for a few years, and is delighted with that country." Unfortunately editor Fetzer failed to print a lengthy interview with Hall. His readers knew Dr. Hall and would be interested in news about the physician's son, but he merely pointed out that Lee would be visiting "a few weeks."[59]

Hall did have an enjoyable visit with family and friends back home. His return on Saturday, November 30, was noted in the newspaper. He was no longer "Mr. Hall" but now identified as "Deputy U.S. Marshal" and had returned "from a few weeks visit to North Carolina, where he has a mother living and other kinfolks." It is unknown why his father was not mentioned, as he was still living. Hall was noted as looking well "and is ready for business."[60]

Sometime during 1873 Hall experienced one of his most exciting yet dangerous adventures. As yet no contemporary account has been located but an account of it was provided by N.A. Jennings, who also came to Texas for adventure and served under Capt. L.H. McNelly and then under Captain Hall as a Texas Ranger in the 1870s. Jennings later wrote a book about those years and selections were published in various newspapers. Jennings had high praise for Hall, and wrote of his finding adventure when he was a deputy sheriff in Grayson County. Jennings recorded that in "a little less than two years [Hall] made 1,060 arrests, killed seven men and was wounded five times." Jennings further wrote that Hall's fame as an officer "spread far and wide" and it became a "foregone conclusion that any man Hall undertook to arrest would be made a prisoner or would be a subject for the coroner." Jennings's story involved a man named Wilkinson, a fugitive from justice wanted for cattle stealing and murder. He had "managed to elude Hall for months" and had sworn he would never be taken alive.

Finally Wilkinson grew tired of continually being the subject of Hall's pursuit and sent a message to him at Denison that if he wanted him so badly he should meet him at a certain place on a certain day and the two of them would fight it out. The only condition was that he should come alone. Hall agreed, and the meeting was to take place on a certain prairie some eighteen miles from Denison at 4 o'clock in the afternoon. Hall mounted up, and armed with a breech-loading shotgun and a six-shooter ignored the entreaties of the sheriff to take with him a companion. Jennings recorded Hall's response: "Wilkinson has made a fair, square offer, and I believe he'll keep his word and be there alone. If a desperado can keep a promise, I think I ought to be man enough to do the same, and I'll meet him on his own terms. And if I come back he'll be with me."

If I come back he'll be with me.

The description of the following gun battle suggests the narrator took some poetic license but perhaps Jennings had heard the account from Hall himself. If Hall did relate what happened to his ranger friend this is the retelling of it:

The place of meeting was a clear space of about half a mile square, surrounded on all sides by mesquit [*sic*], chaparral and liveoak [*sic*] woods. At precisely 4 o'clock Hall rode out from the southern edge of the chaparral onto the prairie, and a minute later Wilkinson rode into view from the north end. He, too, was armed with shot-gun and revolver. The men were within plain sight of each other but too far away to exchange shots. At the same instant they urged their ponies into a gallop and made straight for each other, both holding their shot-guns ready for action.

Further details, which were at least in the mind of Jennings if not in reality, were that no more evenly matched men had ever met in a duel to the death; both were expert horsemen and excellent shots with either pistol or rifle or shotgun. Neither Wilkinson nor Hall "knew the meaning of fear." Quickly they were within shouting distance of each other but "not a sound escaped their lips; they were there for action, not words." When close enough to use the shotguns each man dropped to the other side of his horse so as to make a smaller target, but were able to still use their weapons over the neck of the horse. Wilkinson's shot tore through the outer coat of Hall, but did not wound him. Hall's shot blasted Wilkinson's horse, causing it to collapse. The rider was able to jump off in time but he lost his shotgun under the falling horse. Hall now rose up in the saddle and wheeled his horse to face the grounded man. "I've got you!" Hall yelled, pointing his weapon straight at Wilkinson. "Give up now or I'll kill you!"

Wilkinson was not ready to surrender, however. "You've got the drop on me, all right," Wilkinson answered, looking into the barrels of the shotgun, "but if you're such a brave man as you'd have folks think you are, get down off your horse and fight it out with me with six-shooters."

Hall agreed, and immediately "sprang from his horse jerking his six-shooter from its holster at his belt." Only a fiction writer could make the denouement more dramatic. Both six-shooters roared at once. Hall was wounded in the left shoulder while Wilkinson was hit in the breast. Neither man fell; again they fired at each other. This time Hall was hit in the left side. But his aim was true: "The desperado pitched forward and fell on his face and Hall sank to the ground."

Fortunately for Hall two cowboys were close enough to hear the gunfire and approached. They found Hall on the ground unconscious and his horse standing "with drooping head over him." The unidentified cowboys managed to get Hall to a nearby ranch where he received some medical attention. Supposedly within a month he was back on duty, "arresting men as vigorously as before." [61] As far as known this was the first man Jesse Lee Hall ever killed.

This certainly had a basis in fact but without any other contemporary evidence providing details it is difficult to determine if it happened in late 1873 or early 1874. Jennings refers to Hall as an acting deputy sheriff of Grayson County. What is known is that the county sheriff, James W. Vaden, appointed Hall as his deputy in early February 1874. During this time it was popular for southern newspapers to report Texas news. An item in the February 13, 1874, issue of the *Southern Argus* of Selma, Alabama, reported that "J.W. Hall," the "new sheriff of Grayson [C]ounty" had appointed Lee Hall as deputy. This was an error as there was no J.W. Hall sheriff of Grayson County. The same newspaper printed a correction in the issue of March 13, stating that "James Vaden is Sheriff and Lee Hall is deputy sheriff of Grayson [C]ounty." Vaden had been elected sheriff on December 2, 1873, and served until February 15, 1876.[62]

Chapter Two

"A moment's reflection convinced him he was a dead man if he resisted"

—*Denison Daily News*, July 3, 1874.

If Jesse L. Hall had been a visionary at the beginning of the year 1874 he could see there would be significant milestones ahead in his career. B.C. Murray, editor and proprietor of the *Denison Daily News*, one of two leading newspapers in Grayson County, would frequently find reasons to place his name in his newspaper columns. As yet he had had no contact with such notorious outlaws as Bill Longley or John Wesley Hardin but that would soon change. In addition Hall would become a staple among the elite of the county, not just a deputy. When James Williamson Vaden became the new sheriff of Grayson County, he was then a thirty-three-year-old stock raiser, born in Tennessee and living with his parents and siblings in Sherman.[1] He saw good qualities in the former school teacher and constable and appointed Lee Hall as his deputy.[2]

Sometimes it is difficult to determine the origins of some adventuresome tale due to the lack of available records. Not every arrest or legal action was recorded at the time it occurred; thus some may be folklore or apocryphal. One such example is related in an 1879 newspaper recounting the early adventures of not only Lee Hall but a brief mention of his brothers who were in Texas by then. It started as a note of praise for Dr. James King Hall but quickly turned to the four sons: Lee, Frank, Will, and Dick. The article noted that all had left for Texas after the war and all were doing well. Dick was then the steward of the insane asylum in Austin at a salary of $1,200 per year. Will and Frank were in charge of a ranch of four thousand sheep, the origins of which they reportedly had bought from Richard King, the "Croesus of Texas." But it was the eldest brother who interested the writer and the editor, who headlined his piece "A Tar Heel Trooper in Texas" showing that the state's nickname is not of recent creation. According to this item the other brother, Lee, after coming to Texas "shortly after the war" was made deputy sheriff and "displayed such courage and efficiency in the performance of his duties, that he was made sheriff and held the office as long as he wished." This aspect of the report is in error as Hall never served as sheriff of any Texas county. Nevertheless the report continued and stated that Hall "never shrank from arresting the worst desperadoes and has been shot at a hundred times." We can forgive the reporter's use of hyperbole, but perhaps Hall indicated that in his various gunfights it *seemed* that he had been shot at that many times.

The newspaper tells of one occasion when Hall with a posse were in search of a desperado when for an unknown reason the posse left him. The result was a "stand up fight between him and one of the worst desperadoes in that State." Naturally Hall was victorious, and then the desperado "presented Lee with a splendid gun as a compliment to his pluck." More likely Hall physically took the "splendid gun" from the desperado without the latter considering his captor's "pluck."

In another story told in the 1879 article, a "blackleg gambler" came to Sherman and soon was "paying his addresses to one of the prettiest women in the place, but who was engaged to another man." The blackleg gambler, never identified by name, had friends who approached the house of the young betrothed couple where other people were gathered and ran off their horses. Then they fired shots at the couple, wounding them so severely that they collapsed on the front porch, allowing the shooting party to believe they had been killed. The ruffians thought they had killed both and many thought that both of them would die. At this point Lee Hall entered the narrative and began the pursuit. In the Indian Nation the desperadoes separated but Hall followed the blackleg gambler's trail, farther into the Nation, into Kansas and into Arkansas, and finally to Hot Springs. Hall adopted a disguise, even to the point of selling his horse and using a buggy for pleasant drives in the country and, over time, developed a friendship with the gambler. On one occasion he asked the gambler to ride with him which the gambler pleasantly agreed to; it was on this occasion that Hall arrested him, handcuffed him, and then "tore off his whiskers and goggles" and identified his true identity. He then returned the gambler to Sherman without having obtained any form of requisition. The gambler was "tried by law and severely punished."[3] A similar rendition of this event relates how Hall tracked the desperado to Little Rock and arrested him before delivering him to Shreveport, Louisiana, authorities where he was jailed.[4]

The first news item to bring attention to the new member of the sheriff's department was when he and a posse entered the community of Pilot Point intending to arrest three men accused of attempting to assassinate Dr. J.H. White of Sherman. The doctor and his friend, a Mr. Dymond, had inadvertently made enemies of a rough crowd. Dymond had been killed and White attempted to provide justice by offering a reward for the capture and conviction of those who had killed his friend. At this point White lived in Pilot Point, a small community in Denton County, but he realized his life was in danger when someone fired shots at him. After this he moved to Sherman, some thirty miles southeast of Denison, thinking it would be safer. Hall investigated and determined a George Stratton and two others were the would-be assassins; how he located their whereabouts is unknown but he planned to arrest the three with a small posse. Hall first grabbed Stratton, who was then charged with shooting at Dr. White. The two others they wanted managed to get away in the nick of time; their haste to flee was so great the lawmen found their beds still warm "from which they had escaped." Stratton was delivered to Sherman where he was placed under a $1,000 bond by Justice J.V. Cockrell and released. He later was tried and found guilty of assault in October 1875. Sentenced to a term of four years at Huntsville he became convict number 4875. He was released from the E.H. Cunningham work crew October 8, 1879, and then disappears from history.[5] The editor of the *Sherman Patriot* commented: "Lee Hall generally brings [in] the game, if he has a half a chance."[6]

But Stratton's arrest did not end the matter for Dr. White, as he had not gone far enough from his enemies. Shortly after midnight on April 23, 1874, assassins shot him down in front of the Western Union telegraph office in Sherman. Dr. White "was walking arm in arm" with a man named John C. Flippin when "cowardly fiends stepped up behind them and fired three shots, producing instant death."[7] Authorities suspected Flippin was somehow involved in the assassination. As White had previously lived in Pilot Point, Hall determined his investigation would lead to the assassins there. An examining trial of John C. Flippin was held in early May, which resulted in his posting bond in the amount of $6,000 to appear before criminal court in July. Another examining trial of a man named Merchants was to take place later that month.[8] Apparently no one was found guilty of the assassination as the 1878 list of fugitives from justice produced by the Adjutant General's office noted that there was a standing reward of $500 offered for the "unknown murderers" of Dr. White.[9]

Earlier in the same year, February 25, 1874, Sheriff James W. Vaden gathered a posse to arrest certain members of the large Holder family who were accused of murdering Jarret Hastings in October of 1873. The posse consisted of the sheriff's younger brother Henry L. Vaden; Lee Hall, J.S. Moody, Robert West, and two others identified only as Welch and Barney. The Holder family lived in the community of Georgetown, then a small settlement in north central Grayson County close to the Red River. The trip to Georgetown and the actual arrest proved to be uneventful with no resistance on the part of the Holders. The posse returned Thursday morning the twenty-sixth having William Lawson Holder and three of his sons: E.V., Jack, and George W. Holder, as well as William Lawson's son-in-law William Jefferson Young. The five prisoners were all placed in the Sherman jail. The matter which led to the killing and then the arrest had started during the late war. William Lawson Holder's brother Lew Holder and Jarret M. Hastings[10] were both hiding out in the brush in order to avoid conscription in the Confederate army, no different than what many young men did to avoid the war. However, Lew Holder made a deal with the conscription officer to turn in Hastings if he (Holder) would not be held for conscription. The officer agreed but intended to turn them both in, in spite of the deal. Holder "arrested" Hastings and was on the road to Sherman to deliver him to the conscription officer. Holder was riding and Hastings was walking when Hastings knocked him off the horse with a rock, then attacked him with a knife and killed him. He then stole his horse and fled the country. This killing took place about eight miles north of Sherman.[11]

The Holders were not a forgiving family and waited for the opportunity to avenge the death of Lew Holder. Hastings, now eight years after the war's end and perhaps thinking all had been forgotten if not forgiven, returned to Grayson County. On October 29, 1873, about three miles west of Denison, the opportunity for vengeance came. Hastings was waylaid on the road, surrounded by E.V. "Evans" Holder and several others and then shot, dying there as his killers waited and watched. The men arrested by Sheriff Vaden avoided a lynch mob but not a legal trial. Of the group E.V. Holder was found guilty and sentenced to five years in prison. Jack Holder did not fare as well as he died of pneumonia on March 12, 1874, in the city's jail. Both his wife and his mother were present at the time of his death. [12] W.L. Holder, the head of household in 1870, had seen his family broken during those early years of the 1870s. Another tragedy for the family was his death on November 23, 1876.

The single line item in an Alabama newspaper read: "Col. W.L. Holder, of Grayson [C]ounty, is dead." [13]

Some actions frustrated Hall, which a decisive man simply had to let alone due to the vagaries of fate. In early March, Lee Hall arrested "Tennie" Hall (no relation to J.L. Hall) and Perry Dumas, charged with threatening to take life. Dumas was a nineteen-year-old mulatto male who in 1870 was living with fifteen-year-old Emma Dumas, in the household of Attorney at Law Silas Hare of Grayson County. No one came forth to prosecute Dumas or Hall so they were released. [14] That same Silas Hare had been appointed Criminal Judge for Grayson, Dallas, and Fannin Counties which might explain why no one "came forth." [15]

The community of Pilot Grove, some sixteen miles southeast of Sherman in southeastern Grayson County, had become well-known after the Civil War as the central point of the notorious Lee-Peacock Feud. The historical marker erected there in 1965 reminds the traveler that the town was founded in the 1850s. By the time Deputy Lee Hall was hunting desperadoes, few people could recall when it was known by the original name of Lick Skillet, before it was changed to Pilot Grove in 1858. [16] Lee Hall arrived at Pilot Grove in April and arrested two men, both strangely identified as John Patterson, either one or both using an assumed name. Whatever their real names were they both were wanted for stealing horses. Apparently the presence and action of Deputy Hall was all the community needed to act forcefully, as some unidentified citizens arrested two other men, Ike and Bill Graves, both "notorious characters." [17] Hall had become an efficient man-hunter and his ability to work well with the citizens of the Grayson County communities proved to be valuable in all his undertakings. Between Lee and the citizens, four men were arrested, all accused of stealing the property of others; Hall needed and utilized the cooperation of all for the betterment of the community. This would become a natural characteristic of the young deputy.

William Andrew Jackson Posey had not been forgotten even though he had left the state of Texas. He had settled down on a farm, ostensibly earning an honest living north across the Red River in the Creek Nation, some twenty miles west of Muskogee in the Indian Territory. He may have made some changes in his lifestyle, working as an honest man, but he may have also been involved in a horse stealing ring as well. Reports were current in North Texas about horses being stolen and rewards being offered for their recovery. The *Dallas Daily Herald* reported that accounts of horse theft were coming in from "all quarters of this and adjoining counties" and surmised that "an organized band of horse thieves" operated in the northern tier of Texas counties, which included Clay, Montague, Cooke, Grayson, Fannin, Lamar, Red River, and Bowie. The thieves would drive their stolen stock into the Indian Territory where it would be held until a large herd was gathered before driving them on into Arkansas or Kansas where they would be sold. Could W.A.J. Posey have been involved in this ring?

That question was not to be answered with certainty, as in early May Deputy Sheriff Hall had other more immediate concerns. In pursuit of a gang of horse thieves he galloped into their camp intending to arrest them all. This time his reconnaissance failed him as there were no men there, only wagons, horses, women, and children; the men were actually out on a horse-stealing raid. He did locate one of the gang in a house in the neighborhood and "secured" him and delivered him to "a group of citizens at Collinsville"; presumably Hall entrusted his prisoner to them since Collinsville had no jail. It was only a village of a few hundred located twenty-five miles southwest of Sherman. Commented the *Sherman Register*: "We have not heard of his being placed in jail, and would not be surprised if his thieving days were not over." The report continued, ominously hinting that a lynching would be appropriate: "The citizens of this county ought to organize a company of militia men, or a vigilance committee for self protection, and it would do no harm to stretch the necks of the scoundrels if their wholesale thieving cannot be stopped in any other way."[18] While lynching in this case would be effective in reducing the amount of thievery, it would be against all of Lee Hall's principles.

The pursuit of horse thieves and other desperadoes occupied much of Hall's time but in May the Knights of Pythias organized a lodge in Sherman. On the night of May 8 Hall became a Knight. The organizers were two men from Houston: A. Ewing and a Mr. Gray. J.S. Van Slyke was elected Grand Chancellor; Lee Hall was elected Vice Chancellor. Others elected included S.N. Zemansky, George B. Greene, Dr. G.G. Steever, Ignatius Fellnor Jr., and J.W. Phillips. Regular meetings were scheduled for every Friday night. Certainly Hall realized that there would be some Friday nights that he could not make the meeting if he was on a man hunt.[19]

Hall and his hand-picked unofficial militia would not give up on the hunt for horse thieves. Mike Gormly was the leader of one of the area's principal gangs of desperadoes and thieves. He had gathered a small group of miscreants and operated in North Texas and across the Red River in Indian Territory. Hall had captured him in May of 1874 but Gormly "gave him the slip and broke for the timber. Being a good runner, he made good his escape."[20] Hall would not give up on pursuing him. On June 2, 1874, Hall and his five-man posse discovered their hiding place at the widow McCay's residence about twenty miles from Red River City on the road to Tishomingo, in the Chickasaw Nation (present-day Johnston County). Hall placed three of his men around the house while he and one other approached it. It was not a peaceful confrontation. Seemingly Hall and his companion had not sufficiently reconnoitered the setting as Gormly and three of the gang jumped out of the brush with six-shooters in each hand. The four outlaws were *behind* Hall but in spite of being taken by surprise and covered, Hall ordered them to surrender while aiming his rifle at Gormly. Gormly and Hall fired nearly at the same time. Gormly's shot went wild but Hall's did not, wounding the horse thief. A few more shots were exchanged before the gang fled with Hall and the posse in pursuit. They did not overtake the fleeing men, but Hall, in examining the site of the gun battle, did find where Gormly had fallen and dragged himself into the brush. The deputy believed Gormly was severely wounded and avoided capture only because his companions carried him away.

Hall granted an interview with a reporter from the Denison newspaper. The editor wrote that Hall "thinks Mike is severely if not fatally wounded. Great credit is due to Hall and his bold companions, for their efforts to rid us of this band of desperadoes, and may God speed them in their good work." It is not known if Gormly survived his wound but he was at least out of commission for a while, probably hiding out in the Indian Territory. [21]

Around the same time as the Gormly gunfight, on the night of Thursday, June 4, thieves robbed the till at Maupin's store[22] in Red River City near the border line. The store was located about a mile south of the river and was operated by two brothers, John and James Maupin. John Rice Maupin had been a member of Quantrill's guerrillas during the war, fighting for the Stars and Bars of the Confederacy. By reputation, when men came with horses from the Indian Territory the Maupins would buy them or exchange whiskey for them. [23] The amount taken was a mere four dollars in change but store owner John Maupin informed Hall and requested he look out for the thief and if possible recover the stolen money. At Colbert's Ferry Hall noticed an elderly German man who looked "suspicious" riding a pony. This was only hours after the encounter with the Gormly gang and Hall's senses were on high alert. Acting on his suspicions, no doubt an early example of profiling, he arrested the man, searched him and discovered the money stolen from the Maupin store. In the scant verbal exchange due to the man's ability to speak only broken English, the suspect took out from his pocket a small bottle and drank the contents. Hall inquired as to what it was and was told it was whiskey and salt. Arriving at Maupin's store the man went to the well and filled the bottle and drank again. Hall wanted to get his prisoner to Sherman without delay but now the man got off his horse and refused to move, saying he was too ill to continue. Hall was running out of patience and ordered the man to get on the horse or else he would be shot. This threat convinced the man Hall was not one to trifle with and he did manage to mount up again. After a while, at Duck Creek, south of Red River City, the man again stopped and dismounted, complaining he was too sick to go on. Hall now realized his prisoner was seriously ill. The two men exchanged a few more words, in which the man revealed he was subject to seizures and that what he had originally drank was not whiskey and salt but morphine. Perhaps knowing the end was near the man further explained that he had taken an overdose, explaining this just before he experienced another seizure, causing him to collapse and die. Now Hall was alone with a dead prisoner and no type of assistance was nearby. All he could do was to take the corpse into Denison for a post mortem. From Hall's time with his now dead prisoner he had learned the man was probably German and his name was either Mead or Smeet. He only spoke broken English and Hall couldn't determine what his real name was. He said he had lived about sixteen miles from Waco in McLennan County. Dr. Sanford, Dr. Julian C. Field, and Dr. Alexander A. Acheson conducted the post mortem.

This incident proved newsworthy for a while and rumors began to circulate about the mysterious man. Some thought he was simply deranged; others believed he had committed a heinous crime and killed himself to avoid being discovered and punished for it. Others thought he was the notorious "Pa" Bender of the murderous Bender family of Montgomery County, Kansas. [24] The news of the Bender family and its numerous murder victims was one of the top stories at this time; in fact, the *North Texas Enterprise* in Bonham in neighboring Fannin County brought the report to Grayson County readers in its prominent report about "the particulars of a horrible murder or series of murders perpetrated in Labette county, Kansas, by a German family by the name of Bender."[25] Photographer W.D. Kirk made an image of the deceased Mead or Smeet in hopes someone might provide positive identification.[26] Finally the rumors about the man being the Bender serial killer became stale and he was forgotten about.

Hall next went to Henrietta in Clay County, Texas, as there were reports of an Indian uprising. Henrietta is about one hundred miles west of Grayson County and two men were reportedly killed and scalped. Hall put an end to the wild rumors on his return to Denison, explaining that the two men killed were John and Charles Jacoby, formerly of Denison, but Indians had not been involved in the killings. The Jacobys were killed by a black man. Clay County Sheriff W.H. Newson arrested the killer and to prevent him from being lynched placed him in the jail at Gainesville, seat of Cooke County. It is not known if Hall took any part in the capture but he did report that "everything [was] quiet on the Wichita." [27]

A little over three weeks after the incident with the German, lawman Hall was again on the trail of Bill Posey. Whether he was a member of a horse-thieving ring or acted solo did not concern Hall, as he wanted Posey either dead or in prison. Hall learned that Posey was living some twenty miles west of Muskogee in the Creek Nation and gathered together a small but resolute group of men to capture him. Deputy Hall led the posse, although Grayson County's William Calvin "Bill" Everheart[28] was a brave man as well; he would become the county sheriff in a few years. In addition to Everheart, Hall had with him Samuel D. Ball and Burt Douglass as well as two blacks acting as guides. On the twenty-eighth the Grayson County men were within five miles of the Posey ranch, but due to a heavy storm they made camp to wait for morning and hopefully a calmer day. At dawn on the twenty-ninth they started out for what might become a deadly gunfight. Hall secreted his posse in the barn and waited until Posey showed himself. Posey left the house to gather up his horses but his mount shied at something and rammed him against a gate post, injuring the arm. The unsuspecting Posey then returned to the stable where Hall and his men stepped out with shotguns at the ready. Another version described how Posey rode out into the lot when the posse "came down on him with double barrel shot guns. Posey was at first disposed to draw a pistol, but a moment's reflection convinced him he was a dead man if he resisted, and so threw up his hands and surrendered."[29] On June 29, 1874, Posey's time as a free man ended. Posey "received the handcuffs with a very bad grace, indeed," as one report described the arrest, but the good news was clear that he was their prisoner. Hall and his men, no doubt pleased with their morning's work, returned to Sherman where Posey was placed in the county jail. There was a reward of $1,500 for Posey, $500 offered by the state and $1,000 offered by individuals whom Posey had harmed. [30]

Posey, convicted of stealing two mules, entered Huntsville as convict number 3644 to begin serving his five-year sentence. If the sentence was fully served he would be a free man on July 11, 1879. But Posey escaped on March 4, 1876, and never met up with Lee Hall again. Posey had not changed during his time in Huntsville but continued his life as a thief and a fugitive. When the law caught up with him on June 16, 1877, his thirty-first birthday, he resisted arrest and was killed in the gunfight.[31]

The year of 1874 was a significant year not only for Lee Hall for law enforcement in general. Following the end of the Civil War the state had been plagued with lawlessness, including Comanche raiding parties creating terror among settlers as well as bandit raids from across the Rio Grande. The Texas State Police, a force created by Governor E. J. Davis, offered some protection during 1870-1873 but the Legislature disbanded that organization in early 1873. After that there was a period when the only law enforcement bodies were county sheriffs and the presence of scattered troops of the U.S. Army. Richard Coke, newly elected Democratic governor in 1873, recognized the seriousness of the degree of lawlessness and created a new organization that came to be known as the Frontier Battalion. This new force was composed of six companies of Texas Rangers, each initially made up of seventy-five men. Governor Coke appointed John B. Jones to head this new organization with the rank of major in May 1874. This force would provide protection all along the frontier line. But Jesse Lee Hall's experience with the Frontier Battalion was in the future. He would continue to hunt desperadoes on his own.

On August 13, 1874, Deputy Sheriff Hall returned to Sherman from Fort Griffin in Shackelford County and Fort Richardson in Jack County having in custody two horse thieves wanted in Grayson County. No details were provided, only that all was quiet among the Indians, it "being the dark of the moon." [32]

Living that close to the Indian Territory guaranteed that he would sooner or later have to deal with conflicts between the Nations. At Muskogee, in the Indian Territory, the contest for the principal chief of the Cherokee Nation was getting hotter every day: it was between William P. Ross and Ouciletta. This was a political conflict turned bloody; since the race began there had been sixteen murders in the Cherokee Nation. Most of those murders had been committed "by reason of quarrels growing out of feuds existing between the Ross and Downing parties." A few of the victims were Jess Foreman, a Mr. Buckeye, Jack Doubletooth, and Richard Fields. They were "prominent Downing men." Richard Fields was shot while in church.[33] One murder was to have an effect on Deputy Hall: that of a prominent Delaware named Isaac Newton Journeycake, frequently referred to vulgarly as "Johnnycake." He was born in 1819 and with a lifetime of honorable conduct was beloved by every member of the Delaware tribe. He was a member of the Delaware Council and for many years was the official interpreter for the tribe. But on the thirteenth of June 1874 Isaac N. Journeycake was riding with "Donald Anderson, a colored man" having visited a friend's house. Calvin Coker, a half-breed Cherokee and some friends had been drinking and seeing the two riding by mounted up and met the pair on the road. Coker told Journeycake to ride outside of the road as he wished to talk with him privately. Journeycake refused to be intimidated and responded to Coker that if he had anything to say to him he could ride along with him on the road. Coker interpreted this response as a challenge and drew his weapon and fired. His first shot missed but Coker fired the second at point-blank range, killing Journeycake instantly. Why Coker acted as he did is not known but it was the general belief that Coker had attempted to draw rations on his wife's annuity without the proper authorization, which refusal developed into the grudge which led to murder. Coker fled the scene of the crime.[34] No details have as yet been uncovered how Lee Hall learned where Coker was and how he captured the murderer. He did and a single news item tells of his success: "Lee Hall, of Sherman, received $1,000 as reward for the arrest of Coker and Bullard, the murderers of the Wyandotte [*sic*] half-breed Johnnycake."[35] How Bullard was involved has not been determined; he may have been one of the men with Coker when the killing of Journeycake took place. This chain of killings beginning with the death of Journeycake was followed in 1875 when Calvin Coker, described as "a border desperado, was shot and killed by an unknown party at Coffeyville." [36] That "unknown party" proved to be one Buck Donaldson. He was tried in Denton County's District Court September 27, 1891, over fifteen years after the killing. The jury took fifteen minutes to bring in a verdict of not guilty.[37]

But then Hall had to make a decision about his future. Would he always remain a deputy sheriff of Grayson County, Texas? Would he occasionally return to North Carolina for visits with his family, or would he travel south to Austin and see more of Texas? He had come to love the country but perhaps Grayson County was becoming monotonous. Occasionally items in the various newspapers provide clues but also frequently raise additional questions. Sometimes concentrated research provides no clues. A brief one-line item appeared in the Sherman newspaper of September 19, 1874, which raises the question of word meaning in the 1870s: "Lee Hall has been relieved of his Deputy Sheriff's office."[38] The transitive verb "relieved," usually in the passive voice, means that someone, in this case the sheriff certainly, no longer needed Hall as a deputy and took that position from him. Was Hall "fired" after only seven months and if so, why? Had he committed some egregious breech of conduct? Not likely. Had he been so successful there was no longer a need for his services in fighting lawlessness in Grayson County? Not likely.

During early September Sheriff Vaden had tracked a Grayson County fugitive to St. Louis. Henry Reilly was his name, and he had had a difficulty with a man in Denison and had been arrested and charged with assault to kill and bailed, but then jumped his bond and fled the state.

Sheriff Vaden learned he was at the Missouri Medical College where Reilly was enrolled as a student. Vaden called him out of the "clinic lecture" classroom and placed him under arrest. The *Galveston Daily News,* in reporting that Vaden and his prisoner had left St. Louis to return to Texas, stated that the prisoner "has, it is charged, been engaged in several shooting scrapes, although but twenty-two years old."[39]

Sheriff Vaden's trek to locate and capture the medical student certainly took some time, and who was in charge of the sheriff's office during his absence? If Hall had been relieved of his duties was a judge or justice nominally in charge? To add to the mystery, an item appearing in the Denison newspaper in December states that Hall had returned from a trip to Missouri and Kansas "last Sunday" which would be Sunday December 6. This was not a pleasure trip, for in Kansas "he came across Ed. Withers, an escaped criminal from this county [Grayson], and arrested him, but he made his escape from the guard, placed over him, and is again at liberty."[40] This was the situation with Withers in late 1874. Fifteen months later a news item from Grayson County indicated that it was not known whether the prisoners who escaped from Sheriff Vaden "some days ago, on their way to the penitentiary" had been recaptured or not. Their names were J.J. Williams, William Jones, Ed Withers, and Van Osborne. No follow up on this matter has been located, unfortunately.[41]

Chapter Three

"Now gentlemen, you can go to killing Rangers, but if you don't surrender, the Rangers will go to killing you!"

—Lieut. J.L. Hall, December 22, 1876

Gatesville, the county seat of Coryell County, is some two hundred miles southwest of Sherman but on April 3, 1875, Deputy Hall arrested a man named Wilson wanted for a murder committed there. Hall made the arrest in a house of ill-fame in Sherman. Although Hall may have preferred to work alone, this time he had two or three men with him; the arrest was accomplished peacefully, although Wilson, armed with an "improved Henry gun" at first showed fight. He then reconsidered when he realized he had no chance against the lawmen. Commented the *Sherman Register*: "He is accused of other crimes, besides the murder . . . , and is said to be a very bad man." There was a $500 reward offered for his arrest and the editor surmised the officers would receive the reward.[1]

At the beginning of October 1875 Hall had received the thousand-dollar reward for the arrest of Coker and Bullard. Realistically with that amount of money he could pay off any debts he may have had and perhaps have a considerable amount of cash left over. That amount of money in terms of buying power in the twenty-first century would be the equivalent of $20,000. Hall was thus flush with cash and, not being a gambler, he invested a good part of it in his future.

But the name of Coker appeared again in the headlines. Whether he had escaped or was out on bail is not determined, but an effort to gain revenge and again kill became his final act. According to Kansas newspapers, Cal Coker met his final fate during a violent altercation with a young Indian boy named Love who was armed only with a knife. Coker chose to kill the youth who had testified against him. Although armed with a revolver he could not inflict a fatal wound on Love. During the affray the youth was severely wounded but managed to strike a more dangerous blow to Coker. When his assailant was down he managed to crawl to safety until found and then received medical attention. He survived. One report stated: "Finally the boy with the little knife struck the fatal spot, and Coker, the desperado, who has been for years a terror to the people of that section, fell a corpse at his feet."[2]

That was in January 1876. In March, Hall was again on the trail of a fugitive from Texas justice. The subject of his hunt was John A. Purnell, the ex-sheriff of Hill County, county seat Hillsboro midway between Dallas and Waco. In July 1870 Purnell was identified by the census taker as a fifty-year-old native of Maryland with the occupation given as "District" —suggesting the enumerator had not finished identifying his role as district superintendent of schools. He was appointed sheriff three months later, on September 5, 1871, by Gov. Edmund J. Davis. The governor, aware of Purnell's strong Union feelings, had honored the veteran with an important responsibility, and Sheriff Purnell may have had the best of intentions when he pinned on the sheriff's badge. For an unknown reason he could not continue in his position as sheriff due probably to the anti-Union feelings among many of Hill County residents. On June 31, 1872, Purnell wrote out his letter of resignation to Governor Davis.[3] In August 1872 a district judge removed John A. Purnell from his office for impropriety in handling the funds collected.[4] As sheriff he had been obligated to assess and collect taxes from county residents. This is where Purnell's apparent weakness entered in as he was indicted for the "embezzling of money collected from taxes." Now a fugitive he took flight from Hill County. On the nineteenth of June 1873 Governor Davis caused to be published a proclamation offering a reward of $500 "for the apprehension and delivery to the sheriff of Hill [C]ounty of JOHN A. PURNELL, a defaulter from several criminal prosecutions for embezzlement."[5] He also was accused of "packing" the Grand Jury and was fined $200 for such action, according to one report.[6] Available records indicate the shortage was not discovered until early 1873.

What Hall was doing from the time the shortages in Hill County were discovered, the reward offered, and clues emerged as to where Purnell might be and his eventual capture is uncertain. It is known that Hall took the trail, obviously interested in cashing in on the $500 reward. Rather than trailing the fugitive alone he took with him a self-styled detective, J.W. Holt.[7] Whether Hall or Holt worked up the case is unknown, but apparently they learned of Purnell's communication to Governor Davis written from Fort Lyon, Missouri, dated July 3, 1873. In it Purnell stated he had learned of the reward offered for him and declared that he would "come and give my self up at any time [if] I can have a fair hearing." He further claimed that he had turned over to the county treasurer every dollar he had collected.[8] That hunt took the lawmen to Baxter Springs, located in extreme southeastern Kansas close to where the Oklahoma, Kansas and Missouri state lines meet. The once thriving community had been a market for the early Texas cattle-drovers, but now was in the early days of decline. Had Hall learned that Purnell was in Kansas by his own sleuthing abilities, or, more likely, someone tipped him off, hoping then to receive part of the $500 reward offered for him? Whichever the case Hall and Holt located Purnell in Baxter Springs and arrested him, apparently with no resistance. They may have quietly arrested their man and left, causing virtually no attention to the citizens of Baxter Springs, which would explain the shortage of press coverage. They then headed back to Hill County, a trek of some four hundred miles, during which time the only major city was Dallas. Hall and Holt may have stopped in Sherman to rest but they then continued on to deliver Purnell to Hill County authorities.[9] All indications are that the reward was paid. [10] Then it was time for a new adventure and Hall looked to travel.

From Sherman to Austin in the mid-1870s the journey was less than 300 miles going through Dallas and Waco and then to the capital city. Hall may have used a buggy or rode horseback; part of the way he may have ridden the rails. Exactly why he chose Austin is not yet determined, but he found employment in the House of Representatives. The Fifteenth Legislature was organizing for its new term in April 1876, and new positions needed to be filled: the Chief Clerk, the Assistant Clerk, the Journal Clerk, the Engrossing Clerk, the Encoding Clerk, the Sergeant-at-Arms, the Assistant Sergeant-at-Arms, the Doorkeeper, Assistant Doorkeeper, and Chaplain. J.H. Cochran of Dallas County nominated J.L. Hall for Sergeant-at-Arms but he did not receive a majority on the first vote. A second vote was taken and this time he received a majority of forty-eight votes and became the new Sergeant-at-Arms of the Texas House of Representatives.[11] What adventures could Hall possibly experience now?

What Hall experienced in the Texas capital was nothing compared to hunting fugitives. Each session opened with a prayer by the chaplain. On the first day of August after prayer there was no quorum yet present. There were thirty-five members absent who were identified in the *Journal* and also in Austin's leading newspaper, the *Daily Democratic Statesman.* Hall was directed to bring them in. He first brought in Mr. Hunter, "under arrest by the sergeant-at-arms" and interrogated by the Speaker as to the cause of his absence from the House without leave. Hunter stated he was unaware that the House needed his presence and that the sergeant-at-arms was looking for him, but "declined to make any excuse for his absence." But Mr. Hunter was only one member returned. The others needed to be arrested and brought in to the House. Mr. Pickett offered a resolution authorizing Hall to do just that, which was approved: "You are hereby commanded to arrest and bring to the bar of the House of Representatives of the Fifteenth Legislature, now in session, the following named members of the House who are absent without leave [here follows the names of the thirty-two members], there to hold and keep said members under arrest until otherwise ordered by this House." Hall performed his duty on the same day he received the command. He wrote on the document: "Came to hand August 1, 1876 and executed the same day by arresting all the within named members of the House of Representatives (except the Hon. D.U. Barziza and the Hon. T.M. Dennis), whom I now have before the bar of the House."[12] It was a good day's work, but hardly exciting or adventuresome.

Obviously after hunting Texas fugitives, being the Sergeant-at-Arms was too tame and another type of work was required for the youthful North Carolinian-Texan. It was necessary to resign rather than merely walk away from his position. During those months spent as Sergeant-at-Arms he undoubtedly listened to some of the debates concerning appropriation for Capt. Leander H. McNelly's Special State Troops working between the Nueces River and the Rio Grande, the dangerous area known as the Nueces Strip. This inspired him to consider another change in his career. On August 11, 1876, after four months working in the capitol, Hall turned in his resignation to Honorable T.R. Bonner, House Speaker, and to the House members, writing:

> Having been commissioned a Lieutenant with special State Troops, I hereby tender my resignation as Sergeant-at-Arms of this House.
>
> Thanking you all for the general and uniform kindness and courtesy shown me while exercising the duties of my office, I am, very respectfully, Your obedient servant, J.L. Hall.

Hall's resignation was accepted on motion of House member Baker and a new Sergeant-at-Arms was appointed. [13]

After serving four years in the Confederate Army, Leander Harvey McNelly had retired to his farm in Washington County to peacefully live out his days. Republican Governor E.J. Davis created the Texas State Police force to curb lawlessness and crime in the state; he and Adjutant General James Davidson needed capable captains to lead. McNelly was selected to be one of the first four captains; he proved to be one of the most respected members of that unpopular force, which quickly became a scourge of the land to many Texans. Ironically in that time and place the rank-and-file included former slaves, Mexicans, and whites. When the legislature ended the force in April 1873, McNelly returned to his plantation, again intending to live out his days peacefully, knowing consumption would probably take his life within a few years. Then the new governor, Democrat Richard Coke, created the Frontier Battalion, a force whose goal was similar to that of the State Police: to reduce the amount of lawlessness and crime in Texas. In addition to the Frontier Battalion, whose specific assignment was to eradicate the hostile raiding of Comanche and Kiowa on the frontier line, he added a special unit and called upon McNelly to lead it. It became the Washington County Volunteer Militia Company A, based in McNelly's home county. At first the headquarters was at Burton where McNelly lived. It was this "special state troops" that Jesse Lee Hall now joined. The force was always dependent upon the legislature appropriating funds for the service. After months of service in DeWitt County dealing with members of the feuding Taylor and Sutton factions, McNelly was called out of service due to the lack of funding. Then in May the legislature acted. House bill No. 83 read: "An act of making an appropriation to pay Capt. L.H. McNelly's company volunteer militia, for sixteen months' service on the Rio Grande to July 1,1876"; the bill was approved on May 25.[14] J.L. Hall chose to leave the safe and peaceful halls of the capitol building to serve with McNelly in the notorious area known as the "Nueces Strip." He was now Lieutenant Hall, Special State Troops.

Hall had missed out on some of the more exciting adventures that the men of Captain McNelly's company had experienced. In mid-June McNelly and his men had charged upon the residence of the notorious John King Fisher on Pendencia Creek[15] and arrested him and those men present. The number of those arrested varied in reports from seven to ten. There was no resistance. George Durham, one of McNelly's men, recalled the incident but remembered arresting only nine men and recorded them as follows: King Fisher, Frank Porter, Warren Allen, Bill Templeton, Al Roberts, Bill Wainwright, Jim Honeycut, and two brothers, Wes and Bill Bruton.[16] The prisoners were turned over to authorities at Eagle Pass while McNelly and his troop moved on to scout between Oakville and San Antonio. Fisher and his men were released on bond.[17]

Hall quickly became accepted by the men of McNelly's company. One of the young men was Napoleon Augustus Jennings, a native of Pennsylvania who at the age of eighteen years visited Texas for the first time and quickly determined that "life would not be worth living outside of Texas." He had received an excellent education and with his father's blessing he journeyed to Texas to seek his fortune. On May 26, 1876, he enlisted in McNelly's force and served until February 1, 1877, a period of nine months. He later wrote of his adventures, which included his experiences under J.L. Hall. Did not Hall as well find Texas so wonderful that he could not live outside the Lone Star State? Although there are serious faults in Jennings's writing, such as invented conversation and his placing himself in certain actions in which he did not participate, much of his memoir, *A Texas Ranger,* we can accept— with caution.[18] Jennings may have instilled in the men that the new lieutenant was a most friendly man, and immediately gave him the nickname of "Red" Hall, but perhaps the men did not use that to his face. He certainly had reddish hair and this may have been a common nickname while in Grayson County as well. Author-traveler Edward King in his 1875 work *The Great South* captioned an engraving as "Red" Hall. Jennings described the first time the new lieutenant came into McNelly's camp, which then was "just below Oakville."

> We had heard that he was coming and that he was a hard man to deal with, but we soon discovered that he was a splendid fellow, full of fun, of charming manners, and only "nasty" when dealing with outlaws. His hair was bright red, and he soon got the nickname of "Red Hall," which clung to him ever after. When he rode into our camp that afternoon, early in August, 1876, the first thing he did was to sing out:
>
> "Say, have any of you boys got a chew of tobacco? I'm Hall."

And the boys, according to Jennings, liked that first impression and welcomed him into their camp. Almost immediately the boys, or privates, played a trick on him by getting him to tell stories of his life in the House of Representatives, and then one by one sneaked off and left him relating his stories to the campfire. When he realized what the boys had done he joined in the laughter of course. The boys "howled in sheer delight" but Hall answered: "'You're a tough lot' . . . with a grin." [19]

As a ranger, Hall could expect to deal frequently with cattle and horse thieves as well as killings and assaults; there was also the responsibility of completing the Monthly Return, describing each month's activities, number of scouts, miles traveled, fugitives captured, and so on. Hall's first return, dated August 31 at Oakville, reported thus: "No arrests made during this month that I have any official information on. Hall has made some. Sheriff of this County has made several calls for men, who were furnished." [20] Hall's company would be broken up into small squads, each under a lieutenant or a sergeant or corporal. Each man was expected to act as a leader if called upon to do so.

Newspaper editors quickly found Hall to be good copy. A single issue of the *Austin Weekly Statesman* provides three examples of print about Hall, either directly or indirectly. Because of McNelly's illness, Hall was in charge of "McNelly's company." In the popular "Texas— Facts and Fancies" column readers found the following:

> Lee Hall, late sergeant-at-arms to the House, becomes a lieutenant with McNelly.
>
> McNelly's company are encamped near Oakville, and the *Tribune* says they are nice fellows and the people are glad to have them around.
>
> Lee Hall has gone to fight Injuns with Horace Rowe and McNelly, over about Oakville, their post office address. Both of them promise to write to the Statesman.[21]

It is interesting that Hall's first Monthly Return was made out at Oakville, the county seat of Live Oak County. He and his men would experience numerous scouts and much action in that county. It had developed a bad reputation, which caused McNelly's men to demonstrate a presence there. Public opinion varied widely about the new unit, the Special State Troops. Some citizens were concerned about the fact that the rangers were "scouring the town and vicinity of rough and ruthless cowboys" while others felt there should be a greater presence. Some felt that there was not then nor had there been lawlessness in Oakville. "A few cowboys from other places have been the cause of the ill-repute under which we live," was one explanation. It was the general belief that the local option law would prevent much rowdy conduct, as whisky was considered the cause of much desperadoism and under local option would not be available "except on the sly." The local community leaders were understandably concerned about the reputation of not only the county but the county seat as well if the rangers spent too much time there.

But what of the land in general?

> Oakville . . . is not an ill-looking place, but it is in the midst of an ill-looking region. No cultivated fields, no fine pastures or other restful objects are to be seen in journeying to and from it. It is said to be an excellent stock country, but the odds must be in

> favor of the stock, as the brushy nature of the vegetation defies successful search.

The town was described as an "oasis" but what of the country after leaving this oasis?

> Leaving [Oakville] is a desert of prickly pear and chaparral, the wayfarer journeys on and on through a country of monotonous silence and dreariness, past Mexican sheep ranchers, past distant flocks feeding on invisible grass, until the new-old town of San Diego comes suddenly to view, seemingly a jumble of thatched roofs brown with age and shingles, yet fresh from distant pineries.[22]

While the landscape meant that capturing cattle or horse thieves was the most common job of the rangers, Hall may have been surprised when he learned the bank at Goliad was robbed. Initial reports indicated that eight masked men had entered the Seeligson Bank of Goliad between two and three o'clock in the afternoon of Tuesday, August 15, 1876, and robbed it of several hundred dollars. Only one employee was in the bank at the time, a Captain Mitchell, and he was ordered to open the vault. Mitchell claimed that the vault was locked and he could not open it as it had two combinations and he knew only one and Mr. E.J. Seeligson knew the other. This lie forestalled the robbers and they grabbed whatever money they could find in the drawers and rode out of town, "whooping and yelling." Captain Mitchell's coolness under duress saved the bank a large amount of money.[23] These eight men would become the subjects of many a ranger scout.

Frank Callison, a cattleman of Gonzales County, was arrested by a posse of citizens in Frio County in early September and charged with stealing fourteen head of horses as well as an assault with attempt to kill.[24] Charged with crimes that could place him in prison for a lengthy term he decided to turn state's evidence and named the eight who robbed the bank. According to Callison, the seven besides himself, were E.L. "Lark" Ferguson,[25] William Cavin, Alford Day, James T. Trimble, Thomas Jasper, John Gruin, and his own brother Thomas Callison. In addition, four others were identified as aiding and abetting: John King Fisher, William Taylor, "Dock" Cornett, and William Brooking.

Rumors of course circulated wildly as to the identity of the bank robbers. E.U. Brooking, best known as Upshur Brooking, did feel in danger knowing the tenacity of some of the rangers to capture a fugitive or even a suspicious man, and visited Lieutenant Hall's camp to ask for protection. He stayed a few days there but then decided Mexico offered more protection, stole a horse and headed south. By leaving he left the wild rumors as well as his bondsmen who would demand his appearance at the next District Court session.[26]

Lieutenant Hall quickly made himself known to authorities in area counties. On September 1 he was called by the sheriffs of Bee and San Patricio Counties to quiet a disturbance at Sharpsburg, a small community a mile north of the Nueces River in south central San Patricio County. Then it was a lively little community but today nothing is left except a ranch headquarters. Hall wrote in his report, "Order restored. No arrests." It appears to be a case of the sheriffs not wanting to get involved; after all, their position is obtained by the voters he represents. On the tenth of September the sheriff of Live Oak County called upon Hall for assistance. Instead of going himself Hall sent a detachment— which could have been two men or a half dozen— and one Mexican was arrested. He was charged with accessory to murder and lodged in the Oakville jail.[27]

During this time period a young man from Goliad County was also becoming notorious as a killer and leader of a gang of desperadoes: John King Fisher. He would eventually change his ways (on the strong advice of Captain McNelly) and then become acting sheriff of Uvalde County. In the seventies his influence ranged from the counties in the Nueces Strip and especially on his home range along the Pendencia Creek. A minor tempest between newspaper editors about McNelly's jurisdiction stressed Fisher's reputation as well as giving Lee Hall an unexpected word of praise. The *Sherman Register* in September of 1876 clearly made its point: "The statement that McNelly's operations are confined to the territory west of the Colorado [R]iver is untrue. He operates wherever sent by the Executive, in Grayson or Galveston [C]ounties, as well as the counties infested by King Fisher and Wesley Hardin. We don't need McNelly, however, and for the reason that we elect good officers and protect ourselves, just as the people of the West might do if they would do their duty."[28] The editor of the *Sherman Register* certainly was recalling the bravery of Lee Hall when he was a deputy sheriff hunting lawbreakers in Grayson County when he composed that opinion.

A deadly incident occurred the night of September 29, and again Hall had sent a detachment to deal with the matter, he having total trust in the effective work of his men. Sergeant John B. Armstrong was in charge of the squad sent to a location known as "ghost lake" but actually identified as Espantosa Lake in Dimmit County. This body of water, "with its arms" was seven or eight miles in length. It was narrow but deep, and "contains almost every variety of fish." The banks were lined with live oaks, "which are heavily laden with the creamy mast." This was how one report described the site where a group of thieves, possibly including King Fisher, had encamped. The plan was simply to arrest them.[29] On the way to the camp Armstrong and his men captured one suspected thief, Noley Key. Approaching the camp about midnight the men dismounted, leaving two men to guard Key. The rangers began advancing towards the suspected outlaws' camp but within twenty yards two of the thieves began shooting at the oncoming rangers. "We responded promptly, and a lively little fight ensued, resulting in the death of three of them and the wounding of another in five places," Armstrong reported. Back at the earlier camp Noley Key attempted to escape in the excitement of the gunfire that startled the horses, but the two guards, after ordering him to stop, shot him down in his attempt to escape. Armstrong identified the dead thieves as John Martin, Jim Roberts, George Muller/Miller, and Noley Key, "all of whom were desperate characters and the terror of this country." A fifth man, Jim McAllister, was wounded in the fight. The rangers were disappointed that King Fisher was not among the desperate men fighting back, but he had left a week before with a large drove of cattle. The thieves had about fifty head of stolen horses and twenty-two yoke of work oxen in Thompson's pasture. They planned to "round up" the pasture the next day.[30] Armstrong had the less dangerous task of returning the recovered livestock to their rightful owners before he could say that the job was done.

While rumors about the bank robbery still flourished in Goliad in neighboring DeWitt County a double killing occurred that would later involve Hall and his rangers as well as marking the end of the shooting phase of the Sutton-Taylor Feud. The shooting marked the beginning of years of courtroom battles, which did not conclude until close to the opening of the twentieth century. The victims were Dr. P.H. Brassell and his son George, who were taken from their home and murdered during the night of September 19, 1876, by a group of *unmasked* men. The Brassell family was a large one known by everyone in the area. At the time the mob came the doctor was ill; some sources say he had only recently chosen the spot where he was to be buried. Why Dr. Brassell was murdered was a mystery to all except the killers. He was a native of Fayette County, Georgia, was a member of the Constitutional Convention of 1866, which would allow the defeated state back into the United States after the Civil War, and a member of the Georgia legislature in 1868, 1869, and 1870. He moved to Texas in December 1870 and located at the little community of Shiloh, some three miles from Yorktown, DeWitt County. Based on the testimony of family members the following five men were identified as members of the mob: Dave Augustine, James Hester, William Cox, William Meador, and Jake Ryan. Those charged appeared for an examining trial at Justice of the Peace C.C. Howerton's court in Clinton with a large number of witnesses present. The five accused were released on bond; two others not immediately identified were later identified and arrested. [31] Before the year was over Hall and the accused murderers of Dr. P.H. Brassell and his son George would face each other with rifles, six-shooters, and shotguns at the ready.

Captain McNelly was now suffering in the last stages of tuberculosis and was hospitalized much of the time. Lieutenant Hall found himself the de facto commander of McNelly's company. Hall at times met with McNelly to discuss his actions. King Fisher was now notorious but there were fugitives of less notoriety to deal with. On October 9 Lieutenant Hall, or an unidentified ranger, arrested J.B. Johnson in Gillespie County and charged him with cattle theft. He was delivered to the Bexar County jail in San Antonio. Charles Fox had shot the proprietor of a hotel in Pleasanton, Atascosa County, for no apparent reason. Lieutenant Hall and five men scouted in Refugio and sought out the wanted man. How he learned Fox was there is unknown, but Hall arrested him, charging him with assault to murder. Robert Rice was arrested also, and charged with theft. A witness to the arrest described it as a thrilling event: "Our quiet town was aroused from the dull monotony peculiar to country villages, and thrown into a fever of excitement the other day, by the sudden appearance of Lieut. Hall and five men, who in one fell swoop, pounced down upon the person of one Charlie Fox, a well-known desperado in these parts, and one Bob Rice, and bore them off unwilling captives in the direction of Goliad." [32] A William Dawson was arrested on a charge of assault with intent to murder; he was arrested in Bee County and delivered to the authorities in county seat Beeville. [33] A note added to the September Monthly Return mentions arrests made on October 3 and October 5 respectively: on the third a squad arrested George McCarty and Wesley Bruton and charged them with theft of horses and cattle; on the fifth perhaps the same squad arrested Charles Bruton who was accused of rape. The prisoners were turned over to the sheriff of Dimmit County. [34] The Brutons frequently were with King Fisher and were frequently the subject of ranger scouts.

Hall kept busy as well as his men. On Sunday night, October 22, he and a posse rode to Gonzales to continue working up the Seeligson Bank robbery case; two suspected robbers were then in the Gonzales jail. Corporal Oliver S. Watson[35] also contributed to the efforts. On the twenty-third, at Helena in Karnes County, he arrested Charles Romaine who was "an important witness in the Seeligson Bank robbery." He also arrested Jake Jones of Bell County, accused of cattle stealing and murder. Watson nearly captured Bill Taylor, accused of aiding and abetting the robbers, but Taylor was tipped off before Watson could get on his trail and managed to escape. Watson had spent four days in and around Helena working up the case. McNelly's men, working under Lieutenant Hall, were "making it hot for desperadoes." [36] Jake Jones learned that his alias was worthless in evading the law. His real name was Quinlan Miller and the Monthly Return shows he was wanted in Coryell County for "Rescuing prisoners" and also in McLennan County charged with cattle theft. Miller alias Jones was arrested in Goliad County on October 30 and delivered to San Antonio for safe keeping.[37]

Dealing with fugitives from justice was no doubt exciting at times, when a second's hesitation might lead to a fugitive escaping justice or a ranger getting shot. On occasion, however, nature acted against humans; a hail storm could be severe and dangerous, especially if the human was out of doors on a horse or on foot with no shelter close by. Such a hail storm struck the afternoon of Wednesday, October 20, 1876. Lieutenant Hall and a detachment were returning from Gonzales when a hail storm struck. The men were about four miles from town. One ranger was struck by a hailstone which was big enough to knock him off his horse, "considerably hurt" as the *Goliad Guard* alleged. Hall dismounted in an attempt to protect himself from the elements but his horse escaped in a panic. Having lost his mount Hall ran to a small nearby tree, which offered some protection. The storm was about a mile wide and generally followed the course of the river. In its path trees were denuded of leaves; the grass was flattened as if wagons had created a smooth landscape. In several places the pasture fence of cattleman D.R. Fant was taken up and then dropped to earth several miles away. Over one hundred panes of glass were broken in the mansion of Judge Claiborne and there were others who lost windows and whose homes suffered damage. But neither Hall nor any of his men were seriously injured from the effects of the October hail storm, despite the report by the *Goliad Guard*.[38]

Hall's men made two significant arrests on November 2, both in Guadalupe County, just east of Bexar County. The two criminals were known as Jack Day and Jake Ryan and both had developed some recognition for their participation in the Sutton-Taylor Feud, which had for years raged in DeWitt and surrounding counties. Jack Hays Day, a blood relative of the large Taylor family, may have participated in several of the gun battles against the followers of William Sutton. Nicholas J. "Jake" Ryan was a solid follower of Sutton and in the following month would be arrested along with six others for the murder of Dr. P.H. Brassell and his son George in DeWitt County, one of the last acts of the feud.

Day and Ryan were arrested in Guadalupe County; two others arrested the same busy day in Blanco County and Wilson County were a man identified as T. Tiner and one identified only as Zapp. Tiner was in reality Martin Tiner and he had earned the dubious distinction of killing Cornelius Fahey, recognized as the first Austin police officer to die in the line of duty. Fahey was a twenty-year-old officer, who had been shot on March 7, 1875, and died two days later.[39] This man Zapp was arrested in Wilson County and delivered to San Antonio authorities. When the rangers delivered prisoners to the Bexar County jail, frequently a newspaper reporter was present to record the event. The *Daily Express* had this to say about the Tiner arrest: "When he was captured, it seems he was out of ammunition, and was going into a store to obtain a supply, when arrested. He resisted, and made a pass at one of the officers of the law with his knife, just grazing his throat and cutting away a good deal of his beard. The rangers captured four others, [*sic*: three others in addition to Tiner—Ryan, Day, and Zapp] accused with various crimes, on this trip. They deserve great credit for their efficiency in the apprehension of criminals, and the southwest owes them a debt she will not regret.[40] It was a busy day indeed, having made seven arrests, with perhaps the most significant one being that of bringing in Tiner who had killed an Austin peace officer.

On November 1 Hall sent a detachment to Caldwell County to investigate the robbery of a store, variously identified as Johnson's store or Mannix's store. Whoever recorded the month's scouts indicated there were six arrests but gave no further details. Elsewhere on the return is listed the identity of the actual four men arrested: Frank Wingate, G.W. Keith, Ed. Wingate, and Howard Little, all arrested on November 7 in Wilson County for robbery of a store and theft. They were delivered to Gonzales County authorities. That did not end the action, however. E.T. Wingate, a Wilson County resident, believed in the innocence of all those arrested and wrote a letter to the *Galveston Daily News* regarding the arrest. He challenged what had appeared in the weekly edition of the *News* of November 13— a telegram from San Antonio dated November 9 —identifying the four men as having been arrested by some of McNelly's men on suspicion that they were connected with the so-called "Harwood robbery." Allegedly Frank Wingate and G.W. Keith were identified by Mr. Jackson, the merchant who was robbed. E.T. Wingate was clearly disturbed that this report was "not only very inaccurate, but misstates facts." He went on to state that Ed Wingate and Howell [Howard?] Little "had to be turned loose by them at once, as there was not a shadow of evidence against either of them," while Frank Wingate and G.W. Keith, instead of being lodged in the Gonzales County jail, were "unconditionally released, without even a bond or bail being required of them." During the robbery Frank Wingate and G.W. Keith had been, according to E.T. Wingate, "some sixty miles off in Lee [C]ounty" and could so prove by "unimpeachable witnesses." E.T. Wingate, who seemingly was the accused Ed Wingate, wrote it was "bad enough for all the parties concerned to have been mistaken for robbers; but it is indeed too bad to have such reports as the one alluded to published all over the country; and you will certainly not deny me, as one of the aggrieved parties, the small boon of correcting and contradicting these erroneous statements through the same columns in which they were published.[41] E.T. Wingate's letter, written on November 15 from Stockdale in Wilson County, appeared in the *News* on page one.

Apparently things had become peaceful in Goliad County, at least peaceful enough for Hall to operate elsewhere. A notice in the Galveston paper stated that Lieutenant Hall with his detachment from McNelly's command had been there in Goliad for two months and would be moving to Oakville. Compliments had been earned and the *Goliad Guard* informed its readers that the "Lieutenant did good service in arresting and bringing to justice violators of the law, and the departure of himself and men is much regretted by our citizens, to whom, they have endeared themselves by their promptness, vigilance and gentlemanly deportment during their stay."[42] Captain McNelly was no doubt proud.

Then on November 20 a shooting cast a gloom over the good citizens of Goliad County. That day Deputy Sheriff Andrew Herriman, a forty-two-year-old farmer by occupation, called on Lieutenant Hall requesting him to assist in arresting two men: Henry Huff, the twenty-four-year-old son of William Huff, and Henry Luderbacker, a nineteen-year-old son of neighbor Cornelius Luderbacker, the latter indicted for killing a young man the previous summer. Hall with four men and the sheriff with three men, a total of nine lawmen to arrest two, arrived at William Huff's home and surrounded it about 8:00 in the evening. Hall and his men placed themselves at the front while the deputy and his posse were at the rear. The lawmen's intention of course was to make a peaceful arrest but due to their insufficient reconnaissance it turned deadly. Close to the house there was a small out-building consisting of one room and a small fireplace. In that building, only a few steps away from the main house, were John Schewitz, a brother of Mrs. Huff, and John Gisler. The parties who were the object of the lawmen's quest were not at home: Henry Huff was at Victoria and Henry Luderbacker was in Cuero to get a load of lumber. The other boys were out coon hunting with the dogs; hence there was no alarm given. Two of the deputy's men went to this adjacent building, covered the men with Winchesters and demanded their surrender. Neither Schewitz nor Gisler knew who these men were but Schewitz exited the building between them, stumbling over a bench when a shot was fired by one of the deputy's men. Gisler, hearing the shooting, grabbed a six-shooter and fired several shots at Hall's men. He hit no one and the return fire also was ineffective. All now approached the small building where the shots were coming from. Gisler, seeing Hall and his men approaching, fired one more shot and then surrendered, probably out of ammunition. He was unhurt. Schewitz was on the ground, badly wounded but still alive. Mrs. Huff, fearing these men would shoot her brother again, threw herself on his body and screamed that if they were going to kill him it would be over her dead body. Lieutenant Hall, recognizing there was no more danger to his men or the deputy's, now informed her they were officers and that no one was going to be hurt. Mrs. Huff and the two young men now informed Hall that they had no idea that they were officers. They admitted that they were afraid the men were of the Brooking party, a group considered thieves and killers, and they feared they would be killed. Now Deputy Herriman and Lieutenant Hall could only offer their regrets, as both Schewitz and Gisler were innocent parties.

Four days later, on the twenty-third of November, an unidentified party, possibly one of the deputy's posse, wrote his version of the tragedy, which was sent to the *Galveston Daily News.* He wrote that the "affair has cast a gloom over this section of the county, and there is a good deal of blame laid on the deputy sheriff for attempting to make an arrest in the manner he did. If he had come there in daytime, or went into the house alone, there would have been no trouble, as the family and the young men would have known who he was, but the men he sent in were strangers to them, and it is reasonable to suppose that they would protect themselves until they knew who they were."[43]

The *Victoria Advocate* and then the *Galveston Daily News* provided a slightly different version of the tragedy. This version reported that the lawmen, Hall's men as well as the deputy's posse, intended to arrest only Henry Huff, charged with murder. Schewitz and Gisler were seated in the small building and were unaware of the men approaching. "So stealthily did the party approach, that no one was apprised of their presence until they had thrust the muzzles of their guns into the open windows and had ordered the surrender of the young men." Schewitz or Gisler did not know who the men were with rifles pointed at them; Schewitz attempted to flee the building but as he passed through the doorway two men fired at him and he ran only a few steps and fell over a bench in the yard. "The party then gathered around him, and while he was down, unable to escape or resist arrest, again shot him, inflicting four wounds upon an innocent victim, from the effects of which he died within two hours." [44] This version varies in the man who was being sought and in its claim that Schewitz died from his wounds.

In the same newspaper, the *Galveston Daily News,* the report that had appeared in the *Cuero Bulletin* provided another version "of the late unfortunate homicide in Goliad [C]ounty." According to this version, the lawmen consisted of "a party of McNelly's men" which was under the command of the sheriff – not a deputy– which surrounded Mr. Huff's house. "The inmates, alarmed at the movement, fired at them, which was returned, and resulted in the killing of Mr. John Schwetz [*sic*], a young relative of the owner." The other young man, Gisler (or Giesler) escaped. All that could be said was that the state troops claimed they acted in self-defense, having been fired upon first. Summarized the *Bulletin*: "The young men were not aware of the character of the party outside, and very naturally supposed they were some desperate men come to attack them." The recommendation was that if such a situation might occur again, the sheriff or his deputy, whichever might be in command, "should have made himself known, and thus calmed the apprehensions of the inmates, who were not the people they were in search of."[45]

No report yet located provides a clue as to where the Goliad County sheriff may have been in late November 1876. The sheriff had been C.P. Miles but he had been removed from office for "incompetence" as the *Galveston Daily News* reported. [46] His replacement was James Lincoln who was appointed on September 26, 1876, and who served Goliad County until November 5, 1878. [47] Perhaps if he had been in charge of the posse, in company with Lieutenant Hall, the entire affair would have ended peacefully. The group should have approached during the day time thus avoiding the tragedy. Of course whoever was in charge of the posse ought to have announced himself by a "Hello, the house!" But none of these actions took place.

Later that month Hall acted in the most important arrest of his career and perhaps the most important arrest during the troubles of the Sutton-Taylor Feud. With McNelly's weakening physical condition preventing him from doing any type of field work, it was left to Lieutenant Hall to act, and he and his men would much prefer working on horseback with the potential of real action than sitting idly in camp. On December 20 indictments were handed down for Hall to arrest the alleged murderers of Dr. Philip H. Brassell and his son George. [48] It would be the task of Lieutenant Hall to arrest these men and deliver them to DeWitt County courthouse and jail, and to safely keep them until their trial. Those named in the two indictments were: David Augustine, James Hester, William Cox, Charles H. Heissig, William D. Meador, Nicholas J. "Jake" Ryan, and Joseph Sitterle.[49] Many citizens were disturbed over the situation, believing that the witnesses could not be so sure of their identity that late at night. Lieutenant Hall developed a plan in which he might be able to arrest the group of seven at one time. A month before, on November 22, William Meador had married Amanda Augustine, daughter of the indicted David Augustine; and Joseph Sitterle had married Malinda Cox, a sister of the indicted William Cox. In addition the bridal couples and their friends and families planned a wedding dance on December 22. This worked perfectly for Hall as the opportunity was there for all seven to be arrested and delivered to the jail in Clinton.

There are several versions of the arrest. Jennings, who may have been with Hall that night, recalled that it was in a drizzling rain and colder than usual when Hall took his squad of sixteen men to where the wedding dance was being held. The plan was simple: surround the house filled with men and women, make the arrest, and then deliver the prisoners to Clinton. No one was to get through the ranger surround. In dramatic fashion Lieutenant Hall entered the main room with his Winchester in hand. The music stopped and all eyes glared at the intruding lawman. Some women screamed. Joe Sitterle demanded: "Do you want any one here, Hall?" Then the lieutenant called out the names of all seven and demanded their arrest. In the following exchange Sitterle asked how many men Hall had, to which Hall answered sixteen. Then for a moment Sitterle seemed ready to fight as the rangers were badly outnumbered, but he then reconsidered when Hall demanded the women and children leave as he only wanted to fight men. With this show of bravado the wedding guests wilted and surrendered. Hall allowed the dance to continue, and the rangers enjoyed the food and drinks and even danced with some of the ladies present, according to Jennings's account. At dawn the lieutenant with his men and the seven prisoners left for Clinton.[50] It is probable that Jennings's comment that some of the ladies present danced with some of the rangers is apocryphal.

George Durham, a Georgia-born lad who had joined McNelly at the age of nineteen and continued under Hall, also left his version of the arrest, and he too may have been present that rainy night. His account of the arrest, first published in 1937 and in a revised version in 1962, generally agreed with that of Jennings. One aspect described by Durham that may have been true was that Hall took one of the seven out and placed him under guard, threatening that he would be shot if any one attempted to escape from the dance. No one made an attempt. Even with the dramatics and conversation between Sitterle and Hall, which may be apocryphal, the seven indicted men were arrested and delivered to jail where Judge Henry Clay Pleasants took over in the court system. Essentially the arrest was peaceful; since two of the accused murderers had been deputies in DeWitt County they both anticipated they all would be released on bond and then the district attorney would eventually drop the charges due to insufficient evidence.[51]

McNelly's Monthly Return for December merely indicated that the seven men were arrested on December 22 and delivered to the Clinton jail. There is no description of the dramatics that other writers described, not even that the arrest took place at a wedding dance. [52]

The famed Western artist Frederic Remington claimed to have had a pleasant conversation with Captain Hall in which the question of the arrest was raised. Remington recalled that Hall had used "secret-service men, discovered the perpetrators, and also that they were to be gathered at a wedding on a certain night. He surrounded the house and demanded their surrender, at the same time saying that he did not want to kill the women and children. Word returned that they would kill him and all the rangers. Hall told them to allow their women and children to depart, which was done; then, springing on the gallery of the house, he shouted, 'Now gentlemen, you can go to killing Rangers, but if you don't surrender, the Rangers will go to killing you.' This was too frank a willingness for midnight assassins, and they gave up." [53]

The arrest of the men charged with killing the Brassell father and son was a significant act not only for McNelly and Hall but for the amount of lawlessness in DeWitt County as well. The double killing of the Brassells was in effect the last shooting directly related to the Sutton-Taylor Feud; with the arrest Hall, if he had been so inclined, could have taken credit for that act, but did not. Arresting the seven indicted men without any shooting was fortunate for all concerned.

Some arrests, however, were deadly. Two of the dependable men serving Hall, Sergeant John Barklay Armstrong and Private Thomas W. Deggs, were victorious in a deadly confrontation at Graytown, Wilson County. The man they encountered was John Lewis Mayfield, convicted of murdering a man named Robert Montgomery in Parker County a few years previously. Armstrong and Deggs encountered Mayfield and informed him he was their prisoner; his response was to the effect that he "would be damned if he was" and he drew his pistol and fired three shots before the rangers' answering gunshots killed him. Either of the two shots would have killed him. [54] This self-defense killing of Mayfield occurred on December 7, 1876.

The specific date of another incident was not recorded in the Monthly Return, merely the notation that "Since Dec. 10 Lt. Hall arrested G.N. Ludebeck [*sic*]." This was later followed by the statement that William Fatheree and William Jacobs were arrested for the murder of a man named Middleton near Yorktown, DeWitt County. One wishes the return was more detailed, but in this case newspaper accounts add details to the incident in violence-prone DeWitt County. The *Statesman* reported in its popular column "Texas—Facts and Fancies" that one Louderbach was accompanied by two other persons, not yet identified, when they encountered John Middleton, "a good citizen of Goliad." A fight occurred, and Middleton was shot and left in the road, mortally wounded. Of course there was much excitement about this matter and "murdering must be repressed." [55] The *Statesman* issued a follow-up item in a later issue, pointing out that John Middleton had been killed near Buzzard Point, in DeWitt County, "a few days ago, in a difficulty with his brother-in-law." [56] Brothers-in-law fighting and shooting at each other? The cause of the difficulty between them has not been learned. The men involved were neighbors: William Jacobs was sixteen when the 1870 Goliad County census was conducted, living in household Number 191; William Fatheree was eighteen living in household Number 192 according to the same census, taken six years before the murder. John Middleton, the "good citizen of Goliad," was a twenty-nine-year-old farmer living in household Number 189 with wife Mary and one-year-old son named Lesley and five-year-old daughter Francis Louderbach. [57] The individual G.N. Louderbach has not been located on any census and one wonders if Hall misnamed the assailant.

Another killing happened shortly after this action, which involved the men of McNelly's command. The Monthly Return reports casually that Corporal Williams[58] arrested Casper "Jack" Wingate on December 20, 1876, in Wilson County, and charged him with several indictments in Liberty County, Texas. [59] Hall's report provided few details: "Whilst carrying him to San Antonio [the] party was bushwhacked & Wingate running to the thicket to escape was killed." A newspaper report was more detailed. In this account Corporal Williams with Horace Rowe[60] and one other ranger captured Wingate. The trio intended to deliver their prisoner to San Antonio when the rangers "in the Salado bottom were fired upon by Wingate's pals, who sought to rescue him. Wingate . . . was instantly killed, and Horace Rowe's horse was killed under him." Of course the rangers returned the fire but none of the shots was effective.[61] It was a dangerous incident indeed; Wingate's pals, intending to rescue Jack, may have shot him when firing at the rangers. The rangers may have shot Wingate in the exchange. The three rangers— Williams, Rowe, and the unidentified one —shooting at the would-be rescuers and they firing back resulted only in the death of the one prisoner and one ranger horse.

The final Monthly Return for the year of 1876 ended with this simple entry that John Mayfield was arrested for murder; no place was indicated or who attempted the arrest, but this telling comment appeared in the remarks column: "Killed while resisting arrest."[62]

Chapter Four

"Cleaning Out the Crop of Knaves and Bloody-handed Scoundrels"

—*Daily Democratic Statesman*, February 18, 1877

The people of Goliad County could indeed show their appreciation for the accomplishments of Lieutenant Hall and his rangers. A representative of the county, undoubtedly a stock raiser, wrote a lengthy report to the editor of the *Galveston Daily News* showing how the work of Hall had made a significant change in the county. Prior to Hall's presence the citizens had "quietly submitted" to the "lawless element" that had congregated there. Goliad citizens had generally refused to react to "the terrorism which prevailed" and "did not dare to express what they felt." But then there was the Seeligson Bank robbery, which seemed to bring about a different attitude in the people, and although the affair was "humiliating" it was a "god send to the county," according to the anonymous letter writer. Hall came to Goliad and a "marked change for the better" was evident over what it was a year before. Even a "few official changes" were made, although unfortunately the writer did not name what the specific changes were. Praise was due Hall for the way he worked up the bank robbery case, and others as well; not only did Hall receive praise, but also the "gentlemanly bearing of his men has won for them the respect of all." In Goliad there was now "a spirit of determination exhibited by the citizens," which certainly gave confidence to the people of the town and the county as well.[1]

This was well and good but there was still important work to be done. Arresting the indicted Brassell killers was only one step in the process of seeking justice. From the Clinton jail, which was notoriously insecure, Hall took them to Galveston for "safe keeping" but there was no room there. Finally, on Tuesday, January 9, he delivered them to the new Travis County jail in Austin. This jail, only recently completed, was considered by some to be secure and the DeWitt County prisoners were to be incarcerated there.[2] The structure was indeed new, and a much improved structure over the old, which had been compared to the Black Hole of Calcutta. In April 1876 the *Statesman* had reported that the new jail was nearly completed and when the iron cages were done they would "seem to be effectual bars to the liberty of man." But there may have been some doubt in the editor's mind, as he continued, seemingly with a sense of assuring his readers too much, "Verily the prisoners placed in the new jail will stay there until removed by law."[3] But there were several escapes before it had been open even five months. On August 29 four prisoners forced their way out and made their way out of Austin. The quartet were an unidentified Mexican, John Redding who had robbed the Comanche bank and then released the notorious Scott Cooley from the Lampasas jail, Joseph Van Wee sentenced to two years in the penitentiary for a robbery in Austin and awaiting an appeal, and one McLeavy, charged with a "murderous assault" the previous March. Then the *Statesman* headlined its reporting: "Our New Jail/All Show and No Security." Indeed, it was certainly not escape-proof, but the DeWitt County prisoners apparently bided their time believing they would win acquittal if they ever stood trial. There is no evidence that any of them attempted an escape.

Although Lieutenant Hall was gaining great respect from the law-abiding citizens of South Texas, Captain McNelly, although still officially in command, was growing weaker and weaker in his terminal battle with consumption, the common nineteenth-century term for tuberculosis. Everyone knew his disease would soon take his life. An added concern was that the ranging company mustered into service on July 26, 1876, under the law entitled "An act to suppress lawlessness and crime in certain parts of the State, and to make an appropriation therefor[e]," would be mustered out on January 25, 1877. That was the first part of General Order No. 14 from the Adjutant General's Office. This did not mark the end of Lieutenant Hall's career, however, as the second part of General Order No. 14 authorized him to "reconstruct a company" which would serve from January 25 for a period of three months, or "unless sooner discharged." This new company would consist of twenty-five men: two sergeants, two corporals, and twenty privates and one non-commissioned officer. If one questioned why this action was being taken, the third part of General Order No. 14 explained: the changes were "rendered necessary, in order to utilize to the best advantage the appropriation for the suppression of lawlessness and crime in certain portions of the State." That may have been sufficient for some people, but for many it was not. The fourth part of the "explanation" was that the governor and commander-in-chief— now Richard Hubbard— "regrets that the ill health of Capt. L.H. McNelly, during the past term of service of his company, as well as the present necessary reduction of his force below the proper command of a captain, indicates that another should be placed in charge of the small force that can be kept in service for even a limited time." There was an explanation that all could easily understand: McNelly was too ill to continue— receiving a captain's pay — and the money was not there. So the final part of the General Order No. 14 was that Captain McNelly would turn over all public property to Lieutenant Hall "who will receipt for the same." He would muster out the old company and then organize a new company.[5]

The rangers were not pleased with the results of the order. Napoleon A. Jennings, who although not actively involved in all the actions he described, certainly knew the temper of the men and wrote: "After the reorganization of the rangers, we returned to DeWitt County and continued to arrest men for whom indictments were found. We also went into other nearby counties, everywhere arresting desperadoes. . . . We had no fights and so did not kill anyone. We couldn't get into a fight in those days, because we couldn't find any men who would fight us." [6] Jennings apparently wished there had been fights with desperadoes, as he was recalling his Texas experiences and wanted to write about actual engagements with outlaws.

George Durham commented on how Hall and McNelly differed in their leadership style. "As a man Lieutenant Hall was all right. He had been city marshal at Denton and had been sergeant at arms of the Texas Senate [*sic*]. He knew his way around. But most of us Rangers felt that if Captain McNelly was being fired either Sergeant [John B.] Armstrong or Lieutenant [T.C. 'Pidge'] Robinson should be promoted. So we didn't fall over ourselves welcoming Lieutenant Hall."[7]

Although the new commander was not welcomed by the men, he was the one who gave the orders for what area needed to be scouted and who would be on a certain scout. If he was popular with the men, fine; if not, that would not distract him from his major concern, which was to reduce lawlessness and crime. If the legislature only gave him three months before ending funding for his company he would work hard for those three months. It became public knowledge that Hall was "a young man in the prime of manhood and thoroughly fitted for the service" and would take McNelly's place.[8] There was now little concern for raids from Indian war parties, but the criminal elements from across the Rio Grande as well as Texas counties, desperadoes and horse thieves and murderers, continued to be of great concern.

The year 1876 turning into 1877 drew many citizens to a dance in Karnes County, which resulted in tragedy, brought on by the combination of too much alcohol, too many six-shooters, and too many angry words resulting in gunplay. The dance was held in the little community of Polecat, now long since disappeared off the maps. What actually started the shooting is unknown but one of the guests, James Word, died. Apparently Word for some unknown reason attempted to kill Will B. "Speckled Bill" Jacobs, a cousin of the Allee brothers. For the first time attention was drawn to these brothers, Alfred Y. and Alonzo R., who later would become notorious. Jacobs managed to avoid the shots, but others joined in the shooting, resulting in a house filled with gunsmoke. Andrew Crockett "Crock" Tumlinson was wounded; James Washington "Buck" Lyons was also there and may have joined in the shooting. In court records it appears that Alfred Y. Allee fired the shot that mortally wounded James Word. Although the dance was held New Year's Eve it is impossible to determine if the shooting was on December 31, New Year's Eve, or January first. The exact date and cause of the ruckus resulting remains unknown, but four men were charged with the murder of Word: brothers Alfred and Alonzo Allee, Will Jacobs, and Buck Lyons. They were arrested on March 7, a good two months following the murder. The reason for the delay is unknown, as the Monthly Return noted simply that they were arrested for murder.[9]

This was not the first confrontation the Allees had with authority, as on the evening of December 13, 1876, Alfred Allee and Buck Lyons were in Goliad, and having "too much whisky on board" rode around the city square flourishing their six-shooters. Allee apparently attempted to get Lyons quieted down in order to leave town, but before he could accomplish that Sheriff James Lincoln and deputy Peter Miller challenged the boys, demanding them to disarm. Lyons surrendered his pistol but Allee, defiantly, responded "I will give you mine this way" and fired, wounding a bystander. Lyons and Allee left town. Sheriff Lincoln, the County Attorney, and some prominent citizens conferred and decided it would be best to contact Lieutenant Hall for assistance. Hall sent Sergeant Linton Lafayette Wright with three men to enforce the law regarding the carrying and firing of weapons within the city limits.

"Ajax" the Goliad reporter commented that with their presence "peace is with us once more." Witnesses could not agree on the cause of the disturbance but Ajax concluded that "Whisky was the main cause."[10] Alfred Allee would appear at the court in Helena and would give bond for his appearance at trial.[11]

In the latter part of February, Hall with a small force was in Goliad, "stirring things up." The unidentified Goliad correspondent who contributed items of interest to the Galveston *News* pointed out that it was becoming "a very unpleasant thing in this western country to kill a man or steal stock" as Hall, described as a "knight of a free lance" would take him in and place him in the new county jail, which had been just completed and had "quite a number of boarders already."[12]

Lieutenant Hall was active in many counties in southern Texas. His Monthly Return for February provided only the bare essentials. During the month of February his men had scouted in the following counties: DeWitt, Gonzales, Goliad, Karnes, Atascosa, Bee, Live Oak, McMullen, Frio, LaSalle, Duval, Dimmit, Zavala, Maverick, Refugio, San Patricio, Nueces, Aransas, Wilson, Bexar, Hays, Travis, Lavaca, Victoria, and Calhoun. He added the results of all those scouting miles: "Making 26 arrests and capturing and restoring about 6000 dollars worth of hides and other property to the proper owners." The *Victoria Advocate* was able to obtain a copy of Lieutenant Hall's Monthly Return and provided an extract of his activities during the month of February. Hall reporting that he had made twenty-six arrests in those counties named may have seemed like a case of braggadocio, but in reality he was merely reporting the facts. Those arrests in the report showed five arrested for murder, one arrested for assault to murder, seventeen arrested for theft, one arrested for cattle skinning, one for carrying a pistol, and one for a misdemeanor.[13]

Ranger captains were obliged to complete an additional form, "Statement of Arrests," some of which have survived and are preserved in the Adjutant General's Papers. For February 1877 Hall reported:

> Attempts were made to arrest members of other parties, among them Geo. M. Jackson and four of the Goliad Bank Robbers. Ferguson,[14] Cavin, & others near Eagle Pass by Sergt. Armstrong also Privates Rudd & Rector came near taking them, on the line of Duval & Live Oak; also Sergt. Watson made scouts after some parties, what their names I am not informed. Sergt. Armstrong arrested two men who proved to be the wrong men on a capias from Fayette County charging them with theft. I have kept eight or ten men on duty at Clinton to prevent any outbreak that might otherwise occur. While the others with myself have been scouting in different directions principally looking after hide & cattle thieves.[15]

The reason Lieutenant Hall had to leave some rangers at Clinton was to make sure that the Sutton-Taylor Feud "outbreak" did not get stirred up again. Apparently the presence of rangers did prevent any new disturbance.

Although there may not have been large rewards offered for the capture of the Seeligson Bank robbers, lawmen were keenly aware of the alleged identity of the accused. Sheriff Albertus Sweet of Lampasas County arrested a man whom he believed was Bill Taylor, an accused bank robber and who had killed Gabriel Slaughter in 1874 in Indianola, and delivered him to the Travis County jail. It was determined, however, that the man was not Taylor but John Cablo, not one of the men included in Frank Callison's confession. Ranger Thomas W. Deggs took him in charge and delivered Cablo to the Goliad jail, apparently believing if he was not the wanted man Taylor he was probably wanted for something else.[16]

On Sunday morning, March 11, 1877, Bee County Sheriff D.A.T. Walton arrived in Galveston to take prisoner John E. Singleton from there to the Bee County jail where he was scheduled to be executed by hanging. Singleton had been jailed in Galveston since June of 1876 because the Bee County jail was not considered secure. Singleton had been found guilty of murder in the first degree; the Galveston Court of Appeals affirmed the decision of the lower court and remanded him back to be hanged. Sheriff Walton and Lieutenant Hall with his company now had the responsibility of guarding the prisoner through his execution. The sheriff reported to the *Galveston Daily News* that all was quiet. He seemed quite defensive about his county, pointing out that the Singleton murder was the only one that had been committed there for many years. Also neither Singleton nor the man he killed were Bee County citizens, but both had been passing through when the deed was done. Walton "speaks very highly of Lieut. Hall and his men, and says they are doing much good in that section in ridding it of lawless men."[17] Singleton was to be hanged on the twenty-seventh of April.

Sgt. John B. Armstrong was one of the most successful men who served under Captain McNelly and who continued under Hall. Most importantly, Armstrong impressed members of the press no more or less than did Lieutenant Hall. On March 25 Armstrong arrested Wallace Carter in Houston County. The Monthly Return only provides the date and place of the arrest and that he was charged with murder, but two days later Sergeant Armstrong was in Houston with his prisoner when a reporter from the *Galveston Daily News* interviewed him. The information gathered was that Carter had "committed a murder in an interior county some ten years ago, and has been dodging the law ever since." That "interior county" happened to be Houston County, county seat Crockett, close to 175 miles from Galveston. Calvin Wooten (or as some newspaper reports spelled his name *Woolten*) "was shot while sitting in his own house; he lived but about two hours when he expired." The deceased was "well known, was much beloved, and had always led an upright, irreproachable life." Suspicions fell on Wallace Carter, "a man of a desperate character" and he was arrested the next day.[18] Although Carter may have been tried and found guilty of second-degree murder, the prison records do not list him as one of Huntsville's prisoners at that time. Somehow he eluded the law and became a fugitive. Ten years later Armstrong fortuitously learned of his whereabouts and went after him. He "slipped upon Carter as he was with a herd of cattle, and since the murder has been engaged as a stock man in West Texas."[19] The writer of the "Houston Local Items," which appeared in the Galveston journal, concluded the article: "[I]f all Lieut. Hall's command are like him [Armstrong], West Texas may be glad to have the company among them."[20]

A woman had been the cause of the animosity between the murderer and victim. Carter and Wooten, a Houston County widower, were both "enamoured [*sic*] of the same young lady" but when she rejected young Carter he threatened he had "but one more thing to do and then he would leave the country." That one thing was to kill Wooten. In the 1860 census Wooten was a respected farmer living in Houston County, a twenty-five-year-old Mississippi native with real estate valued at $960 and with personal estate valued at $16,570, a sizeable fortune. His wife at that time was twenty-year-old M.A. Wooten, from Alabama.[21] When she died is uncertain, but in late December 1866, then-widower Calvin G. Wooten joined her in death, shot by Wallace Carter. Carter was tried and convicted of second-degree murder; he appealed the verdict but the superior court affirmed the lower court's decision. Carter was convicted February 8, 1879, and entered Huntsville penitentiary to serve his sentence as number 7399. He was thirty-four years of age. The prison record shows he escaped from the Rusk system on June 7, 1880.[22]

Back in early March 1877 Hall intended to visit Grayson County to see friends and family. It had been several years since he had been in northeast Texas and he certainly deserved a vacation. On the tenth he had telegraphed Adjutant General Steele requesting a leave of absence for ten days, which was granted. Even during his absence, however, he still received publicity in the press. The *Victoria Advocate* reported that "Peace and quiet reign in our midst, thanks to the vigilance of our county attorney and Capt. Hall's command." The newspapers were not always accurate in giving Hall's rank, often calling him "Captain" when he was still a lieutenant. The *Advocate* made no specific mention that Lieutenant Hall had been promoted to captain after June 1, 1877. Even the service records merely show a change in rank: from January 25–June 1, 1877, Hall was lieutenant. From June 1, 1877, through February 29, 1880, he held the rank of captain. The law, evidently, "is being better enforced now than it has been for many years past." Most everybody recognized the fact that liquor frequently started arguments that turned into gunplay. There was a temperance committee in Goliad County, which was "now in a flourishing condition" with many persons joining. The captain had joined "last Friday night"[23] before heading out of town for his leave. Hall perhaps explained to the new committee that he had been a member of a Temperance Union back in Greensboro, North Carolina, before he was Texas-bound. Certainly the Goliad citizens welcomed Hall in their midst.

On the thirteenth of March Hall's men arrested Ben and N. Fairchild in Gonzales County on a capias from Lee County. They were wanted for murder and theft; they were able to give bond. A news item from Gonzales stated that a squad of Hall's men with Deputy Sheriff John H. Lewis had brought in the two Fairchilds, who were charged with "assault with intent to commit murder."[24]

Life for J.L. Hall was not limited to just hunting desperadoes and man-killers, for the young man did have a life outside of scouting and sleeping in tents on the ground. On the sixteenth of March while on leave he was in Dallas and stopped in to visit with acquaintances at the *Daily Herald* office. He was on his way to Sherman where he paid a brief visit with relatives and friends. The conversation naturally turned to his command down in South Texas: one detachment was in DeWitt County, one in Bee County, and one in Live Oak County, probably eight men in each detachment. In his opinion if the company could remain there for six months or a year longer then it would be safe to move it elsewhere. Further, in those counties where the local option prevailed, things were quieter as "a large percentage of the troubles were directly traceable to the intemperate use of whisky." Troubles with raiders from Mexico were not then as extreme, as they were "rather busily engaged" with a revolution, but there would be troubles with the Mexicans again, according to Hall. With conflict along the border reduced, "farmers and stockmen feel a security as new and novel, as it is delightful." The editor concluded his report on the visit by pointing out that Hall was "a meritorious officer, and well worthy to succeed the gallant McNelly, who, we are sorry to say, is rapidly passing away with that dread destroyer, consumption."[25]

While Hall was in Dallas, an editor in Victoria was finding fault with the lieutenant's activities. Edward D. Linn, editor and publisher of the *Victoria Advocate*, composed an editorial entitled "Lieut. Hall's Report" dealing with the February Monthly Return. As noted, Hall had identified a number of counties he and his men had scouted in during the month and had "effected arrests." One of the counties was Victoria and editor Linn now stated that the "scouting operations" in Victoria County had been "confined to the limited extent of one personal visit to our city from this officer, unattended by his men." Linn continued by stating that in effect Hall was not needed in Victoria County as the voters had chosen an "efficient, energetic and tireless officer" identified as Sheriff Thurmond, one who "never fails to do his duty at all times and has yet to request the services of State troops in the matter of effecting arrests in this county."[26] In essence Linn was stating that as far as Victoria was concerned the troops were an unnecessary expense to the State of Texas. Their presence could be used much more beneficially further west. Furthermore, Linn noted that Hall and his detachments were active in the twenty-eight days of February but made only twenty-six arrests, less than one a day. The command should be confined in those counties where there was the most crime. Linn concluded that "For the present at least, Victoria can dispense with this officer's services."[27] Editor Linn may have been echoing the prejudice of his readership; twenty-six arrests in twenty-eight days gives no indication of the severity of the crimes nor the value of property recovered.

How long Hall stayed with friends and relatives in Sherman is unknown, but he was back on duty by March 28. In the meantime his men were working at reducing the number of desperadoes running loose. Sometimes prisoners escaped, even from jails that were supposedly "escape proof." In January 1876 members of the Horner Gang—Joe, his brother George and William Z. Redding—had robbed the bank at Comanche, Texas. Joe and George Horner were captured some weeks later in San Antonio and lodged in the Bexar County jail. Joe Horner was tried, found guilty, and sentenced to ten years in Huntsville. During the night of April 1, 1877, Joe Horner escaped from jail with two other prisoners, Bob Peel and a man named Brown. It would fall to Ranger Hall to find and capture Joe Horner, who by 1877 was considered a noted outlaw.[28]

Arresting and bringing to trial thieves, desperadoes, and murderers certainly was for the good of the community at large from the point of view of providing security to honest citizens. But there was more, as Mr. E. Seeligson would gladly attest, in opposition to editor Linn's negative view of Hall. Seeligson was in Galveston visiting and buying his spring stock of goods. A reporter inquired of things in Goliad and he reported there was a good deal of improvement going on. Farming would be successful if "the grasshoppers do not eat them out" which would give the farmers a "good year." Quite a number of immigrants were moving in to Goliad, but more importantly, Lieutenant Hall and his men were doing good work, as "there is not a week but that they pick up refugees from justice." According to Seeligson, Hall and his men "have saved the State of Texas thousands of dollars, besides giving protection to life and property since he has been operating in the county." The positive results from Hall's presence would only continue, but if his company was disbanded or moved elsewhere Seeligson feared the lawless men would move in and "commence their old business again."[29]

Citizens of Goliad may have been pleased with the changes from the old wild days to a more peaceful setting but around the capital things were different. Thieves were brazenly stopping and robbing stagecoaches, and that represented a danger on the highway. Travelers could be robbed of their money and potentially their life. On March 7, between Waco and Gatesville, north of Austin, a stage was stopped at gunpoint; not only were the passengers robbed but also the U.S. mail was stolen. Then twelve days later on the nineteenth the stage between Georgetown and

Salado in Williamson County was stopped but there were no passengers or mail so the lone highwayman let the stage continue on its way. The highwayman now was operating closer to the capital. Four days later the McDade to Bastrop stage was stopped and passengers robbed. For him it was another disappointing stop for he obtained but little money. After sending the driver on his way he realized that he had not checked the U.S. mail bags and *then stopped the stage a second time*, but again it was a disappointment as the bag held only letters, no registered mail. On March 26 two stages were robbed by the same man: in the morning the stage from Austin to Lockhart in Caldwell County and then in the afternoon the stage from Austin to San Antonio was stopped. This time the robbery resulted in over a thousand dollars being stolen. It was the first time the robber could feel that his "work" was successful. Instead of disappearing some distance from the scene of the crime he foolishly decided to spend the loot lavishly, however.

Ham White was the man who had chosen to rob stagecoaches as his career. He met a friend named John Vaughn and the two of them started on a spending spree, which ended up two days later in the village of Luling in southern Caldwell County.[30] Luling then was a small community only three years old, the railroad having reached there in 1874. In early January 1875 a fire wiped out an entire block of businesses, but by the time White and his companion arrived the town was rebuilding. Besides the depot there were livery stables, saloons, a few stores, and residences. During the years after the railroad's arrival the population gradually grew until it neared a thousand by 1880. Ham White the stagecoach robber and his friend Vaughn thought they could now relax for a short time. It was the twenty-eighth of March 1877.[31] Unfortunately for Ham White, his robberies had taken place close to the headquarters of the Frontier Battalion and the Special State Troops in Austin, where Gov. Richard B. Hubbard and Adjutant General William Steele had their offices. They were keenly aware of not only the lawlessness in the state but that it looked bad that the highwayman was active so close to Austin. General Steele, recognizing the need, assigned Lee Hall to bring in the stage robber. He took with him rangers J.F. Pendleton, George H. Allen, and Samuel A. McMurry.[32]

To determine the highwayman's identity and where he could be located required some detective work, but Hall began the job immediately. There had been no training available for detectives on the frontier but Hall had learned some special skills during his years as a lawman in Grayson County and working in South Texas. He now could put them to good work. Hall visited the site where the Austin to San Antonio stage was stopped and found clues: he determined certain horse tracks could be the trail of the robber, leading in the direction of Caldwell County seat Lockhart. The hunters followed these particular horse prints some miles before losing the trail, but then found it again. They met a traveler who recalled meeting a man on a bay horse, which Hall suspected could be the man they were hunting. The rangers continued on towards Luling, only some sixteen miles south of Lockhart. By now their horses were jaded and they stopped in "Jackson's" livery stable[33] to allow their horses some needed rest. There in the stable they noticed a man saddling a bay horse and "the moment they looked at him sharply he appeared nervous and uneasy." Hall slowly approached, suspecting he was the man they were after. As Hall got closer the man said, "Don't come near me" and raised his hand towards the inside of his coat. Hall, undoubtedly suspecting he had a pistol, said, "Why, you appear frightened" to which the man responded: "It is enough to frighten anyone to be surrounded by three or four men." That amounted to a signal to the rangers who drew their pistols while Hall grabbed the man by the wrist. He was quickly searched and the six-shooter taken from him. The saddlebags were also searched. What they discovered on his person as well as the saddlebags convinced Hall they had the stagecoach robber in custody. They found nearly nine hundred dollars in currency. They also found a memoranda book which proved to be a record of the robberies. Hall had gotten his man.

Besides Ham White, they also arrested John Vaugh, who had been posing as White's brother and who denied any involvement in the robberies. White and Vaughn had made inquiries as to when the stage would be leaving. Hall inquired of Vaughn where he got his money to which he responded, "It's none of your business." From Luling on March 28 Hall telegraphed Adj. Gen. William Steele the good news: "Have captured the stage robber & most of the money— will be in Austin tomorrow." From Luling the rangers traveled the sixteen or so miles north to Lockhart where the prisoners were confined in the county jail.[34] Before surrendering their prisoners Hall discovered White had secured several iron saw blades around his legs which would be put to use to escape if he should be captured. The Austin reporter gave great praise to Hall and his men for the important work. Pointing out that he "and his brave men deserve the thanks of the public for this great work, fraught with danger and fatigue, but for them the desperado and bold highwayman, Ham White, would yet be at large. This service alone argues volumes in favor of the keeping up for a year or two, at least, an efficient State guard organization. The rangers have more than earned the $1250 reward offered, and we are glad to know that Marshal Purnell [35] and other Federal officials will urge the authorities at Washington to add another thousand to it." The prisoners were delivered to federal authorities on Thursday, the twenty-ninth of March. White was tried in the United States District Court on the sixteenth of April. The jury was out ten minutes and returned a verdict of guilty on all counts. Judge Thomas Duval sentenced him to a life term in the West Virginia Penitentiary at Moundsville. [36]

The good news of the stagecoach robber's capture became news in Hall's home country. The Wilmington, North Carolina, *Morning Star* reported the capture, as well as the *Greensboro Patriot*. The *Patriot* reported that Hall had "just added another to the number of his bold and dare-devil undertakings by following up and arresting a couple of highwaymen who had gone through a stage and robbed the passengers. He went on the trail and on the eighth day out [*sic*: it was only two days] got his men and booty and brought them safely into Austin." As if any further praise of the Greensboro boy was needed, the *Patriot* concluded its report:

"The Texas papers are filling Lee's hat full of feathers for this last of his gallant exploits."[37]

Frequently Hall and his troops were called to protect judges when they traveled from one court to another as well as assisting local officers on an election day. An added responsibility was to provide security at public executions. In April, Bee County Sheriff David Alfred Theophalis Walton[38] requested rangers to help preserve order at the scheduled execution of John Edward Singleton,[39] a convicted murderer sentenced to be executed. Singleton was convicted of murdering John C. Dwyer in July of 1875. Dwyer was on his way to Rockport for supplies when he stopped at Beeville. Dwyer, a well-known merchant of "Dogtown" in McMullen County, and Singleton met and developed a friendship. They left Beeville together in Dwyer's buggy. Later the mail rider came into Beeville and informed authorities that the men in the buggy had shot at him. A posse quickly formed and eight miles from Beeville they discovered the body of Dwyer, stretched out on the road with two bullet holes in his forehead. He had been robbed of all valuables. The posse trailed the buggy for several miles but then lost the trail. Few details of the capture have been located, but suspicions quickly fell on Singleton as the murderer and he then was arrested.[40]

Once in custody Singleton was guarded carefully; at his trial he was found guilty of murder in the first degree. He appealed to the Superior Court in Galveston, which upheld the ruling of the lower court; a date was set for his execution. It was at this point that Sheriff Walton requested assistance, and Lieutenant Hall, "who will assist him to guard the prisoner until he is executed" responded. Although guarded, Singleton and two other prisoners planned an escape. On Friday, August 18, Josh Speight "the notorious," Singleton, and John Sharp, two murderers, planned to force their way to freedom. The latter two prisoners had on leg-irons, but Speight was not ironed. Jailer Miller routinely inspected the jail "to see that everything is all right" before going to his lunch. That day he found that something did not look right and called in deputy sheriffs Seifert and

Owens and another guard, James Hunter for assistance. They inspected the prisoners and found that Sharp and Singleton had filed their leg-irons in two, and were "all prepared to make a desperate dash for liberty as soon as the jailer had gone." They were ready to pry open the last door and kill the guard if necessary, but the plot was discovered in time. Until execution the leg irons would be changed daily and a closer watch kept on them.[41] Commented a Galveston reporter: "[They] are rough customers, and if they once escape from their cells they will give the jail guards a rough deal before their permit themselves to be recaptured. With them it will be a terrible exemplification of the revolutionary watchwords, Liberty or Death."[42] But the prisoners did not escape even though they threatened heavily the guards that they would. When it neared the execution date Singleton was transported back to Beeville for execution. Sheriff Walton and Lee Hall with his rangers continued to guard Singleton closely.

The day of the hanging was typical of the era: entire families gathered as at a picnic, with men, women, and children. On the scaffold the condemned man called for the sheriff, two rangers, and the reporter from the *Goliad Guard.* He there confessed that he had done the murder, that he had no thought of killing Dwyer at first but he killed him for "only a slight provocation."[43] Hall's Monthly Return noted that nine of his men had been retained in Bee County "guarding the jail from the 20th of March to the 27th of April, when Singleton was executed." He wanted Adjutant General Steele to fully appreciate why the number of arrests was lower this month than before, thus the explanation, writing, "This accounts for the falling off our column of arrests as compared with previous months." His return showed only five arrests that month. Not surprisingly, there were no disturbances at the execution; it was Hall's, as well as Sheriff Walton's, first execution. It would not be Hall's last. Walton spoke very highly of Hall and his men, saying "they are doing much good in that section" in ridding the country of "lawless men."[44]

The April return reveals some frustration for Hall. He notes the arrest in Wilson County of Scott Raider who was wanted for murder, and was then delivered to Bee County. Then Hall notes: "I was absent during this month [March]. One week in furlough in Northern Texas and the remainder of the month delayed in the trial of Ham White while my entire company with the exception of eight men left in this county, were guarding prisoners at the Courts of Bee, Live Oak, San Patricio, Refugio & Goliad."[45]

Hall and his men were active, which resulted in much success in the field. Hall and his company did much better in May, with a higher number of arrests. He with sixteen of his rangers delivered eight "noted scoundrels" to the Bexar County jail in San Antonio, all desperadoes captured between San Antonio and Eagle Pass. They would be delivered to the counties where there were indictments for them, which meant in many cases miles of travel guarding them, or sending word to the sheriff to come and get them. Four were delivered to Goliad "under a strong guard" while the others were sent to Austin. One of the prisoners was John Murray, who, "assisted by another ruffian," had severely wounded a black man and then "ravished his wife and daughter— the latter a mere child." That crime had been committed in Pleasanton, Atascosa County. Commented the editor reporting this event: "The Rangers present a very soldierly appearance, and have the bearing of gentlemen. There is ample work for about two hundred of them."[46] There would never be two hundred Texas Rangers together, not even in the worst situation.

Just in case there was thinking in Austin to further reduce Hall's force, citizens of DeWitt County started a petition to forward to Gov. Richard B. Hubbard to keep Lieutenant Hall and his rangers. According to the citizens, the services of Hall and his men had "been great in this section of the State, in assisting the civil officers and good citizens in maintaining law and order in our midst; and, as we are [of the] opinion that security to life and property cannot be maintained in this section without co-operation and continuance of said command, and that the reign of terror that has so long afflicted our citizens, in the organized bands of lawless men depredating upon us, can not be suppressed or punished unless said troops be retained in the State service until the criminals in the hands [of] the law are brought to trial, we earnestly petition your Excellency to retain said troops in the State service until the dangers threatening the life and property of the law-abiding citizens of this section may be obtained, and law and order established."[47] Several hundred citizens signed the petition. If the troop was disbanded, if DeWitt County was left with only the local sheriff and deputies to preserve law and order, then desperate men and "refugees from justice" would flock to DeWitt and join the lawless element.

Hall was of course responsible for every item of the state's property in the possession of his company. His reports usually listed how much camp equipment the company had, the condition, how many mules, tents, and so on. In May one of the mules was lost and what happened to it had to be reported. Besides the mule the report showed one less field glass, and Hall dutifully explained why. "The field glass was presented to Fralosa Garcia, commandante of the Piedras Niegres [*sic*] Division of the Rio Grande as a bonus for turning over prisoners who had taken refuge in Mexico." This particular action was not dated other than merely in Hall's May 31, 1877, Monthly Return. At this time Lieutenant Hall had one other lieutenant, two sergeants, two corporals, and twenty-four privates in his command.[48]

In May Hall noted that "Generally Speaking" the country was quiet, and he had divided the company into detachments: Lieutenant Armstrong with five men; Sergeant Parrott with five men, and Hall with eight men. The detachments started from Beeville on May 28 scouting through Live Oak, Wilson, Bexar, Medina, Frio, Uvalde, Kinney, Dimmit, Zavala, Maverick and McMullen Counties. They were scouting for some fifty or sixty criminals who were "advertised on the published list" (a list of criminals from the various counties, their crimes, rewards, and so forth) but failed to find any of them. "We also arrested and kept under arrest for several days about thirty suspicious characters whom we were not able to identify and were unwilling to detain them any longer on account of the expense and trouble, although convinced there were charges against them in some portion of the State, as they were avoiding officers of the law." Hall admits they were arrested because they appeared guilty of something, certainly a technique which is discouraged today.

The weather, at least the extreme heat, could also have an effect on the men, as noted: "Our duties were very arduous, especially in guarding prisoners at Eagle Pass, as we had at one time under guard as many as thirty-three. In consequence of which our expenses have been double the usual amount." But Hall had good news to report also: "There seems to be a feeling pervading the entire western County, to enforce law and order if properly sustained."[49]

The evening of May 21, 1877, Captain Hall with about fifteen of his command arrived in Victoria. They spent the night there and headed for Corpus Christi the next morning where Hall would re-organize the command. The *Advocate* noted that "Satisfactory arrangements have been made by Gov. Hubbard for the payment of Hall's men, and they will be retained in the field. Now look out for another growl from Throckmorton editors."[50] Lieutenant Armstrong, with S.F. Grimes, the county attorney of DeWitt County, and J.M. Mathis of the firm of Coleman, Mathis & Fulton, of Rockport, arrived in Victoria and checked into the Taylor House. When the company had to be re-organized because of the lack of legislative funding, Hall had to merely select the last ones hired to reduce the company in numbers. Occasionally stockmen gathered the necessary funding to support the company of rangers, and this is likely the situation here.

On June 5 Sergeant Parrott, with a detachment of four men, headed for Lavaca County searching for a man identified as Hawkes, but failed to find him. All was not lost, however, as they did capture William Frazier who was charged with murder in Goliad County. The detachment was back at camp by June 9. Corporal George H. Allen with one other man started for Richmond on June 7 in pursuit of Upshur Brooking. This was a successful scout as Brooking as well as J.D. Bell were arrested at Flatonia, although the men had to travel 225 miles. Prisoners Brooking and Frazier were delivered to Goliad for safe keeping. Prisoners could be kept in camp for short periods but it was certainly preferable when they could be placed in a secure jail. On June 15 Hall sent out a detachment of thirteen men to Austin to deliver the accused murderers of Dr. Brassell and his son, from the Travis County jail down to Cuero for trial. When that action of the court was finished the prisoners had to be delivered back to Austin "for safe keeping." Sergeant A.L. Parrott and twelve men left Cuero on the twentieth and delivered them without incident. They would be the responsibility of the rangers through numerous court appearances. The publicity surrounding the 1876 case and trials would give them the name of "the DeWitt County prisoners" and all would know who was referred to. Hall's final comment on the Monthly Return for June: "My men have all been engaged almost the entire month in reorganizing and guarding De Witt Co prisoners."[51]

For the purposes of keeping track of Hall and his men the Monthly Returns provide few details. When completing the July return Hall had no remarks to add, other than placing his location in Castroville, Medina County. The "Statement of Arrests," however, does provide information on his activities. He was "detained" in Austin as a witness in Federal Court, "consequently was not actively engaged with my company." Sergeant Parrott and his twelve men were conveying the DeWitt County prisoners from DeWitt County back to the Travis County jail. They were then ordered to report to Castroville in Medina County to guard King Fisher and other prisoners and to deliver them to Uvalde. A final notation for the July report indicated that part of the company scouted in Mexico, crossing over "in pursuit of the Trimble murderers."[52] In the August report Hall noted that he had arrived on July 31 at the camp of Captain Neal Coldwell near Frio City, Frio County. On August 1 he left for Eagle Pass accompanied by Sergeant G.W. Arrington of Coldwell's company with a detachment of eighteen men. On August 3 they "surrounded the town making several arrests." Then on the next morning they surrounded the filibustering camp of Pedro Valdez, arresting 118 men, nearly all of whom they released. "The work this month has been exceedingly arduous owing to the extreme heat, scarcity of grass & water & Sick men constantly on my hands." [53] In August he was in Rio Grande City, Starr County, and still there in September as well. Hall had no arrests to report for September but added: "Most of my company being on duty here the rest a small detachment attended the courts with Judge Pleasanton [*sic*, Pleasants] and Guarded the jails in Goliad and Dewit [*sic*] Counties [and] several unsuccessful scouts were made by squads at Goliad and Cuero . . . ." Those squads sought fugitives in the counties of Lavaca, Gonzales, DeWitt, Goliad, Bee, San Patricio, Nueces, Refugio and Live Oak. [54]

In early August one of numerous mysteries began, which were never satisfactorily resolved. Two Mexicans were found hanging from a tree in Capt. Richard King's *Puerta* pasture, some twenty-five miles east of his ranch headquarters. King requested assistance and Sergeant Watson and seven of Hall's command proceeded to the spot where they were found but were unable to ascertain anything further than that they had died with their boots on. They buried the unrecognized bodies. Someone had determined they had been involved in the murder of a shepherd and provided rough justice to them. [55]

This was only one example of vigilante justice practiced in the Nueces Strip, but of course it was not unique to Texas. Sometimes as well a murder went unresolved for years. For instance, in 1858 a man by the name of Vare was killed by one Beardsall on the Pecos River. At Beardsall's trial in 1859 in San Antonio it was determined that the murdered man had recently been paid $24,000 at Fort Lancaster. He then proceeded to San Antonio accompanied by Beardsall and Draper. On the road Beardsall killed Vare believing that he had that amount of money on his person, but he did not. The jury determined Beardsall should hang for this murder. Beardsall managed to escape and with the Civil War approaching he was able to avoid being captured, although what he did during those years is unknown. In August 1877, almost twenty years after the crime, "the vigilant Capt. Hall arrested him at Piedras Negras." Beardsall now was "to have his sentence carried into execution." [56] Beardsall was not kept in San Antonio but delivered to Austin to await his fate in the newly constructed Travis County jail.[57]

A potentially greater concern was what was happening on the border, what was headlined "The Last Mexican Outrage." A special from Rio Grande City reported that on a Sunday morning in August an armed body of fifteen men entered the city, broke open the jail, shot the jailer and Judge Cox, the county attorney, and released two notorious criminals, murderers and horse thieves. A Brownsville special to the *Galveston Daily News* indicated that this "Rio Grande Outrage" was part of General Escobedo's plan "in order to interrupt the friendly relations existing between the officials of the Diaz government and those of the United States on the frontier."[58] The civil authorities asked the military for assistance. Major William R. Price acted swiftly and had 100 troops on the trail before daylight and then demanded of Mexican authorities the surrender of the raiders.[59] The next day General Benavides answered that the Mexican government "will do all in its power to capture the raiders who liberated the prisoners at Rio Grande City; that he had sent troops in all directions and that if they are caught they will be held subject to the Texas authorities under the extradition treaty with Mexico."[60] In addition Governor Richard B. Hubbard was notified and acted as he should have. The *Advocate* reported that his "prompt tender of the military power of Texas to Gen. Ord on the occasion of the late invasion of the State by Mexican banditti is highly creditable to him as an official. Within a few hours of being notified of the outrage two companies of the frontier battalion and Lieutenant Hall's command were *en route* for the disturbed section." Further, the *Advocate* reminded its readers that when Captain McNelly had "carried Texas authority to the opposite side of the Rio Grande, he assumed no function not in accord with the doctrine of self preservation, and at the same time established a precedent which the authorities of Texas should never hesitate to carry out."[61]

Once having arrived at "the disturbed section," Lieutenant Hall began working to secure the arrest of the raiders. He proposed to cross the river at Camargo but unless orders were to the contrary would do so without the regular army. This was no different from what McNelly had done in 1875, establishing a precedent that rangers could carry out their duties across the border, as the *Advocate* noted above. Rumor spread that Hall had told the Mexican authorities that there were 25,000 Texas volunteers organizing for a campaign against Mexico, a statement which could not be true, but might have been part of Hall's strategy to get the Mexicans to surrender the raiders. What was not rumor was the formal demand from Texas Governor Hubbard to the Mexican authorities for the Rio Grande raiders. By now the names of some of them were known: Rafael Garcia, Gregoria Garcia, Seferino Juarez, Rafael Trevenio, Pedro Rodriguez, Pablo Perra (Parra?) and one whose last name was given as Obispo (Brigido Oliveras?). The two prisoners who were taken from the jail were Segundo Garza and Rudolfo Esproceda (Esponseda?).[62]

Hubbard was receiving praise for his consideration of Lieutenant Hall and his command. The governor was presenting a "wise policy in retaining this force in the field under adverse circumstances and in providing for its pay and comfort"; his actions "cannot be extolled too much." After all, it was one of Hall's men who had captured the notorious John Wesley Hardin that very month of August in far off Pensacola, Florida. "After the capture . . . of such a man as Hardin, it will require but little special pleading to render the maintenance of the State police force an exceedingly popular step with the people, who are so effectually served by it." With this amount of praise, which first appeared in the *Dallas Herald*, described as "the most influential journal in North Texas," another item stated that Mexican lawyers had advised General Servando Canales not to surrender the Rio Grande City raiders, for the reason that "as actual *bona fide* citizens of Mexico they do not come within the provisions of the extradition treaty."[63]

Hall expressed his view on the border troubles to a friend in Austin, Miss Julia Pease, the daughter of Governor E.M. Pease. Communicating with her from Rio Grande City he wrote:

> On the eve of my leaving Eagle Pass . . . I rec'd an order from the Adj. Genl. to repair at once to this place, on account of the recent raid from Mexicans of which you are familiar from the news papers. When we first came, there was a slight war cloud, which notwithstanding it has virtually vanished, the situation is delicate and may lead to war between the Mexican Republic and our Govt. The Mexicans are still concentrating troops on the opposite side of the river and should an outbreak occur, we being at the front would get the first taste of it, and I am not I confess much [illegible] to such as termination of the negotiation now going on between the two Republics, although I would like to be considerable [illegible] before war is declared.[64]

This is from one of the few letters written by Hall which are now extant, and reveals his education as being a fine one from the vocabulary he uses.

On September 22 the *Advocate* could report that three of the parties concerned in the jail breaking had been delivered to the United States authorities at Brownsville. They were identified as Rudolph Esponseda, one of the escaped prisoners, Pablo Parra, and Brigido Oliveras. These three were, however, considered "the most unimportant of the whole, not being popular and having no great reputation as criminals."[65]

While Hall and his men were busy dealing with the Rio Grande City troubles a deputy sheriff of Nueces County, Thomas A. Shaw, was killed while conveying a prisoner from Concepcion to Corpus Christi. The prisoner, Martin Rodriguez (alias "Chiquito"), escaped. The prisoner's wife drove the wagon containing Shaw's body into Corpus, claiming that a number of men attacked them and in the *melee* Shaw was killed and her husband escaped. Authorities suspected she was implicated in the killing and was placed in jail. Sheriff Thomas Beynon offered a reward of $500 for the arrest of Rodriguez.[66]

Sheriff Beynon conducted an informal inquest and determined Shaw had numerous stab wounds on his body and evidence of a blow to the head. Also the spot where the killing had taken place was visited. There was evidence that a deadly struggle had occurred and blood and "pools of gore here and there." There were no bullet marks on Shaw's body or on the wagon that had been used to convey the prisoner. The wife of the prisoner, Francisca Lopez, did confess that it was her husband Martin Rodriguez who committed the murder. She explained that both men stopped the wagon to light a cigarette, that she heard her husband yell in rage and he then drew a knife and stabbed Shaw. Shaw then drew his pistol and fired at Rodriguez who then grappled with Shaw, overpowering and killing the smaller man. Sheriff Beynon placed her in jail awaiting the action of the next grand jury.[67] Meanwhile the murderer Rodriguez was a liberated man, perhaps already in Mexico. He would become an object of Hall's scouts, seeking him to pay for his murderous act.

Among all these troubles on the border, no one had forgotten the celebrated John King Fisher. A reporter in late September visited the jail in San Antonio where he was being held and was able to hold "an interesting interview" with him. He described him as twenty-five, of dark complexion, medium stature, with "a well knit frame, and has a very pleasing countenance, in all, he is quite a handsome and somewhat polished man." Fisher expected to be released on a $25,000 bail to appear at the October term of District Court in San Antonio. In spite of his reputation as a thief and killer the reporter noted that he had "numerous friends, among them some of the largest and most influential stock men of Western Texas, who will strain every nerve to bring about his acquittal."[68]

By the middle of October Lieutenant Hall and his company arrived in Cuero. The Cuero editor complimented them on their "good service in arresting outlaws and fugitives from justice." He noted that the members of Hall's company were "all young men of respectability and well known characters, and wherever they go they are welcomed with great cordiality and respect."[69] In the same issue an item from the *Goliad Guard* reported that several of Hall's men had lost their horses during their work on the Rio Grande, due to the lack of grass and water and by forced marches. One of the horses died after arriving in Goliad. The *Guard* editor stated his belief that the State should pay for the horses, "as the men get little enough anyway." They had been in a "region where both men and beast must suffer for food and water."[70]

By November, Hall had moved camp to Nueces County where the command would be stationed through December. For an unspecified reason the November monthly return was prepared by Sgt. John B. Armstrong who was well on the way to recovery from an accidental self-inflicted bullet wound. The company was divided into detachments: six men at Cuero, seven men at Banquete, and eight men at Lagarto. The balance was at Corpus Christi guarding the jail and assisting the sheriff in getting witnesses for district court.[71]

Chapter Five

Hall retaliated and John Price was "everlastingly pounded up."

—*Austin Daily Democratic Statesman*, January 18, 1878

Adjutant General Steele required his ranger captains to prepare returns that gave an accounting of their activities each month. The amount of detail given in these returns varies greatly. Hall provided a frustratingly sparse amount of information, as if he had little time to spend on paper work. At the end of March 1877, for example, he wrote: "arrested Ham White, stage robber, Bastrop" and the next line "arrested Jno. Vaughn, stage robber, Bastrop." Why did he write "Bastrop" when he knew full well that he arrested the two in Luling, Caldwell County, not Bastrop? Be that as it may, Hall's statement of arrests for the month of April 1877 explains why there were so few arrests, assuring the adjutant general that his men were not neglecting their duties. Hall explained that one week he was "on furlough" in northern Texas and during the remainder of the month he was attending the trial of Ham White in Austin. As for the rest of the company the rangers were guarding prisoners and assisting at courts in Bee, Live Oak, San Patricio, Refugio, and Goliad Counties. Nine of his men were "detained in Beeville guarding the jail from the 20th of March to the 27th of April, when Singleton was executed." Only five arrests were recorded during that month.[1] On the twenty-ninth he recorded: "arrested Matt Thompson, murder, Polk Co."

Fortunately we have newspaper reports that give greater detail. The *Galveston Daily News* frequently provided summaries of news from other counties in the state, and the issue of Wednesday, April 18, 1877, is an excellent example. The editor chose to give his contribution separately from other counties and made a headline in bold print, giving Hall greater attention: "The Latest Captures by Hall's Men." The story consisted of a special telegram to the *News* dated at Flatonia, Fayette County, April 17. Two men of Hall's company, Privates T.W. Deggs and J. Jenson,[2] had passed through Flatonia with prisoners Matt Thompson, charged with murder in Polk County, and another unidentified man, also charged with murder. The pair had been arrested in DeWitt County by Private Deggs.[3] Matt, the son of J.T. and Mary Thompson, was about twenty-eight years of age when arrested, based on census records. The family members, according to the 1870 census, were residents of Natchitoches Parish, Louisiana. Mr. Thompson was a farmer and his wife Mary kept house; neither Matt nor younger sister Mary Nancy gave an occupation, although they were certainly old enough to work outside the home, twenty-one and nineteen years of age respectively.[4] Perhaps Matt grew tired of farm work and left. The distance from his home parish to Polk County was less than 200 miles, but all we know for sure is that he was charged with murder in Polk County, Texas. According to the prison record, Thompson was twenty-three years of age when entered into prison, fair complexioned, blue eyes and dark hair. He had received a "common education" with his occupation as laborer. He had been convicted June 16, 1875, and was sentenced to eight years for the second-degree murder in Polk County. Thompson was received in Huntsville on November 7, 1877, and was pardoned by Governor Hubbard in September 23, 1878.[5]

The *San Antonio Daily Herald* and Austin's *Daily Democratic Statesman* shared news items, or at least clipped them from their respective columns. A fine example is one from the *Herald* which appeared in the *Statesman*, listing some of the arrests of Hall's men. "Jones, *alias* Williams, connected with Joe Horner in his stage robbing; William C. Bruton, against whom about a round dozen of indictments have been presented in Goliad [C]ounty for cow stealing; Jim Lewis, connected with Bruton in sundry above cases[;] J. Burditt, who is wanted in Travis [C]ounty; G.H. Thayer, an escaped swindler from Grimes [C]ounty; John Murray, who lately escaped from the Atascosa [C]ounty jail; Buck Dorn *alias* Fitzpatrick [*sic*, Kirkpatrick] in whom the people of San Patricio [C]ounty are interested, and John West, another innocent [looking] young man of eighteen summers." This was quite a number of arrests made in a relatively short period of time. The *Herald* added that the most notorious of the lot, King Fisher, was arrested at Eagle Pass and conveyed to the Castroville jail for safe keeping. The indictment charged him with murder in the first degree.[6] If convicted he would face the hangman's noose. The "J. Burditt" was James Burditt who with Ben Thompson caused a ruckus in the Capitol Theatre in Austin, which resulted in Thompson killing bar owner Mark Wilson and severely wounding his bartender Charles Mathews during the Christmas holidays in 1876.[7]

Due to the small number of rangers under his command Hall frequently had to divide his men into even smaller squads in order to cover more territory. In May he recorded his activities in the "Statement of Arrests" in which he tells of dividing his men into three groups: John B. Armstrong with a squad of five men; Sergeant Parrott with a squad of five men, and Hall taking eight men. They started from Beeville and scouted through Wilson, Dimmit, Zavala, Maverick, Live Oak, Bexar, Medina, Frio, Uvalde, Kinney, and McMullen. There is a degree of frustration in his report:

> We made attempts to arrest fifty or Sixty noted criminals who are advertised in the published list, but failed. We also arrested and Kept under arrest for several days about thirty suspicious characters whom we were not able to identify and were unwilling

> to detain them longer on account of the expense and troubles and though convinced there were charges against them in some portion of the State as they were avoiding the officers of the law. Our duties were very arduous, especially in guarding prisoners at Eagle Pass, as we had at one time under guard as many as thirty three. [8]

Jones, *alias* Williams, real name J.T. Jones, was arrested in Piedras Negras, Mexico across the Rio Grande from Eagle Pass, for theft of horses and stage robbery. He was escorted to the Travis County jail for safe keeping. That arrest was made on May 12. Hall suspected he was involved with Joe Horner in a recent stage coach robbery. Others arrested on May 12 were John Murray, charged with murder and rape and then escorted to Bexar County and placed in the "Bat Cave," as the county jail in San Antonio was frequently called. William Bruton and Robert Lewis were two others delivered safely to Texas soil from Piedras Negras. Both were charged with theft and returned to Goliad County.[9] What is interesting about these arrests is that they were made in Piedras Negras, Coahuila, Mexico. Did Lieutenant Hall have orders from the adjutant general or the governor to cross the Rio Grande? He certainly wasn't in "hot pursuit," which might justify crossing the international boundary. Surprisingly the press did not make great mention of his crossing, and little note of the arrests. The Austin newspaper provided a disappointing one-line item: "Capt. Lee Hall followed Horner into Mexico, and captured him."[10]

Additionally in June the notorious Upshur Brooking was arrested in Harris County, and charged with theft. The Monthly Return is more informative indicating that "Up" Brooking was arrested on June 9 in Houston. He was taken to Goliad where he was able to give bond and was released.[11]

Conflicts in Mexico were frequently erupting in revolutionary activity; filibusters caused havoc; the dangers of Lipans, Apaches, and cattle thieves raiding into Texas ranches were commonly reported. When President Benito Juarez died in 1872 Sebastian Lerdo de Tejada (always referred to as "Lerdo") became the country's ruler, but in late 1876 Porfirio Diaz returned from exile and defeated Lerdo. In 1877 he was elected president and began to establish his power, which he held almost continually until 1911. In mid-1877 the conflict between Lerdo's followers and the opposition party of Diaz erupted. Many Texas outlaws sought to find refuge in the troubled border states of Coahuila, Nuevo Leon, and Tamaulipas. Matters first came to Hall's attention in July 1877 when Pedro Valdez planned to assist in a conference with *confrere* General Naranjo. On August 4 Hall and his men surrounded the camp of Pedro Valdez and made some arrests, although later they released them as they had no specific charges against them. "The work this month has been exceedingly arduous owing to the extreme heat, scarcity of grass & water & sick men constantly on my hands."[12] This was Hall's assessment of the month's work in his Statement of Arrests.

The Monthly Returns typically provide no details, only the date, name of the person arrested, the charge and where the arrest was made, but they reveal that Hall and his men were effective man-hunters. They also fail to stress how dangerous the work could be, as often a fugitive resisted arrest. Hall, as well as Steele and the governor, also knew that accidents could happen with so many young men handling so many firearms. A gunshot could be fatal or merely take them out of action for a long period of time. An accidental gunshot could be dangerous, and such an event happened not only once but twice in the same period, meaning his small command was reduced by two. The "accidents" happened to Oliver Simpson Watson[13] and John Barklay Armstrong.[14] Sergeant Watson was accidentally shot in the neck on May 17 at Yorktown in DeWitt County. A pistol had been placed on the store counter, and it accidentally fell off. On landing the pistol fired and the ball went into Watson's neck. Armstrong's wound may have been more embarrassing for him as it happened "while he was carelessly handling his pistol." Armstrong was at Goliad when it happened. "The ball entered just below the groin, striking the hip bone near the joint and up to this time the doctors have been unable to ascertain the location of the ball, but think it is lodged back of the hip bone."[15] This is in essence Hall's explanation to Steele, knowing perhaps that there would be an increase of medical bills charged to the company. The wound of Armstrong was perhaps more dangerous than that of Watson's, but in either case two men were unable to work for an uncertain period of time. Some feared Armstrong would be unable to mount a horse and have to use a cane the rest of his life.

Armstrong was not one to sit around and take life easy while recuperating from his pistol wound, however. By mid-summer he had devised a plan to track down the West's most notorious man-killer, John Wesley Hardin. He was aware that Hardin's wife, Jane Bowen Hardin, had family in Gonzales County and he decided he could find clues there from family members. He assumed the role of a tramp looking for work and met up with Neill Bowen, Hardin's father-in-law. He made Bowen's acquaintance and by trickery managed to intercept a letter from Bowen to a "John H. Swain" in Alabama. The clues added up that Hardin, who had a $4000 reward for his capture, was there. Armstrong telegraphed professional detective John Riley "Jack" Duncan to come get him and the two of them left Texas intending to capture John Wesley Hardin. Armstrong was still using his cane when he, Duncan, and other Florida officers captured the fugitive on August 23, 1877, in a violent encounter leaving one associate of Hardin's dead.[16] They brought Hardin back to Texas to stand trial for the killing of a Brown County deputy sheriff three years before. Hardin was found guilty of second-degree murder and sentenced to twenty-five years in Huntsville's state penitentiary. When entered into the prison his description was carefully noted: five feet nine inches tall, weighed 160 pounds, but more interesting for identification there were scars on his right knee, left thigh, right side, hip, elbow, shoulder, and back.[17] In 1894 he was pardoned by Governor J.S. Hogg, and wandered across Texas until in August 1895 he was killed by John Selman Sr. in a personal quarrel.[18]

Armstrong was still using his cane when he captured Hardin in August 1877, but he was apparently in full strength in October. He and a detachment of six men passed through Gonzales, the county seat of

Gonzales County, "having in charge the notorious Bill Taylor" whom they would deliver to Indianola, Calhoun County, for trial charged with the murder of William Sutton in 1874.[19] William Riley "Bill" Taylor and his cousin James Creed "Jim" Taylor had found their hated enemy William M. Sutton on March 11, 1874, on the deck of the steamer *Clinton* as he was intending to leave Texas for Kansas. Sutton and his companion Gabriel Webster Slaughter were both killed in a flurry of shots. Later, Taylor was arrested and jailed in Calhoun County waiting his trial, but during a terrific hurricane that damaged the town of Indianola, Bill Taylor escaped, but not before he was able to save some people's lives. Texas Rangers caught up with him again in early 1877 in Coleman County and safely delivered him to the Travis County jail.[20] From there Lieutenant Armstrong and his detachment were to deliver Taylor to Indianola. Commented the *Castroville Era*, in an exchange published in Austin, "Bill Taylor, the 'desperado'. . . did one noble act. 'While the storm was raging, at the risk of his life and recapture (which was the same), he saved the lives of two drowning women, whose prayers will ascend for him— desperado and murderer as he may be— as long as they live.'"[21]

Occasionally newspaper editors found reason to add levity in their reporting of news events. In June the *Statesman* reported that the "notorious James Bracken" was "bagged" by Lee Hall and placed in jail at Goliad "where he robbed a bank in broad daylight." Readers may have thought he was one of the Seeligson Bank robbers, but the editor stressed that he would "break no more faro banks and rob no more of the breaking sort until he escapes from the penitentiary." So he had held up a card game instead of the Seeligson Bank.[22]

One who did participate in the Goliad bank robbery was Frank Callison (frequently spelled Kallison). Of the children of Samuel and Martha Callison who apparently spent their entire lives in Gonzales County, Frank and younger brother Thomas became notorious. Frank was born in 1853 and younger brother Tom was born three years later. Holding up the Goliad bank was certainly Frank's idea, but after the robbery was completed he willingly gave up his companions in hopes of receiving a lighter sentence, or none at all. That effort failed and he was tried, found guilty, and sentenced to nine years in prison on October 18, 1877. When he entered Huntsville as number 6308 on October 26, he was twenty-four years of age, weighed 145 pounds, had dark hair, blue eyes, and a light complexion. He used tobacco and was intemperate. He had received a common education and had no occupation other than laborer. He was transferred to Rusk on January 1, 1883.[23] Once in prison he was forgotten about. The last attention given him appeared in the *Victoria Advocate* when it reported that Goliad County Sheriff James Lincoln "passed through this place on last Tuesday with two convicts for the State penitentiary. One of the prisoners, Frank Kallison [*sic*], was convicted of being implicated in the Seeligson bank robbery of last year and sentenced to a term of nine years. The other, Elsoy Brown, was convicted of horse theft and sentenced for a term of five years."[24]

The shooting phase of the Sutton-Taylor Feud may have been over but after the arrest of the murderers of the Brassell men the courtroom phase began. Special escorts were necessary to deliver the prisoners from court room to jails, from Austin to Cuero and elsewhere when the case was moved on a change of venue. This aspect of the feud would continue into the 1890s when Dave Augustine, one of the seven alleged murderers, was on his way to Huntsville but was pardoned by the governor. The Monthly Returns do not reflect the dangers nor the excitement Hall's men would possibly experience. On these escorts the rangers never knew when a rescue attempt would be made. Or when a mob might attempt to take prisoners from them to administer "swift justice" by lynching them. On June 15 a scout of thirteen men went to Austin to escort the prisoners from the Travis County jail to Cuero. Hall recorded this as a 200-mile trek. Then on the eighteenth Sergeant A.L Parrott with an escort of twelve men "reescorted [*sic*] same prisoners to Austin again" and then in early July Parrott with eleven men escorted the same prisoners from Cuero back to Austin. Hall neglected to record the exact dates in July for these escorts, but noted Sergt. A.L. Parrott and the same men of the escort then guarded King Fisher from Castroville in Medina County to Uvalde for his trial. Several men of this guard then scouted in Medina, Uvalde, Frio, Atascosa, and Maverick Counties, even crossing into Mexico in search of the Trimble murderers.[25]

The murder of Robert Trimble[26] was a particularly heinous crime and received much attention at the time. Trimble was from Benton City, Atascosa County, and was robbed and murdered. Some travelers found the body after noticing buzzards circling and investigated. Evidence showed Trimble had been stabbed several times near the heart, his body then dragged two hundred yards by the feet, then abandoned. The mules were cut away from the wagon and turned loose while two horses were substituted. Commented "Prickly Pear," a correspondent from San Antonio: "After circling about for awhile the murderers drove into the road and took the direction back to town. Their object was, no doubt, to leave the wagon at a distance from the body to divert attention from the vicinity of the place where the crime was actually committed." Prickly Pear did not know Trimble but thought he had "quite a sum of money with him" when attacked by the men who killed him. Trimble was described as an "industrious, good man" and left a widow and several children. He had served during the Civil War in Company A, Thirty-third regiment of Texas Cavalry. To conclude his report Prickly Pear stated that "It appears from this horrible crime that the gang that has infested the outskirts of this county still exists, and a revival of some very ominous conversation about vigilants maybe looked for."[27]

No gathering of "vigilants" rose up and took the law into their own hands, but the murderers of Trimble did receive a brutal sort of justice. Stationed in Uvalde County at this time was Lieut. Pat Dolan of the Frontier Battalion with thirteen men who were there to assist the sheriff in guarding the jail and preventing an escape. In addition there were men in Parrott's detachment; together it was a formidable force that began their search for the murderers. Private G.K. Chinn and four men went to intercept the party who killed Trimble and on the road they met a party of five Mexicans with the wagon suspected of belonging to Trimble. They arrested them and sent the prisoners with two men, Privates E.L. Temple and Richard Chute, to Uvalde. Near Uvalde one of the prisoners drew a rifle from within the wagon and shot both Temple and Chute. That happened on the twelfth of July. Three days later Private Chute and future captain of Company D of the Frontier Battalion Frank Jones were on the trail of the Mexicans which led to the Rio Grande. Dolan's Monthly Return indicated that one Mexican was killed and two wounded.[28] The Atascosa newspaper differed in relating the results: it indicated that some rangers, accompanied by David Young, Robert Ragsdale, and Medina County Sheriff Ferdinand Niggli, pursued them into Mexico. "It is said," the article concluded, "that the pursuers made two lucky shots, and that they returned with two horses and two saddles."[29] Questions will probably always remain about the final act of the pursuit of the Trimble murderers. Were they captured but shot while "attempting to escape" or did some get away? Unfortunately we have no record of Hall's thoughts on this whole sad affair.

Possibly Hall was also in the hunt for the Trimble murderers. Texas newspapers are strangely silent on Hall's activities at this time but perhaps some reports filtered back to Greensboro. Charles E. Jones, editor and proprietor of the *Charlotte Daily Observer*, frequently found items from Greensboro's *New North State* of interest. Jones reported that Hall, "who has created so much excitement in Texas and Mexico, for the past ten days, is a son of Dr. Hall of this place. It has not been many years since Lee left here for his new home in Texas. He has since gained much distinction as a brave and discreet officer in that State." This was not enough for editor Jones as he continued with what perhaps was of the greatest interest:

> A short time ago the Governor of Texas placed Capt. Hall in command of a company and instructed him to capture or kill Mexican marauders who had been committing murders and depredations on the Texas borders. Capt. Hall, in carrying out his instructions, has pursued the Mexicans to the Rio Grande, and it

> seems, was about to follow them into Mexico, but was detained by orders from Governor Hubbard, to learn the result of application for the extradition of the Mexican offenders.[30]

Even when the rangers were not in pursuit of a noted desperado, newspaper editors found them good copy and Hall's actions generated good publicity. For instance, in mid-November Hall sent a detachment to Cuero under the command of Lieutenant Armstrong apparently merely to show their presence. They drilled every day in the city hall square, opposite the office of the *Cuero Bulletin*. Armstrong had them going through "the military evolutions like old veterans."[31] To the modern ear this sounds odd, especially when rangers were generally in hand-to-hand gunfight situations, not in battle formation like large armies, but it made excellent copy for the newspapers. Also, an unusual felony noted in ranger records regarded fraudulent land titles. At this time there was a group of individuals involved in this offense and on November 5 Hall or one of his men arrested James W. Maddox and delivered him to Austin, charged with being implicated in the notorious land fraud case.[32] This has received little attention from historians but it involved numerous individuals in different counties working together. The *Austin Daily Democratic Statesman* reported that Maddox was charged with "being connected with the Kansas City ring of land thieves." The arrest of Maddox was not the only one of the ring. Others arrested and charged with complicity in this conspiracy included brothers James and William McCollough, Thomas E. Tullis, B.F. McDonohough, T.J. M. Richardson, D.H. Francis, and two others named Ham and Hatch, first names unknown. Their charges included not only forgery but violating U.S. postal laws, which made it a federal case. Some received prison sentences and at least one of the men charged committed suicide. This represented a rare example of rangers during the "frontier period" working against white collar criminals.[33]

While Armstrong was stationed at Cuero, Corporal G.H. Allen was stationed at Corpus Christi. On November 23 Allen received credit for the arrest of Henry Perkins, who was indicted in Goliad County for hog stealing and who forfeited his bond at the previous term of district court. He was delivered to Goliad and jailed on December 3.[34]

In December Armstrong took his detachment from Corpus Christi to Cuero, via train from Indianola, to then pick up the "Brassell prisoners" from the Travis County jail and take them to Cuero for trial. The editor of the *Cuero Bulletin* had this to say about the facility to hold them in Cuero: "The jail now building here will probably be completed for the occupation of prisoners within a month, as the contractors have now sufficient stone to finish the structure. It is a fine looking building, strong and well built, and will no doubt answer the purpose in every particular, and save the county the expense of sending prisoners off to other points for safe keeping." At some point Captain Hall joined Armstrong; in fact he may have been in Austin and together he and the lieutenant delivered the prisoners to Cuero for their trial.[35] This was encouraging to the DeWitt County citizens but if the jail was not finished then rangers had to guard the prisoners even outside the courthouse during the trial.[36]

The good work of the rangers did not go unnoticed, but occasionally Hall was praised indirectly, through mentions of the men he led. One Henry C. Thompson was in DeWitt County in December, spending a few days about the town of Cuero, and returned home to Houston where he visited the newspaper office. From what he observed, Lieutenant Armstrong "and his men have brought about a great change for the better in that region of country. Half a dozen years ago everybody there went armed with at least one six-shooter hung to his waist. Now you hardly meet on the road a man with a pistol on." The change was "attributable to the presence of State troops more than anything else" according to Thompson.[37]

Armstrong also impressed the editor of the *Cuero Bulletin*. "As a gentleman and soldier he is greatly esteemed, not only by the citizens of DeWitt [C]ounty, but all over Western Texas. The young gentlemen composing the company of Captain Hall, are all selected men and well known as of the highest character and respectability. The services of this company have been invaluable to the West and should be retained in the service."[38] The idea that the State Troops depended on the legislature for their pay was never too far from the thoughts of all who depended on them.

Some jails in Texas were notoriously inadequate for holding prisoners. Newspaper columns were filled with reports of prisoners escaping, or how a mob raided the jail and released the prisoners or took them out and lynched them. Somehow four prisoners, including King Fisher, in the Castroville jail in Medina County obtained saws and cut through their cells and entered the jailer's room. Once inside they armed themselves with a shotgun and pistols, intending to shoot their way to freedom. One of them, named Jasper Merritt, was about to scale the wall when Sheriff Ferdinand Niggli appeared and fired two shots at Merritt, wounding him severely in the side and back. Merritt fell and the other prisoners, realizing they had no real chance of escaping, threw down their arms and returned to their cells. Physicians considered Merritt's wounds very dangerous.[39]

The public perception of the Texas Rangers is one of daring men dealing with lawlessness with their six-guns and Winchesters blazing, and Hall was quite capable with those weapons, but occasionally he resorted to his fists. On January 17, 1878, while in Austin, Hall and "Captain" John Price, already developing a reputation as a detective, got into a difficulty. What initiated the matter is not specified, other than the witnesses reported that Price had been going about the city all morning verbally abusing Hall, "making savage threats against him," and even ignoring the advices of friends that he should cease and desist his abusive talk. Price continued his verbal abuse, saying it would continue until he found Hall— and then perhaps the words would turn to gunplay. Once the two men met, Hall tried to reason with him, saying he did not want a difficulty, that he was a peace officer, but this did not assuage Price's anger. "This seemed to add fuel to the flames that were blazing in Price's bosom or stomach, and he burst out in a fresh blast of savage fury, using the most abusive and offensive language" as the *Statesman* reporter wrote.

Then Hall retaliated against the abuse and resorted to his fists. Price attempted to draw his weapon but Hall, resisting the urge to draw his own weapon, finished the fight without any shots being fired. Price was "everlastingly pounded up."[40] The news of the fistfight travelled as far away as Brenham in Washington County, the *Banner* describing Price as being "very handsomely thrashed" with the ignominious punishment.[41]

The winter months frequently caused changes in tactics for lawmen, at least in the northern parts of the state. But for Hall who seemed to be operating more in the southern part of the state that would not be a great change. Hall planned to keep his headquarters at Corpus Christi during the winter, but "his headquarters will be mostly in the saddle." Or so reported the *Statesman* of Austin, who could keep informed of what the Texas Rangers were doing by simply visiting the adjutant general's office a few blocks from the newspaper offices.[42]

Nefarious activities were taking place on the Texas coast, which would soon bring in Hall's men. A band of thieves was recognized as killing cattle for their hides in the Long Mott neighborhood, no different than the wholesale slaughter of the buffalo of a few years earlier – killing the animals for their hides alone, wasting the remainder of the beasts. An early arrest was of John Wacker of Calhoun County, arrested by a squad of State troops for being in possession of a lot of stolen hides. He was delivered to authorities in Indianola. Later that month of February a squad composed of three of Hall's men— William L. Rudd, A.S. McKay and Theodore S. Hillyer— were noted as passing through Victoria on their way to Calhoun County.[43] They would be able to report their success in March.

Not all the action dealt with guns and fists. Hall on occasion mixed with the upper social classes of the city. In February his lieutenant, John B. Armstrong, set the date for his wedding to Miss Mollie Durst. The wedding took place at St. David's Episcopal Church in Austin the evening of February 20. Among the well-dressed attendants was Jesse Lee Hall escorting Miss Pattie Townes, a twenty-one-year-old school teacher in Austin.[44] Other attendants included former Ranger Netteville Devine escorting Miss Ella Mabry, daughter of noted cattle baron Seth Mabry; another ranger, Lieut. Samuel A. McMurry escorted Miss Florence Jackson. Robert J. Kleberg of the King Ranch was an attendant with Miss Julia Pease, daughter of former Gov. Elisha M. Pease. It was a brilliant affair but unfortunately no photographs of the bride and groom let alone the attendants were made. Following the wedding, the group retired to the home of the bride's mother "where the evening was spent pleasantly."[45]

The excitement of the February 20 Armstrong-Durst wedding and pleasant evening following could not last long for Lee Hall, as there were criminals needing to be captured or killed. One priority for lawmen in early 1878 was how to find Sam Bass and end his career. By coincidence at that moment the gang was planning to rob the train at Allen, a small community in Collin County, an area that Lee Hall certainly knew well. On the night of February 22, train No. 4 of the Houston & Texas Central left Denison in Grayson County, its several passenger cars holding 175 travelers. In addition there was a mail car and an express car. Train No. 4 pulled into Allen about 9 o'clock that night and Sam Bass and his men were waiting and immediately attacked. Initially there was considerable confusion among the passengers and some resistance from the express car messenger, one James A. Thomas. On threat of being burned out of the car, however, Thomas finally surrendered and the robbers entered the express car and took what they wanted before riding off into the night. Estimates of the amount of loot they stole ranged into the many thousands, but Sam Bass, who was there, later admitted that there were four in the gang and they equally split $1,280, a mere $320 each.[46]

Governor Hubbard reasoned that, if only for political reasons, he had to act fast, and he immediately offered rewards for the train robbers. He notified the Texas railroad officials that he would offer a reward of $500 for the capture of each of the robbers and requested they provide transportation for Lee Hall, who would start at once to the scene of the crime.[47] Once the governor had offered the rewards, the Houston & Texas

Central Railway and the Texas Express companies showed they could be just as liberal and offered $1,500 for each of the four. The rewards were offered "to induce the most determined efforts to catch the thieves."[48] Lee Hall, feeling determined to grab the rewards, picked four of his men and left for Allen in order to get on the track before the trail grew cold. The Monthly Return provides only the following: "Feby 23— 4 men at Allen Station hunting for train robbers until Apl 1st."[49] It would be months before anyone received any of the promised reward.

The year 1878 would prove to be a banner year for law enforcement in Texas. John Wesley Hardin, the state's most notorious man-killer, would be tried, found guilty of second-degree murder and sentenced to a term of twenty-five years in the state's penitentiary in Huntsville. His brother-in-law Brown Bowen would be found guilty of a murder and would pay the price on the gallows in Gonzales, with Hall and several rangers keeping order. Another noted man-killer, Bill Longley, who boasted of more murders than he had actually committed, would be tried and found guilty and suffer death by hanging in Giddings in Lee County. Perhaps the worst man who never killed a man, Sam Bass, but who had robbed trains and stage coaches, also was run to earth in July of that year. Others received credit for the bullets that led to Bass's death, such as Rangers Richard C. Ware and George Herold, but Hall was also there at Round Rock and participated in the gunfight and pursuit of the gang.

That exciting action took place in July but two months earlier Hall was in Austin meeting with Major John B. Jones of the Frontier Battalion. Most recent reports were that Hall was in Austin "seeking to effect arrangements whereby the command may be retained in service." Their concern was how to convince the Legislature to continue funding the rangers so they could continue their good work. There was no question that the counties in West and South Texas needed the rangers, but the eastern counties did not have the same issues of lawlessness, and they were against spending state money on the rangers. A Dallas newspaper reported that the state was six months in arrears to the members of Hall's command and feared that "a number of them contemplate withdrawing from the force" in order to find some other employment where the pay was more regular.

An effective leader must count on dependable men and Hall was no exception to this rule. There were times he had to be in Austin while his men continued to scout for fugitives. During the months of December through February a detachment led by Lieut. William Rudd was working in Calhoun County, on the coast, planning to capture a gang of cattle thieves. Three men were of particular interest: Frank Hartman, considered the leader, Frank Gordon, and Charles Ernst. These were not their real names. For some time cattle had been killed for their hides, "but no evidence sufficient to convict the suspected parties could be obtained." Finally, Private William T. Cavin "was detailed to ingratiate himself into the good graces of the suspected desperadoes for the purpose of establishing sufficient evidence against them upon which to secure a conviction." Cattle was not their only interest, as on the night of Saturday, February 23, this trio planned to break into the mercantile store of Charles M. Holden of Fulton and take a lot of the retail grocer's goods.[50] On the night of the planned robbery there was to be a performance at the Fulton Opera House, and "everybody was supposed to be at the concert."[51] Ranger-spy, Cavin, was actually placed outside the store as the "lookout" while the others ransacked it. As soon as possible he went to alert Lieutenant Rudd and the others but they were too late to actually trap the thieves inside the store. Cavin, however, was able to lead the rangers to where the thieves had hidden their horses.

Arriving at the spot where the horses had been secreted Lieutenant Rudd's command to surrender was answered with a flurry of shots. Perhaps thirty shots were exchanged, the rangers being at a great disadvantage as they were only able to fire at the flashes of the guns the thieves had as they were hidden in the brush. No one was wounded in the fiery exchange. Late Sunday morning gang member Charles Ernst, apparently not tough enough for gunfights in the dark, surrendered to authorities who promptly turned him over to the rangers who jailed him in Rockport. That evening the rangers continued the hunt for the other thieves and traced them to St. Joseph's Island, knowing they had stolen a boat to get there. This time the thieves had somehow escaped, but they lost all their horses and stolen goods to the rangers.[52]

Ranger A.S. McKay[53] was resourceful and persisted in scouting after the gang's leader, Frank Hartman, and finally located him across the bayou from Indianola. Hartman "manifested a disposition to resist arrest" but after a twenty-minute talk with McKay he wisely decided to give up and surrendered his weapons. He was delivered to the jail at Rockport, where his companion was confined. On February 25 a man named Huffington "landed" Gordon Franks, one of the Fulton burglars, on the shore of Long Mott. He may have believed he had eluded the Rangers but as soon as he stepped on the shore they arrested him and delivered him to Indianola. A reporter expressed the belief that even with this capture there was still one more gang member in the vicinity "but he and his pal might as well try to evade bloodhounds as Hall's ferrets."[54] Indeed, Lieutenant Rudd and Aransas County Sheriff Samuel Z.J. Beetley delivered the remaining robbers to the Nueces County jail in Corpus Christi for safe keeping: Charles E. Wittinbirt,[55] George Franks, and Frank Hartman. "Coloma" Franks was left in the Rockport jail as he was too badly wounded to be moved.[56] At the time of the night time gunfight it was believed no one had been injured, but apparently one robber had been, as it was now learned Coloma Franks had received a bullet wound.

Perhaps at this late date we must accept the identities as given in the official prison record of Huntsville, which housed the Fulton store robbers, rather than their various aliases. They are listed as Charles Withenbert, # 6770; Charles Franks, #6771; Frank Hartman, #6772; and Gordon Franks, #6773. The true identity of these men is confusing, as perhaps Charles Withenbert was really Ernst who had earlier surrendered. This is how they were identified in the prison records at any rate. On being received they were shaved and all scars and marks recorded as well as their education level, occupation, whether they smoked, were temperate or not, married or not, where they lived, and when they would be released.

Among the Huntsville prisoners at this time was John Wesley Hardin who was serving a twenty-five-year sentence for second-degree murder. As would the Fulton store robbers, Hardin learned that bad behavior in Huntsville resulted in severe punishment. Withenbert, #6770, was punished August 5, 1878, for disorderly conduct and spent one hour in the stocks. On December 29, 1878, he spent twelve hours in a dark cell for "insolence" and was punished again December 31, 1878, for disorderly conduct. He was discharged October 20, 1881. Charles Franks, #6771, was punished for "bad work" on May 24, 1878, and punished again in July 1878; he escaped on May 29 but was quickly recaptured on May 31, 1880, and punished on September 18, and again punished– "whipped"– in September 1880. He too was discharged early on December 31, 1881. Frank Hartman, # 6772, evidently behaved himself avoiding punishment but managed to escape July 16, 1878, and was not recaptured. The fourth, Gordon Franks, # 6773, also avoided physical punishment and he too escaped August 31, 1878.[57]

The rangers were not inclined to take all the credit, as they acknowledged the "valuable service" of Calhoun County Sheriff F.L. Busch, his deputy Ben Evers, Mr. Clayborne Garner, Justice Kleinecke, and other citizens, "who rendered timely assistance."[58] The Monthly Return as usual provides no details, but does give the names of those four arrested, at least as they were so identified: Charles Withian (Withenbirt or Wittinbirt), arrested February 24; Gordon Franks, arrested February 25; Coleman Franks, arrested February 26; and Frank Hartman, arrested February 28. Their crime: "Burglary." From a variety of sources one learns that besides Rudd and McKay there was former McNelly ranger Charles Brown McKinney involved in the pursuit as well as the "ranger-spy" William T. Cavin[59] who had infiltrated the gang.[60]

Concern for payment due to the actions of the State Legislature was an almost continuous concern for ranger captains as well as the men.

Without sufficient pay for their hazardous work, the men would naturally seek other employment. Such was the case again in early 1878 when Honorable Ellsberry Richard Lane introduced a bill in the Senate providing for the organization of a company of sixty men to be placed on the Texas border with Mexico to protect the frontier. The *Goliad Guard* editor commented that "None are better acquainted with the situation of the people on our exposed frontier than Mr. Lane and the people of West Texas will appreciate his efforts in the legislature in trying to have their lives and property protected from marauders that infect both sides of the Rio Grande." At the same time rumors were afloat that Hall's company was to be disbanded, but the editor hoped that "our Senator will doubtless use the power of his eloquence in effecting its passage,"[61] meaning Lane's bill establishing the force of sixty.

In December 1877 William Vollrath was murdered while asleep in his bed at his rancho, twelve miles from Lodi in Wilson County. No motive was ever determined for the crime, but authorities followed the tracks leading ultimately to a house occupied by Benjamin Goodwin. He was arrested on suspicion of murdering young Vollrath and jailed in Wilson County but escaped. Louis Vollrath, the murdered man's father, immediately offered a reward of $250 for the capture of Goodwin; in addition, Sheriff Robert C. Houston offered a reward of $100. Additional rewards were soon offered. In late February 1878 Goodwin was captured near Oakville with a stolen mare in his possession. It is likely that some of Hall's men made the capture. By this time the reward had increased to $1,100.[62] He apparently escaped his captors or else was released on bond for in mid-summer of 1879 Goodwin, now identified as Warren Goodwin, was reported to have been arrested in Lee County but escaped, then was arrested in Montgomery County "for murder done long ago in Jefferson [Marion County]." No motive was given for either the Wilson County or the Marion County murder. Lee Hall had pursued Goodwin but never caught up with him. Commented the *Statesman*: "They don't let Warren Goodwin have peace. Lee Hall pursued him and he fled from

Corpus Christi. . . . There is no rest for the wicked, and Warren's is a hard road to travel."[63]

Occasionally unusual actions occur when dealing with criminals. Apparently Sergeant William Rudd was one of several rangers assisting at the court in Refugio at the punishment trial of murderer Juan Antonio Hernandez in April. Hernandez was convicted of the murder of two men, Waelder and Maton. He heard the verdict of guilty and punishment of hanging and then "pulled off his shoes and carefully wrapping them up in his coat, gave the bundle to Sergeant Rudd with the request that he hand them to his (Hernandez's) wife." The doomed man "supposed the hanging was to come off immediately."[64] Hernandez was not executed until October 8, 1878, at Refugio, however, with between 400 and 500 men on horseback as witnesses. The *Victoria Advocate* failed to identify any ranger as being present but the Monthly Return indicates there were four members of the State Troops there assisting Refugio County Sheriff Jeptha Williams and his deputy.[65]

The activities of John Wesley Hardin as well as those of his brother-in-law Joshua Robert "Brown" Bowen received a great amount of attention in the press of the day, sometimes overshadowing Hall's actions. Bowen was found guilty of the murder of Thomas Haldeman and his letters denying his guilt received attention. Bowen's letter claiming he had not had a fair trial was printed in the *Victoria Advocate* as well as other journals in the issue of April 20. It was followed in the Wilson County newspaper by just a brief news item: "Moore, charged with an attempt to murder in this county [Wilson], was arrested in Goliad [C]ounty by Hall's men." In his monthly report Hall was just as taciturn, recording in his report merely that Sam Moore had been arrested on March 31 for murder, with no details.[66]

On a more personal note, the trial of James D. Whitney charged with assault with intent to kill Jesse Lee Hall was taking place in Grayson County. Details have not surfaced but the attempt was made in Whitesboro in April of 1871. Whitney had been captured in the Indian Territory by Sheriff William C. Everheart, Constable Spence, and posse.[67] Strangely at the time of the attempt there was no newspaper coverage, at least none as yet has been found. The main sources of information are reports of the trial seven years later.

When Sergeant Armstrong captured John Wesley Hardin in Pensacola, Florida, in August 1877, he also made arrangements to have Hardin's brother-in-law Joshua Robert "Brown" Bowen captured. Bowen was wanted for an 1872 killing in Gonzales County. Ranger Armstrong arranged for his capture and he was returned to Texas where he stood trial, was found guilty and sentenced to hang. While waiting for the results of his appeal he was kept in the Travis County jail; in the same jail was Hardin, as well as several other desperate men: Bill Taylor, Mannen Clements, and Pipes and Herndon of the Sam Bass gang. When the appeal was denied Bowen was sent to the Gonzales jail to await his execution. Then Hall and his rangers were sent to guard the jail and prevent the prisoner from escaping. The Monthly Return indicates there were five men of the Special State Troops there: Hall and J.B. Armstrong are listed but the return does not identify the others. The reporting in the *Gonzales Inquirer* identifies, besides Hall and Armstrong, William L. Rudd,[68] A.S. McKay, and Theodore S. Hillyer.[69] Brown Bowen, on May 17, 1878, would mount the gallows. The reporter who witnessed the execution gave exciting headlines to the article: "As the Law Takes a Life" and "A Scene a Thousand-fold More Terrible than a Murder by a Mob" and "A Vast Crowd and Guard of Rangers." At the time of the execution inside the jail yard were Sheriff Alonzo T. Bass, Hall, Armstrong, Rudd, McKay, Hillyer, deputies Bruton and Lewis and several others not identified.[70] Over a thousand persons observed the end of Bowen and the presence of the rangers prevented any disturbances. Curiously the popular New York publication the *National Police Gazette* provided a large illustration showing what other newspapers missed—captioned "Fracas at the execution of the desperado Brown Bowen at Gonzales, Texas, between the friends of Bowen and those of the murdered man." This shows what appears to be nine men fighting, four of them holding what appear to be rifles. In the distance is silhouetted the gallows with Bowen standing with the noose around his neck.[71] The execution of Bowen received considerable press coverage, not only in the *Gonzales Inquirer* but numerous other journals as well. Bowen was allowed to give a lengthy speech prior to the execution, first asking Rev. Eli Y. Seale to see that his body was taken care of, thanking him for his kindness and "Christian consolation to me while in a felon's cell." Bowen wanted his body taken to his father's farm and Judge Christopher C. DeWitt would assist him in so doing. Surprisingly, Bowen remembered those who had placed him in custody back in 1877. "My heartfelt thanks to Capt. Lee Hall, Lieut. Armstrong and their faithful followers, for the kindness they have shown me. They are doing good for the country. May they ever prosper. My prayers are with them." And finally his last words were advice to others: "Good-bye all; I do hope you will all pay attention to these my dying statements; there has been no attention paid to them during my life. Farewell, all." Then the trap door was sprung and Bowen died.[72]

Hall recorded in May, "Since my last monthly report my company has done very little scouting that done by Sergt. Parrotts detachment in Northern Texas, and no other duty except attending the execution of Brown Bowen in Gonzales & the courts at Rockport, Corpus Christi, and Indianola. I reorganized my company on the 25th (all except those that I wished to discharge) agreeing to enlist on the terms offered by the Governor. I have at present one detachment of five men under Sergt. Parrott in the neighborhood of San Antonio watching Nathan Underwoods ranch as I had been informed by telegram from Northern Texas that the Bass gang had gone in that directions & knowing that they would stop there in case they came this far South."[73] Neither Hardin nor Bowen ever achieved popularity during their lifetimes, but the train robber Sam Bass did become a folk hero. Ranger Lee Hall and his company as well as many other lawmen were anxious to have the opportunity to capture or kill Sam Bass— not only for the reward, which they might never receive, but more for the sake of establishing law and order in their homeland.

The career of Sam Bass needs no review other than to say he began by robbing stage coaches in the Dakota Territory, then in 1877 he and his gang pulled off a successful train robbery in Nebraska, netting them $60,000 from the Union Pacific. In North Texas Bass and other gang members struck terror among officials by robbing several trains and were seemingly able to escape the law's clutches every time. The end finally came when Jim Murphy, a member of the gang, betrayed them by informing Major Jones that they planned to rob the Williamson County Bank in Round Rock, only a few miles north of Austin.[74]

The Bass gang at this point in mid-May consisted of Bass, Seaborn Barnes, Frank Jackson, and Jim Murphy. Sam Pipes and Alf Hearndon, two members of the gang, had been captured and were securely placed in the Travis County jail. About this same time Hall had five men attending district court in Corpus Christi, one man was in northern Texas looking after stolen cattle, two men were in Burnet County delivering prisoners, and the remainder were in Banquete or Corpus Christi. To Hall parts of the state were relatively crime free. "No murders have occurred in Nueces County since we went there last fall," he recorded. "This Section of the State is quieter & the law is thoroughly in force in every County except Live Oak & San Patricio. We will have no service apparently to perform except to secure the attendance of witnesses before the courts & enforce order at Such time."[75] Hall would soon see violent action in Williamson County, as much as he would handle.

Major Jones knew approximately when the gang would attack the bank, and wisely wanted some rangers present when they struck. The closest company was that of Lieut. N.O. Reynolds in San Saba County. Jones sent Corporal V.C. Wilson to get to Reynolds and have him come as fast as he could with the men with the best horses. Reynolds was ill at the time and consequently he rode in a wagon, which slowed the group down, but they did get to Round Rock. Major Jones, fearing Reynolds and his men would not arrive in time, telegraphed Lieutenant Hall to come to Round Rock; he arrived there at 1:00 p.m. on July 19 and conferred with

Major Jones. For further fire power Jones then telegraphed Sergeant J.B. Armstrong to bring some of Hall's men and come to Round Rock also.

One of the rangers was ordered to keep watch on the bank. While in position he noticed three men entering Koppel's General Store. The coat of one of them flared up and the ranger noticed what he thought was a pistol. Wearing weapons within the city limits was against the law in Round Rock, and the ranger, with deputies Maurice B. Moore[76] and Ahijah W. "Caige" Grimes, confronted the three who had entered the store. The trio, who may have had the appearance of cowboys just into town, heard the challenge asking if they had pistols. They all three answered "Yes" and then drew their six-shooters and fired at the lawmen. The battle of Round Rock thus began almost by accident. Moore later explained what had happened: "I immediately drew my pistol and commenced firing at the one who shot me. After I fired my first shot I could not see the men on account of the smoke. They continued shooting and so did I, until I fired five shots, then they ran out of the store."[77] The two deputy sheriffs of Williamson County had done their duty, to challenge the three who were suspected of defying the law. Grimes paid for it with his life; Moore was wounded, but not critically. Major Jones was in the telegraph office when he heard the shots. Lieutenant Hall was in a hotel lying down but when he heard the shots he grabbed his pistol and Winchester and ran for the street. The outlaw trio never had a real chance to get out of town unscathed. Out in the street, Ranger Richard C. Ware took deliberate aim at one of the robbers— Seaborn Barnes— and fired, the shot entering his head and killing him instantly. Bass was severely wounded in the side and hand and unable to mount, but companion Frank Jackson managed to get him mounted and the pair galloped out of town. Major Jones, Hall, and various citizens who had obtained weapons fired at the fleeing bandits. Those who began the pursuit had to return to town when their horses gave out; Hall also had followed the trail of blood drops but lost it in the onset of the evening, and returned as well. The next morning some of Reynolds's men continued the search and found the dying outlaw. He asked them not to shoot, and admitted: "I am Sam Bass."[78] Ironically, Sam

Bass, train robber and would-be bank robber, became a popular figure in Texas. The grave of Bass, alongside that of companion Seaborn Barnes, is a popular tourist spot today. The grave of Deputy Grimes, in the same Round Rock Cemetery, is only occasionally visited.

It was as easy to criticize public figures in the nineteenth century as it is today in the twenty-first century. The *Victoria Advocate* noted that while the Legislature was organizing some of the in-house positions, someone placed the name of Captain Hall in nomination for sergeant-at-arms. A West Texas delegate remarked that "Capt Lee Hall should be on the frontier" rather than being safely in the halls of the capitol building. Ignorance of where Hall was at that moment was apparent, as just two days later it was determined that Hall had been fighting the would-be bank robbers at Round Rock, eighteen miles north. So, concluded the *Advocate*, "it was discovered that Hall was in the right place after all." [79]

During this period when the name of Sam Bass was on virtually everyone's lips, outlaws in other areas of the state could operate freely. A band of "noted horse thieves" had been operating in Victoria and Goliad Counties and drew the attention of the press by mid-August. In early August the gang gathered nineteen horses near Goliad; on the ninth, six men joined as a posse to follow the thieves and caught up with three of them: Braxton "Brack" Cornett of Goliad, a man named Bell from Matagorda County, and an unidentified Mexican in possession of the stolen horses. The trio were taken to Goliad and lodged in the jail while the sheriff took charge of returning the recovered stock. Commented the editor, "These men are said to be connected with a gang of horse thieves operating between here and Red River, and officers of the law are on the trail of others of the band, and expect to effect their arrest before they succeed in escaping from the country."[80] Of this gang of thieves only Cornett would gain any notoriety; in a few years he would join up with Bill Whitley and others and move up from stealing horses to robbing trains and banks. He was eventually killed by Alfred Y. Allee on Allee's ranch in Frio County.[81]

In September Captain Hall was in Victoria, "having just returned from a long trip to the counties west of the Nueces." He reported that the country was peaceable "in that direction."[82]

The news from the adjutant general's office frequently indicated the State Troops would have to be reduced in numbers due to the lack of funding appropriated by the Legislature. On October 10, 1878, Goliad County citizens held a public meeting "for the purpose of taking into consideration" the recent action to reduce Hall's company from thirty to fifteen men. Three men were appointed to form a committee to draft resolutions expressing the citizens' desires to present to Governor Hubbard. The committee appointed was made up of Judge Pryor Lea, D.F. Merriwether, and David Hardeman, all highly respected citizens of the county. The resolutions adopted were to the effect that the community of Goliad felt "aggrieved" at Hubbard's recent order reducing the number in Hall's command; further the committee felt that more than thirty were necessary "to ensure adequate security to the population of the Southwestern portion of the State." A few years before "crime and lawlessness was so prevalent" the civil authorities were unable to preserve the peace; then the small forces under McNelly and Hall had restored peace and quiet. Granted, at present law and order reigned supreme, but a reduction in the number of troops would result in the country relapsing again into its former condition. The "crime and disorder of the past would be reenacted" and in sum, the command should be kept "at least several years longer in service." Of course the proceedings of the meeting should be "respectfully communicated" to the governor.[83] How would the governor react?

How Governor Hubbard reacted is not recorded—at least no documentation has been located—but he and his adjutant general certainly discussed the resolutions. On October 15 William Steele wrote out the official response. He began by stating that the protests of reducing Hall's company had been received; he was "fully persuaded" that the concerns of the Goliad citizens were not overstated and that a much larger force than Hall had "could be usefully employed." He also reminded the citizens that earlier when the force was to be disbanded a number of merchants and stockmen had promised to provide the necessary funds to keep the company in force— but those "promises have been but partially fulfilled." Steele made it clear that there was "no money to pay the necessary expenses of small parties that it has been habitual to send out in all directions after felons." Steele, however, continued giving hope: "The force now left being without ability to send out detachments, I think is sufficiently large for any action in a body." He reminded the citizens that they were certainly aware that there was "much objection" in various parts of the State "to the keeping this company in service." By now Steele could have concluded his response but he took another paragraph and a snipe at the commander: "Had Capt. Hall carried out the instructions sent him without publishing it to the world, malefactors would not have learned of the reduced force before the meeting of the next legislature and the incoming of a new administration, the opinions of which on this subject are unknown."[84] So Hall's force would be reduced due to economic reality as well as political influence from certain portions of the state, presumably counties in the eastern half of Texas.

Hall would continue to eradicate thieves and murderers no matter the size of his company. The Rio Grande always posed a problem for lawmen. There was no extradition treaty between Mexico and the United States; hence it was illegal for lawmen to cross to capture a fugitive. This was common knowledge among thieves and murderers. Sometimes lawmen did cross over and managed to avoid an international incident; sometimes once the fugitive had crossed over he was forgotten about, for the time being at least. Such a case was that of finding Martin Rodriguez, alias *Chiquito*.[85] Rodriguez was the alleged murderer of Nueces County Deputy Sheriff Shaw. On December 17 Corporal Rudd with two men crossed the river at Brownsville "for purpose of arresting and extraditing Martine Rodriguez the Mexican who murdered Dept Shff Shaw of Nueces Co. some 13 months ago. He succeeded in having him arrested in Matamoros but failed to have him extradited as the Mexican authorities refused to give him up. Not with standing he was a naturalized citizen & had voted for years in this county."[86] A newspaper report is a little more informative, pointing out that Rudd was assisted by Cameron County Sheriff William Scanlon.[87] The pair arrested Rodriguez on the Mexican side of the Rio Grande but could not deliver him back to Brownsville. The *Rio Grande Democrat* confidently stated that "there is no doubt that, through the exertions of vice-counsel Valls, he will be turned over to our authorities."[88] All was not a wasted effort, however, as Hall concluded his Monthly Return with this: "[Rudd] succeeded however in arresting Carlis Vela the Mexican who shot and mortally wounded Mr. Maestrot a New Orleans drummer & killed his driver and is now returning with Vela to this place."[89]

Illustration 2. Jesse Lee Hall

JESSE LEIGH "LEE" HALL (1849 – 1911)

Courtesy Jack DeMattos, first published in *Real West*, August, 1984 and *Real West Yearbook* 1986.

Illustration 3. Dr. James King Hall, *circa* 1885

Courtesy the Greensboro History Museum.
Dr. Hall, father of the future Texas Ranger, was a surgeon during the Civil War, serving with the 22nd North Carolina, C.S.A. After the hostilities he became a prominent physician of Greensboro, North Carolina.

Illustration 4. The badge worn by J.L. "Red" Hall during his early years in Grayson County.

Courtesy Kurt House Collection.
The front merely indicates his position as deputy.

Illustration 5. Reverse of badge worn by Hall during his years in Grayson County, showing "Texas/Red Hall."

Courtesy Kurt House Collection.

Illustration 6. An engraving of Lee Hall during his early years in Grayson County

From *The Great South* by Edward King.
Engraving by artist James Wells Champney who accompanied King on his journeys throughout the south.

Illustration 7. Champney's drawing of a Denison saloon

"Men drunk and sober danced to rude music." [Page 177.]

In *The Great South* artist James Wells Champney captioned this drawing of a Denison saloon "Men drunk and sober danced to rude music." Desperate men and women found recreation and perhaps plotted illegal activity in such businesses during Hall's time.

Illustration 8. Champney's engraving of "Playing Keno"

James Wells Champney entitled this engraving of a Denison gambling game as "Playing Keno," showing a young lady as dealer. Not only were the men daring at the edge of the frontier, but women were also.

Illustration 9. Earliest known image of Hall

Courtesy Kurt House Collection.

An exquisite image of Lee Hall, Texas Ranger, Indian Agent, ranch manager, and U.S. soldier. The photograph itself is a mere .5" x 1" held in a 2.75" x 1.75", gutta percha frame of floral design. Was this a gift from Hall to Bessie C. Weidman . . . or someone else?

Illustration 10. Notorious desperado of the Nueces Strip John King Fisher.

Courtesy the Western History Collections, University of Oklahoma, N.H. Rose Collection, # 2152.

This image was made in the early 1880s when he had turned his life around to serve as a sheriff of Uvalde County, Texas.

Illustration 11. Artist's drawing of the capture of John King Fisher

PURIFYING THE BORDERS.

THE TEXAS RANGERS RAIDING A HEADQUARTERS OF HORSE THIEVES, CATTLE-RUSTLERS AND "BAD" MEN.

From the New York publication, *Life*, December 19, 1901. *Courtesy Larry Shaver.*

Fisher and his gang are depicted being captured by Captain L.H. McNelly. Note there are at least thirteen rangers depicted. Note also the sign above the residence: "King Fisher His Shack." And the ranger identified as "Field Secretary Jennings" taking notes and rolls of paper in his saddle bag; this he used for his work *A Texas Ranger*.

Illustration 12. Napoleon Augustus Jennings

This particular drawing appeared in the *Salt Lake Tribune* of Salt Lake City, Utah, July 9, 1899.

Jennings as he appeared long after his ranger days, now a successful writer. This image and accompanying article appeared in numerous publications including the *Rochester Democrat and Chronicle*.

Illustration 13. Espantosa Lake

Author's photograph.
One of the dangerous gunbattles between Hall's men and outlaws occurred near this site. This is a view of Espantosa Lake in north central Dimmit County. Four outlaws were killed during the engagement and one seriously wounded. The rangers were led by Sgt. John B. Armstrong.

Illustration 14. Captain L.H. McNelly

Courtesy the Albert and Ethel Herzstein Library, San Jacinto Museum of History, La Porte, TX.

McNelly's successful methods of leadership in fighting *banditti* from across the Rio Grande were followed by Lee Hall. Original image by James Inglis, Montreal, Canada, 1872.

Illustration 15. Thomas William Deggs in the late 1860s

Courtesy Roger Kaland Collection.
Deggs joined the Special State Troops as a private under Captain L.H. McNelly February 1, 1876.

Illustration 16. Thomas William Deggs in 1874

Courtesy Roger Kaland Collection.
Deggs served under Lieutenant J.L. Hall from January 25, 1877, to August 31, 1877.

Illustration 17. Horace Rowe

Courtesy the Austin History Center, PICB 10200.
This image of Horace Rowe shows clearly the youthfulness of most of the men who became rangers under McNelly and Hall. This is undated but probably made during the early 1870s.

Illustration 18. Texas Ranger John Barklay Armstrong

Author's Collection
Armstrong served with McNelly and Hall and received state wide recognition for his capture of John Wesley Hardin in 1877.

Illustration 19. Julia Maria Pease

Courtesy the Austin History Center, PICB 06790.
Julia Maria was the daughter of Governor E.M. Pease, and friend of Lee Hall as she appeared about 1875. Image was made in the New York Studio of Napoleon Sarony, 680 Broadway, New York. She attended Vassar between 1870 and 1875 and possibly this was a graduation picture.

Illustration 20. Bee County Sheriff D.A.T. Walton and family

Image courtesy Archives of the Big Bend, Sul Ross University, Alpine, Texas. As sheriff he and Captain Hall ensured an orderly execution of convicted murderer Singleton at Beeville. Back row from left, J. David and Paloma, with hand on father's shoulder; middle row from left, Ella, D.A.T., Amanda, Nanni; front row, from left, Lula, William Baylor in father's arms, Norine, and James Allen.

Illustration 21. Thomas "Black Tom" Caffall and Robert J. "Brown" Bowen

Courtesy the Wittliff Collection, Texas State University.
A beautifully framed image of two men who were the subjects of Hall's scouts. At left Thomas "Black Tom" Caffall, who eluded ranger patrols, and a young Robert J. "Brown" Bowen, brother-in-law of John Wesley Hardin. Hall and his rangers prevented any disturbances at the legal execution of Bowen in 1878.

Illustration 22. John Wesley Hardin, 1875

Courtesy the Robert G. McCubbin Collection.
The notorious John Wesley Hardin as he appeared in 1875, a fugitive hiding out in Florida.

Illustration 23. Sheriff Charles Brown McKinney and former Texas Ranger George W. Farrow

Courtesy the Brush Country Museum. Cotulla, La Salle County, Texas.
La Salle County Sheriff Charles Brown McKinney at left, and former Texas Ranger George W. Farrow. McKinney and Hall were instrumental in forging a "peace treaty" at Paso de Las Isles in the Rio Grande, in 1885. McKinney was assassinated December 26, 1886, by James McCoy and George W. "Bud" Crenshaw.

Illustration 24. Linton Lafayette Wright

Author's Collection.

Wright began his service under Captain McNelly on January 1, 1875, and continued to serve under Capt. Jesse L. Hall. He later became the sheriff of Duval County, Texas, elected November 2, 1880, re-elected four times, serving until November 4, 1890.

Illustration 25. Lee Hall's younger brother Richard Moore Hall

R. M. HALL.

From *Personnel of the Texas State Government*, compiled and published by L. E. Daniell, 1889.

This shows Richard Hall as he appeared during his term as Commissioner of the General Land Office, Austin.

Illustration 26. Engraving of the General Land Office of Austin in the 1870s

The Land Office of Texas—Austin.

Engraved by James Wells Champney, this illustration appeared in King's *The Great South*. Lee Hall's younger brother Richard M. Hall served here as General Land Commissioner.

Illustration 27. William Sidney Porter

Courtesy the Austin History Center, PICB 07214.
Porter who would later become known as "O. Henry," is depicted as he appeared in 1884 as a resident of Austin. His health had improved greatly after spending time on the Dull Brothers Ranch managed by Lee Hall. Photograph by noted Austin photographer Samuel B. Hill.

Illustration 28. Texas Ranger and one-time Austin City Marshal James E. Lucy

Courtesy Richard Lucy, great-grandson of James E. Lucy and Austin History Center, PICB 19634.
The image is undated, but note badge visible at left lapel. Photo by Samuel B. Hill, who operated in Austin from 1878-1901 on Congress Avenue.

Illustration 29. Dr. Owen Clinton Pope

Courtesy Hardin-Simmons Special Collection.
The photo depicts Pope (1842–1901), who with Lee Hall and Charles Brown McKinney engineered a treaty with Mexican officials to reduce the lawlessness on the Rio Grande frontier. Pope was later president of Simmons College from 1898 to 1901.

Illustration 30. Patrick Dargan Hickey

Courtesy the Brush Country Museum, Cotulla, La Salle County, Texas.
Hickey served many years as La Salle District and County clerk. The Irish-born native on one occasion drew a pistol on Jesse Lee Hall but friends interfered and prevented any bloodshed. Hickey was "used up" in this fracas with the former Texas Ranger captain.

Illustration 31. Quanah Parker, Yellow Bear, and others

Courtesy the Lawrence T. Jones Collection, DeGolyer Library, SMU.

This cabinet card image was made by Augustus R. Mignon, a Fort Worth photographer in December 1885. Quanah Parker is standing at far left; Yellow Bear is seated at left. Isa-Tai is seated at right. Parker and Isa-Tai were both at the Battle of Adobe Walls during the Red River War. The other three are unidentified but George W. Briggs may be standing next to Parker.

Illustration 32. Ranger Captain Joseph Shely and members of his Company "F" in 1882.

Courtesy Western History Collections, University of Oklahoma Libraries, N.H. Rose Collection # 1409.

Seated from left: Washington W. Shely, younger brother of the captain; Tom Mabry, Robert Crowder, and Cecelio Charo. Standing from left: James M. Buck, first sheriff of La Salle County; Samuel E. "Pete" Edwards, dangerously wounded during the assassination of Sheriff C.B. McKinney; Captain Joe Shely; George W. Farrow, William T. "Brack" Morris and Charles Norris.

Illustration 33. Captain Lee Hall, 1898

Courtesy the Western History Collections, University of Oklahoma Libraries, N.H. Rose Collection, #1265.

This depicts Hall as he appeared in his uniform during the Spanish-American War.

Illustration 34. Father James W. Kirwin, Chaplain of the First United States Volunteers.

From the *Daily Picayune*, New Orleans, Louisiana, August 7, 1898.

Illustration 35. Captain Lee Hall in Philippines Insurrection uniform

From the *San Francisco Call*, September 26, 1900
Newspaper image of Captain Lee Hall as he appeared in his Philippines Insurrection uniform following his return to the United States. This is how he appeared during his interview with Nan Byxbee.

Illustration 36. Hall's grave

Author's photograph.
Final resting place of Jesse Lee Hall, alongside Bessie C. Weidman Hall. Their grave is in the National Cemetery of San Antonio, Texas.

Illustration 37. Map of North Texas

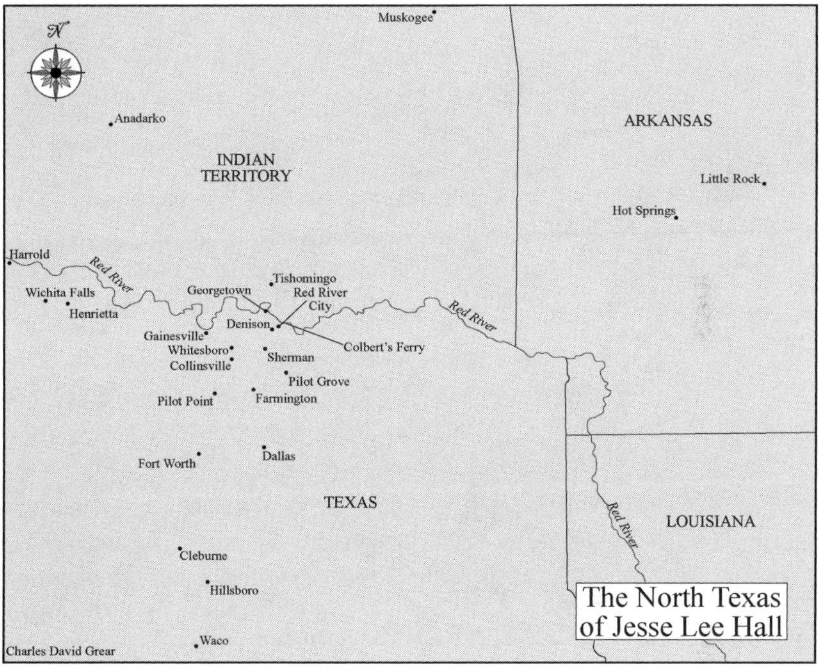

Map courtesy Charles David Grear.
The northern area of Texas in which "Red" Hall worked.

Illustration 38. Map of South Texas

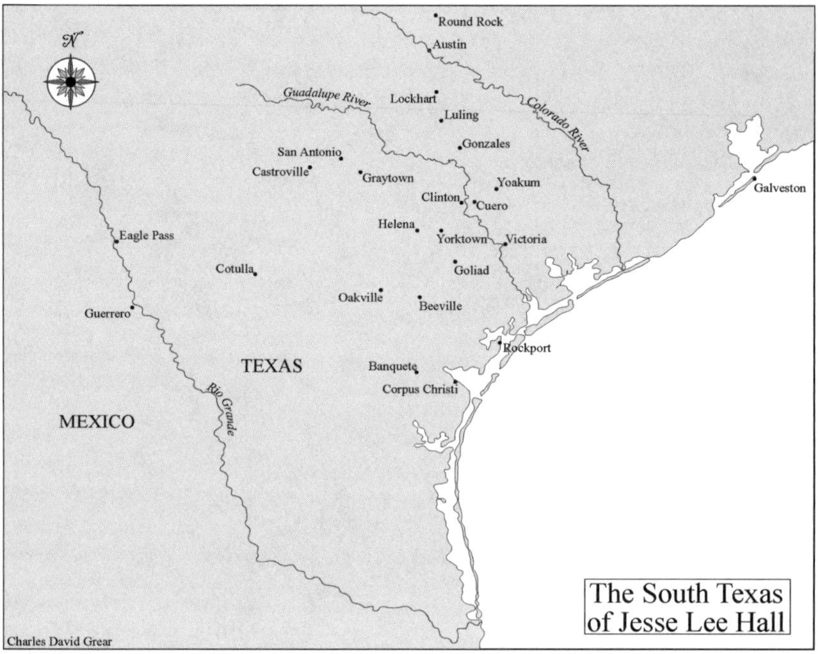

Map courtesy Charles David Grear
The southern area of Texas in which "Red" Hall worked.

Illustration 39. Map of the Philippines

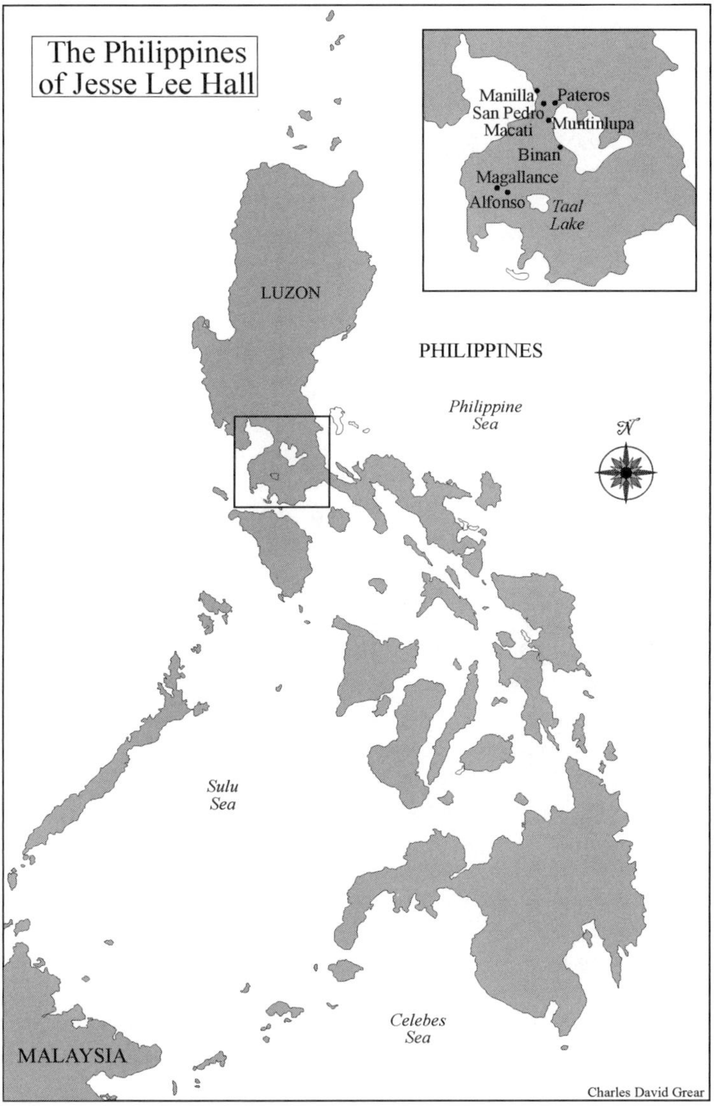

Map courtesy Charles David Grear
The Philippines where Hall served during the Philippine Insurrection where he was so badly wounded he was forced to leave the service.

Chapter Six

"Battle Royal between Robbers and Rangers"

—*Galveston Daily News*, November 8, 1879

Once the dust had settled in Round Rock and train robber Sam Bass had been found and brought into the town where he died on his twenty-seventh birthday, life may have seemed anticlimactic to the rangers and townspeople. The bandit chieftain was buried the next day, his grave next to that of robber companion Seaborn Barnes. Through the years souvenir hunters chipped away the headstone of Bass until it was next to nothing. The most recent one apparently will survive for decades as it does not yet bear the marks of vandals.

Although ending the career of the train robber brought additional recognition to Major Jones and his Texas Rangers, at times the actions of a ranger could bring ignominy to the force. A foolish prank could result in tragedy as Private George W. Talley learned. On August 1, 1878, in the small community of Banquete, near Corpus Christi in Nueces County, a young man named Joshua E. Peters[1] stopped at a store. He had with him his wife and small child, for whom he had sought medical attention. While Peters was occupied with his business someone tied a tin can to the tail of his horse. Peters discovered the "trick" and commented to a group of men standing close by that he could whip the man who had done it, and carried on. Amazingly, George W. Talley,[2] one of Hall's men, accepting the remark as a challenge, drew his pistol and fired at Peters, the ball striking him in the stomach. Initial reports indicated that the wounded Peters then struggled with Talley who, in trying to shoot Peters again, accidently shot himself in the leg. Peters became weak from loss of blood and then fell to the ground. Talley then shot him again, this time in the head, killing him. Talley was unable to catch a horse to flee before other rangers arrested him and delivered him to the county jail. Joshua Peters was described as "a quiet gentleman, young, energetic, and of an unblemished reputation." Witnesses showed "great indignation" at what appeared to be a cold-blooded murder.[3]

Initially County Judge Joseph Fitzsimmons, after the examination was concluded, set bail at $10,000. Then Talley applied for a habeas corpus hearing before District Judge John C. Russell who then reduced the bail to the amount of $5,000. The evidence before Russell was conflicting as to whether Peters had reached and grappled with Talley before the first shot, thus making it a bail-able offense, or if Peters, even though shot, grabbed Talley's pistol and shot Talley through the leg. Talley was released on bail.[4]

Ranger George Durham, who may have actually been an eye-witness to the whole affair, later recalled that Talley had been drinking tequila and then looked around for some devilment. He found that devilment in the form of Peters's horse. He tied a tin can to its tail, which spooked it and somehow hurt the horse. In Durham's recollection, which is very different from the initial newspaper one, the shooting took place in the following way. Peters came upon Durham and Talley playing cards and demanded to know who had spooked his horse. Peters was "fingering his pistol and frothing" when Talley drew his weapon and fired, killing Peters with a shot through the heart. Then Ranger Talley left the scene and disappeared for forty years.[5] Durham's memory played tricks on him as Talley returned to Texas after only a twenty-six-year disappearance.[6]

During his disappearance he had worked in Mexico but occasionally worked across the river in Texas. In 1905 he was in Corpus Christi visiting a saloon when someone tipped off the Nueces County sheriff that Talley had returned. Sheriff Mike B. Wright[7] and a deputy investigated and arrested the suspect. This time Talley stood his trial for the Peters killing. The jury could not agree and it ended as a mistrial; the second trial resulted in his being sentenced to seven years in prison but on appeal he was tried for the third time; this time the jury, after being out about twenty minutes, found Talley not guilty.[8] Talley had managed to avoid the prison term; he had killed a defenseless man but had spent years on the run as a fugitive. The press seemingly found it important to note that Talley had been a member of Hall's Ranger command.[9] There is no mention of Talley becoming an object of Ranger scouts in Hall's Monthly Returns.

The work continued with scouting for men accused of murder and theft. Hall ordered three men to assist the sheriff of Karnes County while court was in session. Captain Hall and ten men assisted court in Live Oak County. Sergeant Wright and four privates assisted stockmen in Live Oak and San Patricio Counties to recover five hundred head of cattle from thieves. Apparently none of the thieves were arrested, "as the owners of the Stock refused to prosecute them, stating it was impossible to get a conviction." In addition to this fact, which must have been frustrating to the commander, he noted that the health of the company was "exceedingly bad" for the past month there were at times more sick men in camp than well.[10]

It was common for newspapers to have traveling agents to seek out news and the *Galveston Daily News* owned and edited by Alfred Horatio Belo was no exception. He posted, and was probably correct, that his paper had a circulation greater than all the daily newspapers in the state. The agents frequently wrote reports of the political races as well as descriptions of the crops, the rainfall, and reports of anything they felt were of interest to the readers. One unidentified agent travelled throughout West Texas and gave a glowing report of how DeWitt County had changed from the lawlessness of the Sutton-Taylor Feud days and how by 1878 it was a peaceful county, thanks to the work of Captain Hall. After a mention of the killing of Sheriff Jack Helm and the treaty of peace, which did not end the feud as hoped, he continued with praise of the ranger captain. "[T]hanks to Lee Hall," he wrote, "and the [fenced] pasture system in cattle raising, old DeWitt is as quiet and orderly as any county in the New England states." His praise continued, "It is hardly credible that where a few years ago lawlessness was a boast, and murder was an every-day occurrence it should now be the pride of a community that it is peaceful and law-abiding." And who should receive the credit for this accomplishment? Lee Hall, "a perfect gentleman, highly educated and accomplished, handsome and athletic, patient and courageous, without the slightest hint of bravado in his composition. With such a compliment of manly virtues, he forced himself on the love of the better classes, and compelled the bad element to fear him." As if this was not enough praise for the lawman, the reporter continued: "To him no distance is too great, no difficulties too discouraging, or danger too great when duty calls, and so rapidly does he move his men and himself that he seems endowed with ubiquity. . . . I take pleasure in assisting your many readers to a knowledge of a man who combines all the qualities of true knightliness in himself." If Hall's Rangers read this hymn of praise did they not shower him with quizzical jests of how they could develop "true knightliness" as well?[11]

The Monthly Return for October 1878 records in most simple terms, "Arrested Antonio Garcia, murder" and one is left to wonder if it was Captain Hall or one of his rangers who made the arrest. The bare bones report fails to reflect the atrocity that ended with Garcia's arrest for the killing of Augustin Amallo (or Anallo), a shepherd in Nueces County, as was Garcia. Often the phrase *cherchez la femme* is employed which is perhaps appropriate in this case, two men wanting the same woman. Amallo had cohabited with Manuela Ariano for several years, a union which produced two children, but he had separated from them when she and the children moved in with Garcia at a neighboring ranch. On one occasion he visited this ranch intending to visit his children; it was then that Garcia lured him away and crushed his head with an axe. It was a cold-blooded deliberate murder committed on September 7, 1878. Garcia was arrested in October and confined in the Nueces County jail. At his trial he was convicted and sentenced to death for the first-degree murder of Amallo. Garcia did not deny the crime; on the gallows he was "defiant to the last."[12]

Even with the clean-up of criminals by Hall's men that was praised in the newspapers, being situated close to the U.S.-Mexico border proved to be a continual problem in the days of the horseback ranger as it is today even with the numerous technologies that did not exist in the nineteenth century. "Frontier Protection" was the title of a lengthy letter written by "A.M.C." at Eagle Pass in early January 1879. The main concern of the writer was that Governor O. M. Roberts was "not well inclined towards frontier protection." If the governor was aware of what the conditions had been and what the conditions were now, then the "natural conclusions from the past and present surroundings of what the condition will be in a short time hence if the protection heretofore given is withdrawn" then if he does withdraw protection it will be "a shameful recusancy of a public duty." Continuing, A.M.C. stressed that two years before, reports of incidents growing out of the "disturbed, lawless condition of the frontier" were virtually a daily reality. Until Captain McNelly and then Captain Hall appeared in the area of Maverick County, the "better part of the community were wholly at the mercy of the desperado element." There were over one hundred "loose characters" who had drifted west from Goliad and DeWitt Counties as well as elsewhere who existed only by "plundering workingmen." But for the coming of McNelly and Hall, "no one proposing to live by honest labor, with the moral courage to assert his rights, and protest against wrong, could have lived until this time in this community. . . . The bad were united by a proneness to violence, while the good were so intimidated that each sought immunity for himself by condoning or apparently applauding the wrongful acts of the dominant element, thus in effect adding to its strength." Now A.M.C. was ready to explain clearly what the results were thanks to the arrival of Captain Hall: "But the 'Hoodoos,' as the gallant Hall and his rangers, came. They came several times, and placed themselves before the public by acts, entitling them to the gratitude of Texas." Hall's arrival provided a "feeling of security" which "now pervades the public mind." A.M.C. predicted that if Governor Roberts continued with keeping Hall and his rangers in the frontier counties "it will be true economy to give the saving to Capt. Hall for future services."[13] What is most interesting about this report from A.M.C. is his calling Hall and his men "Hoodoos," an unusual term, also spelled "Hoo Doo." The bloody feud in Mason County, Texas, of the 1870s was frequently referred to as the Hoo Doo War, which was in its simplest terms a conflict between German settlers and Anglo settlers, although it had personal feuds and other matters involved. Feud historian Dave Johnson explains that the origin of the term Hoo Doo "has been lost to history."[14] Historian C.L. Sonnichsen noted that the term referred to a vigilance committee, or simply a mob.[15] Further, it was applied to members of the Ku Klux Klan.

It is thus strange that A.M.C. would refer to the Hall ranger company as "Hoodoos" as they never donned a mask to obscure their identity. They may have instilled fear within a desperado, but always with their faces bared and guns drawn. The A.M.C. letter remains of great interest.

John Wesley Hardin, captured by Ranger Armstrong in Florida, had been tried, convicted of second degree murder, and sentenced to serve a term of twenty-five years in Huntsville penitentiary. He was received as prisoner # 7109 on October 5, 1878. He had received a better education than many of the other prisoners and fortunately the letters he wrote to friends and family members were preserved. We have no substantial record of Ranger Hall visiting the notorious man-killer, but his name does appear in the correspondence. On May 11, 1879, Hardin wrote a letter to Emanuel "Mannen" Clements, a first cousin, which contains the following intriguing statements:

> Mannin I have No nuse of interest to communicate [to] you at present onley this Leaves me well and in Hopes of Better Days [.] When you go to austin See Lieu[tenant] J B Armstrong & Capt Lee Hall [.] Tell them with proper management the Scrap Taylor case can be worked up to a certainty [.] you can imagine How I am informed [.] the party Says that if allowed He wil Show up also [.][16]

Rufus Pitkin "Scrap" Taylor was one of the cowboys who had been arrested following Hardin's killing of Deputy Sheriff Charles M. Webb in Comanche in 1874. Taylor was lynched with two other cowboys near Clinton; apparently Hardin believed that even from his prison cell he could influence others to bring charges against certain DeWitt County citizens for the lynching. As yet we have no record of Clements meeting with Armstrong and Hall.

But the claim was made that Hall did visit Hardin in prison. N.A. Jennings, who was a ranger under Hall and wrote of his adventures in Texas, claimed that the only time Hall ever ran from a man was when he went after Hardin. Jennings claimed that Hall wanted the $4000 reward offered for Hardin and "determined to get it." He and a posse found Hardin and some five or six men with him at the edge of a lake. Hall ordered his men to "run right in on them" and have the outlaws captured "before they know it." The charge was made but the posse faltered, leaving Hall galloping in alone. Hardin and his men shot at him and laughed to see him run. Hall then spent the day searching for his cowardly posse and, finding them, gave them a chewing out which the posse "submitted to with becoming meekness."[17] There does not seem to be even a tinge of truth in Jennings's claim that this incident happened.

Frequently newspapers welcomed well-written letters from travelers describing their journey west. One such letter came from a native of Raleigh, North Carolina, sent to his home paper. Editor J.W. Goslen of the *Union Republican* of Winston chose to reprint it in his issue of June 12,

1879. In addition to witnessing a "fearful shooting scrape" in Marshall, the correspondent told how he had registered at a San Antonio hotel giving his Raleigh address and in "less than half an hour" a gentleman came up to him and introduced himself as Lee Hall from Greensboro, North Carolina, and the son of Dr. Hall of that place. Obviously Hall impressed the traveler, as he wrote: "He is the leader of the Texas Rangers, and has been for four years. He has the biggest reputation in Western Texas, and the mention of his name on the frontier is a guarantee of protection to the outer colonies." He continued by telling how Hall introduced him "to all the United States Army officers," who provided him with the flattering information. He concluded by stating that he had "never met a cleverer gentleman in my life, and he made my stay exceedingly pleasant."[18]

Watson and Armstrong were not the only ones who had to endure the pain and suffering of dealing with an accidental self-inflicted pistol wound. The notorious desperado John King Fisher who had faced McNelly as well as Hall experienced being shot as well. As he was well-known the newspapers had fun with it. Fisher, described as "the desperado of former years" but "now a quiet, placable, industrious rancher" felt "the devil getting the better of him a few days ago and rather than have any trouble or shoot anybody else he shot himself through the thigh and is now lying up to cool off." The jocularity did not end there as the reporter concluded Fisher "may be a priest yet."[19]

George Durham, when writing of his service with McNelly and Hall, recalled the physical appearance of King Fisher, especially the first time he stood face to face with the man. He noted Fisher "was the most commanding picture I had ever seen. He stood around six foot, and weighed, I judge, about 180 pounds. He had black, wavy hair; and while he was just now turning twenty-one years of age, he was growing one of them mustaches that he trained down his cheek." Fisher's wearing apparel also impressed young Durham. "He wore a *tres piedras sombrero* with a solid gold, coiled rattler, for a band; and gold tassels. His shirt was of that heavy, Mexico City silk, opened at the throat; and a silk, red bandana was knotted on his neck."[20] Durham may have been impressed with Fisher's outward appearance but Lee Hall was not. In August 1879 he issued an order that forbad the wearing of sombreros, fancy top-boots, and carrying of white-handled revolvers in his command. Those things were forbidden because they were "characteristic of the desperado, and he wishes his boys to look like civilized people."[21]

During court, judges and other court officers were generally pleased with the presence of a few rangers in the courtroom. During district court in September, Sergeant J.W. Warren and Privates John McNelly, Sam Graham, and J.A. Gibbons were in town and would remain until court was adjourned. Captain Hall was expected in a few days, according to the *Victoria Advocate.*[22]

Although *Victoria Advocate* editor Linn had his occasional differences with Hall as a commander he at times offered him praise. On Tuesday, September 23, Linn reported:

> That gallant ranger, Capt. Lee Hall, put his smiling countenance and red head into our sanctum on last Tuesday. Lee is one of the best fellows in the world as a private citizen, and one of the bravest, most energetic and intelligent officers at present in the State service. His consistence to duty, his skill and unquestioned personal courage has, within the past three years, restored to Western Texas peace and good order within her borders, where before existed in bold defiance of law, the greatest outrages and crime. Capt. Hall is on his way to San Diego, which place he will make his headquarters for a short time. Success to you, Captain.[23]

In the same issue of the *Advocate* an exciting bit of news from Cuero reported that Jim Thomas was arrested by Hall's men and jailed. This arrest took place on September 18, 1879. The Monthly Return only noted he was arrested for theft of a horse.[24] Lesser known desperadoes received attention during this time as well. John Evitts, charged with horse stealing, was arrested by Captain Hall in Goliad County. Deputy Sheriff Chriswell delivered him to the county jail in Cuero.

John Sharp, charged with the murder of Alfred Cone during the earlier troubles of the Sutton-Taylor Feud, was captured and delivered to Helena in Karnes County. This was an important arrest because of its connection to the feud. Sharp and Cone had apparently argued over a gambling debt and Cone shot and severely wounded Sharp. Cone, hoping to evade retribution from Sharp, moved to a ranch twenty-five miles south of Helena belonging to T.M. Dennis. His plan did not work, however, as four men, including Sharp, located him in his field and shot him dead. A posse managed to capture Sharp and placed him in the Helena jail. Later he was moved to the more secure Gonzales jail. On learning that "J.S. Sharp, the murderer of Alfred Cone" was taken from Helena to Gonzales his friends promised to rescue him. It didn't happen, although editor John Cardwell of the *Statesman* commented: "It makes decency shudder to read of such facts constantly recurring, and yet the legislature would not shock the sensibilities of mankind by appealing to the branding iron, stocks and whipping post to exterminate thieves, and to the gallows, in behalf of the security of life and property. Why not hang horse and cattle thieves and common highwaymen?"[25] Sharp was not branded nor whipped nor placed in stocks but was found guilty of the murder and sentenced to life imprisonment in Huntsville. He appealed the verdict but the appeal from district court resulted in the conviction standing. Hall's Monthly Return is informative: "Oct 1st 3 men left Cuero to convey prisoner Jno. Sharps to receive sentence for life in Karnes county."[26] Sharp, received at the prison on October 9, was entered into Huntsville's records as prisoner # 7936. He was twenty-seven years old, five feet and ten inches tall and weighed 147 pounds. He was described as having a dark complexion, hazel eyes, and black hair. He was not married, used tobacco, and was intemperate. He had received a "Fair" education and his occupation was listed as a laborer. The expiration of his sentence was noted as "Death" but Gov. John Ireland chose to pardon him on March 28, 1886.[27] What John S. Sharp did with his life after being pardoned is unknown.

King Fisher may have mended his ways but he still had to appear in court on various charges. In September, Corporal George H. Allen and two other rangers were to deliver him to trial in Laredo; somewhere on the trail he saw an opportunity to escape and took it. It was fortunate for him that the rangers did not shoot at him, which one might expect to happen. Lieutenant T.L. Oglesby had the responsibility to prepare the semi-monthly report this time and recorded what happened: "Corporal Allen left camp with two men for the purpose of committing to Jail at Laredo King Fisher. Fisher made his escape Eight miles from Laredo on the evening of the 3rd."[28] A later report, written years later, stated that Fisher escaped by stampeding the pack mules and in the confusion made his escape from the rangers. Fisher thought better of his action and surrendered to authorities. The *Galveston Daily News* chose to consider this an important event, headlining its special telegram report from Uvalde: "King Fisher Surrendered." The report pointed out that Fisher had escaped from the rangers but now had surrendered and would stand trial on "the other indictments."[29] King Fisher, charged with many crimes, was altering his ways as he realized his career as a desperado could only result in a tragic finale. As proof he composed a letter to the *Castroville Quill* in which he explained his action. The letter itself has not survived but numerous journals reported it. The *Gonzales Inquirer* was one:

> King Fisher, the noted west Texas outlaw, writes to the Quill his excuse for escaping from the rangers while being taken to Laredo. He says opinion runs so strongly against him in that place that if taken there the Mexicans would mob and kill him. Furthermore, on the same day he was to be in Laredo he was wanted in Uvalde to answer a more serious charge than that preferred in Laredo, and that he immediately went to Uvalde, where he is willing to be tried, as he does not fear the law, but only mobs.

The editor commented: "Well, we hope he will have a first class chance to test the claws of the law upon him."[30] It was a wise decision, but it would not be until 1881 when he became a free man. All indictments against him were dismissed; where he did stand trial he was acquitted. Afterward, "the once noted desperado" as the *Statesman* described him, was "living quietly on a farm on the Nueces, attending to his own business, and taking no more scalps."[31]

How could such a noted desperado as King Fisher manage to escape from the men of Hall's command? How could they have been so careless? The Monthly Return offers no explanation, merely reporting "Sept 2 to 6. Corpl Allen & 2 men escorting King Fisher to Laredo (escaped in route)."[32] A report printed in the *Castroville Quill* does not clarify the matter either, reporting that King Fisher, "while being taken to Laredo by three of Lieut. Oglesby's men, made his escape."[33] What he did then is uncertain, as he did not go immediately to the Uvalde authorities as he had written. He may have taken some time to thoroughly consider his options as apparently he surrendered only in mid-October. The Uvalde report, dated October 15, indicated he was there to stand trial.[34] Ranger George Durham, who was in a position to know, merely wrote that after Fisher had been arrested somewhere along the river on the road to Laredo he stampeded the pack mules and then spurred his mule into the brush and fled across the Rio Grande. "There was another big scare piece in the newspapers about this escape, but I was damn glad. Because King was a better man than Allen."[35] The "big scare piece" has not been found. It is uncertain if Durham was one of the rangers responsible for delivering Fisher to Laredo; if not then he was only reporting hearsay. It is difficult to see why Durham had such a low opinion of the corporal. George Henry Allen was born the second son to Clemens and Mary Allen on July 8, 1853, in Colorado County, Texas. He mustered into McNelly's Washington County Volunteer Militia Company A as a private on June 22, 1875, and was honorably discharged on February 31, 1877. He then mustered into Hall's Special State Troops on March 31, 1877, and served until November 31, 1879, having served from August 1 as a corporal.[36] Nothing in his record indicates the escape of King Fisher from his squad was an act of carelessness. Perhaps Durham's attitude toward Allen was simply a matter of personality differences. After Allen left the Ranger service he continued in the field of law enforcement, acting as city marshal of the city of Weimar, Colorado County, "for some time."[37]

King Fisher may have received much of the attention of the rangers but there were others who were considered as important to capture or kill. Thomas Dix Jr., charged with murder in Zapata County, was arrested by Corporal Allen that October month. At Burns Station, then a small community in DeWitt County, Sergeant Warren, with privates John McNelly, Sam Graham, and William T. Cavin, arrested P.H. "Bud" Dowlearn for assault with intent to murder in Travis County. He was wanted for other offenses, mainly in DeWitt County.[38] The *Cuero Bulletin*, the editor of which certainly should have known the Dowlearns, reported that Warren and his men "captured Bud Doolan [*sic*] last Sunday morning [October 11]. He is charged with several offenses against the laws of the land." Continued the *Bulletin* editor, "Doolan has evaded arrest for several years."[39] During the bloody days of the Taylor-Sutton Feud Patrick Hayes "Bud" Dowlearn was considered a member of the Taylor faction, and family tradition indicates he may have been involved in the ambush slaying of Cox and Christman in 1873.[40]

Captain Hall arrested a black man, not identified in the Monthly Return nor in the press, but one who was charged with assault with attempt to murder in Bastrop County. On October 12 Eli Collins was arrested as well, charged with fraudulently disposing of mortgaged property in Hill County. Private Sam Platt made the arrest in Goliad County. He was delivered to the sheriff in Travis County.[41] Collins was unwittingly fortunate in not being placed in the Goliad jail. The Goliad grand jury conducted an investigation into the conditions of the jail in October. Their report follows, in part:

> We find the jail in a filthy condition; also find that the prisoners are short of sufficient covering, and they have not been properly fed, and they all say that they have been furnished with but little bedding whatever by any official, and complain bitterly of not having enough to eat. We found ten men in one cell and three in the other. We had the jail physician, Dr. [Leonidas Star] Lipscomb, before us, and he says that it is injurious to the health of the prisoners for so many to be confined in one cell. . . . We also find

> one of the prisoners, Jose Ramos, in the last stage of consumption, and if permitted to remain much longer will hasten his death and be injurious to the health of the inmates.[42]

Dr. L.S. Lipscomb was a physician in his early fifties and perhaps recognized consumption frequently; he also may have treated gunshot wounds frequently as it hadn't been so long since Goliad County experienced true frontier conditions.[43]

About this same time don Rafael F. Salinas, a thirty-one-year-old sheepherder in Duval County, was returning from his camp just after dark when he was fired upon and killed.[44] Investigation revealed that the body of Salinas was "found [and] that he was killed by a party of five men; had four bullets through his body." The murderers traveled some fifty yards from the body and then scattered, each one going his separate way. Apparently those investigating determined the number of murderers from the amount of horse prints left.[45] No further details have been discovered about this crime but on October 18, Florentina Garza and Marguerita Garza were arrested near Concepcion in Duval County by Private C.W. Johnson and two others.[46] Curiously the Monthly Return does not give a clue as to what was done with the two prisoners, as would normally be added to the return.

But all the action did not take place along the Texas-Mexican border. To the immediate south of San Antonio was the community surrounding Campbell's store in Atascosa County. Ireland-born John Campbell had arrived in Texas in the 1840s, survived various fights with Indians and the Civil War and then established a mercantile store as well as raising stock. His store was located mid-way between Pleasanton, the county seat, and Oakville in Live Oak County; in time it became the relay station for the U.S. mail from San Antonio to Oakville and points south. In 1879 the store served as a post office with John Campbell as postmaster. By that year Campbell had a wife and four children and his store became the object of a gang of thieves.[47]

Campbell's store is over two hundred miles due north from Santa Maria in Cameron County. Hall learned of the attempted robbery from one of his undercover men, never identified, although probably William T. Cavin. That explains how Hall managed to be there when the thieves struck. Hall and his men arrived November 4. The clerk on duty, a man named Kemper, informed Hall that there were five suspicious-looking characters around and he anticipated a robbery that night. Kemper was not acting alone but already had a man named David Young there who would help fight off the bandits. Hall and his men and the several other citizens who were ready to combat the quintet of robbers when they galloped up, waited in silence. Kemper was then working at a desk while the others hid themselves around the store. The robbers may have been surprised to find Kemper working at his desk but this did not prevent them from continuing with their plans to plunder the store. They bound Kemper, who offered no resistance. At this point Hall rose up and demanded the surrender of the thieves; the surprised thieves answered with a shot. Quickly the store was filled with gunsmoke as Hall and his rangers and the other citizens fired back. Citizen Charles Westerman was wounded; Luis, identified by the press as "a Mexican thief" was killed, and another, John Smith, alias Alexander, was wounded while another identified as Archie Huir was also wounded. The other two "thieves," actually rangers who were working with Hall, had stayed with the horses and when the gunfire erupted they disappeared into the brush.

The Monthly Return of Captain Hall is informative.

> Capt Hall received information at Santa Maria that an attempt would be made to rob Campbells store [in] Atascosa County[.] left that place for said store with 2 men and instructions for 2 men to join them from Oakville but they did not arrive in time. The robbers came and in attempting to Make their arrest and they refusing to surrender two of them were Killed Jno Smith Louis Varejal and also Hare only wounded and lodged in Pleasanton Jail. Capt Hall and 2 men to appear before Grand Jury and returned to San Diego via Oakville.[48]

Private Sam Graham, who served under several noted ranger officers, including Hall from August 1, 1879, to February 29, 1880, was at the Campbell's store fight and in the 1930s wrote of his experiences while serving with the Texas Rangers. Obviously impressed with being a part of the action Graham recalled what had happened in this manner:

> [W]hen we arrived The Proprietor had been notified by the Capt[.] The Capt came about 15 minutes after we arrived. It was all timed to arrive after night & by different routes, one outfit was lost & did not arrive until after the whole thing was over. We were secreted in the store. Martin[49] & I in [a] side room with a door opening in about the center of the store. The robbers came about 8 Oclock, took the drop on the Clerk, took him out side & started to loot the store. We stepped to the side door and ordered them to surrender (Thinking they would, they generally did) but the answer was a shot. They dropped behind the counter. Our shots brought them out of there. Then it was a running fight, they running for the door. One a Mexican [Luis Varejal], fell dead on the door [floor?] with his pistol full cocked in his hand. He had fired all the loads out of it. One of the others fell about 50 yards in front of the store. He died about 3 days later [Smith alias Alexander]. another was wounded so badly he could only get about 75 yards. He lived to go to the penitentiary. The man that took the Clerk out got away on his horse. none of us were injured.[50]

The news of this gun battle received considerable press coverage. The report from San Antonio was telegraphed November 7 and appeared in the Galveston newspaper the next day, headlined "Thieves Taken in the Act" and sub-headlined "Battle Royal Between Robbers and Rangers." Of the thieves, Luis died on the floor; Smith alias Alexander and Archie Huir were wounded. Of the two, Smith was most seriously wounded and a later report stated he "passed in his checks" in the early morning of November 22, thus ending his many days of suffering.[51]

Occasionally a wanted man would elude the best efforts of the rangers. Such a man was Thomas Caffall, a stockman of the Gonzales and Karnes Counties area, wanted for theft in Burnet County. Sergeant Warren and one other ranger hunted for him December 3 and 4 but failed to find him; then again Private John McNelly and one other man scouted for him on December 12-15, 1879. On January 8 and 9 Private Graham and one man again were scouting for him but to no avail. Stockman Caffall was a family man and one wonders if the rangers had a Jack Duncan working the case they would have been more successful. Curiously the Monthly Return fails to show he was ever arrested and perhaps the state ultimately decided not to prosecute.[52]

Lieutenant John McNelly, nephew of famed L.H. McNelly, was now serving in Hall's command. He had a prisoner in charge— William Clark — arrested in Live Oak County charged with a Travis County murder a number of years before. The Monthly Return indicates only that Oglesby's detachment made the arrest but there is no indication as to how it was accomplished. John McNelly delivered him safely to the Travis County jail in Austin.[53]

Lee Hall began the year 1880 as a captain of the Texas Rangers but that would soon change. His work naturally caused him to be on the Texas coast occasionally, an area attracting thousands due to the promise of many pleasures for tourists as well as for desperadoes. The only community of any size in the area was Corpus Christi, seat of Nueces County. The details have been lost but on one of those occasions Captain Hall was at the home of Richard Emanuel Halter, a forty-three-year-old officer of the Coast Survey Team. He and his wife, the former Sarah Weidman, a decade younger than her husband, were both from the east: she from Pennsylvania and he from Washington, D.C. On this occasion the younger sister of Mrs. Halter was there visiting, and that is where Captain Hall was introduced to Elizabeth Cook "Bessie" Weidman. She was the daughter of General John and Emma R. (Grant) Weidman of Lebanon, Pennsylvania. Bessie C., the sixth and last child of General Weidman, had older siblings: Grant, Martha, Sarah, Emma, and Mary. Bessie was born October 4, 1857. Mr. Weidman abandoned his career as district attorney "when the rebellion broke out [and] he raised a

Company of Cavalry for three years' service, which was accepted by the Government, and assigned to the Army of the Potomac. He served gallantly in the Union's Peninsular Campaign of 1862 and other battles but after more than a year's service contracted a disease which obliged him to resign his commission" and return to his home to recuperate. But no amount of tender care at home was sufficient as he succumbed to the disease on April 23, 1863.[54] Thus Bessie C. Weidman, now fatherless, grew up without her father's love and guidance.

Older sister Sarah Ann Weidman of Lebanon and Capt. Richard E. Halter of Washington, D.C. met and in about 1870 were married. He was a member of the Coast Survey Committee, a federal agency created in 1807 to provide nautical charts of the new country's coastlines; soon other concerns were added, namely the "national boundaries, commerce, and defense." By 1878 the agency was officially named the Coast and Geodetic Survey.[55] When Halter entered this profession is unknown but eventually he rose to the rank of captain and was highly regarded in his calling. His profession required him to spend lengthy periods of time away from his Washington home. As early as September 1876 a Lebanon news item reported that Halter and his wife would be leaving for Texas that month "and will take with them Miss Bessie Weidman, sister of Mrs. Halter."[56] This "visit" may have lasted more or less four years, as a later Pennsylvania news item reported that Captain Halter and family had "recently returned from a four years' residence in Padre Island, Gulf of Mexico" and "were "sojourning" in Lebanon during the summer.

The question must be asked: was Bessie with her sister and brother-in-law and their children all of those four years, or did she occasionally return home to spend time with her widowed mother? Articles in the Pennsylvania papers suggest she frequently was away from Padre Island. In October 1877, for instance, she attended a "soiree musicale" at the residence of Col. Joseph L. Stichter in Reading, Pennsylvania. The guests of this parlor concert, actually a benefit for the local Ladies Aid Society, gathered in the "sumptuous parlor" of host Stichter. Bessie was listed as among "the *elite* of the city"; others were among the "distinguished guests from neighboring towns."[57] During July of 1878 the Reading newspaper noted that she, along with Cyrus G. Derr and his wife, were leaving for Cape May, New Jersey, and would stop at the "Stockton," among the most elegant hotels of the area.[58] In December 1879 the Reading paper reported that Mrs. Emma R. Weidman, the mother of Mrs. Henry W. Zimmerman (nee Emma Weidman) and of Mrs. Cyrus G. Dee (nee Mary Virginia Weidman) would go to Texas to spend the winter and spring with their other daughter Mrs. Richard E. Halter. Mrs. Weidman would be accompanied by "her youngest daughter, Miss Bessie."[59]

Whether it was at a Christmas gala that December of 1879 or some other social event we don't know, but on December 22, Hall left camp at San Diego to go to Corpus Christi and Lagarto "to look after parties implicated in Cattle stealing."[60] Hall then returned on December 26 having traveled a distance of 200 miles according to the Monthly Return.[61] Possibly it was during this time that he met Captain Halter who invited the ranger captain to his Corpus Christi home. It would soon be apparent that this gentle invitation would go beyond friendship and the life of Jesse L. Hall and Bessie C. Weidman began then or very soon after; probably it was love at first sight. During one meeting Captain Hall literally fell into the enticing snares of Miss Weidman; once the question of marriage was raised she made it clear that if he wanted to marry her he would have to resign from the rangers. She did not want to daily worry if her husband was going to return after a scout or if he would fall from a desperado's bullet and leave her a young widow. Possibly the same thoughts grew in Hall's mind; what if a desperado's bullet found him as its mark and he was left to die on some lonely prairie or in a thicket of mesquite growth? Lee Hall would retire from the ranger service in exchange for Bessie's hand in marriage. She was no doubt a brave woman but she was not like the wife of fellow ranger Captain Dan W. Roberts, who spent time with her husband in camp, and later wrote a wonderful record of her life with Texas Rangers.[62] In time Bessie would understand that the man she would marry was a man who needed action, whether there was danger or not.

Occasionally individuals sought Hall's camp to be in a sort of "safe house," knowing that whoever the man feared would not attack the camp. Such a situation probably resulted in concern for her future husband's safety. She certainly learned of the affray in Atascosa County and the incident with Sheriff Timon would have only increased her concerns. In mid-January Sheriff Hughbert "Hugh" Timon, an Irish-born ex-Confederate who had been a resident of the county for thirty-two years, attempted to arrest a man named Andrew Hart. In addition to the warrant Timon brought along a Winchester and a pistol, and was reportedly under the influence. The details are sketchy and controversial, but Timon approached the house where Hart and his wife were, intending to serve the warrant. Perhaps Timon called on Hart to surrender and then fired a shot from his Winchester through Hart's door, and then Hart returned fire from his pistol, shooting Timon. Or perhaps Hart shot first in answer to Timon's demand to surrender. Mrs. Hart's version agreed with her husband's, that Timon shot first. Whatever the truth, Timon was seriously wounded. Dr. E.A. Spohn of Corpus Christi did what he could but Sheriff Timon died February 2, 1880. Census taker U.R. Wallace, who also prepared the county mortality schedule, noted that Timon was a white male, thirty-nine years of age, married, was from Ireland and was a stock raiser. His death resulted from the effects of a pistol shot.[63] Public opinion was that Timon was in the wrong. Commented the *Galveston Daily News*: "There is no more important law on the statute books than that providing for the punishment of public officers for drunkenness. Dismissal from office for a single violation of the law would not be too much."[64] The sheriff left a wife, Kate, thirty-four years old, and three children: Patrick, six; Margaret, four; and Hughbert, two years old.[65] What eventually happened to Andrew Hart is uncertain. A report from San Antonio later placed Hart in company of Hall's rangers "presumably for protection."[66] Bessie C. Weidman was by now thinking of becoming the wife of Texas Ranger Hall, but did not this incident of Timon's death cause her to realize that her husband as a ranger could be shot to death at any time? Whether alcohol would be involved or not Bessie C. must have experienced concerns for being the wife of a lawman.

Hall prepared his Monthly Return on January 31 at San Diego, Duval County, some fifty miles west of Corpus Christi. It showed an aggregate of twenty-seven men: one captain, one lieutenant, two sergeants, two corporals, and twenty-one privates. This return may serve as an example of the more detailed reports, so different from the earlier years of Hall's captaincy when a few sentences seemed sufficient to advise his superiors what he was accomplishing. On January 1 Captain Hall sent one man from San Diego to Corpus Christi to get certificates of brands and marks of stolen cattle belonging to parties in Hidalgo and Cameron Counties. The next day he sent two men to Carrizo Springs to attach witnesses for Frio County court and assist the sheriff of Frio County, J.C.B. Harkness. The unidentified rangers returned on the sixteenth, having logged in a total of 225 miles. On January 2 Sergeant Rudd and one man left on a scout to Las Animas "for instructions." No details as to instructions on what or from whom. On January 3 Hall sent Corporal Samuel Malcolm Platt and one man to Cuero to look into parties depredating near there. On the sixth, Private James A. Gibbons went from Cuero to Clinton to arrest Robert Davis, who was charged with disturbing the peace, and placed him in the Cuero jail. On January 7 Hall left San Diego to go to Cuero via San Antonio, arriving there on January12. On January 8, back at San Diego, Corporal McMurry and one man left camp to go to San Patricio "to look after and locate parties engaged in stealing Cattle, returned on 12th." On January 8 Sergeant Rudd arrested Marcus de Luna, charged with two indictments in Hidalgo for assault with intent to murder. De Luna was placed in the Edinburg jail. Also on January 8 Sam Graham left Cuero with one man to scout in Karnes County after Thomas Caffall, charged with theft of cattle in Burnet County. As noted above, he was never captured. Then on January 9 Sergeant Rudd left Santa Maria for Brownsville to attend the examining trial of the McCampbell brothers. These were Joseph, Chance, and Ed McCampbell who in late December had been arrested by Lieutenant Oglesby and his detachment for "wholesale horse stealing."[67] On January 9 Sergeant Platt and a detachment left Cuero to arrest Bill Taylor, "Top" Chisholm, Charles Middleton, and Frank Blair, "charged with Rape of a negro Girl in Clinton." They were arrested and placed in the Cuero jail. On January 14 Hall sent two men from San Diego to attach witnesses for County Court at Oakville; the pair returned the next day. Also on the fourteenth Lieutenant Oglesby returned from Brownsville. On the fifteenth Hall sent two men, Horace Mabin and W.D. Martin, from San Diego to arrest Anastaisa Lasose, charged with murder in Hidalgo County. They arrested him and placed him in jail in San Diego. On the fifteenth Sergeant Rudd sent two men from Santa Maria to scout in Hidalgo County. On January 17, Sergeant McMurry and six men from San Diego went to Oakville to attend court. On the twenty-second two men from Santa Maria went to Rancho Catillo to investigate horse stealing, but this turned out to be a false report. Back on December 28, 1879, Sergeant J.W. Warren with one other man had left Cuero to scout in Lavaca, Fayette, Colorado, Wharton, Fort Bend, Jackson and Victoria Counties, searching for fugitives and stolen cattle. They recovered 250 head of cattle in Fort Bend County belonging to stockmen of Gonzales, Lavaca, Victoria, and DeWitt Counties. The two men returned to camp on January 12, being out fifteen days on what turned out to be a profitable scout.

Some scouts were not profitable, as a hunt for Short Day on Irish Creek turned out to be a waste of time and energy; he was hiding elsewhere.[68] Captain Hall sent two men from Cuero to scout in Frio County after fugitives. They arrested Davis Grumbles on the Siestedero Creek on the twenty-fourth and confined him in San Antonio's Bexar County jail.[69] He was tried on a habeas corpus hearing on February 24 and released after providing bond of $3000.[70] On New Year's Day William Treadwell joined by enlistment; on the eighteenth he arrested William Dunman in Goliad County, who was charged with carrying a pistol and disturbing the peace. He also arrested Dave Dunman, charged with intent to murder and placed him in the jail at Goliad. More serious charges were brought against the Dunmans: William was charged with a murder in Kimble

County and taken there in irons; Dave was charged with horse stealing in Williamson County.[71] On the eighteenth Treadwell arrested Harry Burris in Goliad County, charged with theft of horses. He delivered him to the Justice of the Peace of Precinct No.2 in Goliad. It was a good beginning for this ranger recruit.

Sergeant Warren was successful as well. On March 14 he arrived in Cuero with William Hunt, *alias* George Williams, whom he had arrested in Refugio County as an escaped convict. Hunt had been sentenced several years before in Victoria County but escaped. Hall's men had tried to locate him before but this time Warren was successful. Commented the *Advocate*: "Serg't. Warren deserves the highest praise for the capture of this criminal."[72]

It would be a good year for Captain Hall as well. Although his thoughts may have turned to young Bessie C. Weidman in Corpus Christi, his main concern continued to be the eradication of Texas criminals and the reduction of lawlessness and crime. During the early days of February he made no arrests but scouted in La Salle, Duval, McMullen, and Atascosa Counties. Corporal S.M. Platt experienced a firefight but no ranger was wounded or killed. Hall recorded the incident laconically in his Monthly Return: "Copl Platt left San Diego for Ft Ewell, Searched in Lasalle & McMullen Co. Killed Mauel Martinez while resisting arrest." He added to the bottom of the return in case it had been missed: "Manuil Martinez was killed by Copl Platts detachment. Resisting arrest."

Actually others did not regard this killing as just another happening in LaSalle County. Hall did not provide a date of the killing but the *Statesman* shared with its readers that it had occurred on February 25 and pointed out that Martinez, the slain man, "was a citizen of San Antonio." A *Statesman* reporter managed to obtain an interview with Captain Hall, who stated that "the rangers had a writ for a man whose name was Martinez, and under the guidance of a person who was acquainted with him, were on their way to attempt his arrest. On coming in sight of the man who was killed he was pointed out by the guide as the one for whom they were looking. The rangers promptly ordered him to halt, but instead of doing so he drew his arms and fired upon them and wheeled his horse to escape. The rangers immediately fired, and as usual, their shot proved fatal. No one regrets the occurrence more than the rangers, and the sad mistake is deplored by all."[73] Additional reporting of this incident appeared in the *Galveston Daily News*, reprinted in the San Antonio paper and subsequently in the *Tri-Weekly Herald* of Marshall, the *Weekly Banner* of Brenham, and the *Dallas Daily Herald*. The San Antonio and Galveston report attempted to explain that the dead man was Manuel Martinez, a well-known and respected citizen of Atascosa County and not the man of the same name of Wilson County. The dead man left a wife and four children.

On Saturday, March 6, Captain Hall was in Austin, and he was able to explain the rangers' action to a reporter, justifying Platt and his detachment. According to Hall, Martinez had "acknowledged being a horse thief to a member of his company who was acting detective, and had agreed to deliver to him a certain number of horses, to be stolen from Hon. Santos Benavides, at five dollars per head, but hearing that the rangers were in the vicinity, he went to the detective and postponed the delivery. Then the rangers determined to arrest him without waiting, and to that end the detective sought him and decoyed him into a trap. When he saw the rangers, he opened fire on them, and they, after being fired on more than once, returned the salutation and killed him."[74]

As far as the rangers and adjutant general's office in Austin were concerned, the matter ended with Hall's explanation. The editor of the *Star-Vindicator* in Blanco, Blanco County, intended to offer the last word on the matter; he admitted that tragic mistakes do happen, but did not touch on the question of how to prevent the criminals from shooting at rangers.

> Mistakes of this kind too frequently occur, which shows that the officers of the law are not sufficiently cautious in this respect; and so as to put a check upon this carelessness, and make men more

> particular in those cases, we think it but right that they should be made to suffer for every such accident. The penalty for taking the life of an innocent man, even through a mistake, should be a severe one, and then, if rigidly enforced a few times, we feel certain such terrible accidents would not so often happen.[75]

Captain Hall had been away from camp since March 3; after concluding his business in San Antonio and Austin— perhaps a conference with Steele's replacement Adj. Gen. Major John B. Jones[76]— he went east to Columbus in Colorado County, then to Cuero in DeWitt County, and then to San Diego, having travelled a total of 420 miles. During his absence Lieutenant Oglesby was in charge and much was accomplished, including assisting at district court sessions, delivering stolen stock to their owners, returning escaped convicts to Huntsville penitentiary, arresting U.S. Army deserters, and scouting after fugitives and recovering stolen stock. Corporal Platt was most active, as on March 27 he recovered thirty-two head of horses and was able to get them returned to their rightful owners. Then on the twenty-ninth Corporal McKinney "in attempting to arrest Marcus Labato shot & killed him." Labato had been charged with assault to murder. Again the Monthly Return provides little information, but the press eagerly presented many details which would perhaps satisfy the editor of Blanco County's *Star-Vindicator.* According to the *San Antonio Express* a detachment of Hall's command rode up to the Crary & Case sheep ranch near Fort Ewell and demanded the surrender of "a Mexican desperado who had been shooting men and stealing in a general way of late." After the arrest the man's friends "attacked" the rangers who attempted to get their prisoner away from them. A gunfight followed in which about thirty shots were fired, "resulting in the killing of two of the Mexicans, the wounding of another, and the fatal wounding of Peter Johnson" the rangers' guide. Peter and his brother Pierce had arrived from Philadelphia some three years before and "embarked in the sheep business."[77] Captain Hall had Corporal McKinney write out what had happened to send to Adjutant General Jones with the March Monthly

Return. This is what McKinney wrote out for Hall to review prior to sending it to Austin.

> Capt J L Hall
>
> Sir,
>
> While in camp on the 29 Pierce Johnson wrote me a note to come up an[d] arrest a Mexican that had shot a Mexican and Stoled [*sic*] a horse. I went up not taking any one with me as I had two others prisoners in camp to guard. In making the arrest, the Mexicans friend come out and made fight. Peter Johnson went with me to Show me the Mexican and do the interpreting. Petter [*sic*] Johnson was seriously Shot. I killed the Mexican that Shot him. I was also Shot through the lapel of my coat. A book in my pocket turned the ball[.] horse Stealing is going on all the time. A Mexican train was robed [*sic*] of four horses last night in four miles of this place [.]

This was McKinney's straightforward explanation of why Marcus Labato was shot to death.

Adjutant General Jones received official information on the affair on the seventh and shared it with a *Statesman* reporter, or perhaps submitted to an interview. The *Statesman* story provides a few details that McKinney left out in his report, although it does not contradict anything McKinney had written. According to Jones, after Labato was found and ordered to surrender, "three other men standing nearby cheerfully ordered McKinney to leave, which of course was contrary to the religious principles of the rangers, and was not to be complied with, whereupon one of them, Gonzales by name, fired from the door of a hacienda, shooting down Mr. Johnson, killing him almost instantly." In the ensuing gunfire McKinney shot and killed Labato and severely wounded Gonzales. McKinney's life was saved by a large memorandum book in his breast pocket filled with capiases and letters. One ball went entirely thorough the papers and glanced off the back cover of the book.[78]

Chapter Seven

Hall and Buckley "by whipping their horses up the bank, barely did save themselves from destruction"

—*Austin Weekly Statesman*, August 26, 1880

Hall may have been somewhat at a loss once he had made the decision to resign from the Texas Rangers. He seems to have had no definite plans for his immediate future. The decision proved to be, as historian Claude Elliott pointed out years later, "the turning point in his life." The life of a Texas Ranger was "the only life for which he was fitted."[1] Somehow word reached Austin that he had been "circulating about Cuero" as was printed in the popular "Texas— Facts and Fancies" column in the *Daily Democratic Statesman.*[2] One wishes the reporter had been more specific, but Hall certainly had friends in Cuero and his "circulating" may have been nothing more than renewing friendships with old companions from earlier days.

Hall paid a visit to the *Victoria Advocate* newspaper in March 1880. He was now described as the "esteemed friend and excellent State officer" paying "the pleasure of a call." Hall informed editor Linn that he was expecting soon to visit the home of his parents in North Carolina, "from which he has been absent for a number of years."[3] Apparently Hall had not kept it secret that he would be resigning; the rumor spread that he was no longer with the Special State Troops, or else that change was imminent. The *Advocate*, citing a report from the *Rockport Transcript*, noted that he had "withdrawn" and had then entered into a contract with a party of northern capitalists to proceed to Mexico and take charge of a large tract of land bought by them in the Sierra Mojada country for the purpose of raising stock.[4] According to the *Transcript*, he intended to gather ten men to accompany him, preferably former members of his ranger command, men whom he could depend on in any dangerous situation. Hall intended the expedition to start about the middle of April 1880. The *Transcript* editor noted that "Hall has been so relentless and arduous in the pursuit of miscreants, many of whom hail from our sister Republic, that in our opinions when the fact of his new move becomes fully known, he will be sadly exposed to danger, and yet fear is a feeling foreign to the nature of Lee Hall, and he is no doubt eminently capable of caring for No. 1. . . . Adios Hall! And may the name that has in the past been your firmest ally, prove your most efficient protector in the future."[5] The plans to visit home may have had to be altered as the *Advocate* reported he had arrived in Victoria the previous Saturday, May 15, and would visit his North Carolina home and then would "accompany capitalists to Mexico who design developing some of the mineral wealth of that republic."[6] No additional mention has been located about this intended visit home to North Carolina, and no additional information has been learned about this venture into the Sierra Mojada country.[7] If this venture developed, it received little publicity. We suspect that it may have been an intended venture but for some unknown reason did not materialize. The *Statesman* noted he was in Austin on May 26, with no comment on what his immediate plans were.[8]

Occasionally the arrest of a fugitive was only the beginning of a series of legal maneuvers that ultimately left only frustration for lawmen. The case of James W. Beardall is one example that touched the life of Hall over the course of many years. Beardall and a companion named James P. Draper were accused of murdering one Louis Vare near Fort Lancaster in Crockett County on February 4, 1858. Beardall told another man named Reagan of the circumstances of the killing, and based on that, Beardall and Draper were arrested and lodged in the Bexar County jail. They were tried in San Antonio in September 1859 and found guilty of murder in the first degree, but before sentence could be passed they both escaped. In July of 1877— eighteen years later— Hall arrested Beardall in Piedras Negras, Mexico, and returned him to Texas. Now he denied his identity and claimed to be James Denman/Dennan. The identity trial proved he was Beardall but on appeal the case was remanded on the grounds that there was no copy of the indictment, as the original had been lost. If Lee Hall was following this in the various newspapers he had available to him, then he must have realized the man would never mount the gallows, as had been the original sentence of the court. By December 1880 James W. Beardall was gone from the hands of the law, being released on a $2000 bond and presumably gone again to Mexico to ultimately live out his life as a free man.[9]

After his ranging days, Hall planned to enter into the stock business, not driving Texas longhorns to northern markets as might be expected, but raising sheep. In early August of 1880, a couple months after he stepped down from the rangers, he and Ed Buckley, a well-known wool buyer of Corpus Christi, with a group of fifteen men, probably including his brother Frank, and wagons, set out for Crockett County in far West Texas intending to locate grazing land for large flocks of sheep. Edward Buckley was an Irishman who had married a South Carolinian lady, Emily, and now had four children at home. They resided in Corpus Christi on Water Street.[10] In addition Hall and Buckley intended to sink artesian wells hoping to locate watering sites in what was considered a "vast territory."[11] It was a "vast territory" in the 1880s and remains such even today, although using the term "vastness" would arguably be an overstatement. When Hall and his group entered what is now Crockett County— not organized until 1891— there were only a few small, scattered settlements, none of any significance. Today there is only the county seat, Ozona; the earlier small settlements had not developed and gradually disappeared. Some two hundred miles west of San Antonio the men explored the barren landscape. It was good land for raising sheep and today Crockett County remains one of the leading producers of wool and mohair.

The Hall brothers and Ed Buckley may have had dreams of raising large flocks of sheep and goats on this barren land but they never materialized. Hall's various dreams in fact would never materialize from this point on in his life.

Hall, the former lawman, must have pondered the point that with virtually no population in the area there would be little danger from desperadoes. Nature, however, could be a problem as although they were in an arid land there were at times heavy rains that occasionally caused flooding. On day Lee Hall and Ed Buckley were in the bed of a stream watering their horses "when they saw the flood coming down upon them, and, by whipping their horses up the bank, barely did save themselves from destruction."[12] The flood waters proved to be perilous and dramatic, as Sycamore Creek "rose over forty feet in a few seconds." This was excitement and adventure indeed; Hall and Buckley, greatly relieved, had had a narrow escape and one of them related their experience to a reporter from the *Kinney News*, the newspaper published in Brackettville, the Kinney County seat. Perhaps not so strangely this issue of the *Kinney News* reached Bessie C. Weidman's home state of Pennsylvania, which found the item of great interest.

> During the late storm Mr. Ed. Buckley and Captain Lee Hall reached Sycamore creek, west of Brackett, and stopped in its bed to water their horses. While the animals were drinking a roaring was heard up the creek, and they saw a great volume of water

> rushing towards them, crushing down trees and everything in front of it. They barely escaped to the hill and looking back, saw one of the most wonderful sights that the average man in a lifetime might expect to see. The creek was full of water, a great river, and where they had watered their horses a moment before was now a rushing current fully forty feet deep.[13]

Sycamore Creek, this "great river," eventually empties into the Rio Grande.

But until his marriage, which would not occur until November 25, 1880, he would continue as a Texas Ranger, captaining his Special State Troops. Hall didn't spend all his time hunting desperadoes. Occasionally he just visited friends and on one occasion his visit reached the columns of the newspaper. On January 13, 1880, he was in Victoria, Victoria County, to visit Edward D. Linn, the editor and business manager of the *Victoria Advocate*. In the Saturday issue readers learned "That worthy officer and esteemed friend, Capt. Lee Hall, stopped in to see us on Thursday, fresh from the West. Capt. Hall is known as one of the best officers of the State, and he makes it a point never to let a criminal escape him. Capt. Hall met a large number of friends here, and returned to Cuero by the evening's train."[14] It had not been so long since Linn had publicly doubted the value of Captain Hall in that section of the state. Strangely, Linn now writes that Hall is worthy of high praise. Perhaps Linn finally realized that Hall was making it safe for citizens of Victoria as well as further west in the frontier conditions of the state. Linn had a remarkable life and is typically unknown today; during his career Hall and Linn apparently developed a lasting friendship. An early interest in journalism developed firmly and after the Civil War Linn became editor of the *Victoria Advocate* and by 1898 was the sole proprietor. He was also interested in politics and among other responsibilities was state senator to the Twenty-fifth Legislature in 1897. He had married "Gussie" West in 1889 and they had four daughters. He was unable to continue his political career due to failing health; he died in Goliad County in 1899.[15] Hall obviously impressed Linn as he was not reluctant to praise Hall whenever he visited the offices of the *Advocate*.

Ironically, in the same issue of the *Advocate*, January 13, appeared a lengthy article about a former fugitive from justice: Bill Taylor of Sutton-Taylor Feud notoriety. Editor Linn editorialized that "Bill Taylor, a character of some local celebrity in this section, was set at liberty and freed of the charge of murder in the well known Sutton-Slaughter case, it was prayed for by his friends, and wished for by the people at large, that he would go to his home to become a better and more useful citizen . . ." but he did not. Hall may not have read this in the *Advocate* but when he got to Cuero that evening he certainly learned of the latest act of Taylor. "In company with several other young men," Taylor entered the house of Cesar Brown, described as "a peaceable colored man," drove him "from his humble cabin" and then "ended the wrong by outraging the young daughter of that colored man." Taylor and his companions were immediately arrested. Taylor and Middleton were sent to jail without bond while a third companion, Frank Blair, established doubt as to his presence and was admitted to bail in the sum of $1,500. Editor Linn concluded his report: "Justice demands that the guilty parties be punished to the fullest extent of the law."[16] The three were eventually cleared of the charges.

Captain Hall prepared his resignation letter and submitted it to Adj. Gen. John B. Jones to take effect the first of June 1880.[17] Hall's resignation was accepted and Lt. Thomas L. Oglesby chosen to take his place with Sgt. Samuel A. McMurry to be his lieutenant.[18] They were both products of serving under Captain Hall. This began a less stressful period for Hall. No longer responsible to the Special State Troops, Hall was finally able to visit home in Greensboro, North Carolina. Exactly how he got to Texas a decade or more before remains uncertain, but this time to return home he rode the rails. Again his presence drew attention in the press, not only in Greensboro's *Patriot* but in the daily *Morning Star* and *Weekly Star* of Wilmington, North Carolina, and the Raleigh *Daily News*. Each pointed out that Hall was the son of Dr. J.K. Hall of Greensboro, and that he had resigned his command of the Texas Rangers, "a position which has given him a name noted throughout the country for courage, capacity and good deeds."[19] Hall's arrival was newsworthy, as well as his departure. The *Greensboro North Star* noted that Captain Hall, "now of Texas has returned home, after spending a few weeks with his relatives and the friends of his youth in Greensboro."[20]

Captain Halter and his family spent several months in Lebanon visiting relatives and friends but would return to Corpus Christi on October 4, 1880.[21] For Bessie C. Weidman and the ranger captain, the wedding plans had already begun. Even once he no longer held that official position, Hall would almost always be referred to as Captain Hall.

Wedding bells were ringing, no doubt about it, but before they rang for Lee Hall and Miss Bessie C. Weidman younger brother Richard M. Hall became the husband of Miss Elizabeth "Bettie" Hughes, of Sherman, Grayson County. They were married on November 17 at Sherman. The *Daily Statesman* gushed forth its happiness, congratulating "the happy groom, and joins with many friends and acquaintances in wishing long life and prosperity to him and his lovely bride."[22] Not surprisingly the news at home received great attention. The *Greensboro Patriot* included details such as they were married at the residence of Mr. P.A. Turner of Sherman with Rev. J.H. McLean officiating. According to the *Sherman Chronicle*:

> Mr. Hall is a gentleman who has long been respected here for his sterling qualities of head and heart. He is at present holding a responsible position in the supervision of the Lunatic Asylum at Austin, and has established a reputation there for honor, integrity and humaneness, of which he has reason to feel proud. Mrs. Hall *nee* Hughes, is formerly from eastern Texas, and is the sister-in-law of Mr. P.A. Turner, at whose residence the wedding took place.

The couple left Sherman on the 2:15 p.m. train for Austin where they would reside. Unfortunately there is no indication what guests were at Richard M. Hall's wedding. Was Jesse L. Hall there for his brother's wedding?

Wedding bells rang out the evening of Thursday, November 25, 1880, for the marriage of Capt. J. Lee Hall and Miss Bessie C. Weidman. Rev. William Dunbar officiated at Zion's Lutheran Church at 9:00 p.m. in Reading, Pennsylvania. The nuptials were uttered among "a brilliant assemblage of friends and relatives." Miss Weidman was attired in a gown of "white satin, trimmed with pearl passementerie." The groom's attire was less observed: he was described as a "tall, dignified and handsome Texan."[23] The bridesmaids were Miss Ella Livingood of Reading, Miss Nellie Gloninger of Lebanon, and Miss Helen Weidman of Pottsville; they were described as "a galaxy of beauty" dressed in white lace and muslin. The groomsmen were Lee's brother James K. Hall of Greensboro, Capt. William A. Thompson of the 4th Cavalry of Baltimore, and Casper Dull of Harrisburg— all attired in "customary black." As the traditional wedding march began the bride entered on the arm of her brother, Grant Weidman. After the ceremony "the bridal couple and suite were tendered a bountiful reception by the mother of the bride at her residence [where] were displayed most elegant and costly gifts, the presents of numerous and devoted friends." Then the happy couple left Lebanon on the 11:40 train "for an extended tour through the South, from whence they will go to their future home in San Antonio, Texas."[24] Curiously, neither Captain Halter[25] nor his wife was mentioned either as having a role in the wedding or whether they attended.

Only rarely does younger brother Francis Rankin Hall receive attention in the columns of a Greensboro newspaper, but one instance appears in June 1881 in the *Greensboro North Star*. Editors Keogh and McCormick "were very much pleased, last week" to see their young friend Frank R. Hall of Texas who had arrived at his old home on a visit to his parents. Frank Hall had done well in his "new home" and spoke "highly of his future prospects." The praise continued, like "all energetic and enterprising persons, he has been quite successful in his undertakings, and is fully satisfied with the change he has made in his home." This appeared in column one and in the adjacent column one learns that Mrs. Capt. Lee Hall "while on her way to her old home in Pennsylvania" visited Dr. Hall, also that Frank Hall came from Texas with her, but "he left his lambs in the Lone Star State."[26] This mention of Hall's lambs was a reference to Hall's involvement in raising sheep in Texas. Apparently the editor would assume the readers would appreciate the humorous reference.

During the next year or so after his marriage little is known of Captain Hall's activities, and the sparse record suggests he and Bessie C. may have traveled extensively. A brief item in the *Greensboro Patriot* of November 1881 indicated they were visiting Dr. and Mrs. Hall, as they were on their return route to their home in Texas, "after a summer's sojourn in the Eastern States." A fairly regular correspondent to the *Greensboro Patriot*, her column identified as "Bella's Letter," summarized the local news and included mention not only of the captain but a paragraph about "Our Doctors" as well. Of the local physicians she wrote: "It would be impossible for me to eulogize one more than the others, nor will I attempt it, for each one in his own capacity excels the other, from our oldest 'silver haired' physician, Dr. [James King] Hall, down to the youngest of the brotherhood, Dr. Charlie Glenn. Our town cannot, as many others, bemoan the fact that we have the *quantity* of doctors and not the *quality*, but can triumphantly boast of both."[27]

A curious item in an Alabama newspaper suggests that Captain Hall may have done some traveling without his wife. He reportedly "passed through" the city of Montgomery on October 31, 1881, about a year after his marriage, "on his way to the Atlanta Exposition." What caught the editor's eye was that he had in his possession a pair of cattle horns, "which are a curiosity in length and keenness. They are beauties of their kind."[28] What was in reality an early "World's Fair" but then known as the International Cotton Exposition (I.C.E.) had been an enterprise intended to show America the progress Atlanta had made after its destruction during the Civil War and Reconstruction as well as new developments in the cotton industry. It was billed as the rebirth of Atlanta as well as the "New South." Over a quarter-million visitors, including Jesse Lee Hall, attended, during the eighty-six days it was open. Presumably Mrs. Hall accompanied her husband but she was not named in the article. We do not know if the seed of separation of later years had already begun, or if Mrs. Hall was innocently visiting family in the east without her husband.[29]

Perhaps all was well within the Hall family. Jesse Lee and Bessie C. arrived back in Texas and moved into their new home. In late April 1882 Dr. Hall and his wife arrived in San Antonio for a visit, which the *Evening Light* of Saturday, April 29, 1882, noted in its listing of "Menger Hotel Arrivals." In the same notice the names of Lee and Mrs. Hall of La Salle, La Salle County,[30] were included, so it was a sort of family reunion. But also perhaps it was on this occasion that Dr. and Mrs. Hall brought along with them "a timid and reticent boy" —suffering now in the early stages of tuberculosis, the son of Dr. William Clark Porter of Greensboro, William Sydney Porter.[31] He had developed the dread disease, the "white death" or consumption as it was often called, and was to spend time on the ranch of Lee and Richard Hall in hopes that the fresh air and activity would keep the disease at bay. Young Porter had been working in his uncle's drugstore and thus was continually confined, possibly exacerbating his medical condition.[32] Both brothers were operating the Dull Brothers Ranch, Lee now having a "safe" position as Bessie C. no doubt believed, while Richard Hall was no longer working as a steward in the State Lunatic Asylum in Austin.[33]

The several years William Sydney Porter, or "Willie" as he was called, spent in South Texas was the best thing that could have happened to the boy, who now was in his early twenties, born September 11, 1862. Dr. and Mrs. Hall spent several months visiting their sons in Texas, but when they returned to North Carolina they left the young Porter boy there to continue life on the 400,000-acre ranch that Lee and Richard Hall operated. The ranch headquarters was not a little line shack but amounted to comfortable living quarters, with plenty of books to read, as hard work was not all that was available. Porter learned the physical work of the cowboys, although the livestock was herding sheep not longhorns; Porter also learned the talk of South Texas, not only the native Texans' tongue—certainly different in accent from his native North Carolina—but also the Hispanics', whose *lengua* was all its own. Porter, now developing into a strong and healthy young man, lived and worked on the ranch and absorbed the stories he had heard related by the cowboys and the Texas Rangers and of the *banditti* of the Rio Grande frontier, until Mr. and Mrs. Richard Hall left to become State Land Commissioner in Austin. Young Porter then moved to Austin as well. Years would pass, and many adventures— some good and some bad— before he became a respected author of popular short stories using the *nom de plume* O. Henry.[34] Capt. Lee Hall would imaginatively figure in some of those popular stories, although being given an alternative name.

Annette Martin Ludeman, late historian of South Texas, described the ranch as "an enormous affair, located in La Salle County, and was typical of the rough, uncultured county that fiction had painted it. Fifteen miles away at Fort Ewell was the post office in a little frontier village known to the Mexicans as 'Dulce Gejetes' (milk candy)."[35] When the time came for the brothers to move on, the now-healthy William Sydney Porter did as well, locating in Austin.

Chapter Eight

"Lee Hall is . . . as brave a man as ever stood"

—*Charlotte Observer*, February 15, 1885

On August 25, 1882, Captain Hall (he would almost always be referred to as "Captain" now) was back in Texas and again "dropped in" on the *Victoria Advocate* editor. He was "looking well" and was on his way to Goliad to see friends there. He planned to return to Victoria in a few days.[1] Hall was now spending his "free time" traveling around the country renewing friendships with people and visiting places where he had been as a ranger.

Apparently the ranching endeavor planned for raising sheep in West Texas had not panned out as anticipated. Actually this period of Hall's life may have seemed like being in a continual state of flux, just the opposite of his years as a ranger. A new venture was soon underway: managing a ranch. This could have been an important deal for the ex-ranger. Through his role as their agent, he had developed a working relationship with the Dull Brothers of Harrisburg, Pennsylvania, James J. and Andrew Jackson Dull, described as "two wealthy Pennsylvania brothers" by La Salle County historian Annette Ludeman.[2] In May 1883, on behalf of the Dull brothers, he concluded the purchase of the ranch of Capt. William A. Waugh for $85,000.[3] How Hall worked this from the beginning is unknown but he certainly had the managerial skills as well as the knowledge of handling men working under him. His years as a ranger had proven that. Furthermore he had developed the essentials of all who work for another— that of generating trust. He was appointed postmaster at Waugh's Rancho on August 6, 1883, succeeding Lawrence W. Earnest who had been appointed June 24, 1879. Postmaster Hall held that position until the following August when Nicholas R. Miller replaced him. No reason is known for the change; Hall may have resigned the position as there was insufficient excitement in sorting the United States mail.[4]

Hall may not have realized it but working in the area where the Dull Brothers Ranch was located would not be that much different from working in South Texas as a ranger captain. The headquarters of the ranch was located in La Salle County, which was a dangerous area, taken over by white men from Indians and subject to raiding parties from south of the Rio Grande, as well as Indian raids. People who settled there had to be brave and courageous. The county had been created in 1858 from the huge Bexar County but was not organized until 1880 when Cotulla became the county seat. The first sheriff was James Madison Buck, a native of Rapides Parish, Louisiana, with a wife and nine children, elected on November 2, 1880. A former Texas Ranger, he served until June 1881 when he resigned the position, as he determined that the sheriff's office required "a man who has no scruples in killing a man whether the law justifies him or not."[5] Buck certainly realized that La Salle County was a dangerous area and chose to opt out of being in a position where he might have to kill a man, justified or not. William O. Tompkins, a cattle raiser from Alabama and also a former ranger, followed Buck into office. He was appointed June 13, 1881, and was then elected on November 7, 1882. Tompkins served until January of 1883 when the office was declared vacant. He ran again for sheriff against Charles Brown McKinney in November 1884. Tompkins had extensive service under several ranger leaders: He was first mustered under Lieut. J.M. Denton's Company A of the Frontier Battalion on September 1, 1876. He then served under Lieut. Guy B. Broadwater, then under Sergt. Thomas L. Oglesby. On August 1, 1879, he was mustered in as a private in Capt. Lee Hall's Special State Troops. He served under Hall until November 30, 1879. Then he was out of the service but rejoined on January 1, 1881, and served until February 28, 1881, under Captain T.L. Oglesby.[6] With such broad ranger experience, Tompkins could have contributed to eradicating lawlessness and crime. The third county sheriff was Charles Brown McKinney, also a former ranger who had first served under Captain McNelly. He was elected on February 3, 1883, following a contested election campaign and then reelected on November 4, 1884.[7] McKinney's term as sheriff began amidst very hard feelings from the defeated Tompkins and his associates. Historian Robert M. Utley termed it as a feud between the "Ranger party" and the "sheriff's party."[8]

The reason Tompkins could not serve continually under the same ranger leader may have had something to do with the fact he occasionally made bad choices. In June of 1883, when he was no longer acting sheriff, Tompkins met Lee Hall on one of the streets of San Antonio; Tompkins was "a little under the influence of liquor" and began to curse Hall, no doubt still feeling injured from the loss of the sheriff's position. It was surmised that "bad blood was engendered in relation to the contest for sheriff of LaSalle [C]ounty." Hall was not a man who would take such abuse and knocked Tompkins to the ground. Before the unsightly public brawl escalated, friends intervened and stopped the fight.[9] For Captain Hall it must have been distressing as both Tompkins and the new sheriff, McKinney, had been rangers, and both had served under Hall. Picking himself up from the street Tompkins realized he had picked the wrong man to abuse; he should not have challenged Lee Hall in any manner. It was fortunate for Tompkins that his verbal assault did not lead to gunplay, which it might well have. He had apparently not heard of John Price's attempt to humiliate Hall on the streets of Austin some time before. Abusive language from a liquor bottle does not lead to success. One wonders if Bessie C. Hall learned of this incident and thought that being out of the ranger service was as dangerous as when he was a captain of the Special State Troops.

All was not dangerous, however— or perhaps it was. In 1884 the Texas Livestock Association met in Austin for their annual meeting and banquet. A great deal of business was conducted with some of the largest and most successful stock raisers entering into the discussion and volunteering to serve on committees. A few of the principal cattlemen and businessmen attending included Henry Seeligson, merchant and banker of Galveston; Honorable Buckley B. Paddock, the former editor of the *Fort Worth Democrat* and future mayor of Fort Worth; cattle kings Major Seth Mabry, John R. Blocker, Christopher Columbus Slaughter, Abel H. "Shanghai" Pierce, and Richard G. Head; ex-Senator William H. Crain, future Texas governor Joseph D. Sayers, and ex-Senator Elsberry R. Lane. A total of thirteen committees were prepared dealing with all aspects of livestock raising, such as "Marks and Brands," "Estrays," and "Protection of Stock from Theft and Frauds." Lee Hall was placed on this latter committee, with C.C. Slaughter chairman, H.D. Sullivan, R.G. Head, W.H. Crain, Berry Gatewood, and P.S. Weatherspoon as committee members. During these various orders of business William Crain, the Sergeant-at-Arms, appointed two others to be his assistant sergeants-at-arms: Lee Hall and B.B. Paddock. At one point in the afternoon Hall announced that the president-elect of the Livestock Association, Joseph D. Sayers, who would become governor of Texas in 1899, was present and he and Paddock escorted the president-elect to the chair to be recognized.[10]

After all this important work some of the gentlemen decided to move to the popular Isaac S. Simon's Restaurant on Sixth Street in Austin for their banquet.[11] What could have been a very satisfying evening turned out to be disruptive and scandalous to many of the citizens of Austin. The *Statesman* may have had a reporter present, or heard a description second-hand. In either case, what transpired appeared in the edition of Saturday, January 12, 1884:

> A highly disgraceful affair occurred yesterday morning in Simon's restaurant. A party of some twenty-five prominent cattle men went to the place about 1 o'clock for the purpose of having a banquet. While they were at the table Ben Thompson came in, and, after a short conversation with some of the gentlemen, walked to the further end of the room and pulled out a couple of revolvers and began to brandish them in a threatening manner.[12]

Ben Thompson was not a cattleman by any definition, but a professional gambler. At this stage of his life he had developed a reputation as a terror, a brawler, and a deadly gunfighter who had emerged the victor in many gunfights. In spite of these negative qualities he had also earned a great deal of respect, so much so that a few years earlier he was elected to the position of City Marshal of Austin. He had no business being present, however, let alone interrupting the banquet, unless the fact that he knew some of the cattlemen and they all knew of him made him assume he had an unwritten invitation to join them. Ben Thompson had at one time earned the respect of the voters of Austin, but such incidents as breaking up the stockmen's banquet caused many to consider him nothing more than an unwelcome brawler.

Various writers have described what happened that morning at Simon's Restaurant but to be fair we will use the description provided by James E. Lucy, an ex-ranger as well as future Chief of Police of Austin who was there and recalled vividly what transpired. He was interviewed in March 1927 by Hugh Nugent Fitzgerald of the staff of the *Austin American*. Lucy recalled, in part: "Throughout all the years the seal of silence has closed my lips, but in justice to myself and the noted Ben Thompson, I have decided to give you the real facts of the story of my clash with Ben Thompson in the long ago. Hundreds of stories have been written by hundreds of writers and all [are] at variance with the facts." Captain Lucy was aware of numerous falsehoods about Thompson and nearing the end of his life felt compelled to correct them, at least those of which he had personal knowledge. Lucy continued: "Now I believe in truth and in justice— in justice even to Ben Thompson, who had enough to answer for without his courage being questioned or his motives impugned. Ben Thompson was a very dangerous man, but a most courageous man. He never showed the white feather in his life."

Here Lucy has said enough of Thompson the individual and begins to relate what happened at Simon's Restaurant, which involved Lee Hall: "The cattlemen of that period, whatever may be said of their faults, were men of unquestioned nerve, men without fear and men who had braved dangers all their lives. After the regular proceedings of the convention there was a banquet held at Simon's Cafe, a noted restaurant on the avenue in those days. Of course, the cowmen were enjoying life and many speeches had been made."

Lee Hall is now brought into the incident, and the cattlemen called on him to make a speech. As Lucy recalled Hall, "mounted a chair. He was a rare entertainer and those present on the side of the cafe reserved for functions, were uproariously applauding his remarks. On the other side of the big room were the tables usually occupied by those not associated with the organizations or associations which gave their affairs at Simon's." Captain Lucy was at one of these tables, seated with banker James A. Hamilton, cattleman and land speculator Frank Maddox, and Col. William Greene Sterett, a long-time newspaper man. Lucy had been in Mexico working on "a big deal" and after a lengthy discussion of their business the men had adjourned to Simon's for dinner. Thus by chance Lucy was there to witness what transpired:

> Captain Lee Hall had been my pal. We had served together in the rangers. We had bunked together in northwest Texas. He was almost as close to me as a brother. There were large strong or screen doors in Simon's cafe. While the merriment was at its height around the banqueting board and Hall was using a chair as a rostrum for speaking purposes, one of the screen doors was pushed inward and revolver in hand, Ben Thompson walked toward Hall. Hall was one of the bravest men I ever knew. He had been given the acid test as a ranger many times. Thompson was in an ugly

> mood. He had not been invited to the banquet. He disliked Lee Hall. He looked upon Lee Hall as a personal enemy. He used his gun as a club, smashing the glass and other tableware and was to all intents and purposes bent upon deadly work.

Then the "most remarkable stampede" Lucy had ever witnessed occurred, with cattlemen deserting the place, anticipating Thompson would start shooting. But Lee Hall did not stampede, nor did he even draw his weapon. Lucy, however, feeling that Hall was in "a most precarious place," did draw and cock his pistol and bravely covered Thompson. Thompson then said: "Captain, this is not your fight. You have no business in it. It does not concern you."

Lucy had no ambition to kill Thompson and did not believe that Thompson intended to kill him, or Hall. It appeared to be a "Mexican stand-off" with two fearless and dangerous men facing each other with drawn weapons, each perhaps wondering how they could terminate the situation and still save face. We do not know what thoughts passed through Thompson's mind with Lucy pointing a pistol at him, but we do know what Lucy was thinking: "Lee Hall was the man I was thinking of. He was my loyal pal and friend. As I have said those interested the most had stampeded the place. Like the Arabians, they had folded their tents or cloaks about them and the place that they had occupied at the beginning of the affair was a banquet hall deserted." Captain Lucy or perhaps Fitzgerald the reporter knew how to add tension in the telling of this incident, as Lucy now stood with cocked pistol in hand facing the dangerous Ben Thompson, and Thompson faced him with a pistol as well. Lucy was not taking any chances, but he did not want to shoot anybody. What transpired no doubt surprised the few remaining witnesses: "There we stood, guns in hand. I did not dare turn to peer into the rear section of the place. All at once there was a rustle or rush and a sound of footsteps. Then a voice rang out, 'Ben, give me your gun.' Then I did look."

Lucy was certainly as surprised as Thompson was; the voice that ordered Thompson to surrender his weapon came from Congressman

William Henry Crain. Without saying a word Ben Thompson surrendered his pistol to Crain. Then Crain turned to Lucy, still holding his cocked pistol, and said, "Will you give me your pistol, Captain?" Lucy of course felt compelled to do the same as Thompson and turned over his weapon. Then Crain, "one of the democratic leaders and orators of his day, departed with the guns."

That did not end the recollection of Captain Lucy. Ben Thompson then called for his body guard, a large black man named Mack, who now gave his boss a pistol. He was now armed, and now Lucy was unarmed. He asked Thompson: "You have a gun. Where do I come in?" Thompson looked Captain Lucy square in the eye without a trace of anger and said, calmly, "There are bad men on the outside. You must protect me. Here is my gun. Are you ready to go? If you are, there is a horse and cart on the avenue in this same block." Gratefully the tense situation had ended with Ben Thompson and James E. Lucy exiting Simon's Restaurant together, both no doubt pleased that the situation had ended with no gunplay; no one had lost face. Lucy further recalled that on Congress Avenue were "four or five men as desperate as I knew in Texas. They had no use for Ben Thompson." The fact that Thompson and Lucy were together obviously prevented these four or five desperate men from causing any trouble for either. Riding in the cart the men now went to a particular place Thompson wished to go while Lucy returned to Simon's, perhaps to continue his visit with his friends.[13]

The *Statesman* expressed great concern over the incident that could have ended with a tragedy. It was described as a "highly disgraceful affair" and remarked: "It is certainly a burning shame that in the capital of the state such a thing should transpire. When any man is allowed to override law in such a manner with impunity, civil government is simply a farce. Where were the police, and why were they not executing their duty? Were they afraid?"[14] That question did not receive an answer. Ben Thompson did appear in the recorder's court charged with "a disturbance of the peace by violent, offensive, tumultuous and obstreperous conduct."

The result was that the jury found him guilty and Ben Thompson was fined $25 and costs.[15] He would continue his violent behavior for two more months; in March Ben Thompson, along with notorious gunfighter but now the acting sheriff of Uvalde County John King Fisher, were both murdered in the Vaudeville Theatre in San Antonio.[16]

How Lee Hall reacted to the deaths of two of the most noted men in Texas was not recorded, but certainly he felt some regret due to the fact that he had known both: Thompson as a City Marshal of Austin and King Fisher when he was fugitive from justice. It was especially painful that now when King Fisher had turned his life around and would most likely have built a reputation for effective law enforcement, he had been murdered. It was a tragic affair indeed.

Hall had become a familiar figure in La Salle County and frequently was in the county seat of Cotulla, now a growing community of nearly one thousand inhabitants. Located on the line of the International and Great Northern Railroad it was about mid-way between San Antonio and Laredo. In 1880 when the first federal census was conducted, there were 789 individuals according to the enumeration by E.R. Nelson. As for stock raising there were some 186 men involved in either raising or herding sheep, compared to eighty-one men involved in raising or herding cattle. Six men listed their occupation as horse herder or horse raiser. A few years later local county boosters described La Salle as "surrounded by one of the finest countries in the State" and "as a stock-raising country, it is considered superior to any portion of the United States— and this is certainly one of the healthiest localities on the American continent for man and beast." In addition to the superior quality of the land the town of Cotulla had a good school building with a Masonic Hall above, a church, a lodge of Knights and Ladies of Honor, a temperance council, religious services every Sunday, prayer meeting every Wednesday night, eight general stores, a drug store, three saloons, one ice cream parlor, three hotels, several boarding houses and restaurants, blacksmith shops, and virtually everything else a community could want. This was a description of the county seat according to "Observer," a resident whose glowing description appeared in the *Galveston Daily News* in mid-1883.[17]

Politics could become heated at times, not only in the halls of Austin's capitol building but in county seat Cotulla as well. An incident described as reaching "fever heat" happened there in September of 1884. The specifics of the argument that led to a near shooting affray were not identified, but what may have been the cause was the question of who should be elected to congress. In the same issue that carried the Hall-Hickey knock-down the campaign opened with speeches and debates by various interested parties: mainly Democrat Joseph D. Sayers and Independent Judge J.B. Rector. On the fourth during a heated "discussion" between Captain Hall and county clerk P.D. Hickey the "disputants came to blows." Hall knocked Hickey down "in the first round" but the clerk intended to continue the fight. As he struggled to get on his feet he drew his pistol. Hall apparently was ready to pummel away in the second round, but bystanders managed to get both quieted down before any shooting was done. Hall still regularly carried a pistol as did Hickey but was reluctant to use it unless absolutely necessary.[18] Patrick Dargan Hickey had been the county clerk and district clerk for several years and would continue in that position for several more years. It was indeed fortunate that Hall was not reckless in the use of his gun.[19] In truth we don't know what started this argument; it could have been anything far removed from the political question.

The press could be harsh on the citizens at times but could also report news in a lighter manner. The *Houston Age* kept up with the activities of the rangers, both in their campaign against lawlessness and crime but also occasionally in their domesticity. The *Galveston News* felt it was worth reporting that Captain Lee Hall, described as "the intrepid and famous ranger commander," was in the city and was the father of two children, but "neither of them will ever command a ranger company. They are both girls."[20] They were Jessie Lee, born October 3, 1882, and Sarah Elizabeth, born December 23, 1883. Both had been born in San Antonio.

Now that he was a father, Hall's activities certainly caused some concern in the heart of Mrs. Hall. After all, she had convinced her husband to resign from the ranger service in order to marry her. In the mind of Bessie C. Hall, by leaving the rangers he would lead a much safer life and not leave her a widow at an early age. Things did not turn out that way, however, as seemingly every new choice of career her husband began was filled with the same amount of danger as when he was a Texas Ranger.

Of course Captain Hall was the one making the choices of what activity to follow, such as when to help lawmen track down horse thieves. In early November 1884, Hall and "an armed squad of brave fellows" left the Bayou City in search of a gang of horse thieves that had "terrorized and robbed the region of Banquete for a long time." Banquete was a small community west of Corpus Christi. Apparently Nueces County authorities had learned the gang's members were now operating further north and east. With Captain Hall was Deputy Sheriff H.R. Glasscock, Ben Keggans, Dave Lubbock, G. Harris, a Detective Daly and Deputy Sheriff Coy of Corpus Christi.[21] The posse went to Willis by train and then to Montgomery, and then proceeded to Hempstead on horseback. It was believed that the thieves could be found in the Hempstead area. "Those who know," opined the reporter, "the desperate character of the band sought for were of the opinion that a battle would have been the result of a meeting." Apparently the wanted men were not found, and Hall and his men retuned to Houston after scouting through Montgomery County. The next day Glasscock and Keggans continued the hunt, but were equally unsuccessful.[22]

The most dangerous incident happened in early 1885 and again it involved troubles along the Rio Grande, close to the counties of La Salle, Dimmit, Webb, and Maverick. Although in 1875 and 1876 Captain McNelly had caused a reduction in thieving raids across the Rio Grande, they had later resumed with renewed energy. Increased raids caused increased fear among the law-abiding citizens situated close to the river, and a portion of Dimmit County touched the waters. After each raid

Dimmit County ranchers lost horses or cattle, or both. There were only four rangers assigned to that stretch of the river with orders to patrol over sixty miles of desolate countryside. In response various cattlemen organized their own type of defense in the form of minute companies, ready to execute any Mexican or Anglo they caught in the act of stealing. A report from Eagle Pass, the county seat of Maverick County just to the west of Dimmit County, stated that eleven Mexican bandits in the last three weeks had been found in Dimmit County "shot to pieces."

On the night of February 5, cattleman Samuel Jones laid in a supply of arms and ammunition to take back to Carrizo Springs, county seat of Dimmit, to be ready in case it was necessary to defend the town. He further reported that just the day before, several officers and stock men had discovered six Mexicans driving cattle towards the Rio Grande. In the ensuing gunfight two of the thieves were shot to death. At that time there were seven bandits jailed at Carrizo Springs and "their friends and the dead men's friends threaten to raid and burn the town." There were some 300 armed men in and around Carrizo ready to provide defense, and rumor had it that the Mexicans were preparing a force even stronger.[23] The degree of fear was rising due to the troubles along the river, a fear both reasonable and unreasonable.

Runners were sent from Carrizo to Cotulla in La Salle County asking for aid "to repel the threatened attack of Mexican bandits." County Sheriff Charles Brown McKinney gathered two "well armed men" to accompany him on the trek over fifty miles to where the invasion was believed to be planned to take place. In addition to Sheriff McKinney, United States Deputy Marshal Fred Niggli with others left San Antonio for Carrizo Springs and Capt. Ed Sieker of the Frontier Battalion gathered twenty rangers from Uvalde to be ready to defend the town. It was difficult to know what to believe with so much activity happening; threats of hundreds of Mexicans fighting against hundreds of Anglos only aroused people's anxiety. According to a report from San Antonio dated February 7, the "whole of the frontier, 200 miles long, is constantly open to predatory incursions, and the United States posts are objects rather of Mexican curiosity than fear. Rapine raids, and counter-raids, murders and counter-murders have been unusually common of late in that section, and the threatened abolishment of the state troops has tended to make them more so."[24]

The abolishment or at least the reduction of the State Troops was a frequent topic of concern among the stockmen on the river as well as in the halls of the capitol. Capt. Lee Hall went there because of his instinct to act again as a ranger, in spite of the desire of his wife that he avoid such dangerous situations. If he intended to not allow Bessie C. to learn of his actions he failed to do so. Rumors quickly circulated, and one rumor that "attained currency" the morning of February 11 was that three rangers had been killed in Dimmit County— Capt. Thomas L. Oglesby, Capt. Jesse L. Hall and Captain Joseph Shely. Three ranger captains had fallen at the hands of desperadoes! Supposedly Mexican raiders had killed them in revenge for the deaths of their thirteen comrades during the previous weeks. Later that same day the report was that only Captains Oglesby and Shely had been killed but Captain Hall "had his leg shot off." The three rangers had been riding together at the head of forty armed citizens when they were ambushed; no reports were available as to the number of armed citizens killed or wounded. A telegram from Cotulla to the *Galveston Daily News* reported that it was Captain Hall who was at the head of the party of citizens, and he was wounded but Oglesby and Shely were both killed. Fortunately, a later telegram from San Antonio to the *News* reported that the killing of the two rangers and the wounding of Hall "was a canard."

Indeed, trying to determine if the situation in Dimmit County was a canard or if there was real danger to its citizens was vexing. All the reports of theft and murder were not fictitious. Contributing to the troubles was the fear that the ranger force would be abolished all together. The senator from Laredo, Edward F. Hall (no kin to the ex-ranger), was intensely against the force and labored to have it drastically reduced if not totally eliminated. The difference between Senator Hall and men like Sheriff McKinney and ex-ranger Hall amounted to a simple fact of life: Hall and McKinney were willing to place their lives in danger while the senator preferred to work from the safety of his office. Later in 1885 on one occasion Senator Hall and Capt. Joseph Shely found each other and moved from mere verbal argument to physical violence. It was well-known the pair had been "at outs for some time" and when Shely approached Senator Hall he slapped him in the face. Both men then drew their pistols and remarkably emptied them inside Holland's Theatre in Laredo. Senator Hall's shots wounded Shely in the leg and shoulder. Senator Hall was not injured in the firefight. Fortunately Shely's wounds were not serious.[25]

The actual facts, other than the tragic killings of raiders caught in the act of stealing, were more prosaic. The reporting of a peaceful exchange between contending groups is less newsworthy than bloody fireworks. Captain Hall was instrumental in arranging a peace conference between representatives from Mexico and representatives from Texas to at least agree to end the bloodshed. The conference occurred on the ninth of February, 1885. The negotiators were Sheriff McKinney and Lee Hall representing the Americans and Dr. Owen Clinton Pope,[26] a Baptist Minister who was highly regarded on both sides of the river, and two unidentified Mexican officials. To ensure an atmosphere of neutrality the men agreed to meet on one of the several islands in the Rio Grande, known as Paso de Las Islas.[27] At the time the river was shallow enough so it was easy for the participants to cross to the island. The special report from Eagle Pass began,

> Recognizing the impossibility of enforcing the law and preventing predatory incursions from both sides on the Rio Grande, and fearing a re-occurrence of the late alarming conditions at Carrizo Springs, under the suspension of the extradition treaty with Mexico, prominent citizens in Mexico asked a conference with a view to a peaceful solution of the difficulties, and on the 9th instant Lee Hall, ex-captain of the rangers, and Sheriff McKinney

> of LaSalle [C]ounty, representing Texas, and Dr. Pope and two Mexican officials representing Mexico, met on an island in mid stream and after a parley of some duration, reached a settlement.

There were numerous important points agreed upon in this settlement. (1) Four of the five Mexican prisoners held in the jail at Carrizo Springs were to be liberated and restored to their friends in Mexico; (2) there was to be no more shooting of Mexicans in Dimmit or Maverick Counties without due investigation of the charges against them; (3) Americans running off Mexican stock in Mexico or committing other crimes in Mexico were to be delivered to Mexico; (4) the Mexicans, on the other hand, were to use all efforts to prevent robbery and pillage of Americans; (5) the Mexican authorities would deliver up thieves now protected by the Mexicans; (6) the Mexicans were to break up the gang of thieves now encamped opposite Dimmit County and return the stock in their possession to the rightful owners in Texas. This indeed was a memorable spectacle, for the armed groups of men on both sides of the river were ready at a moment's notice to open fire if the "parley" turned ugly. Perhaps the men on the island had a pre-arranged signal to indicate it was time to end negotiations and open fire on those on the opposite side.[28]

The report from Eagle Pass, however, stressed that the men on the island were unarmed, but at one time "it seemed as if an agreement would not be reached and a fight was imminent. The issue, however, was peaceful and both parties departed for the interior without exchanging any angry words."[29] The news of this "Arbitration on the Border," as the *Dallas Daily Herald* sub-headlined its report, reached numerous other Texas newspapers as well as those in other states. The *Wise County Messenger* of Decatur, Texas, concluded its reporting of the affair with this caution: "Time will test the effectiveness of this new mode of international treaty."[30] Captain Hall returned to Cotulla the night of February 11 and reported "everything quiet at Carrizo."[31]

Ironically the *Galveston Daily News* of February 10 placed an editorial—before news could have reached its offices of the negotiations on Las

Islas— stressing that the "state of affairs on the Rio Grande has not been so serious for a long time as it is now. Instead of the rangers being in part disbanded the force should be used to the utmost and doubtless needs increasing." That Texans had to defend themselves was a given and if the rangers were disbanded they would be left "to their own resources," which of course could result in Texas ranchers taking the law into their own hands. The agreement made on Las Islas would be held if both sides prevented vigilante law.[32]

Curiously others who were aware of this action in later years recalled the event in such a way as to make themselves a participant. Ranger Captain James Abijah Brooks performed notably in south Texas but recalled the incident quite differently. "Capt. Shely, Lieut. [William] Scott, ex Capt. Lee Hall, [and] Capt. Lam Sieker was the party to meet with them [Mexicans on south side of the river]. Capt. Scott suggested that I go along with them, which was one of the proudest moments of my life."[33] In spite of what Brooks recalled in his later years and recorded in his memoirs, his presence on the island, and that of Scott and Sieker, has no contemporary source of confirmation. Captain Joe Shely made no mention of the affair in his February and March monthly return.[34] Former Sergeant Ira Aten recalled the incident when writing his experiences as a ranger and sheriff in 1941. Aten recollected that due to an "urgent appeal" for help from Dimmit County citizens he and members of Lieutenant Frank Jones's detachment made a "forced night ride" in answer to their call for help. Aten mentions that the call had also been sent to Captain Hall and Sheriff McKinney, "two old, tried, and hardened ex Ranger captains of many years' service." Aten counted and noted that the Anglo group meeting at the river was "some forty of us" and to their surprise "found about the same number of Mexicans lined up on the opposite [side] of the river." Apparently somewhere around eighty men were on the banks of the Rio Grande. Aten recalled:

> After some parleying we agreed to exchange notes on the situation. This was done by having each side ride into the middle of the

> stream carrying a white flag, a handkerchief, tied to the muzzle of his carbine. The rifle was held above his head. Meeting in the middle of the river each rider would exchange notes and return.
>
> After several exchanges of these notes a peace treaty was agreed upon and five members of each party were to ride to the middle of the river, still under the white flag of truce, to sign the treaty. While our representatives rode into the river to sign this treaty, the remainder of the troop lay in the brush ready for action should any trickery develop. The water ran high up on our horses' sides, filling our boots with water.

In his chapter relating the incident, entitled "A Treaty with Mexico Signed in Midstream of the Rio Grande," Aten wrote, "The treaty was signed, and as far as I know, this is the only such peace document to be signed in midstream of the Rio Grande between the United States and Mexico . . . . thereafter peace and quiet reigned in Dimmit County and the territory in Mexico just across the river.[35] Obviously the several versions of this "Arbitration on the Border" are in disagreement, but the one point which all agreed on is that Dr. Pope, Hall, and McKinney were all there on Las Islas.[36]

The news of this action on the border reached Hall's home country of North Carolina within days. "Capt. Lee Hall," a Charlotte newspaper stated, "whom one report says was killed, and another says had his leg shot off in a fight with Mexican marauders who crossed the Rio Grande, is a son of Dr. Jas. K. Hall, of Greensboro, and as brave a man as ever stood in boots." This was not enough, as the report continued with its praise: "He moved to Texas some twelve years ago or more, and soon established a reputation for dauntless courage that made his name familiar throughout the State. His conflicts with desperate characters, outlaws, Mexican marauders, highwaymen etc., would make an interesting narrative. We trust the reports about his ill fortune are unfounded."[37] The former ranger captain was receiving great publicity for his work in dangerous situations, perhaps no different from when he was an active ranger.

Captain Hall could not have spent much time at Cotulla as another tragedy unfolded in Central Texas. On Saturday, February 21, 1885, U.S. Marshal Harrington Lee "Hal" Gosling was assassinated while delivering two prisoners from New Braunfels, Comal County, to the more secure jail in San Antonio. Prisoners James R. Pitts and Charles Yeager had been sentenced to serve life terms and were desperate, having nothing to lose in an escape attempt. Through the assistance of family members the two had been able to obtain pistols and at an opportune moment attacked Gosling on the train transporting them. It became a deadly firefight in close quarters as others in the car had pistols as well. Gosling was killed instantly and Deputy James F. Manning[38] was wounded. One of the prisoners' accomplices was shot in the stomach and died the next day. Although the prisoners were able to escape from the train James R. Pitts died of his wounds and his wounded companion, Charles Yeager, continued in a feeble effort to reach safety. Word reached San Antonio and when the train reached the depot "a large concourse of people were awaiting. . . . As soon as it arrived at the depot a rush was made to get on the car and hear the details of this horrible tragedy."[39] Immediately posses from San Antonio and Austin were formed to run down the remaining fugitive, Charles Yeager. Attention was given to Leon Springs in northern Bexar County as that is where Yeager lived. Captain Joe Shely with a posse was first to arrive in New Braunfels where the pursuit would begin. About the same time Captain Hall headed a "relief force" from Austin. Now Shely and Hall organized their men so as to cover the most ground. The next morning members of the Shely posse found the bloody footprints of the dangerously wounded Yeager. Captain Shely was able to get within pistol range before announcing his presence to the fugitive, who promptly surrendered and loudly informed his captors that he was unarmed. It was somewhat of a letdown for Hall and his posse, having seen no real action, but Gosling's murderer was now a prisoner. Yeager was delivered to the penitentiary at Chester, Illinois, where he was pardoned out in 1903 and then returned to San Antonio where he died in 1931.[40]

Hall now seemed compelled to seek a new venture. His days as a ranger captain were behind him, although he frequently worked with and for rangers as he had done at Paso de Las Islas, and in pursuit of the murderer Yeager. His ranching venture on the Dull Brothers acreage was ending. Perhaps work for the federal government rather than the State of Texas would be rewarding. North in the Indian Territory the need for Indian agents on the various reservations remained. First a visit home was needed and that could be combined with a trip to Washington. By July, Hall was back in North Carolina and of course his presence was newsworthy. First he paid a visit to his parents at Greensboro and then took his mother to Lenoir to visit his sisters.[41] Many not only in Texas or North Carolina but in the Indian Territory believed he was already an Indian Agent in July. In Muskogee it was reported that new agents were being appointed: J.L. Hall for the Kiowa, Comanche, and Wichita agency; C. Osborn for the Ponca, Pawnee, and Otoe agency; Frederick Hoover for the Osage; and T.A. Burns for the Yahkma agency.[42] Then it was announced that his "friends and admirers in Lenoir" would be "glad to know that he has received the appointment of Indian agent at Cheyenne, to apply for which he came east."[43] This was somewhat premature as a correction followed pointing out that Hall would "soon receive an appointment as superintendent of the Indian reservation in Wyoming with headquarters at Cheyenne."[44] But that would have to be corrected as well, as someone else received the Wyoming appointment. Hall would be dealing with the Comanche and Kiowa in the Indian Territory and in so doing he would meet up with the most famous Comanche of all— Quanah Parker— the son of a white captive and Comanche warrior. Being a superintendent of an Indian agency would mean submitting reports annually to the Commissioner of Indian Affairs. In addition to working with reservation Indians he would receive a salary of $2,300 a year plus expenses. Some considered his responsibility "the best Indian agency in the gift of the government," but that would remain to be seen.[45] In theory Captain Hall and his family could live very well in the Indian Territory without the ever-present dangers of leading state troops in south Texas or hunting the murderers of men like Marshal Hal Gosling.

Chapter Nine

"All of a sudden one drew a knife and the other a pistol"

—*Galveston Daily News*, September 27, 1885

Although becoming the Indian agent was a new career move it was not a drastic move in terms of geography nor responsibilities. The agency was situated about 140 miles straight northwest from Sherman, Grayson County. Back in the 1870s Hall had been in the general area hunting horse thieves or other types of desperadoes. Hall probably found living quarters on the reservation not much different than when he was a ranger, living in a tent in pursuit of outlaws. In other words, the change was not a difficult adjustment to make, although it would have been for his family. But now the agent had a house, which provided more comfortable quarters.

Captain Hall took over his duties at the Anadarko agency on September 1, 1885. He quickly learned that stealing horses was a serious problem; in August agency deputies had arrested C.E. Mallard and J.H. Roberts for horse theft. At their examining trial before the United States Commissioner's Court they were released after supplying a bond of $500.

Colonel Biggers had appeared for the defense and Major Hunt for the government's prosecution. Hall had replaced Biggers as agent.[1]

Captain Hall was not one to remain comfortable in his office as new Indian Agent, but found that some improvements should be made immediately. "The captain had his hands full of work, and was mastering it like a man who felt himself perfectly at home," or so wrote the editor of the *Cheyenne Transporter*, a weekly of Darlington, near El Reno, Indian Territory (now Oklahoma), established in 1879 by George West Maffett and Lafe Merritt. The editors introduced the new agent with praise: "Capt. Hall hails from Texas, and is a gentleman of high attainments, he having served many years as a public officer and is well spoken of in his state. For some years he was captain in a company of rangers, in which capacity he achieved considerable fame as an officer of nerve and ability." The new agent was "fast becoming familiar with his new charge and every indication points for him a successful administration."[2] Glowing words indeed from a journal located some fifty miles north of Anadarko.

But before Hall actually got to the grounds at Anadarko he visited Sherman for a "grand send off." Politicians gave speeches promoting themselves or policies. Spending time at Sherman must have brought back memories to Hall of the days when he was a new Texan, and a school teacher as well as his beginning days as a lawman. There had been a "grand jollification" there with Judge James Q. Chenoweth,[3] United States District Attorney Charles B. Pearre and Hall, each being honored. At 9:00 p.m. on August 25 the Sherman cornet band marched in to the elaborate Binkley Hotel for the purpose of giving the people a serenade. Several overtures "in a most creditable manner" began the evening's festivities. Judge Chenoweth was called up to speak and for ten minutes he addressed the crowd in a "pleasing strain." Chenoweth evoked nostalgia in his talk as he reminded his audience of a former time in Sherman "which was not so far back, when this was a mere village, and following the growth of the State until the present, when he says it is the best, the bravest and most glorious ground the sun sheds its rays upon."[4]

Lee Hall could certainly remember the times fifteen years before when Sherman was a village and he was a brand-new Texan teaching school.

Hall was not allowed much time to savor the memories of his first years in Sherman, however, as he was then introduced and called upon to speak. Thinking of his new position in charge of the Comanche and Kiowa reservation, he said, revealing he was not always serious, "he had no interpreter, so he could not talk, but if those present would visit him at his wigwam he would try to make things warm and interesting for them." Hall did have a sense of humor which, on that occasion at least, was appreciated by those in attendance. District Attorney C.B. Pearre then informed the crowd that he was well pleased with Texas and the policy of the United States government. Hall then may have removed himself from the limelight.[5]

By Saturday, August 29, 1885, Hall was at Henrietta, Clay County, with his clerks, ready to travel to Anadarko, Indian Territory, over a hundred miles due north. His first activities would be to explore the grounds of the reservation and meet the chiefs of the several tribes. He may have recalled his ranger days as he now rode horseback and certainly was armed. An incident on September 18 erupted which could have ended badly for the Kiowa tribe as well as a possible tragic beginning for the new agent who had virtually no experience with Indians.

Recently two young Kiowa men were suspected of stealing horses. On September 18, 1885, Hall got the pair into his office under the pretext of him wanting them to take messages to his scouts. At the same time he dispatched a courier for some troops, probably stationed at Fort Sill, a good forty miles south of Anadarko. "The bucks remained patiently in the office four hours when all of a sudden one drew a knife and the other a pistol." The pair, thus armed, made for the door but before they could escape Hall and his chief clerk W.C. Merrill grabbed them and managed to disarm both of them. During the struggle the pair yelled for assistance and over one hundred Kiowa warriors started to "assault" Hall's office. Several deputy marshals "put in an appearance and quelled the outbreak." Hall and Merrill held the two offenders while the crowd was dispersed by the deputies and some Comanche warriors.

A special report that appeared in the *Galveston Daily News* indicated that Hall or Merrill notified the United States District Attorney— Charles B. Pearre— asking him to investigate the incident. Pearre telegraphed U.S. Marshal William L. Cabell, marshal of the northern district of Texas, to hold them there at Anadarko to await the opening of Federal Court at Graham, Young County Texas, some 150 miles south.[6] Hall had handled the incident wisely, not allowing it to escalate beyond a struggle in his office, which he and Merrill had contained. Some thought the incident "came very near bringing on a conflict between the federal civil authorities and the Indians."[7] No such conflict developed.

During the first week of November Hall visited the agent at the neighboring Cheyenne and Arapaho agency: Capt. Jesse M. Lee.[8] Captain Lee had replaced the previous agent, Daniel B. Dyer, who had been suspended. Hall was accompanied by General Pfeier, superintendent of one of the schools, and a Mr. Hendrix, agency farmer. Among other points of interest was the group's visit to the Arapaho school.[9]

An unidentified reader provided occasional correspondence to the *Cheyenne Transporter*, pointing out that the "government employees are kept busy at their respective work, especially so this week, it being annuity week, attended with its accustomed crowds of Indians." Hall was causing improvements to be made. Under his supervision, "work in each department is being rapidly pushed forward, and ere long we hope to rival your well conducted Agency, of which you are so justly proud."[10]

Hall was not long in his new position when sad news arrived from North Carolina. Dr. James King Hall, the "eminent Greensboro physician," passed away on November 13, 1885. He had been suffering "for some time" with Bright's disease and his death "had been expected to occur at any time for a week." He was survived by his wife and sons. Mrs. Hall and her sister, Mrs. G.W. Harper, were at his bedside when he passed.[11]

Certainly Dr. Hall's sons were notified of his imminent passing and could have arrived in time but there is no mention of them being present for the funeral in the contemporary press. Dr. Hall's remains were interred in the First Presbyterian Church Cemetery in Greensboro where a huge concourse of friends and citizens attended the services.[12] Rev. Dr. Smith conducted the services with the church "crowded to its utmost capacity, and many failed to gain admittance. . . . It was the most impressive scene ever witnessed in Greensboro. Old and young, white and colored, rich and poor, joined in this last mournful ceremony— the final tribute of a mourning people to one of the best and noblest of men."[13] We suspect Hall was not able to leave the agency to visit home during this time.

Although Captain Hall may not have been able to return to Greensboro for his father's funeral another death in the month following did require his presence. In late December, Quanah Parker, the "most influential man in the Comanche nation," Yellow Bear, the father of Quanah's first bride, and Agent Hall met at the Pickwick Hotel in Fort Worth. In spite of any custom of the day prohibiting Indians from staying in a white man's hotel, the group had rooms. W.E. Kennedy was manager of the Pickwick and perhaps due to the prominence of Quanah Parker and Lee Hall Manager Kennedy welcomed the Comanche men as guests. The Pickwick was not an average hotel of the late nineteenth century, but "The Leading Hotel of Ft. Worth" as well as being "unsurpassed by any hotel in North Texas for commercial travelers, transient guests and family accommodations." It was to be a negotiation meeting for the purchase of a large amount of wire and fencing material as well as consulting in regards to collecting rents from Texas cattlemen. It was the beginning of the era of fencing large tracts of land; another topic was how best to collect rents from cattlemen who were grazing their herds on Comanche lands.

Rancher Dan Waggoner brought the Comanche together and one of the activities was to visit photographer Augustus R. Mignon's studio for a group portrait. Certainly the group visited the studio at 208 Main rather than Mignon coming to the Pickwick. The image exists today in the format of a large cabinet card showing Quanah Parker, Yellow Bear, and Isa-Tai the medicine man along with another unidentified Indian and two unidentified white men. All are dressed in the clothes of the white man. The exact date when the image was made is unknown but it had to be only a day or two before the tragic accident.[14]

The day was peaceful and uneventful and on Saturday evening Yellow Bear retired to their room in the Pickwick. He was unfamiliar with the modern gas lighting system and thinking it was similar to a candle blew it out instead of turning it off. Sometime during the night Yellow Bear died from carbon monoxide inhalation. Quanah Parker retired to the same room but considerably later and "lit the gas, and on going to bed, turned it off. The only supposition now was that in removing his hand from the cock, the chief must have turned the gas partly on again." Although they both were in the same room, Parker was nearer the window; otherwise he might have succumbed as did Yellow Bear. Hotel personnel discovered the pair in time to save Quanah Parker from death but they were unable to revive his friend Yellow Bear. It took Parker some time to fully recuperate, and he was watched carefully by a physician.

Hall was notified of the situation and visited Parker during his recuperation. Before Hall could exit from the Pickwick a reporter from the *Fort Worth Gazette* "sauntered" in to inquire about Quanah Parker's condition. He took care to advise his readers of the prominence of Lee Hall: "This gentleman's name is a household word in the West, where his long service for the state in upholding law and order and suppressing the vicious elements of society endeared him to the people." Hall, who "not long ago" had become Indian agent, "chatted freely about his present relations, and the status of the Indians."

Hall informed the *Gazette* reporter that he was in charge of about 1,600 Comanche, about 1,100 Kiowa, and about 1,500 Wichita and other tribes. The territory was "in round numbers" about 8,000 square miles; Hall was impressed with the land, as "the sun never shone on a more beautiful and fertile region." The reporter was curious about the present and future level of civilization of the Indians, as most of his readers, he rightfully suspected, considered all Indians as uncivilized people, many still living in a state of savagery. Hall could only be honest in his answers, and explained that their progress was slow but in the short period of time he had resided there he had "observed some hopeful indications." The Wichita were the best farmers and education and agriculture would be the main factors in their advancement to a more civilized way of life. What was needed most at this point was the acquisition of implements to use to cultivate the rich soil. If supplied with tools, a great many would not know how to use them, as they had never been taught. If the government provided instructors to handle tools of every sort, they could then learn "the use of harness, teams and scores of other things about which their minds are a howling wilderness." The idea was to transform the Indians from "savages" into peaceful farmers.

Educating the adults was one thing, but Hall believed the most important thing was the education of the children. "It is to the rising generation that we must look to see all savage customs and barbaric ways shaken, and this can only be effected by teaching them book learning and to talk English." Hall was optimistic in this regard. At Anadarko there were two individual schools in successful operation. There were over two hundred boys and girls in attendance at these schools. The boys were taught farming and the girls were taught sewing, cooking, washing, and "domestic duties generally."

The notion that there was still in white society an "Indian problem" was a topic Hall was somewhat reluctant to address, but the reporter posed the question and he felt obligated to respond to it. Opening up reservation lands for white settlers was what many white settlers desired, but agent Hall replied artfully: "Those with whom I have talked express a contrary opinion. They seem to want the government to adhere to the agreement by which they and their children were to have [the land] as long as 'grass grows and water runs'." Hall expressed the positive belief that "with the march of time and softening of manners, doubtless a change will come about."

The reporter at this point realized that his time was running out and got to an important question, which perhaps was most important to him: which was the leading tribe in Hall's district? Hall did not hesitate, and he stated that the Comanche were the leading tribe "by long odds." Hall was certainly aware of the great prejudice against them, and that "in former times" the Comanche "bore a hard name" and yet they "are in every way a superior class of red men." The Comanche men "take first rank and they have kept good faith with the government ever since going on the reservation." Hall pointed out one characteristic the reporter and whites in general were unaware of: "One excellent characteristic with the females of this tribe is their chastity, which virtue obtains among them to a larger degree than with the others."[15]

One wonders if during this interview Captain Hall couldn't help but look back on his own efforts at teaching children in Grayson County. Did the Fort Worth reporter know of this area of Hall's background? Hall certainly had the opportunity to share his own teaching talents with the two industrial schools where hundreds of boys and girls were in attendance. Hall must have pondered this while preparing to accompany the body of the deceased Comanche to Harrold, Wilbarger County, by train.

Captain Hall took charge of Yellow Bear's remains and with Parker took the train to Harrold arriving in the evening of the twenty-second.[16] Many of the town's citizens were disappointed when they learned that Yellow Bear was not to be buried there but in Indian Territory. Cattleman Samuel Burk Burnett telegraphed friends in Harrold to advise the families of Yellow Bear and Quanah Parker of the calamity; couriers were sent out to bring them in to meet the body when it arrived in Harrold.[17] Some twenty-five Indians met the train at the Harrold depot, who then escorted Parker and the remains of Yellow Bear to their home in the Territory.[18] Few realized that a burial in Harrold "would have violated one of their sacred customs."[19] Due to the prominence of Quanah Parker numerous journals reported the death of Yellow Bear. Most gave the cause of death as "inhalation of gas" but a few used the term "asphyxiation" as to the cause.

The year of 1885 revealed the respect Hall had from virtually all aspects of society: besides acting as a man-hunter again he had helped negotiate an unofficial treaty on the Paso de Las Islas and now was trusted by the Comanche to return Yellow Bear to his permanent home. A piece in the *Fort Worth Daily Gazette*, however, suggested that the year ended on an ominous note for Capt. Lee Hall. The article reported that United States Attorney Pearre of the Northern District of Texas and Captain Hall were in Dallas and were "closeted all day with Marshal Cabell. They had been reading and discussing a large book entitled *The Statutes of the United States*." The reporter had to admit that while none of them would talk to him, "the inference is that there is something the matter up in the Indian Territory."[20]

Actually, Hall was in Dallas prosecuting thieves who had been stealing horses from the Indians and then selling them in Texas. A reporter was able to gain an interview with the agent, who spoke of what he felt was necessary for the Indian to succeed. "What is needed most to make the Indian a farmer is for him to work side by side with white farm hands. I would rather have fifteen white farm boys to work with my Indians than all the college graduates and theoretical farmers in the country. The Indian is an imitator, and the plan I suggest would make a fine farmer of him. If adopted at all Indian agencies the problem of civilizing the Indians would be solved in eighteen months. A few months' practical farm experience at the agency is worth more to the Indians than all the theory farming that can be taught in as many years at the Indian schools of the east." He conjectured that his ideas on how to make the Indian civilized would result in them becoming self-supporting in less than three years. But this was only one problem that the Indians could not solve by education. Hall had served less than one year, but he had examined the books at the agency and determined that thieves had stolen

700 horses from his wards, mainly thieves from the Chickasaw nation and white men from Texas. The natural result, in Hall's mind, was that the Indians would want to retaliate, but how to convince them retaliation was wrong? As agent was he obligated to teach them Christian morality? He had heard his Indians say "we are not on the war path. The white man steals our ponies. Why should we not steal from him?" Hall explained that he could only tell them it was wrong to steal, but he could not go much further against this type of traditional cultural behavior. Hall told the reporter that he intended to get the thieves punished, but he needed help from Washington. "I think with them I can manage to make it uncomfortable for the thieves."[21]

It is not surprising that thieves would look upon the reservation as a hunting ground, since many a white rancher and settler still considered the Comanche and Kiowa tribes savages. A thief would consider stealing from them a justifiable act, remembering the Red River War of a decade before. But J. Lee Hall, U.S. Indian Agent, as he now signed his name, prepared for the possible raiding parties. The federal government also was concerned about happenings in the Indian Territory. One thing that was happening in defiance of the laws of the government was that Anglo ranchers permitted their cattle to graze on the Indian lands. This amounted to a free open range system: cattle could fatten at no cost to the owners. The Indians however, who owned the land itself, were not receiving the payments promised them by the government for allowing cattle to graze on that land. The cattlemen were in the process of rounding up their herds to be transported to markets. The situation that would become an issue in the spring would be what would happen when agents of the government demanded payment for that grazing on Indian lands? Hall did not go to Washington for instructions: he gave out orders that the round-ups would not proceed until the rent was paid. A potential fight was in the making.

Captain Hall did not become so engrossed with his work that he forgot family matters. Mrs. Hall did spend some time with her husband although her presence was rarely noted. In all likelihood the wife and girls spent time at the agency but also frequently visited friends and family in Pennsylvania. On one of the times at the agency, in February 1886, Mrs. Hall gave a "progressive euchre party at which a delightful time was had." She and the captain "did everything possible to make it pleasant for their guests."[22]

In April 1886 Hall and many cowboys and cattlemen were in Wichita Falls, perhaps to celebrate the "first great driveout" being over. Most of the cattle that had been using the free grass had been rounded up by Texas sheriffs under writs of attachment. Hall would leave on April 11 for Henrietta.[23] He and other assistants had supervised the round-ups as there were thousands of cattle being held in their herds "to prevent them being rushed across Red river into Texas before pasturage is paid for to the Indians." The report telegraphed to the *Galveston Daily News* from Wichita Falls on May 8, 1886, noted that Hall, as Indian agent, "is supreme, and over the vast property in his hands has nearly the power of an autocrat." The Wichita Falls reporter added that Hall "seems to be a clever gentleman, though, and says that he wishes to annoy no one, but intends to see that the process of ridding the territory of cattle not belonging there shall be done as quietly and thoroughly as possible."[24] In case readers were skeptical of Hall's ability, there was no doubt expressed in the *News,* as the editors headlined the article "Bouncing the Barons" in bold upper case with the sub-headline "Captain Lee Hall Clearing the Indian Territory of Texas Cattle." Not so long before as a ranger the headline might have read, "Clearing South Texas of Desperadoes."

In Austin the actions of Agent Hall could be treated lightly. The *Statesman* reported that "Capt. Lee Hall, aided and abetted by deputy U.S. marshals, is engaged in the interesting competition of firing cattle that have no business there, out of the Indian Territory." While Hall was doing this, officers on the Texas side, "armed with sundry legal documents, are quietly waiting to gobble the business as fast as they cross the line." The *Statesman* concluded with mock sarcasm: "Verily the free grass rustler is having a hard time of it."[25]

Creditors on the Texas side were pleased with this action. The cattle owners had driven their herds into the Indian Territory and let their stock range freely on what amounted to free grass. It was asserted that "the herds were driven there to evade the foreclosure of mortgages and the execution of other civil processes, and also to obtain the use of the most luxuriant range on earth without paying rent." By the end of May 1886, Hall, and Indian Agent Owens of the Chickasaw Nation, had driven herds across the line where they were seized by creditors. A rumor was circulating that the Secretary of the Interior had issued a stay of proceedings for sixty days, which would allow the cattle to remain that length of time. Supposedly the reasoning was that the creditors had solicited this stay to enable the cattlemen "to pay up."[26]

Apparently no violent action was taken on either side of the line between cattlemen and creditors. Perhaps Hall's reputation, combined with deputy U.S. Marshals and U.S. soldiers, prevented any violence. Did the potential for violence bring about a rift in the relationship between Lee and his wife? She was finding that the dangerous life of a Texas Ranger was essentially no different now that he had left the ranger service. Life in the Indian Territory of 1886 was very different than what she was used to, although there were occasional amusements that may have offered her some pleasure. A celebration in El Reno, Oklahoma, for instance, attracted the Halls, or at least Captain Hall and his little four-year-old daughter Jessie Lee. No mention was made of Mrs. Hall, so she may have stayed home with the other daughter.[27]

But "family time" could only last so long and in August Captain Hall delivered a number of witnesses to court for a case of horse stealing. The witnesses included Quanah Parker, Big Bow, and other important members of the tribe. The accused, a young warrior named Bone, was bound over in the amount of $5000 to appear at the next term of court.[28]

The comfortable east still appealed to Bessie C. Hall and in September she with her two daughters returned back home to Pennsylvania. The *Reading Times* noted that she had arrived on the evening of the twenty-fifth and intended to stay "for several months."[29]

Captain Hall had different concerns now. A delegation of twelve Kiowa and Caddo Indians, under the leadership of Tehuacaua Jim, stopped in Sherman on their return from Dallas where they had been involved in an important land case, dealing with matters in the Anadarko agency. As they knew no English, interpreters were constantly with them and Hall accompanied them. Obviously the Indians trusted Hall totally in "assisting them in getting things arranged."[30]

Being an agent required providing reports to the Commissioner of Indian Affairs in Washington, D.C. J. Lee Hall on August 26, 1886, concluded his first annual report. Being properly schooled in communication, he began, "Sir: I have the honor to submit this my first annual report, together with statistics, as required in your circular letter dated July 1, 1886."[31] He first reminded the commissioner that since taking charge of the Kiowa, Comanche, and Wichita Agency on September 1 the previous year he had visited all portions of the reserve and had seen nearly all the heads of families who lived on the reservation. This was important as he was thus able to report only what he saw from personal observation. Hall's reserve comprised a total of 2,968, 893 acres of land; his wards numbered 3,088 Indians. Of the Comanche there were 707 males and 885 females; of the Kiowa there were 556 males and 608 females. Of these 1,164 Hall noted that about one third of them "were making rapid progress towards civilization, but as a whole they beg, lie, and steal, and their women are depraved."[32] In contrast, Hall noted the superiority of the Comanche, "from being the most cunning, bloodthirsty, and warlike of all the plains Indians, have become the most tractable, and are making greater strides toward civilization than any tribe of blanket Indians within my knowledge." The Comanche were obedient, truthful, and honest, and in contrast to the Kiowa, was "the unquestionable chastity of their women."[33] The only Comanche Hall identified by name was their chief "Sun-Boy" who had, when Hall began, exhibited viciousness and insubordination, influencing the others to resist Hall's rules. However, exhibiting Hall's leadership, "a firm and decided stand, coupled with an intimation that he would be removed from the reservation for an indefinite time, had the effect of bringing him to terms, and he has since made no open opposition to the advancement of his people."[34] Clearly, J. Lee Hall was the ideal man to be the agent; he wisely used all the skills he had developed to control a challenger to his authority.

Of the others, Hall made no special comments other than providing the commissioner with statistics. Of the Apache there were 332 males and 332 females; there were members of smaller tribes, the Wichitas comprised of Wacoes, Towaconies, and Keechie. Of the Wichitas Hall noted that they all spoke the same language, had the same habits and customs, "have intermarried until they have become one and the same people." They numbered about 480. This group was obedient, and "with the exception of the manner in which they treat their women, which is frequently cruel and unjust, they are well advanced upon the road to civilization."[35]

Hall provided considerable information on the government buildings in which his charges lived and worked and also the condition of the school buildings. The facilities in which the children were to learn is a constant theme in his report. Of the buildings Hall was clear: "There are none in anything like a decent state of repair with the exception of the agent's dwelling and the Wichita school building, both of which have been recently built." The building for the Kiowa and Apache school was badly in need of repair, "which will be absolutely necessary before winter" in order to provide some comfort for the children and employees. Besides the buildings there was a need for fences. Fences were also out of repair when Hall came to the agency, but under his direction eighty acres had been fenced and all fences had been put in serviceable condition. He also had directed the construction of a "good, substantial saw and grist mill during the year."

Of stock Hall recorded that there were over 8,000 head of horses and nearly 5,000 head of cattle, which averaged out to two horses and one head of cattle to every man, woman, and child. Although the livestock was owned or controlled by the chiefs, "a large proportion of the squaws have brands of their own, as well as quite a number of the children." Hall complimented the herd owners, pointing out that they respected the owners and "their property is as secure from interception as that of any of the others." He unwittingly provides a note of humor in his report, perhaps, stressing that the Indians take very good care of their herds, "and when hungry will never eat one of their own, but one of their neighbors."[36] Traditionally this was a fact of life common among all cattlemen: never eat one's own beef when there was meat on the hoof of a neighbor.

Besides the matter of livestock there were other concerns that had the potential to become problems. Gambling, especially the game of *monte*, was the "besetting sin of these people," but it was on the decrease. When Hall arrived at the agency it was a daily occurrence to see large groups crowded around the traders' stores, on the porches and in the doorways, "so that ingress and egress was difficult, on account of the *monte* games." The games ran day and night, attracting men, women, and even children, sometimes two and three hundred engaged at a time. Not surprisingly, "Some of the Indian police were among the most expert." Hall put a stop to gambling immediately, but he had to constantly lecture them about the evils of gambling and "have succeeded in stopping public gambling." He was not naïve, however, as he knew they still played in secret, but it was obviously drastically different than when he first came to the agency.

In addition to gambling another thorn in his side was their abuse of alcohol. He had seen a few cases of drunkenness but determined the liquor had been obtained from soldiers at neighboring Fort Sill. Another problem was the use of what he termed "wo-so-wist" which came from the tips of a certain kind of Mexican cactus that, when eaten, produced the same effect as opium, sometimes causing the user to sleep for twenty-four hours. Another change that Hall could claim was the reduction of polygamy, or, as he stated, it was at least "growing into disfavor." He was aware that it was not only his influence but that the women were becoming more independent; if there was a relationship complaint they brought it to the agent. Hall made good use of his diplomatic skills by adding: "I make it a rule whenever there is a dispute over a woman to leave the decision of choice to her."

In general all aspects of Hall's work as Indian agent that first year were encouraging and productive to his wards as well as the commissioner in Washington. The police force was becoming more and more efficient. Due to their recovering stolen property and making arrests, Hall recommended their monthly pay be doubled in the future, to $16 per month. In concluding his report Hall was "sorry to state" that there had been no missionary work done since he arrived and none for some time previous. He hoped that this fact would attract some of the Christian denominations to the wants and needs of his wards.[37] If asked, Agent Hall would probably have urged missionaries from the first Presbyterian Church in Greensboro to labor in his agency.

Meanwhile, there had been hard feelings down in La Salle County when Hall had been there, and they had not been resolved. At first Frank Hall, Lee's brother, was believed to be involved, as well as an old enemy of Sheriff C.B. McKinney: William O. Tompkins. The first victim of the hard feelings between some of the Cotulla residents was Charles Brown McKinney. The sheriff with his deputy, Samuel Vaughn "Pete" Edwards, had left Cotulla by train to investigate a reported rape of a young girl, which was later determined to be a false report. At the Twohig station they detrained and rode horses to the scene of the alleged assault. McKinney and Edwards unknowingly had ridden into a trap, as two men had set up an ambush: James McCoy and George "Bud" Crenshaw. At a prearranged signal Crenshaw fired his Winchester into McKinney while Coy fired his pistol into Deputy Edwards, severely wounding him.

Edwards's horse panicked and both horse and rider fled the scene while McKinney's body collapsed on the ground. Both murderers fled.

The report of the killing shocked Cotulla's citizens. Adjutant General King ordered Captain George Schmitt of the Frontier Battalion to Cotulla to keep order while posses went out to find the murderers. Telegraphic reports indicated that if the murderers were captured they would probably be lynched immediately. At the coroner's inquest on the body of McKinney it was determined that George W. Hill, Bud Crenshaw, Jim McCoy, W.O. Tompkins, and Headley White had been together the night before the assassination. Further, the same men were known to be together the night after the assassination. These facts, once known, led McKinney's father-in-law, Silas Hay, to plot his revenge against Hill whom he believed was behind the assassination of his son-in-law. While Captain Schmitt and his rangers and local posses searched for McCoy and Crenshaw, the grieving Silas Hay acted. George W. Hill had made "explicit and direct threats" against Hay and on the night of January 2, 1887, Silas Hay— in company with Frank Hall— met Hill to settle the matter. Hill attempted to draw his pistol but his overcoat prevented him from drawing and shooting first. Hay drew his and shot Hill. In Hay's statement he claimed he had not intended to kill him; he only wanted him to know that if he were killed his friends would know who was responsible. Hay also stated that Frank Hall "had nothing to do with it whatever"; he only happened to be with him when the killing occurred.

Captain J. Lee Hall certainly read the reports of these violent acts in the newspapers but we have no record of his intending to travel to Cotulla to give support to his brother. Actually Frank P. Hall was not in any trouble, as Silas Hay clearly made it known he only happened to be with him when he shot Hill. Martial law was not declared in LaSalle County, although it may have seemed that way: Captain Schmitt and his rangers patrolled the streets at night, and ordered all the saloons to be closed by 6:00 p.m. Ultimately Crenshaw's location was discovered and he was killed while resisting arrest. McCoy, who had previously lost one leg in an earlier gunfight, finally surrendered and was tried and convicted for the murder. He was hanged in San Antonio in 1887. Silas Hay was not charged with the murder of George Hill.[38]

The Indian Agents had to submit to an annual visit from the Office of Indian Affairs to determine the quality of work the agents were performing. The Agency at Anadarko was no exception and a Professor Charles Cornelius Coffin Painter conducted his tour in the summer of 1887. Professor Painter began his description of his visit to Hall's Agency with praise: "The Agent here is Capt. J. Lee Hall, of Texas Ranger fame. He is a native of North Carolina, but has been in Texas for a number of years, and did that State excellent service in the work of clearing it of outlaws. He is a man of nerve and reckless personal daring, and of untiring energy."[39]

Painter's opinion of Hall did not diminish as he continued his visit. "I found in Capt. Hall the best agent in this part of the Indian field, so far as his work among and for the Indians is concerned. He is not a class leader nor is he a teetotaler. I suspect he quietly sips his strong tea oftener than is good for him, but do not think he gets drunk. I never heard him swear, but am confident that he is an expert in that line."[40]

C.C.C. Painter was not the only individual who made note of Lee Hall and his "strong tea." Rev. John Jasper Methvin, who was bringing the gospel to the Indian Territory, wrote that although Hall was "generous to a fault, full of hospitality, of fine physique, vigorous of mind and body," he had one destructive quality: he was "a great man in ruins on account of drink."[41] The Methodist missionary had been a Confederate soldier during the late war and had intended to pursue a career in the field of law, but received the call and answered it. In 1870 the Methodist Episcopal Church, South, licensed him to preach. By 1885 he and his family had located to the Indian Territory, but due to several conflicts with superiors Methvin was forced to make his living as a circuit-riding preacher. In 1887 the Methodist Conference named him as Missionary to the Western Tribes where he established a church and school, administering mainly to the Kiowa. These varying experiences gave Methvin a good insight into the foibles of mankind, and his notice of Hall's drinking was only one example.[42]

Perhaps Hall had developed respect among all his charges so that resistance to his leadership was rare. An incident occurred in April of 1887, which had the potential of marring that good record, however. According to Capt. Wells Clifford Morrill, a forty-three-year-old store keeper and cashier of the Agency and one-time City Policeman in Denison, Grayson County,[43] some members of the Kiowa tribe objected to certain of Hall's policies. Termed an "emeute," this action, led by a man J.J. Methvin termed a "new prophet," named Pa-ing-ya, garnered more attention on the Texas side than it really deserved. There was a faction among the Kiowas that objected "to restraint of any kind" and protested the practice of leasing land to any outside parties. Some actually felt this protest justified them to kill beeves and to commit other unlawful acts. The "new prophet" claimed to have special powers, such as the ability to raise the dead and to bring back the buffalo. This conduct was strictly the action of the Kiowas; Morrill made it clear that the Comanches were not involved and they actually disliked what the Kiowas were doing. In this instance agent Hall called in a company of United States troops who went after the Kiowas and rounded up about a hundred. There was no battle, not even any shots fired.

Hall gave the "rude redskins," as they were called, "a very plain talk." He told their chiefs that he would hold them personally responsible for the conduct of the six or eight ringleaders who had started this most recent action. Hall determined that his practice of leniency would cease and he now would hold them strictly responsible for "every bad break." He would, in the future, "exercise his authority so that offenders may reckon on punishment for every transgression." Calling out the U.S. troops was simply a precaution, as Hall had not seen there "was really any need of their presence."[44] Methvin summed up the "emeute," stating undramatically that Hall persuaded the Kiowas by this "very plain talk" to return to their dwellings and wait there for whatever was expected to happen. "The day finally came and passed with nothing but the usual happening, and henceforth Pa-ing-ya was discounted as a prophet."[45]

In spite of the excellent work by Captain Hall as Indian Agent, his troubles grew. The government accused him of "abuses in his office." Supposedly he was "short" $25,000 in his accounts. What he supposedly did with this huge amount was never stated, but for those who knew Lee Hall the news was received with "surprise and indignation." In Sherman and Denison it was was accepted that the accusation was nothing more than a "persecution" and that Hall would "come out all right."[46] On the fifteenth of October the Secretary of the Interior requested the Attorney General to institute criminal proceedings against J.L. Hall, agent for the Kiowa, Comanche, and Wichita Indians in the Indian Territory. The charges in general terms were malfeasance in office. An inspector of the Interior Department and a special agent of the office had investigated the affairs of the agency and determined Hall had presented false, fraudulent, and vicious vouchers in his accounts. He had converted to his personal use moneys instructed to him as agent, colluded with beef contractors, and conspired with certain employees of the agency to defraud the Indians under his charge and appropriated large sums of money for his own use, funds which had been placed in his hands by cattlemen for the use of their pastures.[47] That report appeared in the *Daily Gazette* of Fort Worth on Sunday, the sixteenth; the next day the *Gazette* reviewed the previous day's item and then pointed out that the item had "occasioned some talk in Fort Worth, but is met with little credence." The accusation was answered with basically a flat denial, as men "who have known Lee Hall for years say that they are satisfied of his innocence of any wrong-doing, and believe the press statement to be a gross exaggeration of the facts." An unidentified gentleman who was "in a position to know" stated that it was impossible for Hall's agency to be short $25,000. The total amount handled by Hall had been only $37,000 and of this amount he had paid out $31,250 for cattle for the Indians, and there were sums in certain banks, which he named, sufficient to equal the remainder.

This unidentified gentleman claimed to have had an interview with Hall and Hall had asserted that every dollar of government money could be accounted for, and that he was not afraid of the results of any trial and would defend his "integrity and fair name to the bitter end." His brother, Richard M. Hall, then State Land Commissioner, and Hall's attorney Robert R. Hazelwood of Henrietta, branded the charges against Hall as untrue and asserted that his innocence "would be fully vindicated."[48]

In neighboring Dallas, people were also slow to believe that Hall had been "caught in crookedness." His bondsmen, most of whom were Sherman residents, were satisfied there was no crookedness. Folks in Austin who were aware of the captain's affairs were eager to affirm that the charges against him could not be sustained.[49] The word in the press was that by the end of the year Hall "will be amply vindicated from all accusations of malfeasance in office."[50]

The trial that would determine Hall's fate was to be held in Waco, McLennan County. In February Hall with his wife and family—now three daughters, Jessie, Sarah, and Martha—arrived in Waco and took apartments at the new McLelland Hotel. On the twenty-third he called at the office of United States District Attorney Charles B. Pearre and told him that if he was charged with any crime he was there to surrender. There were indeed charges. The information came from Special Indian Agent Eugene E. White that on or about the first day of November 1887 at Anadarko, Indian Territory, Jesse Lee Hall with "force and arms, unlawfully, knowingly and feloniously did receive public money he was not authorized to retain as salary, pay or emolument, and did fail to render his account as provided by law and did embezzle the same, . . . presenting false vouchers to the United States government, and also colluding with other parties to defraud the United States contrary to the form of the statute in such case made and provided." This was sworn to by J.H. Bull, deputy U.S. Marshal, before J.H. Finks, Commissioner of the Circuit Court of the Northern District of Texas.

A warrant was issued and served by Bull; that afternoon Hall in the custody of Bull went to Dallas. Various businessmen offered to give bail for Hall but he declined as "he had a reason for desiring to give bond at Dallas." Captain Hall's case was set for trial at Graham, Young County, at the next March term of the U.S. District Court.[51] First Hall had to provide bond to answer five charges in five different indictments in the sum of $2,000 in each of the five cases. Two of the indictments charged him with presenting false claims against the United States; three were charges of embezzlement of the respective sums of $30, $150, and $500. Hall's clerk for the agency, W.C. Morrill, was charged as an accomplice with presenting false claims against the United States; he also gave bond for $2,500. The cases were transferred to the Graham docket by formal order of the court and were to be tried in October 1888. Why the delay and change to Graham? At Waco the grand jury had "declined to find any bills." In case the public was forgetting who the defendant was, readers were reminded that "Captain Jesse Lee Hall was for a long time Captain of the Texas Rangers, is very noted and popular in the west. His friends are confident that he will prove himself innocent of the charges preferred against him."[52]

It was not published extensively, but J. Lee Hall was, by the end of 1887, no longer an Indian Agent, no matter how the trials might turn out. A report from Washington, dated February 1, stated that President Cleveland had approved the suspension of J.L. Hall from the office of agent.[53] School teacher, sergeant-at-arms, Texas Ranger, sheep rancher, Indian Agent . . . what would be the next career for Lee Hall? That knowledge would have to wait a while. Many thought it was no more than political shenanigans that cost Hall his position. A correspondent who signed his contributions only as "R.T" announced "sad news" for all "old frontier friends who have known and admired the gallant Texas ranger, Captain Lee Hall, late government agent of the Comanche Indians." Noting his suspension by the president, R.T. stated the year previous "he became entangled in the intricacies of government red tape and was removed." Further, there may have been indiscretions by Hall, but anyone who knew him "for fourteen years as I have, and has witnessed his relentless warfare on outlawry and banditism, upon the John Hardens [*sic,* Hardins] of northwest Texas [*sic:* Hardin was primarily active in East and Central Texas], or the American and Mexican thieves on the border, will never believe him dishonest."[54]

Hall was gone from Anadarko but another change was happening there: an increase of horse and cattle theft. On April 14, 1888, John F. Kimbell of Greer County, wrote Governor L.S. Ross a letter that contained disparaging news. "I wish to call your attention to the stealing and killing of cattle and stealing of horses belonging to settlers along the north fork of the Red river above the junction with the Elm fork, by the Kiowa Indians," the letter began. To Kimbell this was serious, as he continued: "Their depredations have become a very serious matter, requiring active and prompt measures to suppress them. The citizens of this section are law-abiding and peaceful, and desire that the lawful authorities will grant them immediate and full protection in the peaceable possession of their property, as is guaranteed them by our laws." Kimbell suggested that the depredations had increased since the change in Indian agents. "While Captain Lee Hall was Indian agent we had but little trouble from Kiowas. Since his removal there has been a marked increase in the boldness and audacity of the Kiowas' raids upon our stock, and the killing and stealing by them is alarmingly upon the increase." Kimbell had only a few cattle and horses and kept his stock on the north side of the North Fork. But recently the Kiowas had killed two of his milk cows near his house. The Indians did not hesitate to come on either side of the river now. Kimbell claimed he understood the "Indian character and know the necessity of a military control over them." As far as Kimbell was concerned, there was no control over the Kiowas, "for they rove at will on both sides of the river."

Kimbell noted in his letter that he had been in communication with the district attorney, a Mr. Miller, concerning the "unprotected condition and our losses of stock." Miller said he would try and get some rangers stationed along the river.

Governor Ross forwarded the Kimbell letter to Senator Coke (former governor of Texas) and (future governor) Samuel Willis Tucker Lanham, with other letters reflecting the same complaints, asking them to "lay the matter before the Interior Department." The situation on the northern border was serious, and retaliation by white settlers was anticipated at any time. The conclusion of many settlers concerned seemed to be that the governor could do nothing, so one had to wait for help from the Interior Department in far-off Washington.[55] It was a perfect setting for an outbreak of violence on the northern border of the Lone Star State. It was clear in the minds of those who lived there: if Lee Hall had been there, the problem would have been prevented.

Lee Hall was not there, no longer concerned with the agency in Indian Territory. He was now in the cattle business. On March 5, 1889, he passed through Austin with a trainload of 300 one- and two-year-old three-quarter blood bulls. He had purchased them in Gainesville and was shipping them to the sprawling ranches of Richard King and Mifflin Kenedy in the Nueces Strip, a land he was certainly familiar with from his ranger days. The month before he had shipped them 400 head and they were going to need more.[56] Hall may not have been aware but one of the rangers from the 1870s, George Durham, was now a *caporal* on the Laureles division of the King ranches.[57]

Hall could not forget that the charges against him as Indian Agent at Anadarko were still hanging fire. Who knew when that matter would be resolved for good?

Although he had resigned from the rangers in order to win the hand of Bessie C. Weidman, he had the opportunity to re-enlist on one of his trips to Austin. We have no details and the press apparently chose not to make mention of it but the "Descriptive List" issued to him shows that he enlisted as a private in Company F of the Frontier Battalion on July 22, 1889, in Austin. He gave his occupation as "Stockman." The document described him as forty-years-old, 5-feet 11-1/2 inches tall, red hair, florid complexion, born in North Carolina. The document was signed by W.H. King, Adjutant General. A separate document signed by Hall provides the oath: "I do solemnly swear (or affirm) that I will faithfully and impartially discharge and perform all the duties incumbent upon me as a member of the Frontier Battalion until August 31, 1888..., unless sooner discharged, according to the best of my skill and ability, and agreeably to the Constitution and laws of the United States and of this State. So help me God." This was sworn to and subscribed before Walter J. Swain, Notary Public of Travis County, July 22, 1889. No other document is available showing how long he served.[58]

On September 13, 1889, a daughter was born to the Halls, named Mary Weidman Hall, in San Antonio. The fifth daughter would be born not in San Antonio but in Lebanon, Pennsylvania, on November 29, 1890, and would be named Virginia Derr Hall. Captain Hall's family was growing, and also his drinking had increased.

Chapter Ten

"Uncle Sam or any other power could not get together a more formidable cavalry than the sun-browned, raw-boned, danger-tried Rangers of the Texas frontier."

—Col. Theodore Roosevelt, 1899

Capt. J. Lee Hall was no longer the agent at Anadarko, although the charges were still hanging fire. In reality his problems were not of any malfeasance on his part. Whatever the final outcome would be his reputation had been stained, and his political career was at an end. He certainly was aware of the pitfalls of politics and it had cost him the position. The accusations had been made that he had committed false reporting in his books which ultimately cost him his job and to some his reputation. In the final analysis it was proved beyond a shadow of a doubt that he had not committed any wrong, but the position was given to someone else. That in the mind of many was politics, which leaves a bad taste in one's mouth. There was no semblance of justice. In preparing his annual reports he proved he could be an outstanding Indian Agent. Now with the New Year of 1891 there was faint rumbling of issues with Cuba and Spain.

Some good news came in 1891. At Graham, in Young County, in the United States court nationally famous criminal lawyer Col. William L. Crawford filed a motion to quash the indictments against Lee Hall. The motion was sustained in three cases and overruled in the others.[1] During this year he helped his brother Richard in his run for governor, but that proved unsuccessful, Richard Hall losing to James Stephen Hogg. Work was necessary: after all his daughter, Mary Weidman, born September 13, 1889, in San Antonio, was daughter number four, and he now had the yearling, Virginia Derr, born November 29, 1890, to care for. His growing family perhaps provided some relief. Then Hall found a means to experience action, similar to the days when he was a ranger. Of course there was an element of danger involved, but apparently Bessie C. approved, or at least accepted.

The story was this: Workers on the San Antonio and Aransas Pass Railway were rumbling about a strike. By mid-November 1891 another conference was held in Houston between committees representing the engineers and firemen and the railroad's general manager; the main topic was an increase of pay for the workers. With no compromise, there would be a general strike resulting in "the greatest railroad strike ever seen in America."[2] The strike began on December 25, 1891, and by the end of December there was no movement of train cars on the San Antonio and Aransas Pass line. Fortunately there had been no violence although the potential was always present. Nor had there been any effort made to compromise.[3] On January 4 the first train on the San Antonio and Aransas Pass Railway passed through Cuero since the Christmas day strike began. Lee Hall was in charge with a force of heavily armed men. He telegraphed to DeWitt County Sheriff Paul Fielding Breeden to have ten well-armed men meet him to go on to Yoakum. The ever-confident Lee Hall said that "he anticipated no trouble, as he intended to talk peace to the men."[4]

Hall with his men rode the train from Cuero to Yoakum to protect railroad property from the angry workers. The passenger train was four hours late at Yoakum, on the DeWitt-Lavaca County line, but it got through, gliding "noiselessly in without the usual ring of bells or whistles." Perhaps it was successful because it was "fairly covered with guards under Captain Lee Hall, who got off here with a number of men." There was a large crowd of strikers at the depot when the train pulled in, but no disorder occurred, no doubt due to the presence of Captain Hall. There was "considerable subdued excitement to be plainly seen in the crowd." A Galveston reporter interviewed Captain Hall on this occasion. He stated he had fifty men under his command, eighteen of whom stayed there with him in Yoakum. Hall claimed to be under orders from Judge King's court "to protect the property and employees of the railroad company." Hall told Yoakum Mayor J.M. Clark the same thing, to which Clark agreed that property and employees of the railroad company would be protected "without further assistance." Hall responded to the mayor that in the event of the city failed such protection "he was here to give it and see it done."[5] Additional reports from Yoakum indicated that strikers had removed essential parts from several engines, and the water tank at Brushy Creek had been emptied, virtually guaranteeing the engine would not be able to move. From the various reports in leading newspapers it appears that Yoakum's Mayor Clark resented the presence of Captain Hall, although this was not overtly displayed. Clark may have felt he could protect his own town and its citizens without "outside interference."[6] In hindsight it appears to possibly have been a "slick political move" as one headline expressed it; he was exhibiting his effective leadership for the voters of Yoakum. Whether it was his leadership being exhibited or if it was Hall's presence with his deputies is a moot point today; no trouble occurred at Yoakum during the strike.

The press gave considerable attention to what was happening. A report from Yoakum dated January 6, 1892, indicated that from "present indications the strike has hardly begun." The San Antonio and Aransas Pass was moving its passenger trains. The strikers seemed not to care about the passenger trains but were concerned about preventing freight trains from moving essential goods. Workers on other lines assured the SAAP (San Antonio and Aransas Pass) workers they would handle no business to or from Yoakum. In previous strikes management had succeeded in using one class against the other, but in this current matter all the labor organizations operating railroads had federated; this was what the "labor philosophers and agitators" had tried to get for the past ten years. At Yoakum, the headquarters of the strikers, things were quiet. Men were kept off the right of way by a patrol of their own men. At the depot, however, there were a "lot of irresponsible fellows . . . who give the 'scabs' considerable 'roasting' as they pass through the town."[7]

Captain Hall remained at Yoakum, still in charge of his deputies, "who look tough enough to frighten most anyone except men who feel that in being beaten it is banishment from their homes, which nerves them to almost any stand necessary to take." The trains that had been reported disabled were operable again, as the parts had only been disconnected, not removed. Any machinist could get the engines ready to move again within fifteen minutes. Hall's tough-looking men prevented any real violence at Yoakum. The strikers were still holding out and claiming that they would eventually win, but the passenger trains still ran. Ten days in to the strike passenger trains were still moving but freight trains were standing still. This had an effect nevertheless. A report from Corpus Christi indicated that "the people of the coast country begin to feel it severely. Stockmen, who had rounded up several thousand head of cattle for shipment, have driven them back to the pastures. People are growing indignant, and their interests are suffering."[8] Management found sufficient "scab labor" to keep not only the passenger trains but the freight trains running as well. A headline on January 20, 1892, announced that both passenger and freight trains were running on time. In Austin the editors of the *Statesman* placed the latest reports on page one, not only for the benefit of the general reader but also for the officials at state level.

Capt. Lee Hall had a calming effect on everyone, with the possible exception of Mayor Clark who seemingly was displeased with the presence of Captain Hall. One report indicated that the mayor of Yoakum had appointed thirty deputy sheriffs among the strikers "to counteract the force under Captain Lee Hall, which was sent down to protect the company's property." Nine-tenths of the citizens of Yoakum were railway people and many suspected that the mayor had done so "to make himself solid with his constituency." Hall had upwards of about twenty-five men; the mayor's thirty deputy sheriffs represented a potential threat to the calming effect of Hall. People were well aware what could happen. A San Antonio reporter reminded the readers that Hall was "one of the most coolly desperate men in the state. If any trouble occurs it will be serious."[9] If there was trouble between the mayor's men and Hall's men that would provide good headlines and possibly benefit the mayor in the view of the citizens of Yoakum. Since there was no trouble reported perhaps Hall's calming effect did diminish Clark's concerns.

Perhaps to the disappointment of the newspaper editors no serious trouble took place. There were no reports of shootings and killings. The news concerning the strike remained on page one during the coming days, with some reports self-contradictory. The first "entire freight train" ran to Kerrville on January 10, as freight had hitherto been carried on mixed trains. Striking men were still quiet and determined, and railroad officials remained the same. There was "not the slightest prospect of a speedy culmination of the trouble by arbitration or in any other way" or so reported the San Antonio press in a special to the *Statesman.* At least the two groups were talking, but "in the meantime business over the greater portion of southwest Texas is practically at a standstill." That was the essence of the report from San Antonio on January 10; the news continued being placed on page one day after day. But on January 19 the headline in bold read: "Strike Declared Off." The lead article announced that the strike against the San Antonio and Aransas Pass Railway was "a thing of the past" and that after twenty-two days "the men this morning laid down their arms and unconditionally surrendered. The strike was predestined to failure and its length of life is surprising." Obviously the exact length of the strike was not agreed upon, and the same report was unaware of the nation's history with railroads, declaring the San Antonio and Aransas Pass strike was "the first of its kind in the history of the United States" and that it likely would be the last "for some time to come."[10]

With the end of the strike Lee Hall again was out of a job. Nearing his mid-forties he still yearned for the adventure that had brought him to Texas when he was half that age. He now had a wife and daughters to support. Later that year Lee Hall became involved in the Gubernatorial Convention at Houston, during the conflict between James Stephen Hogg, the sitting governor, and George W. Clark. The convention intended to "reorganize the Democratic party of Bexar County and to select delegates to the state convention at Houston." The convention convened at Rische's Theatre with about 700 people present on the morning of July 4, 1892. Following Col. Columbus Upson calling the convention to order, Capt. J. Lee Hall was elected the sergeant-at-arms.[11] It was an unusually exciting convention because of the competition between Governor Hogg and his rival, George W. Clark. A lengthy article in the *Abilene Reporter* headlined its major article with one word in bold: "Split" followed with additional bold headlines: "Texas Democracy and Clark Factions at Houston. / Two Candidates and Two Candidates for Governor. / Both Nominated and Both Accepted!" The convention hall could not have been calm and peaceful; it certainly was noisy. At one point, Captain Donovan of Eagle Lake rose to deliver an address: "Capt. Donovan . . . made a fifteen minute speech, not a word of which could be understood owing to the confusion." Lee's brother Richard M. Hall was also present at the convention.[12] It all may have provided Lee Hall with some excitement but in the end James Stephen Hogg was re-elected governor of Texas. During his four years as governor Hogg did much to strengthen public respect for law enforcement.[13] With Hogg's reelection the political career of George W. Clark was over.[14]

Lee Hall again now was looking for a new venture. Again he found work with the railroad, but now as a guard on the San Antonio and Aransas Pass line. In August he was appointed traveling freight agent at the Galveston, Harrisburg and San Antonio line with headquarters in San Antonio.[15] No job description for him has survived but it could not have been an exciting profession for an ex-Texas Ranger who had had gun battles with desperadoes as well as managing a peace treaty on an island in the middle of the Rio Grande.

The old case of the government against Hall arose again about this time. It was shown that Hall "did not receive credit for about $18,000 worth of property on the reservation which he turned over to his successor and did not get a receipt for" as well as there being other credits for which he never received. It was now accepted that the problems arose from "confusion in bookkeeping,"[16] and that Hall was not guilty of any of the charges. This may have cleaned up the record but J. Lee Hall could not go back to his old position.

Historian Dora Neill Raymond described how the occasional family reunions were of great joy, but Hall had found success on the open range where there was action, and he now was suffering from inactivity. In 1894 after one visit with Bessie C. and the daughters in San Antonio, she and the girls returned to Lebanon, Pennsylvania. Raymond claimed that "there was no hint of farewell in the parting, but from this time on the home was broken."[17] Lee Hall remained alone in San Antonio. The couple were not only physically but emotionally separated, but neither ever filed for divorce. The bottom line was this: Hall had agreed to resign from the rangers at Bessie C.'s request; they later realized that this was not good for a healthy marriage, but they remained in their union although it was not one filled with happiness.

While Hall saw his life and career wasting away due to the poor choice of retiring from the rangers back in 1880, he could look on the bright side by considering the situation of men whom he or his men had captured. At least J. Lee Hall was not a prison number in Huntsville. But in February 1894 Hall could not help but learn that John Wesley Hardin would be released. An item from Huntsville suggested that Hardin's release might "cause many a Texas officer a feeling of uneasiness."[18] Duncan and Armstrong could take good care of themselves; they had proven that in capturing Hardin. Did Hardin's release cause "a feeling of uneasiness" within Lee Hall? Reading the newspapers, Hall also learned that Hardin would visit his three children who were in the Gonzales County area and then visit other friends and relatives. An item in a Karnes County newspaper described Hardin as "once the most noted desperado in the state" and now he was visiting relatives there accompanied by his daughter. He was as "pleasant and affable a man as one would care to meet." He said he had "had enough of the old wild life and that he proposes to live as a good citizen of the country from this time forward." Everyone wished him to live "an exemplary life." Hardin would have "plenty of time to make up for past misdoings and shortcomings."[19]

As evidence of his reformation, on July 14 Hardin was examined in Gonzales and passed the bar examination; he was now an attorney-at-law, a subject he had studied while in his cell in Huntsville.[20] Hardin was forty-one years of age with three children; Hall was forty-five years of age with five daughters and searching for a successful career. Instead of a feeling of uneasiness Hall may have experienced envy.

Hall was not one to remain inactive, however. Although we do not know his specific activities during the late 1890s the newspapers kept up with his travels. An Oklahoma newspaper noted that Hall was in Ardmore on the day before, January 14, 1894. The same journal, the *Ardmoreite*, later noted he was there again, having "come up from Gainesville."[21] A Fort Worth item informed its readers that Capt. Lee Hall was in the city, reminding everyone that Hall's name "is a synonym for bravery in Southwest Texas."[22]

Historian Darren L. Ivey, who has researched the Texas Rangers from their beginning up to the modern era, wrote of the decline of the ex-ranger. "Disenchanted with his financial failures," Ivey wrote, "and possibly with his heavy drinking, Bessie began to make more frequent and prolonged visits to her mother and older sisters in Pennsylvania. When she and the girls went to Lebanon in 1894, her stay there became permanent."[23] Both she and her husband could have avoided hard questions from others about their marital relationship, each telling curious folks that she and the girls were only visiting relatives in Pennsylvania. Likewise he could explain to others that they were in San Antonio while his work kept him traveling. Certainly close acquaintances realized that Mr. and Mrs. Hall were no longer together, physically as well as emotionally.

Hall could not have avoided the press that tracked his travels, although he didn't necessarily have to explain what his purposes were. Much of 1895 was spent in the Houston- Galveston area as well as San Antonio. In April he was at the Grand Central Hotel in Galveston; a month later he again was noted as "in the city." In early July it was reported that "Captain Lee Hall has returned from a trip to the interior and is at the Lawlor [Hotel in Houston]." Again Hall "is in the city" suggesting he had been absent for about a week. By July 22 Hall was "in the city again after a trip through the State and has apartments at the Lawlor." A week later Captain Lee Hall had returned from a trip to San Antonio and was again at the Lawlor. Sometime during this period Mrs. Hall and his daughters paid him a visit, suggesting the reason he had "apartments at the Lawlor."[24] Regular news items from Houston appeared in the Galveston paper, and on August 30 the curious would read that "Mrs. Lee Hall and children left this morning for Harrisburg, Pa., to visit relatives." The very next day, however, we learn that Capt. Lee Hall "has returned from a business trip to Velasco and is at the Lawlor." Journeying from Ardmore, Oklahoma, to San Antonio and Houston and Velasco represented a great deal of time on the rails.

Hall may have ignored the little news items that told people where he had been and where he was going, but he could not have ignored the reported death of John Wesley Hardin, shot dead in an El Paso saloon the night of August 19, 1895. That became front-page news all over the state. Hall had allegedly visited the notorious man-killer while he was in Huntsville prison, but if he did we have no record of what was said or when it happened. In 1900 N.A. Jennings penned a story about how Hall and a posse were chasing Hardin and his gang of half dozen or more. Typically, according to Jennings, Hall ordered a charge onto the desperadoes' camp with him leading the charge. Quickly he discovered all his posse had left him to face the outlaws alone, which caused him to turn and run amidst bullets whistling all around him. When Hall visited Hardin in prison, the convict reminded Hall that one time he had made him turn tail and run. This story first appeared in the popular *Saturday Evening Post* and then was carried in numerous newspapers throughout the country. We believe it was a creation by Jennings to help sell his writing.[25] In spite of N.A. Jennings's claims no solid evidence exists that the two men ever met. In spite of some reports, Hall did not experience any feelings of unease, whether it was when Hardin was released, or now that he was dead. On the contrary, Hall may have welcomed the opportunity to meet face to face with the notorious man-killer Hardin. Hall's man Armstrong had captured him in 1877 and that would have been an interesting topic of conversation if the two men met. Certainly nothing in Hall's make up suggests he was uneasy about the possibility of meeting John Wesley Hardin. In mid-December the *Houston Daily Post* reported that Hall "has been quite sick" for several days. He left on December 12, 1895, "for the west, but was very weak."[26]

Fortunately he was back in the Alamo City in late 1895 when Frederic Remington, one of the greatest American artists, not only in painting but sculpture, visited, and he, Hall, and Capt. Joe Shely met in the San Antonio Club. We know nothing about how the three men met but their visit was rewarding for all. From this three-way gathering Remington wrote the informative article, "How the Law Got into the Chaparral." It appeared in the December 1896 issue of the popular eastern publication, *Harper's Magazine*. We know the conversations took place in the latter months of 1895, as by January 1896 eastern publications began announcing the forthcoming contents, stressing that the December issue "presents a holiday appearance in its cover of white, gray and gold, and the illusion is not dispelled by an examination of its contents, beginning with a frontispiece in color."[27] Remington was in New Orleans by mid-January. In the "Gossip Gathered in Hotel Lobbies" column, the *Picayune* alerted all that "Mr. Remington is the well-known artist for Harper Brothers, and his sketches of soldier and western life are familiar to the reading public." Hall at this stage in his life was in his late forties, but Remington, or so the *Picayune* reported, "is a large, smooth-faced fellow of youthful appearance . . . [and] does not look over 30 years of age and is inclined to be stout." Remington had browsed about the French Quarter all day the day before. He then continued his tour of the various western army posts.[28] Remington recalled that Captain Hall was "a gentleman of the romantic Southern soldier type, and he entertained the highest ideals, with which it would be extremely unsafe to trifle, if I may judge."[29]

The years prior to the heroics of Captain Hall in the conflict with the Spanish remain elusive. A mysterious 1898 item in a Salt Lake City, Utah, journal reported that Hall, described as "a noted Texan" had been spending several months in Denver, Colorado. No additional information has been learned about why Hall was in Denver, but quite possibly it was to visit his younger brother William P. Hall who was employed there as a clerk. W.P. Hall was then a lodger in the Larimer Street Hotel and held the clerk's occupation for some time. He remained in Denver until his death on September 19, 1917.[30] Lee Hall could not remain long in Denver visiting his brother as a most significant event happened, not only for Lee but for all Americans. He was summoned "to the South . . . to take command of a large body of Texans" which was being organized for "a descent upon Cuba."[31]

The battleship *Maine* had exploded in Havana harbor on February 15, killing 266 Americans. Whether the destruction was an on-board accident or the result of an enemy torpedo was never positively determined, but the press mesmerized American thought into the belief that it was an enemy attack and the deaths of those hundreds of patriots had to be avenged. On April 25, 1898, the United States declared war on Spain. Events then happened rapidly. On May 1 Commodore Dewey emerged victorious at the battle of Manila Bay, defeating the Spanish fleet in the Philippines. On June 22 the first United States troops landed in Cuba for on-the-ground engagements. Eight days later, on July 1, the troops defeated the Spaniards at San Juan Heights. Two days later the U.S. fleet destroyed the Spanish fleet off Santiago Bay in Cuba. On the seventeenth of July the Spanish surrendered at Santiago. The "splendid little war" had proved to be of short duration.[32]

Lee Hall enlisted on May 25, 1898, as Captain of Company M of the U.S. Volunteer Infantry. One of the last things required of all field and line officers was to pass a physical and tactical examination, and all did except two: Capt. Lee Hall of San Antonio and Capt. Stephen P. Allen of Palestine, due to hernias. This was a great blow indeed to the two men, but petitions were forwarded to President McKinley. According to the *Austin Daily Statesman*, "Both officers are greatly beloved by their men and petitions are out tonight appealing to the president to commission them notwithstanding their failure to pass."[33] The petitions were sufficient in spite of the ailments and both were allowed to accept the commissions.[34]

Seemingly Captain Hall could not avoid trouble wherever he went as on the thirteenth of June 1898 he and a streetcar conductor had an "altercation." The man was E.L. Jacobson of the Denver Resurvey Car Line. Some issue began between the two and to settle the matter Conductor Jacobson stopped the car in front of the office of Line Manager Baer. At this point the argument was still relatively peaceful but then Jacobson "applied an opprobrious epithet" to the captain and "struck him repeatedly in the face." Jacobson was a much larger man, and Hall would not submit to the beating and drew his knife. He slashed Jacobson across the face and then gave him a deep wound in the neck beneath the left ear. The bleeding Jacobson was taken to St. Mary's Hospital where his wounds were dressed; doctors deemed the wounds serious — two on the face, one on the neck, and one on the back of his head— but not life threatening. Hall was taken to court where he was released on a $500 bond. Witnesses were reportedly pleased with the action, saying Jacobson "got what he richly deserved; that he had been brutal and insulting to the soldiers [who rode the cars], and unaccommodating to the patrons of the line." Jacobson had attempted "to run a bluff" on Hall but "he woke up the wrong man." The *Times-Democrat* reporter concluded by praising the victor: "While Capt. Hall is quiet, unassuming and gentlemanly in his conduct, his reputation as a courageous and desperate fighter is State wide."[35] Within days the incident had garnered additional publicity. Now the word was that Jacobson had been "carved up while making an assault on Capt. Lee Hall" but his recovery was assured. Following the difficulty, the local union of the Amalgamated Association of Street Car Employees met to take action on the matter between Jacobson and Hall. They met the night of June 15 and the local union decided to telegraph Samuel Gompers, president of the American Federation of Labor, urging him to meet with President McKinley and the Secretary of War to prevent Lee Hall from receiving a commission in the Galveston regiment. Gompers certainly received the telegram but chose to avoid meeting with the president over what he must have considered nothing more than a senseless brawl.[36]

Whatever Samuel Gompers may have done in the matter of the street brawl Lee Hall received his commission, as all the men he had recruited wanted. While the war in Cuba was ending, finally the Texans received their genuine weapon— a .45-caliber single-shot rifle. Although this weapon had been in service for over twenty years and was no longer issued to regular troops, the men welcomed them, probably glad to throw aside the wooden sticks that they had been drilling with. They also received a small amount of ammunition. It made them all feel more like capable soldiers.[37]

The descent upon Cuba would not be right away. In the meantime, citizens enjoyed themselves in the usual ways. Several months later, for instance, the news from Pennsylvania was quite different from the reports of men brawling and preparing to go to war. Mrs. S.E. Fox and Mrs. J. Lee Hall were chaperones the night of July 20 along "the Cool Swatara" near Brock's boat house, the trip being made "in a large 'bus." Most people, of course, referred to this tributary of the Susquehanna River in east central Pennsylvania as the "Swattie." All attending spent the day fishing and enjoying other activities. Among the fun-loving party were Misses Jessie Hall and her younger sister Elizabeth, two of the captain's daughters, and other young men and women. The party had started from the home of Mrs. Hall.[38] Only a few days later, on July 23, Mrs. J. Lee Hall left for New Orleans where she would pay a visit to her husband. She was going to travel alone; the several daughters saw her off at the train station.[39] Even though separated, the couple managed to maintain some sort of communication, in spite of the distances. That would become even greater with the political situation between the United States and Spain.

The visit was agreeable but not long. Everyone was concerned about when the men would leave for Cuba. One news item stressed that one company in the waiting regiment was composed of young men, many of whom had given up good-paying positions in San Antonio to become soldiers. The company was Company M, or better known unofficially as the Texas Rangers.[40] Some were sons of prominent merchants and some were crack shots. The captain was Lee Hall; the First Lieutenant was Thomas Netteville Devine, Second Lieutenant J.U. Rogers, and First Sergeant C.W. Starck. Many were beginning to worry that that since there had been no word about when the regiment would move out, they would not get to see any action. This inactivity could result in desertions or fights, as the camp of Colonel C. J. Crane, colonel of the Ninth United States Volunteers "Colored Immunes," was composed totally of Blacks.[41]

The ex-ranger was able to get leave and make a visit to his mother and other relatives; such visits were always news to the hometown newspaper, which reported that he was now a captain in the volunteer army.[42] On October 3, Hall visited the War Department in Washington, D.C. to discuss the First United States Volunteer Infantry, known as the "Immunes," or men who had already had a bout with yellow fever and were therefore supposedly immune from contracting it again. He was anxious that his regiment be sent to Cuba where his men would see active service. He had for years commanded men "who held at bay all intruders on the Texas boundary," which was acceptable hyperbole. Because his regiment was too far west at the beginning of hostilities they had not been sent to Cuba. Hall visited Greensboro before going to Lebanon to visit other family members.[43] From Captain Hall's perspective, Cuba was getting farther and farther away.

This was early October and the battles of San Juan Hill and the Heights and Kettle Hill had already taken place; there would be no fame for Lee Hall charging up San Juan Hill in Cuba. On December 10, 1898, the war was ended with the Treaty of Paris. The United States was now recognized as a world power, and racial differences would be temporarily set aside, at least on the battlefieds. The Spanish Empire relinquished Cuba; Puerto Rico, Guam, and the Philippines were now possessions of the victorious United States. But it was not yet time for all soldiers to head home, as there was an insurrection in the Philippines. Hall may have pondered if he was destined to remain in Texas or somehow get to see action in the far-off islands. His muster cards reveal he was discharged from Company M of the U.S. Volunteer Infantry on October 28, 1898; having enlisted on May 25, 1898, he had served five months. Under "Additional Services" the roll stated he had served in the "Frontier Battalion" company, the "Texas Rangers" regiment.

Chapter Eleven

Lee Hall "is an old captain of the Texas Rangers"

New Orleans *Daily Picayune*, July 24, 1898.

An ideal situation for Captain Hall would have been to become a member of the Rough Riders, an opportunity that he felt he deserved. Meeting in San Antonio in May, word from Washington came that no less an individual than John Jacob Astor, known as "Jack," had offered to join the regiment and bring with him from Washington "a complete battery of rapid firing guns, and that his offer had been accepted." Understandably Astor and the "complete battery" would arrive at Galveston ready to be transported to Cuba. Plans were to gather the necessary horses for the cavalry and other necessities and be ready for Cuba and action within days. Captain Lee Hall offered a complete squadron of Texas Rangers and other frontiersmen "organized and ready to march within a few days." Hall and Colonel Leonard Wood met and consulted on May 13, but no decision was immediately made. Uniforms had arrived and distributed among the men, and already six hundred horses had been secured for the regiment. But, sadly for Captain Hall, Colonel Wood, and Roosevelt, the cavalry regiment became a dismounted group in spite of the available horses; neither Colonel Wood nor Colonel Roosevelt felt there was a need for the experience and talents of Jesse Lee Hall. The Rough Riders could go on to fame without him. Most of the Rough Riders were young men, and Hall, being now fifty years of age, was considered too old for the work expected of the Rough Riders.[1]

Then on May 31 Hall's company boarded a Southern Pacific train for Galveston. There were actually only sixty-five men, quite a few less than the 200 that Hall had envisioned. Hall failed to pass the medical examination due to a hernia affliction that he had had since the early 1870s.Thanks to the men in his command their petition resulted in his being accepted in spite of his failed exam.[2]

On the morning of July 16 Colonel Charles S. Riché "sprang a surprise upon his regiment and friends" by getting married to Miss Susan Norton Gadberry of Denison, Texas, Lee Hall's old "stomping grounds." The nuptials took place with only a few intimate friends and relatives of the bride and groom at St. John's Methodist Episcopal Church in Galveston. Colonel and Mrs. Riché would return to Galveston by Monday evening, the eighteenth of July, "in time to leave with the regiment for New Orleans."[3]

Lee Hall and the men of Colonel Charles S. Riché's command arrived in New Orleans from Galveston on July 23, believing they would soon be in Santiago de Cuba. Captain Hall was "new" to the Crescent City but the *Picayune* eagerly found him good copy, advising that he "is an old captain of the Texas Rangers, and enjoys a great reputation for bravery; in fact, any man that could hold the position of captain of Texas Rangers in those days must have been a brave, trustworthy man, and a man of quick action. Captain Hall, although following a life of hardship and danger has lost none of his good looks. The young ladies . . . appeared to have fallen in love with him, and he was hugged and kissed by some of the prettiest girls, until he blushed red to the roots of his hair. After the feast was over, the men were ordered back into the coaches, and guards were stationed at the platform, to keep the men from straggling."[4]

But, as in many things relevant to the military, plans were changed. The First U.S. Volunteer Regiment of Infantry, known commonly as "the Texas Regiment" broke camp the morning of the twenty-fifth of July and began to embark on the Texas and Pacific transfer boat *Gouldsboro*, to then transfer to the transport ship *Berlin*. All proceeded well; Major W.T. Levy was in command of the transfer as Colonel Riché was undergoing an examination for promotion in the Regular Army. At 11 o'clock the paymasters went aboard and began to pay the men of the regiments. In four hours every man had his pay. Before payment, it was trouble free to keep the men on board, but once they had their money in their pocket "their only thought and aim was how and where to spend it." The result: the guard was doubled and they were given orders to shoot any man who refused to halt, although even so many men broke through the lines. At 5:30 p.m. Hall was named provost marshal and sent armed patrols throughout the city with orders to arrest every man and return him to the ship. Hall was not anxious about any of his men deserting; rather his concerns were that if the men happened to be in a drunken state they would be left behind.

In addition a grave concern was with the available water supply on board. Surgeon W.F. Starley seriously objected to the quality of the water supply and insisted on having pure water for the men; he obtained it, apparently without any difficulty. Mrs. John Everett, a member of the Women's War Relief Association, "grasped the situation and at her own expense had four barrels of distilled water . . . placed accessible to the men, near the guards of the ship." In addition "a large box of books, periodicals and clothing were also unpacked and sent aboard." On a more personal note Mrs. Lee Hall arrived on the twenty-fifth from Lebanon, Pennsylvania, "to see her gallant husband off; they had not met for two years, but Captain Hall was too busy to devote much time to her, as his duties were of a decidedly onerous nature." Mrs. Hall, "a most admirable woman, and imbued with much of the captain's patriotic sentiments . . . took the matter philosophically and will enjoy every spare moment of her husband's society until his leave." The couple spent at least one night in the Grunewald Hotel as their names were included as "Lee Hall and wife San Antonio" in the "At the Hotels" column.[5] One cannot help but wonder just how philosophically Bessie C. Hall accepted this situation; her husband, now nearing fifty years of age, had resigned from the Texas Ranger organization for her, but now he was getting ready to become a soldier in far-off Cuba, or wherever he would end up. Was one career choice any safer than the other?

She and her "gallant husband" had to be philosophical, as "Riché's Regiment" nearly every day provided a report on the command in the columns of the *Picayune*. The command had been taken off the *Berlin* and were now "encamped at the Fair grounds, and the prospects are that it will remain there some time." Even though the men went through "a most trying ordeal" the previous day, "a very large proportion of them were not too tired out to break away from the camp and run amuck through the tenderloin, where they made the denizens of that locality feel as if a band of Apaches had been turned loose on them." No details were given about the "trying ordeal."

In order to move the troops to the fairgrounds, the transport was moved to the head of Mandeville Street and the men were marched ashore, certainly glad to leave their close confinement aboard the ship. It would be months before Hall and the men of his command would see action. Shortly after noon the men began the march towards their camp, moving down the broad Esplanade Street with the sun beating down "with midsummer fierceness" and "as all the men were loaded with every particle of equipment which they could carry the march was a fatiguing one." Numerous sweating soldiers dropped out, overcome by the heat; some slipped away to enjoy a little liberty, knowing that where they were going would not allow them that relief. It took them two hours to march to the camp "and when they got there they were pretty well exhausted." But it was necessary to set up their shelter tents, which resembled dog houses. Once even partly established the arrangement of the tents appeared similar to a little white city. By five o'clock everyone could congratulate themselves on getting organized, but then the clouds opened up and a drenching rain fell. Soon the camp was transformed into a marsh; every man was chilled whereas only hours before they were sweltering from the heat. "Of course, the rain could not interfere with the work of putting up the tents and the mounting of guards, and it was really pitiful to see those men running around, getting soaked to the skin, and laying themselves liable to sickness. Before night there were a dozen of them in the hospital." In spite of the weather, and the fact that all soldiers were forbidden to leave the camp and with guards posted, some dozen or more men "hied themselves towards the city, where they made things howl as soon as they had gotten sufficient stimulant aboard."[6]

But another concern was not overlooked by Colonel Riché. Adjacent to his regiment's quarters were those of Colonel C.J. Crane who was in charge of a black regiment. If the two groups were kept apart there should be no problem, but what if there was some kind of "issue" between them, would the privates keep their heads cool or would there be a conflict between white men and black? In a state of mild anxiety Colonel Riché visited Colonel Crane and the two agreed that they would both keep their men within their own limits of the camp grounds, and "the guards were given special precautions on that score." The concern was that some white private would refuse to salute a black officer and a riot might be the result.[7]

The officers were quite satisfied that they did not go to sea due to the horrible conditions aboard the *Berlin.* They stated that "it was inhumane to expect human beings to live in that boat, penned up like hogs." The alternative was the men would be living in a crowded camp and by chance enduring heavy rains. Capt. Stephen A. Allen was made officer of the day, the same Captain Allen along with Captain Hall who previously had not passed the physical but then had his rejection overridden. Allen issued strict orders that no man was to leave the camp, but even so a lot of men did manage to break through the lines. Due to a variety of factors a number of men were in the hospital, in need of delicacies and nutritious food. Surgeon Major Starley expressed the hope that "those kindly disposed towards the soldier boys to bring them some milk, as that is not included in the hospital rations, and some of the men are badly in need of it." Poor John Emmert was buried on the twenty-seventh, having died aboard the *Berlin*, as a result of the horrible conditions prevailing there. He had been in poor health over a month or more but was not considered dangerously ill. Father James W. Kirwin held services at the Ursulines Convent before the body was taken to Chalmette where it was laid away with military honors. Emmert was a bridge builder from Sherman, Texas where his company F was raised. The young soldier was only thirty-five years of age. This lengthy article about the frustration of being held ashore concluded with a compliment to the residents of the town: "The men are grateful for the kind treatment they received from the residents along the route of march, on Esplanade street. The long march had made them very thirsty and buckets of ice water were most welcome. These boys will be here sometime, and anything the good people of New Orleans will do for their comfort will be appreciated by the officers and men."[8]

One should never judge others by their looks. This seems to be the message as the reporter claimed there would be a "reversion of opinion" that would occur "by their present appearance." How different they would be at their homes. Supposedly there was one present in the regiment who the previous year sold at one time 10,000 head of two-year-old steers, all of them of one color. He had been to Europe several times. But even more surprising than this, in the regiment there was "a certain captain, who, upon his arrival in Cuba, will ask the commanding officer in charge of the troops there to give him 150 men, all mounted, to detach them from the command and let him act independent of the army. He has his men all picked out, all in Riché's regiment. He says he will do the rest, and if they don't carve out a name and render good service it will not be their fault."[9]

The colonel found a new place to drill the men, the City Park. Drills began at 7:00 a.m. for two hours and then again at 4:00 p.m. for two hours.

Again a shower drenched officers and men, "but that did not disturb them, for they went on marching and wheeling about and executing movements as if it was a bright, pretty afternoon in the cool of the fall." Spectators who were there to watch were driven to shelter by the rain. On August 2 the remains of Private Thomas Smith of E Company were interred. Smith had been shot by a guard when he refused to halt on his command. The young soldier survived long enough to admit that he knew he should have halted at the guard's command, but did not. No reason was given for this refusal. Father Kirwin was with him when he expired after giving him last rites. At the cemetery the priest said a few appropriate words, after which a detail gave the customary salute of twenty-four rounds. Then the bugler sounded taps and Private Thomas Smith, Company E, First U.S. Volunteer Infantry was laid away "to rest with honors that befitted a soldier and an American."[10]

The rain continued and due to the incessant downpour the camp was turned into a "wet, sloppy mud hole" with puddles at times ankle-deep. A small lake had formed in front of the headquarters tent and "the only way of reaching headquarters was by wading." How long these miserable conditions would continue no one could say.[11]

The weather did change and drills did continue. The camp on August 4 was renamed Camp Houston, although this did not alter the condition of the ground nor have a bearing on the hateful mosquitoes. The best news and most important event was the arrival of one thousand mosquito bars, which protected the men from that insect. The *Picayune* reporter noted that the one complaint of the men was the mosquitoes, which were "bigger and bite harder out at the camp than . . . in any other part of the city, and the poor fellows who, being unused to the variety that they have encountered out there, and having had to lie down to sleep and rest of nights without bars, have endured untold misery." With the mosquito bars in place the men could "lie down to pleasant slumbers, disturbed only at reveille." In addition to the arrival of the mosquito bars the fourth of August was pay day and that day several thousand dollars would be turned over to a regiment who would leave the greater part of it in New Orleans. The reporter was a realist and could appreciate that the soldiers would not save their money but spend it, either wisely or foolishly. By the end of the day the rain had been fairly absorbed into the ground and one "could walk about camp without bogging into mire several inches deep. On every side were to be seen tents with flaps thrown back and sides hoisted, in order for the sun and wind to dry things on the inside. Another such day as yesterday and the camp will be in shipshape condition."[12]

The best news for the regiment was not only that pay day had arrived and that the sun was shining but that word had come from Washington that Colonel Riché and his regiment would soon be on their way to Santiago de Cuba. For Captain Hall and every man there this meant they would see action, even though it might result in casualties in battle as well. In case there may have been a false report, Colonel Riché sent a telegram to the Adjutant General in Washington: "After learning the sanitary conditions in Cuba from General Shafter's report as published in this evening's paper, I have been requested by the officers of this regiment to inform you that the officers and men of this regiment are universally anxious to be permitted to go where they can render the greatest possible service to our army and our country." This was dated August 4. A telegram in reply came from Washington dated August 5, and was posted in front of headquarters: "Colonel Riche, New Orleans: In reply to your telegram to-day, I am instructed to say that the department appreciates this ready response of your regiment for duty in Santiago. The Berlin is en route for New Orleans. As soon as she reports you will embark your regiment without further orders or instructions from here. Report return of the Berlin and your departure." This was signed H.C. Corbin, Adjutant General. So now it was apparently only a matter of days before the regiment would pack up their tents and any other belongings and leave New Orleans, the mosquitoes, and the mud of Camp Houston. This bit of news "seemed like the good gift from some kind fairy" wrote the *Picayune* reporter. That same day Capt. Lee Hall of Company M was named officer of the day, and, as usual, the regiment was drilled morning and afternoon at the City Park. Until the *Berlin* arrived and the men embarked, it was to be a continuous routine. But certainly it would not be more than a week or so until they all shipped out to go to the battlefields of Santiago de Cuba.[13]

Occasionally Captain Hall experienced unusual activities at Camp Houston. On the night of Saturday, August 6, shortly after midnight, the guards reported to him as officer of the day "that a man on horseback was riding at breakneck speed up and down that part of the race track within the lines. Every time he would get in hailing distance of the sentinel he would wheel the steed about and go galloping off in the direction of the sentinels placed on the other side of the course. The night was so dark than the rider's identity could not be learned." This at least required Hall to investigate, and it was also a call to action. Taking with him his officer of the guard, Lieutenant O'Keefe, Hall stationed himself where the sentinel had been when he halted the mysterious rider. Hall was barely in position when out of the darkness appeared a giant figure on horseback, bearing directly down upon him. Hall jumped to one side to avoid being trampled and demanded "Halt! Who goes there?" "Begorra, and it's the colonel himself, sir" came back the response in pure Irish brogue. Hall ordered the guard to put "that colonel" in the guard house and have the horse locked up. Thus it happened that Lieutenant Colonel H. Hunt McCaleb, represented by Murphy, spent a night in the guardhouse.[14]

Incidents such as the mysterious rider galloping down on the captain were only a minor concern, only an interlude in the monotony of camp life. Of greater concern was the health of the regiment. The men were confined to an area where malaria was a real threat. Even the *Picayune* reporter recognized that, and expressed the fear that if the command were to remain a week longer with no change in the present conditions the "assertion may safely be made that whenever the First Regiment of United States Volunteer Infantry does leave New Orleans, it will leave filled with malaria." Each day more men were delivered to the hospital, the diagnosis being malarial fever, having been brought on, according to the beliefs of the day, by the wet ground upon which the men had to sleep.[15] Even Captain Hall suffered, indicating that he as captain had no better quarters than the men of his command. He informed the *Picayune* reporter who made a daily visit to Camp Houston that his feet had been wet for the last seven days, and that he was "not feeling at all well." None of the officers were extremely sick, but only suffered from "slight touches of malaria, due to wet feet and heavy mists."[16]

When would the steamer *Berlin* arrive? That was an unknown; as of the tenth of August it was still in quarantine. Perhaps it would arrive in New Orleans that evening or the next day, but it would have to be inspected and if there was a need for repairs or cleaning that would take some time. Otherwise it would be ready for the regiment to move out. A reporter for the *Times-Democrat* anticipated the *Berlin* would leave the New Orleans port for Santiago "not later than Monday [August 15]."[17]

Colonel Riché was receiving a significant amount of press coverage, even revealing the amount of money his volunteer troops were sending home, rather than spending their pay in a reckless manner. The *Times-Democrat* noted that in Company M of his regiment soldiers had deposited $327, "a substantial part of the balance drawn being sent away the same day." In Company C the "showing of frugality was remarkable." The entire regiment was tending to send much of their pay home to families. Captain Hall of Company M stated that about $3,000 was sent out of the city on pay day through the Wells, Fargo & Co.'s express alone. The total amount estimated being sent out of the city was between $6000 and $7000, "mainly consigned to wives and parents and dependent ones at home."[18]

No definite word had been received as to when the *Berlin* would arrive to take the regiment to Santiago de Cuba. The campgrounds were still difficult to walk on due to the rains and mists. In the meantime the men could try to find a place to dry their belongings. The number of men in the hospital increased during this time of waiting. Conditions in the hospital were far from ideal, although the Women's War Relief Association did continue to deliver items to those in the hospital. On August 11, they delivered twenty-five cots as a "free will offering."[19]

Still believing that the departure from Camp Houston was imminent men began preparations to leave. The thinking on Sunday the fourteenth was that by Tuesday or Wednesday they would be "steering down the river" to embark on the *Berlin*. This could not come too soon, as besides the privates who were filling the hospital floor and the few cots available, the officers were on the sick list. Lieutenant Chubb, Captain Hall, Lieutenant Colonel McCaleb, and others were suffering from malaria. The *Picayune* reporter was favorably impressed with the Texans, as he wrote that the trouble, "which is only malaria, is nothing serious. That more are not ill is a remarkable illustration of how exceedingly hardy and strong these Texans are."[20]

Hardy and strong the Texas regiment may have been, but a big disappointment was to challenge the entire body. The white soldiers who were looking forward to sailing away from New Orleans were astonished and disappointed to learn that it was Colonel Crane's "negro regiment," which was ordered in their stead to take to the ship. The whites would not be going to Santiago. The order making this abrupt change had been "sprung" at the last moment and without any kind of advance warning. It seemed to some that the War Department had "expressly intended to inflict a disagreeable surprise on the white troops who were eager to the last degree to get to the front." There was no apparent reason for the sudden change on the part of the military authorities in Washington. Many thought it was an intentional slight to the white Texans. Whether the thinking was right or wrong many of the Texans felt that the authorities in Washington intentionally mistreated the Texans as well as New Orleans, the "metropolis of the South." Their action reduced the possibility that they might gain prominence and public applause and attention. The only good result of this change of orders was that the regiment would not be sent into the "pesthole" from which General William Rufus Shafter, the "favorite of the Secretary of War" —Russell

Alexander Alger —was "fleeing." The *Picayune* advised that the Texans should not and must not seek to make the black troops responsible for their disappointment, as they had been powerless to work any change in the orders which sent them to the *Berlin* instead of the white troops. The responsibility entirely "comes from the War Department, where the war has been made from the first a game of politics and a means of advancing the Secretary's favorites." Thus was the conclusion of the *Picayune.*[21] Would Capt. Jesse Lee Hall ever see action again?

The steamer *Berlin* left the docks of New Orleans the evening of the seventeenth of August. One of the officers produced an appeal to the Secretary of War asking him for an investigation into the reasons why the white regiment was left behind. The communication was to be delivered in person by "a certain official from the city" to Secretary Alger. It was now a matter of seeking justice for the white regiment. Some believed the change was made because of the perceived want of discipline and insubordination among the whites. This thinking could not be the reason, opined the *Picayune* reporter, as even if there was some misconduct each man "would be branded as a man unfit to serve his country," which seemed to be an impossible act.

The regiment command became active. On August 17 Captain Hall traveled to Washington on the Louisville and Nashville Railroad to fight for the right to go to Santiago. Three days later, on Saturday the twentieth, Lieutenant Lewis R. Featherstone planned to leave for Washington, and Colonel Riché himself intended to follow shortly thereafter. "Who else will go is unknown, but no stone which might secure a trial by a court of inquiry will be left unturned" or so stated the *Picayune* reporter. The results of these actions would have to wait as Colonel J.W. Scully had completed arrangements with the Southern Pacific Railroad to move the regiment to Galveston. They would leave on August 18 to the new grounds, which they named Camp Hawley, named after Congressman R.B. Hawley.[22]

What were the charges leveled against the Texans who were now facing the possibility of being mustered out and sent home? A special report from Galveston published in the *Picayune* provided the list against the regiment, now identified as "Riché's Immunes." The charges were not to be discussed or revealed by those officers who had gone to Washington or had learned what they were, but the *Picayune* reporter learned from "a reliable source" what the alleged accusations were. They were as follows:

1) some members of the regiment had insulted respectable women on Canal Street of New Orleans;

2) some members of the regiment had attempted to take "improper liberties" with these respectable women on Canal Street;

3) there was the absence of a provost guard to search and take to camp recreants who had overstayed their leave;

4) there was the absence of a majority of the men from camp most of the time;

5) some soldiers had terrorized the town by shooting off their pistols in the streets and other unruly conduct;

6) the officers and men were guilty of failing to salute "the negro officers of Crane's immunes";

7) the officers of Riché's command did not show respect to each other in calling each other by their given names;

8) there was "promiscuous shooting" of guns and pistols in camp at all hours of the day;

9) the officers spent their time at the hotels instead of in camp with their commands.

These nine offenses were not all, but the "reliable source" could not recollect what the other charges were. As a result the officers held a meeting to determine what to do about these allegations. The result was that they denied them in toto and demanded an investigation to provide justice to the regiment "which has been maliciously maligned without reason." Congressman Hawley, whose name was now given to the Galveston camp, and who had been active in getting the regiment mustered in, now declared that if in his power the regiment would not be mustered out without a court of inquiry.[23]

Court of inquiry or not, the First U.S. Volunteer Infantry commanded by Colonel Riché was mustered out on Thursday, October 27, with most of the men leaving on the outgoing trains for their respective homes. Although most of the men were "highly gratified" to be civilians again, they also believed that they had been "shamelessly treated" by the War Department. Colonel Riché intended to assume the position of U.S. engineer in charge of harbor improvements in Galveston. He would hold the rank of captain in the United States Engineer Corps.[24]

An event of major importance which seemingly would prevent Hall from ever experiencing action again was that Spain and the United States came to peace talks by late December of 1898. The peace commission had met in France and by December 20 a translation of the Treaty of Paris was published in the *Washington Times*— even before the U.S. Senate had approved the final language. The treaty in full consumed nearly the entire page one of the *Times*, but essentially the points were that Spain renounced "all right of sovereignty over Cuba"; when evacuated it would be occupied by the United States. In addition Spain ceded to the U.S. the island of Guam as well as that of Puerto Rico, in addition to the archipelago of the Philippines. After the ratification of the treaty the United States would pay Spain $20,000,000. Colonel Theodore Roosevelt and Commodore George Dewey had become heroes because of their action in this "splendid little war" but Hall and his Immunes had missed out on all the action.[25]

The end of the "splendid little war" in Cuba was made official with the signing of the Treaty of Paris in 1898, but while this was taking place a young nationalist named Emilio Aguinaldo y Famy rose to power and declared Philippine independence on June 12, 1898. With Spanish territories now under its control the United States would not recognize Aguinaldo and consequently on February 4, 1899, Aguinaldo declared war on the United States. This young patriot, born in 1869 when Lee Hall was already earning his livelihood as a school teacher in Grayson County Texas, had now declared war on the most powerful nation on the face of the earth.[26] But now Aguinaldo was miles away where the action was.

Captain Hall like many others did not have a secure position to change to after being mustered out. He did return to Lebanon, Pennsylvania, at an unknown time. In response to the new war forming in the Philippines, Captain Hall was needed to raise companies and this occupied his time after the conflict in Cuba had ended. Hall's service record indicates he was mustered in as first lieutenant of Company L of the Thirty-third Regiment of U.S. Volunteer Infantry on July 28, 1899. With the recruits gathered in San Antonio in August 1899 the regiment numbered 1,090 men. Col. Luther Rector Hare received information on August 17 that led him to believe that the regiment would sail for Manila on or about October 25. Company L was organized with first lieutenant J. Lee Hall in command,[27] but for an unknown reason the captains were changed and the official roster shows Lee Hall as captain of Company M. T.N. Devine and J.U. Rogers were first and second lieutenants respectively. C.W. Starck was first sergeant. Five sergeants and one quartermaster, eight corporals, and sixty-eight privates made up the command under Captain Hall.[28]

The Lebanon *Semi-Weekly News* reported he had been spending "several days with his family" when he received orders to report to San Antonio to take charge of his company, attached to the Thirty-third Regiment, again made up entirely of volunteers. The regiment was now being filled up to its full quota and reportedly would be "among the first which will be sent to the Philippines, and is expected to leave inside of a week or two." Hall now could make definite plans; he would leave Saturday evening, July 29, 1899, going to Harrisburg where he would take the train to San Antonio.[29]

At San Antonio the regiment was in "Camp Capron" and shortly before riding the rails to San Francisco, some wrote letters home. Gilder H. "Reddie" Fields of Company L, Thirty-third U.S.V. Immunes, wrote to his hometown newspaper the *Mexia Ledger* about his experiences. He listed every part of his uniform and equipment, and pointed out that "the warmest thing of all is the Krag Jorgenson rifle. It is a beautiful little thing for the boys to amuse themselves with by keeping it clean." He mentioned two others, Willie Davenport from Hearne, Texas, and John Mayben, the first duty sergeant, and pointed out that he didn't think the company would sail before January 1, 1900. Unfortunately, of Captain Hall he only noted that he was in his company with no additional comment. But he obviously had respect for the captain thanks to the captain's concern for his men. He wrote, "Well I will tell you of my misfortune [.] I went out to a dance at Muth's garden last night and stayed until the guard lines were closed and got arrested and got put in the 'Pound Shop' —guard house, but only stayed in three hours and Capt. Hall came and got me out, so won't go to Muth's garden any more." Muth's Concert Pavilion was combined with a Beer Garden on Grayson Street. The talented proprietor Carl Beck brought not only popular music to the Alamo City but occasionally works by classical artists. One wonders if Private Fields that night enjoyed familiar songs or some works by Verdi, Beethoven, or Grieg.[30] Private Gilder H. Fields closed his letter with "I am your loving Reddie" suggesting nearly everyone knew him back in Mexia.[31]

Captain Hall didn't waste any time getting to his destination. In San Francisco, on September 30, the *Examiner* announced that the transport steamer *Sheridan* would sail for Manila with the Thirty-third Regiment of infantry and three companies of the Thirty-second. On the next day, Sunday, the *Glenogle* and the *Charles Nelson* were scheduled to move out with the remaining companies of the Thirty-second Regiment. The *Sheridan* carried nearly 2,000 volunteers; the other two ships carried 1,000 to 1,200 volunteers. The soldiers had left the Presidio Saturday afternoon, marching through San Francisco to the water front.[32] Finally Captain Hall would see action again, after the long voyage to the Philippines was over. Although Spain had ceded the Philippines, many of the Filipinos felt that the Treaty of Paris had only prevented their land from being occupied by the once superpower of Spain, but now was occupied by the United States, the world's new superpower. The fighting of the guerrillas, followers of a young patriot known as Aguinaldo, would last three years, not ending until 1902. Captain Hall would experience sufficient action in this conflict. Over 4,300 Americans would lose their lives and an untold number of Philippine fighters as well.

On their way to Manila, the troops stopped at Honolulu. There, the daily newspaper, the *Pacific Commercial Advertiser*, published a lengthy account of the arrival of the United States army transport, *Sheridan*, en route from San Francisco. From the California port to Honolulu on to Manila was a voyage that took weeks. Here is what the Honolulu newspaper had to say, in part, about the arrival of these soldiers: "Of all the new volunteer regiments that have come for a brief stay in Honolulu before departing for the battlefields of Luzon, there is none the individual history of whose men forms a more romantic chapter in the story of American valor than the command recruited from the plains of the southwest, which yesterday entered upon a short stay in Honolulu." The Thirty-third regiment of American volunteers docked at Oceanic wharf on Saturday, October 7, and set sail for Manila on October 8. The Honolulu paper continued:

> Col. [Theodore] Roosevelt, from a knowledge of his subject, said at the beginning of the recent war with Spain that "Uncle Sam or any other power could not get together a more formidable cavalry than the sun-browned, raw-boned, danger-tried rangers of the Texas frontier. And this is the stuff of which the thirty-third is largely made. It makes little difference that it is a regiment of infantry and not cavalry, for these picturesque stalwarts from the Lone Star state, the Indian Territory and Arkansas fight equally well afoot or ahorse. Many of them are direct descendants of the hardy Texans, who, under the leadership of brave Sam Houston, won freedom for the republic of Texas from Mexican rule. It was then that they took the name of Texas [R]angers, an organization

> which has been perpetuated to guard the state from incursions of Indians, raids of Mexican banditti and pillage of cattle thieves.

Captain Hall received special individual attention:

> A fine example of the Texas [R]anger is Capt. J. Lee Hall, who, as first lieutenant [*sic*], is in command of company L. Tall and sinewy, with face tanned by the frontier winds, he presents a commanding figure. He . . . has probably had more desperate encounters with border ruffians and desperadoes than any other man now alive. So thrilling have been his experiences that the Harpers have made him an offer to write the story of his life with Frederick [*sic*] Remington to illustrate the work.[33]

Unfortunately if indeed *Harper's Magazine* made the offer it did not materialize into a published product. Remington was able to add glory to those who climbed San Juan and Kettle Hills in Cuba, but so far as known he neither drew nor painted scenes of Lee Hall fighting in the Philippines. There he could have found wonderful subjects of western men in action, but that never occurred.

From California to the Hawaiian Islands is a lengthy journey but it is merely a third of the distance when traveling to the Philippines. From San Francisco to Hawaii was over two thousand miles; then from Hawaii to the Philippines was over five thousand. Doubtless many of the young soldiers crammed into the *Sheridan* were aware of that, but perhaps being young and seeking the glory of the battlefields the distance was of no concern. And how many were aware really of the makeup of the Islands, so many thousands of miles away? The Philippines were not just a small group of islands, but an archipelago, consisting of over 7,000 islands and islets. Manila was the capital city of a country prone to earthquakes and typhoons, altogether a different setting than most of the U.S. that soldiers were accustomed to. This country in Southeast Asia had been Spanish ever since the arrival of explorer Ferdinand Magellan in 1521 leading a conquering fleet for the Spanish empire.

Few details have surfaced relating Hall's actions in the Philippines. We know he acted heroically because he was brevetted captain of volunteers for gallant service in late 1899. Because of this he was ordered to San Francisco, California. General S.B.M. Young, under the Lawton expeditionary brigade, made the following recommendation in his official report,

> Lee Hall, First Lieutenant 33d Infantry, U.S.V., to be brevetted captain of Volunteers:
>
> For gallantry and meritorious service in action at Aringay, Province of Union, Luzon, P.I., November 19th, 1899, where, with great gallantry and good judgment, he led his company forward in the dark, waded the river under a strong fire from a superior and intrenched [*sic*] hostile force, and materially assisted in demoralizing and completely routing the enemy and capturing the works and the town, I recommend that First Lieutenant Lee Hall, 33rd Infantry, U.S.V., be brevetted captain of Volunteers.
>
> At Batagnos, a city of 15,000 inhabitants, Capt. Hall, with 20 Macabebes, held the enemy at bay for three hours until American troops came up. It was Company L, of the 33rd regiment, under Capt. Hall's command, who broke the record at target practice in San Francisco before they sailed for duty in the Philippines.

This received publicity in the *Lebanon Daily Times* where Mrs. Hall and daughters lived and was then reprinted in the *Greensboro Telegram*, Hall's hometown.[34] All of Hall's friends and family certainly became aware of this historic action.

Chapter Twelve

"There is the stamp of the battlefield upon his face"

—Nan Byxbee, *San Francisco Call*, October 14, 1900

In the Philippines Hall experienced an entirely new terrain and a new enemy. In this new landscape he experienced fighting in rice fields and enemy-filled irrigation ditches hidden by tall bamboo. Besides the common bolas there were the Krag-Jorgensen and Mauser rifles, weapons very different from the Colt .45s and Winchesters so common in Texas. Hall had a brand-new group of scouts to work with in the fight against rebel leader Emilio Aguinaldo y Famy: the Macabebes scouts. Cornelius Gardener, colonel of the Thirtieth Infantry, U.S. Volunteers, wrote in his report to Adjutant General Theodore Schwan: "The Macabebe scouts, under Lieutenants [William C.] Geiger and Hall, were attached to my command during the greater portion of the time. These officers were frequently exposed to fire and displayed courage and coolness. The Macabebes, although valuable in discovering an enemy, are very poor shots."[1]

William C. Geiger, a lieutenant of Schwan's Expeditionary Brigade, prepared a report of action in early January 1900. This detachment, consisting of five officers and 140 men, was divided into two companies, commanded by First Lieutenant J. Lee Hall of the Thirty-third Infantry, and First Lieutenant James A. Blount Jr., Twenty-ninth Infantry. The command left San Pedro Macati during the afternoon of January 4 and marched beyond Pateros and there camped for the night. On January 5 they reached Muntinlups without any resistance. On January 6, about one and one-half miles from Muntinlups the enemy fired on them from rice fields on the front and from a high hill to their right. Hall's company was sent to the left of the road to engage the enemy who were entrenched in an irrigation ditch, which was concealed by very thick bamboo. The second company was sent to the right of the road to engage the enemy on the high hill. The skirmish lasted about thirty minutes. Colonel Gieger estimated the enemy numbered two hundred but they were driven off, retreating toward Binan. He estimated the enemy had lost fifteen killed and wounded and lost fifteen rifles.

On the morning of January 9 Lieutenant Hall and fifteen hand-picked Macabebes were ordered to report to Colonel Gardener, Thirtieth Infantry. During the next few weeks Hall and the scouts scouted and occasionally engaged the enemy. Gieger reported that by February 3 thirteen guns had been captured and 1200 rounds of ammunition. In addition he included this cryptic line: "Fourteen horses fell into our hands, which we were unable to give receipts for." Lieutenant Geiger concluded his report by complimenting Lieutenant Blount with his good work, and "The work of Lieutenant Hall . . . during the whole expedition was of the highest order."[2]

On January 9 Hall with fifteen Macabebe scouts under his command and a squad of sharpshooters under command of Lieutenant Guy A. Boyle, proceeded by way of Alfonso and Bailen to Naic. The group left Indang at 5:00 p.m. and reached Alfonso three hours later, without incident. They made camp at Marajou for the night. The next morning they discovered the enemy was advancing. Preparations were made for a battle.

> Battle formation, with Lieutenant Hall and Macabebe scouts, and advance guard under Lieutenant Tompkins, as a first line, and company L, Captain Newberry, as right wing, and company K, Lieutenant McCabe, as left wing, of the second line, was quickly made without halting, and firing was commenced on the enemy, who deployed and returned the fire, and then broke and fled precipitately. Colonel [Crisostomo] Riel and 5 of the enemy were captured during the skirmish. Colonel Riel was colonel of the Second (insurgents) Regiment of the rear guard of General Trias' army, retreating from Noveleta. Pursuit of the enemy was kept up for about 1 ½ miles, until stopped by a ravine.[3]

Lieutenant Hall also prepared a report of this action but did not date it. He reported that he had left Silan the morning of January 9, attached to Colonel Gardener's command of the Thirtieth Infantry. He and his scouts first marched to Indang and then on to Alfonso. On the tenth they left Alfonso and continued on to Magallance. "About 4 miles out from [Magallance] surprised and captured two outposts of the enemy, taking 3 prisoners, with their arms. About 300 yards farther on we captured Colonel Riel, the commander of the Insurgent battalion, together with 3 soldiers, 1 rifle, and 2 horses."

Then, after only a short distance, Hall and his Macabebes came in contact with the advance guard of the enemy battalion. They charged and engaged— "dispersed after a short skirmish." Then two miles farther on they came upon the enemy outside of the town of Magallance. "A few well-directed volleys from my scouts and a company of the Thirtieth Infantry disposed them promptly," Hall wrote. Then Hall and the command left Magallance on the morning of the twelfth and marched on to Bailen and then on to Alfonse. They continued with a march to Bayuyungan on Lake Taal. They left there on the morning of the thirteenth and marched on to Talisay where they were joined by General Schwan. Hall concluded his report by saying they then marched on to Santa Tomas, then left for Janauan where they joined up with the main body of the Macabebe scouts.[4]

Much later, after Hall left the Philippines and was in San Francisco, California, noted journalist "Nan Byxbee" interviewed Captain Hall for the Sunday edition of the *San Francisco Call*.[5] Not only was this an important contribution to knowledge about this period of Hall's life but an artist was employed to illustrate what was certainly a near fatal accident. It was this accident which resulted in his being honorably discharged.

We are to presume the interview took place in a comfortable setting with reporter Byxbee taking copious notes and Hall calmly smoking his pipe. He had only recently returned from the Philippines. Byxbee quotes Hall: "Yep," began Hall, "that was a wild night— that night with the Macabees,[6] when I went over the precipice, horse and all, and got crippled in this way. I have gone through many a thrilling experience since the year of '70, but that took the shine off of all of 'em.[7] I have fought the redskins out in the Territories, chasin' 'em with the Texas Rangers and doing a lot of hair-breadth escape acts, but nothin' ever seemed to come home to me and make my hair come so high a-standing up on my head as the doings of that night did."

Byxbee's questions are not recorded so one receives the continued narration of Hall's adventures:

> We were out after a tough set of insurgents— you know the Macabee Scouts were organized by the Spaniards before Uncle Sam took a hand in that little Philippine game. The Macabees were the loyal Filipinos and they wuz fightin' against the rebellious Tagalos, which were headed by Aguinaldo and his gang o' cut-throats, claiming to represent art, music and literature in the highest degree. We hev knocked some of that foolishness out of 'em in the course of the past two years. The Macabees came over to the Americans when we run the Spaniards out, and Uncle Sam put 'em to work. Well, these Macabees wuz sailin' in and fightin' like good fellows, when I was sent down there to take charge of 'em on the island of Luzon and I found 'em a mighty husky lot.

Byxbee may have interrupted Hall any number of times, suggesting thoughts to him that he might not otherwise have mentioned. He again referred to his experience with American Indians.

> I knowed a good deal about Injuns and the kind o' scouts they made in the old Texas Ranger days, and the Macabees can come pretty nigh to holdin' a candle to the redskins for cunning and endourance [*sic*]. A white man, you know, wouldn't ever set more'n an hour in one place, keepin' his eyes peeled for events and situations— he hain't got the patience— but one of them little brown devils'll set and set all day, never movin' an eyelash, watchin' over the p'int of some ridge and skinnin' his optics for some insurgents and their plans. He knows where to troll and where a dog loses scent he can take it up by his infernal spy instincts and folly it out to the end, and here is something interestin' at the end, too.

Captain Hall had indeed learned a great deal about Indians, especially from his brief tenure as agent at Anadarko, Indian Territory.

> Ah' my! But them fellers are heatherns! They hain't far behind the Injuns for cruelty, and the main trouble thet Uncle Sam had after he began usin' em against the insurgents wuz in restrainin' 'em. They would light out and kill everything in sight, never stoppin' at wimmin and children, or hesiatin' about doin' the most dastardly things. They reveled in that sort of thing, but they made mighty good scouts when they wuz under proper control.

Perhaps at this point Bixby chose to get to the main thrust of the interview, that being Hall's own action that resulted in his being injured. Bixby had perhaps heard enough about the heathen aspects of the Macabebes. Hall continued:

> Well, this night which I wuz startin'to tell y'u about, we wuz chasin' a lot o' the brown devils that had played smash with some of Uncle Sam's boys— the sneakin' things had crept up and surprised a small detachment of the boys in blue,[8] and hed caught some o' 'em away from camp. They wa'n't content to kill 'em, they hed let 'em live, but had cut the poor fellers all up— it's a trick

> o' theirs to cut the leaders in the heels, renderin' the victum's legs useless forever. Well, they had fixed three ov the boys thet way, and they had killed some more. The poor fellers came crawlin' into camp draggin' themselves along, weak from loss of blood and knowin' themselves hopelessly crippled for life. I heard of it and hed orders to get out and give chase. I rounded up my scouts, about twenty-five of 'em, and we started out. We didn't know how many o' the enemy we hed to look for— but thet was our business to find out. It was one o' them nights with patches o' clouds hangin' round and shuttin' out a stragglin' moon; we knew the devils had skinned out pretty lively and thet we had a journey afore us. The Macabees was wild, an' I hed to keep a sharp eye on' em. I called 'em all up an' gave 'em the speel about what 'ud happen to 'em if they disobeyed orders— Uncle Sam wa'n't goin' to hev no foolishness, and they knowed who was runnin' thet expedition, etc.

One cannot help but wonder just how much of Hall's "speel" the Macabebes really understood.

> They took it all in, sayin' nothin' but gruntin' and restless to get at their trailin'. I started 'em out in different directions, afoot, and kept to the middle myself, as I war' the only officer with 'em that night. I was follyin' a little brown feller named Sam-bo-lan— we called him "Sambo" for short. He hed eyes like a spaniel, little and sharp and well peeled. I could see him ahead by the patches o' moonlight, sneakin' through the grass and squattin' patiently at every sound for half an hour to see if it wa'n't somethin' worth investigatin'. When he'd half straighten up his naked body and give the quick little beckonin' sign I would come along behind, on my horse. When I couldn't see him he would rise up and let out a funny little screechin' sound thet meant it was all right.

Hall at this point appeared to be attempting to heighten the excitement of his narrative with descriptive words.

> Waal, it kep' getting' darker and darker and the clouds wuz skimmin' along the sky all fired fast, fur a wind hed sprung up and

> a storm wuz threatenin'. The calls kep' comin' across the knolls, low and soft, but so you could hear 'em a long ways. The Macabees wuz follyin' the trails. The call wuz a peculiar sound thet none but a Filipino can make— a kin' of a long drawn out note, soft and melodious— "coo-ee, coo-ee." Every time it 'ud come Sambo 'ud answer, from the middle of the line, and we kep' creepin' along. When we hed been out two ur three hours the big drops o' rain begin to splash and it didn't take us long to git soppin' wet, but thet did'nt faze the Macabees. Waal, I wuz joggin' along on my horse, thinkin' o' nothin' in particular, when I see Sambo straighten up, just a little ways ahead, and give a half-dozen o' the calls, kin' o' alarmed like, and scentin' danger. He was answerin' a call from the scouts off to the left. I hedn't heard it at all. There wuz trouble ahead. They hed come up on a bunch o' insurgents of the art, music and literature class, and there wuz somethin' doin'. I hed all I could do to keep up with Sambo. The little brown feller heeled it like a hound after a hare. We went tearin' over the slick grass, the big raindrops fallin' and my horse guessin' at where he wuz goin' to put his feet next. In two or three minutes the fun begin, and we could hear Mauser rifle bullets a-singin' around in all directions. It wuz like a hornet's nest they hed run into, and the hornets were objectin' like the dooce. Just about thet time the lightnin' begin to flash, and light things up. We hed got into a clump of trees, a regular jungle, where hangin' vines wuz stretched across to throw a feller down, and the brush and things scratched us up, but we got down to fightin' and it didn't take us long to get them fellers runnin'. There couldn't a been many o' the insurgents, and I guess the noise we made shootin' into their camp made 'em think we wuz a whole army. A jagged flash o' lightnin' come acrost the sky, and I see three dead insurgents layin' in the grass, and one feller hed throwed up his hands and was fallin' to the ground right ahead o' my horse, not more'n a hundred feet away. Then the Macabees went wild.

One can almost feel Hall himself getting more and more excited in narrating this incident.

> They wuz goin' after that camp o' Aguinaldo men to beat the band, clost handed, with their long blades, and was prepared fur

killin' and lootin' to the queen's taste, but I yelled out at 'em to stop it or they'd get Government bullets through their black hides, and p'intin' my gun at one o' 'em thet hed a woman by the hair I commanded him to throw up his hands. Thet put a stop to that kind o' business, but a lot o' my scouts were missin', gone on the dead run chasin' the fleein' Filipinos.

There wuz the dyin' woman and some more dead insurgents in the camp, but the rest had fled and had made a stand further on. I heard the shootin' and yellin' and made tracks through the brush as fast as I could get thar, bein' half dragged off the horse and scratched with the brush an' thorns, an' Mausers comin' uncomfortable close with that friendly zip o' theirs. Well, the devils were cornered and they hate the Macabees wors'n the Americanos. They wouldn't surrender ez long as they could put up a ghost ov a fight. I see by the lightnin' two of our scouts layin' dead and more of 'em fightin' hand to hand with blades. I went tearin' on in the dark, lashin' my horse and tryin' to round up my scouts fur some system of fightin' or withdrawin' until we could see what to do, but they wuz at it good and hard an' I might as well o' tried to get hold o' so many whirlwinds. Nex' thing I knew I wuz right in the midst o' the enemy an' wuz gettin' fired at and two fellers wuz after me with knives. I knocked one of 'em flat with the butt of my rifle and put a bullet through the other one. I had got hit in the arm an' it wuz stingin' like fury— the flesh all tore away with one o' them darned Mausers. Then there was a mighty thrillin' minute fur me. A deafenin' big peal o' thunder come and then a flash o' lightnin' and I see dead Filipinos all around me, more a fightin' an' a gun barrel leveled at my head. Just at the same minute my horse reared up an' I see I wuz on the edge of a precipice by the flash o' lightnin,' the tops o' trees and scraggy shrubs down below, and my horse leapin' wild, payin' no attention to the bit, fur I had lost control of him with the terror o' the fight, the storm and the dark all combined. I am sure I can't say I war fond of the combination myself, especially the next minute, when I heard that gun go off and could feel myself reel in the saddle, the horse leapin' in the air, and then I went down and down till it seemed like I'd never stop and landed at the bottom, senseless. The gun hadn't hit me, but the horse had jumped over the precipice, and when I begin

> to git conscious with the rain beatin' in my face and that howlin' storm and fightin' still goin' on, I thought it wuz all up with old Cap. Hall, who wuz said to be a hero of two wars and hadn't ought ter die that way.
>
> I shet my eyes and tried to make out if I wuz hurt much or not, but I wuz about done up. My leg was numb and I couldn't move it. The next flash o' lightnin' showed me why. My dead horse was layin' on it. After a while, ez I was layin' there, indulgin' in the luxury of a quiet groan, as I thought unbeknownst to anybody. I heard a sneakin' noise in the bushes, and lookin' up I see a naked brown form of a Filipino crawlin' toward me with a big shinin' knife. It looked mighty like a wicked face, peerin' through the brush at me, in the light o' a jagged streak o' the lightnin', and I can see him yet peerin' round with them sharp eyes o' his'n', one hand braced ag'in a long vine stringer thet wuz stretched across, and the other a-holdin' the long knife, with his body crouched and creepin' toward me. I guess I must a-swooned.

At this point Nan Byxbee as well as the readers of the *Call* must have breathlessly wondered how could Captain Hall survive this predicament, and Hall, who has revealed he had a sense of humor relating this experience, was enjoying the suspense as well. He continued:

> When I next knowed anything I found myself on a stretcher bein' carried by them darned scouts o' mine, joggin' along over the rough places and bouncin' around on the stretcher, but they wuz true blue, and they carried me ten mile back to camp. The little brown fellers wuz skeered because they had gone wild and wuz afraid that I would hev 'em all killed, but they wouldn't walk off and leave me there to die any way. The Filipino I had seen comin' to kill me wuz only Sambo comin' to drag me out. They had put the insurgents to flight, what they hadn't killed, and wuz ready to go home and take their lickin' like a small boy for the devilment they had done. O' course, they got their lecture, but somehow after they hed carried me through thet storm, over thet rough wild country, when I wuz more'n three-quarters dead any way, I couldn't seem to be very stern with the little brown devils, and I hed to let 'em

> off with a lecture. But they hed played the dooce with thet crowd o' insurgents. Thar wan't much left o' thet camp, I tell you. If you give them a chance them little brown Macabees will knock most anything a-windin' — all they need is to be turned loose.

At this point Captain Hall paused in his narration, sat back, refilled his pipe and straightened up — standing all of five feet and ten inches. He had finished and had provided the reporter with good copy. Byxbee noted that "there is the stamp of the battlefield upon his face, and though his gray hair and his 55 years entitle him to the life of a peaceful American citizen out of the military, it is a life of which Captain Hall knows little." But Lee Hall was still a soldier, and it was with "the greatest reluctance that the old man has obeyed orders to report at Washington, where he is to be honorably discharged for disability." Byxbee continued by explaining that opposite his name on the military records there was a note of many brave acts during his service, "and not the dullest among them, as told by the captain himself, is the tale of his night with the Macabebes."

Hall had the last word: "It's pretty tough" he said regretfully, "it's pretty tough for an old warhorse like me to hev to go back to the stable. I'm not very badly knocked out, and you needn't be surprised to see me turn up in the next war, if it comes in the course of the next twenty years. I ain't dead yet."[9] Was the dramatic incident of the heavy storm, the killings and precipice a truthful account? Some readers may have doubted the truthfulness, but an affirmation that what Hall told to reporter Byxbee had already appeared in the hometown newspaper of Mrs. Hall, so we believe the incident happened; Bessie C. Hall may have learned of it from reading in the *Lebanon Courier*. That article's headline read simply "Injured Himself" and reminded the readers that Hall, "former captain of the Texas Rangers" had arrived at El Paso from Manila, on leave, pending his discharge. "He has been in charge of the Maccabee [*sic*] scouts" the article continued, "and while leading a night scout several months ago fell over a cliff and was injured."[10]

Hall had left El Paso and was back in San Antonio, a much more familiar territory by Sunday evening, September 30, so reported the *San Antonio Express.* He met many friends and talked "interestingly and instructively of the Philippines and their people, and of events that are transpiring over there." The subject of the upcoming election was also discussed. "There is no organized force in opposition to the United States authority in the islands but the soldiers are being harressed [*sic*] by bands of bushwhackers, who waylay our men in unexpected places. Even this show of resistance would not obtain were it not for utterances and policy of the democracy on this side." According to Hall, the Tagalogs, enemies of the Macabebes, were under the impression that if candidate William Jennings Bryan were elected the American president forces would be withdrawn and returned to the United States, leaving them in "undisputed possession." But if McKinley were elected the Tagalogs "would surrender without a murmur." Believing that those soldiers fighting in the islands were friendly to the present administration, that they were "tired of chasing outlaws who are promised immunity from punishment if they can keep out of sight until a new power is created in Washington which will forgive them sedition, rebellion and the rest of it," Hall admitted being a Democrat, "but I don't like the policy of a party which incites armed rebellion, even indirectly, to one's country." President McKinley, Hall's Commander in Chief, was a Republican.

Hall set aside politics at this point, saying of the Texas men now in the Philippines: "[T]here are no braver or more efficient soldiers under the flag than these men. Their record is among the best, for the death rate has been larger . . . in action or from wounds received than any other regiment's[.] . . . Their valor and readiness is already a matter of history. I am now speaking of the thirty-third regiment."

Of the Philippines, Hall pointed out that they were "the most beautiful country in the world and some times I think they are worth the blood and money paid for them." It would be okay for Americans to invest in the Philippines whenever quiet was restored, as Manila, a city of 500,000 people "under the fostering care of American institutions" would become "the queen city of the Orient." In case the reader did not already know, the *Express* pointed out that Captain Hall was in San Antonio on sick leave and would possibly leave the service due to being "permanently disabled by a fall from a precipice not long since, while on detached service on the islands." Hall was the center of attention that day, and seemingly everybody wanted to shake his hand.[11]

Hall had gained considerable experience in the Philippines but what he had accomplished was only a small part of the larger military feat. Brian McAllister Linn sums it up succinctly: "[Hall and the] 33rd's experience in the Philippines was primarily that of a counter-insurgency force. Most of this anti-guerrilla work was spent as a garrison force in a relatively small area. Most of the men continued to see the war in very simple terms, bordered by the confines of their station and the surrounding areas. . . . Although probably resented as an occupation force, the 33rd's men did not provoke protests or uprisings in any of the towns. Rape, billeting, looting, the taking of hostages, deportations, mass arrests, and other abuses often associated with military rule did not occur in the 33rd's area."[12]

From San Antonio and the excitement of hand-shaking, Captain Hall returned to Lebanon to visit his family. He had not seen his wife and daughters since before leaving for the Philippines, so it must have been an extraordinary happy reunion. He was not only with his family but society wanted a piece of him as well. A report from Lebanon appeared in the *Reading Times* of Reading, Pennsylvania, which stressed Hall's change from being a lifelong Democrat to supporting Republican McKinley as he had "repudiated Bryan doctrines." Hall explained that in July 1898, "with a number of other Democrats," he enlisted for service in the Philippines, believing that the conflict there was a war, but when he got there he realized that the United States soldiers were fighting small bands of guerillas. After a few months in the Philippines he found that a number of Democrats and leaders of the Democratic party were sending documents saying that if Bryan was elected, the Filipinos "would have absolute freedom, and intimated that if the war was kept up it would have a bad effect on the chances of McKinley." To Hall this was an "underhand method" and "the traitorism disgusted me with Democracy and its followers. I went to the Philippines as a Democrat. I fought, bled and almost died for my country, and I came home believing that McKinley is right and that such treachery as adopted by the Democratic party will only add to his majority." In Hall's mind, if the insurgents following Aguinaldo were victorious, they believed they would have complete freedom. "Give them freedom and one of the blackest pages of bloodshed ever recorded in history will be written."[13]

The Good Samaritan Hospital of Lebanon endeavored to have Hall give a lecture on the Philippines.[14] The advertisement indicated that there was a "movement on foot" to induce Hall to give a public lecture on the Philippines for the benefit of the hospital. The notice pointed out that Hall "has a splendid record as a soldier and his experiences in the Orient would form an interesting lecture. We trust he will consent to give such a lecture in the near future . . . . The man, the lecture and the cause would be a strong combination."[15] We presume Hall did give a lecture; it was definitely a fundraiser as a later announcement about it said the Good Samaritan hospital was "in need of more money."

Capt. Lee Hall appeared as a witness before the Senate Committee on the Philippines, which was a standing committee of the U.S. Senate and held testimony from 1899 to 1921. It had been established by Senate resolution on December 15, 1899, five days after the Peace Treaty of Paris had been signed but before the treaty had been ratified. Its purpose was to oversee the administration of the Philippines.[16] The main question apparently was the treatment of the Tagalogs who were the deadly enemies of the Macabebes. The questions concerned the use of what was called "the water cure." Hall testified on May 15 and claimed he had only heard of instances of this method of torture but had not seen one in use. To Hall, the water cure was no worse in its effect than the native wine. According to Hall the Filipino prisoners were treated as well as American soldiers, except that those prisoners were made to work.[17] Senator Charles Henry Dietrich of Nebraska called attention to an illustration published in *The Commoner*, a newspaper of which William Jennings Bryan was editor and proprietor. The illustration showed a typical Macabebe scout— "Our Ally" —as "a naked negro" holding a short knife with Aguinaldo— "Our Enemy"— in full uniform holding a sword. These were not photographs but drawings by an unidentified artist. The caption under the Aguinaldo drawing read: "Whatever can be said of the Filipino insurgents can be said of the Apache Indian. Everything that can be said of Aguinaldo could have been said of Sitting Bull." The quotation is credited to one of President Roosevelt's campaign speeches. Beneath the drawing of the Macabebe was the caption: "The heartiest praise is due large numbers of natives for their steadfast loyalty. The Macabebes have been conspicuous for their courage and devotion to the flag. I recommend that the secretary of war take some systematic way of aiding these crippled in our service and caring for the families of those who are killed."[18]

The drawing was less than accurate. Hall informed the committee that the Macabebe was a Malay, not a Negro, and that when he was serving as a soldier he was clothed, not "naked" or wearing only a loin cloth. He also informed the committee that the Filipino was not ready for self-government. Hall further explained that he had had a conversation with General Henry Ware Lawton in which the general had said that the natives should be treated considerately, because "by and bye they would be our people."

The "water cure" apparently was of real concern to members of the committee. Some form of torture using water had been in use since the 1500s but during the Spanish-American War the torture consisted of forcing the victim's mouth open, his nose pinched shut, and a funnel placed in the open mouth. Water, brine, or urine was then poured into the funnel. The victim had to swallow it in order not to drown. It resulted in gastric pain to the extent that sometimes it resulted in death to the victim.

Hall could only explain that he had known of cases of this treatment being administered to prisoners, but the use of it had been "largely discontinued by the natives toward the latter part of his stay in the Philippines."

As for the comparative mortality of the American and Philippine forces in battle, Hall indicated that in general there were three natives lost to one American killed. A final question from Senator Fred Thomas Dubois of Idaho dealt with independent government. Captain Hall responded that he considered that there was much good in the native Filipino, but there was no immediate chance for an independent government, but that "in time they would come to be a good people."[19] Hall reportedly also said that he considered the Filipinos "much like the Mexicans of 25 or 30 years ago and felt that for the present at least they would require a strong government."[20]

With Captain Hall out of the service he realized the wounds from previous adventures would affect him the rest of his life. He now experienced real concerns about his future. He was in no position to remain in Lebanon where his family was, at least Bessie C., so the conclusion was that he would have to enter into some type of employment. A career in Washington with its politicians was not for him, even though he might have made some type of a relationship with President Theodore Roosevelt, the former vice president who took over the top position after the assassination of William McKinley on September 14, 1901. Hall did do some traveling, although perhaps more in search of employment than enjoyment. He was in South Texas in late 1903. The *Victoria Advocate* reported that he was in the city from Kansas City "to mix for a few days with many friends here."[21] No explanation as to why he was in Kansas City has yet been located. Five weeks later he may have still been in the area as the *Advocate* now reported he was in the city and "intends to remain several days."[22]

Glimpses of what the man was doing are occasionally found in the newspapers. On May 22 he was in Austin on business "of a nature that smacks of the old time perils which he was wont to encounter in his more youthful days." Did not the reporter suggest what he was about to do was as dangerous as when he was a ranger captain? While in Washington and New York for the several months before, he had met a representative of a wealthy mining company, possibly Gideon Giroux, who owned mines in the Yaqui Indian country of Sonora, Mexico. The result was that Hall now had a contract to guard the gold shipments from the mines to the railroad. Hall was in Austin trying to find some of his companions to hire as guards of the gold bullion car. Hall needed six men and he called at the adjutant general's office to help him find where the men were now. "I have been overwhelmed with applications from men who want a job in the dangerous work, but I have turned them all down. I want to obtain the services of some of my old men if possible, men who have been tried in Indian fights before and found to be all right."

The job required brave men to haul the bullion from the Giroux mine to Carbo Station in an armored automobile that Giroux had especially built for that purpose. The distance of this dangerous trek was twenty-eight miles. Hall and the guards would not ride in the car but along on horseback. All traffic between the mines and the railroad had been suspended due to the raids of the Yaqui Indians. During the first ten days of April shipments from the Sultana mine had been attacked several times, with five teamsters killed. An incident happened in April that may have been the reason the Giroux firm chose to hire an experienced fighting man like Hall. On April 14 a dozen Yaqui Indians attacked a small party on the road between the Sultana Mine and Rayon, Sonora, Mexico. Samuel Williams was killed, riddled by numerous bullets; Bert Cunningham, an employee and son-in-law of the mine owner, was seriously wounded; Louis Giroux, the son of the mine superintendent, heroically defended the ore wagon and the other passengers— Mr. and Mrs. Bert Cunningham, their child and accompanying nurse. The Mexican teamster and two members acting as an escort hurriedly fled from the scene. The young Giroux, not yet quite eighteen, proved his valor in bravely standing by his people and preventing the massacre which would certainly have happened if he had not defended the group so well.[23] The position was indeed a dangerous one, just what Hall liked and needed. For his services Hall would receive an annual salary of $5,000. Hall left for San Antonio the night of the twenty-second.[24]

The armored car was to be ready by June 1, 1906. By mid-June he was in San Antonio where he was organizing the guard. News of the Yaqui attack was still fresh in people's minds and rumors floated about that Hall was organizing his rangers to *exterminate* the Yaquis; wisely the press attempted to squash those rumors. A special from San Antonio printed in the *Dallas News* of May 28, 1906, reported that the captain had been in San Antonio to organize a guard for the shipment of gold from mines in the Yaqui country. Hall selected five men, all of whom had been members of the Thirty-third regiment "and their courage and endurance have been proven." The group planned to leave on the Southern Pacific Railroad for El Paso on Thursday morning, May 31. The guard proved to be Claude S. Bullock of Denison; John C. Carlisle of San Antonio; Henry L. Ransom of Hempstead; Robert L. Haggard of Denton County; and William Resner. Their destination was Sonora, Mexico.[25] Hall certainly appreciated being the commander of a small group of men who would engage in protecting a valuable shipment of gold from thieves, bringing back memories of protecting Campbell's store back in Atascosa County in 1879.

On June 5 Hall and his five guardsmen passed through El Paso en route to the Sonora country with high hopes for real action. The *El Paso Morning Times* added this curious line in their report: "He expects to shortly be joined by his family."[26] Does that mean Bessie C. and the daughters intended to join him in Mexico? Perhaps there would be accommodations in Carbo, state of Sonora, a community which had been founded in 1888 after the railroad reached there and which became a supply depot for the area merchants. Hall and his guard knew there would be danger, as Mexico was in the throngs of another revolution, not to mention the probability of angry Yaquis, *bandidos*, and numerous other forms of riffraff eager to pillage whatever they could from Anglos, such as the guardian of the ore shipments, former ranger Jesse Lee Hall.

In spite of what the El Paso newspaper reported, the *Austin Statesman* of the same date indicated facing danger would be a real threat to Hall and his guard. "With the recent slaughter of Americans by Mexicans" advised the press release from San Antonio dated June 4, "the mission of Captain Lee Hall and his handful of men for the Yaqui country to guard the gold to be taken from the mines to the railroads for shipment is regarded as a more perilous undertaking than was at first supposed." The advisory continued by warning that Hall's guard, consisting of only six men, was "fraught with danger from the time they set foot on Mexican soil" and judged the number was insufficient, that "the guard should be composed of sixty men." Captain Hall did not want any more than the group he had selected because he "did not wish to arouse the suspicions of the Mexican government officials that he was making an invasion of the country."[27]

In spite of recent news reports and rumors, the danger did not appear. The men of Hall's command riding along outside the armored "gold car" had no difficulty riding from the mine to Carbo Station. There were certainly men who would prefer to challenge the shipments but it soon became obvious that Hall and his men presented too great a risk for the *bandidos*. Frank Mathews, former San Antonio policeman, visited the Yaqui country and wrote to friends in San Antonio that since his arrival there he had not seen a single Indian "who seemed to be dangerous." He wrote that he had seen a number of men "who looked like ordinary Mexicans and who were pointed out to him as Indians" but they were tame. Although the country was very wild they were all having an easy time. Captain Hall also wrote that he wanted another good man, and two who were intending to join Hall were Leonardo Garza Sr. and his son José Garza who were preparing to go to the Yaqui country to accept "good positions" under Captain Hall.[28]

The contract with Captain Hall lasted less than a year, which meant that after that time he was again in a position of searching for new opportunities, or at least a new job. A report in the *Houston Post* mentioned Frank Mathews, "recently a member of the Lee Hall company," as having come from protecting the armored car from Yaqui attacks and now planning to have a little vacation. He predicted that there would be serious trouble on Mexican Independence Day, September 16. The feelings of animosity against the Americans had grown to "a deep hatred" and the "peons" were only waiting for the right opportunity to strike against them. If serious trouble did arise then the Americans would truly be "on their own."[29]

What influence Captain Hall and his brave guard had on the region that the bronco Yaqui made so dangerous cannot now be determined. Apparently anyone intending to attack the armored car with Hall and his men guarding it changed their mind as they experienced no attack. Historian Dora Neill Raymond asserted that with Hall in the area the region became so peaceful that his services were no longer needed, and consequently he was again unemployed. Perhaps the presence of Hall's guards protecting shipments from the mine to the railroad resulted in the country becoming peaceful, but there may have been other factors involved. [30]

Hall and his men had become known as La Sultana Rangers,[31] certainly a throwback to the days of Hall leading the Special State Troops of the 1870s. By April 1907 the group, "famous" according to the San Antonio and Austin newspapers, were to be disbanded, having been in existence more than a year. A review of the force reported that Hall recruited the company and with "twenty picked men he undertook to guarantee the safe transfer of the bullion." During that year the company did not lose "a single load of bullion." Reportedly "Hall's men had more than half a hundred encounters with the Indians . . . but came off victorious in every instance." Further, only three of the original Las Sultanas Rangers were killed in the attacks, but "possibly more than 100 of the Yaquis were killed." No matter how effective Hall and his rangers were, once the railroad spur connecting the mines with the main branch of the Sonora line was completed, there was no need for Hall's services.[32]

Research has failed to determine if this report was totally accurate; no other source references three of Hall's men being killed in action. An additional statement remains suspect, but is not improbable considering the social mores of the time and place. José Garza, a San Antonio recruit, had returned home to San Antonio by April. He stated that "during the time the rangers were not guarding the armored auto they spent their time in the mountains hunting down the Yaqui Indians like they would wild beasts. The savages were tracked from one place to another and shot down wherever seen."[33]

Chapter Thirteen

"He never sent his men where danger was greatest. That part of the work he assumed himself"

— *San Antonio Express*, March 18, 1911

The final years for Jesse Leigh "Lee" Hall were not happy ones. Pondering his past he could see that he had not left a legacy for his family, other than his reputation as a Texas Ranger. He was suffering from old wounds— some from his ranger days and some from the Philippine Insurrection days. In spite of saving fortunes in gold from Yaqui marauders he was far from being financially independent. His family was back east and although he could enjoy occasional visits with Bessie C. and their daughters he felt estranged from them.

During this depressive period of Hall's life the entire Texas Ranger force was threatened. There was the real threat of their being disbanded because their *raison d'être* had been the protection of the frontier; now in the early years of the twentieth century the frontier no longer existed.

In fact, many newspapers ran a lengthy story entitled "Passing of Texas Rangers," first appearing in the *St. Louis Globe-Dispatch* and then in numerous others, such as the *Washington Post* and the *Yorkville Enquirer* of York, South Carolina, and perhaps many others. How the public reacted to this report is problematic but the fact remained that Gov. Oscar Branch Colquitt had intended to reduce significantly the number of Texas Rangers. In early 1911 the governor had reduced the force to a total of thirteen men: Company A under Capt. John R. Hughes with five privates and Company B under Capt. John J. Sanders with one sergeant and four privates.[1] But by this time Hall could no longer think of continuing any form of leadership of fighting men, Texas Rangers or La Sultana Rangers.

There are questions as to what actually Captain Hall did after the dangerous experience as a guard with his La Sultana Rangers. The article "Passing of the Texas Rangers," which was repeated in so many newspapers, informed readers that after he had worked as a mine guard in the Yaqui Indian country, he then took a position as manager of a ranch in a remote part of Lower California and "He is there to this day."[2] Another reported that after returning from the Philippines he "was employed in the secret service of the Wells-Fargo [Company] and was frequently in El Paso."[3] If this was true there is no way to confirm or deny as the records of Wells Fargo were all destroyed during the 1906 earthquake and fire. As to his health, the same journal reported during the summer of 1909 "he spent several months in El Paso undergoing treatment for a cancer."[4] His hometown newspaper, the *Greensboro Patriot,* noted his suffering during the last days was due to "kidney and heart trouble" but of course the medical diagnosis could have included several different troubles.[5] Another journal reported that after his tenure as Indian Agent at Anadarko, I.T. he returned to San Antonio and "engaged in the coal business." A San Antonio publication reported that after Hall returned from the Philippines he "engaged in the oil and real estate business."[6] Seemingly all accounts had him engaged in different occupations, none of which became successful.

Whether he was suffering from a specific disease, an undetermined illness, or a mixture of maladies, the press, friends, and family members knew Lee Hall had not long to live. The press release from San Antonio on March 16, 1911, headlined the inevitable: "Captain Hall Worse." He was at the Santa Rosa Infirmary and "had a very bad night and was reported very weak this morning." Brother Richard M. Hall and eldest daughter Mrs. Isham Keith were at his bedside; it was generally understood he would not survive much longer.[7]

He survived until 9:15 p.m. the night of March 17. The *San Antonio Express* perhaps treated his passing the most honorably, headlining its long article in bold and upper-case letters "Capt. Lee Hall, Famous Texas Ranger, Is Dead" with a smaller headline "Fear Unknown to Him." He was described as one of the best and most courageous of the Texas Rangers. He had been ill for a long time and during the previous two months he was admitted to the infirmary where everything possible had been done for him, but he was unable to successfully combat the disease that brought about his death. The *Express* pointed out that few of his old comrades were still alive, and named Capt. W.A. Pitts, Capt. Dave Wilson, and Assistant Adjutant General E.M. Phelps, all of Austin.

The funeral took place 10:00 Sunday morning, March 19 from the Sloan & Hagy parlors with interment in the National Cemetery of San Antonio. Father Kennedy, chaplain of the Twenty-second infantry, officiated. Captain J.L. Hall was buried with full military honors due to his service in the Philippines. From the military records he was #143 in the record book: "Hall, Jesse Lee Capt M, 1st U.S. Inf. S.A. W[ar] March 17, 1911. Grave Site A-1660."[8] On the monument erected much later this was reduced to "U.S. Vol. Inf. / War with Spain."

For many months the grave of Captain Hall remained unmarked. It was not until June 1912 when a committee was formed to raise the necessary funds for a monument. An initial press release from San Antonio on June 11 indicated that "The matter of a monument was started through the efforts of Gen. Jesse M. Lee, one of the intimate friends of the late captain."

Stockmen of the state were "to be given opportunity to contribute toward a fund of $200 for the monument." Stockmen were considered most likely to donate as "in the early days he was their guardian angel."[9] Judge Thomas M. Paschal, former Congressman from that district, chaired the committee. According to the *Austin Daily Statesman* the committee intended to raise a fund of $2,000 for the project.[10] Members of Judge Paschal's special committee were identified as Charles Graebner, J.H. Savage, T.L. Conroy, and J.F. Carter; perhaps they were prominent stockmen.[11] The *Houston Post* confidently reported that they had "the matter in hand, and no difficulty is anticipated in quickly raising the sum required."[12] Whether the original intent was to raise $200 or $2,000 is undetermined, but in June 1912 the grave remained unmarked. The committee sent out letters to members of the Cattlemen's Association asking that they contribute not more than $5 each to the monument fund.[13] Today, gazing at the impressive marble monument one suspects it is not the one erected in the early twentieth century, but one made to replace the original. It is a short distance from the entrance to the National Cemetery, which is located at 517 Paso Hondo Street. If one visits the grave today, beside Lee Hall's large marker is a smaller one for his wife, Elizabeth "Bessie" C. Weidman Hall.

Bessie C. had been in feeble health for a number of years before her passing on October 11, 1926. Death came while she was living with her daughter Jessie Hall Keith at Warrenton, Virginia. Brief funeral services were held at Warrenton and then the body was shipped to San Antonio to be placed beside her husband's in the National Cemetery. Mrs. Hall's passing was considered important news, and curiously the Lebanon, Pennsylvania, report gave her husband's service as a Texas Ranger prominence, without mentioning his service in the Philippines. "Mrs. Hall," the Lebanon report began, "was the widow of Captain Jesse Lee Hall, a veteran of the famous Texas Rangers. She was the daughter of Captain John Weidman, of this city, a Civil War figure, and well-known in his day as a Lebanon lawyer."[14]

The historical marker at Lee Hall's grave has the following inscription:

"Captain Lee Hall

"(October 9, 1849 – March 17, 1911.)

"Heroic defender of honor of Texas and the United States.

"Born in Lexington, N.C., came to Texas in 1869. Gained national fame as Grayson County marshal and deputy sheriff, 1871-1876.

"Served with Frontier Battalion, Texas Rangers, 1876-1880, hunting such outlaws as Sam Bass, King Fisher, John Wesley Hardin and feuding Taylor-Sutton Gangs.

"In Spanish-American War (1898-1900) was cited for his gallant service in the Philippines.

"Recorded— 1970"

Epilogue

Jesse Lee Hall is best known today as a Texas Ranger in the tradition forged by his captain— the reckless and demanding Leander H. McNelly. Hall replaced the dying McNelly and continued his brave service to the state; this enabled him to be selected as a member of the small group representing the "Ranger Ideal," an honor today recognized in the Texas Ranger Hall of Fame and Museum in Waco. How he deserves that honor is somewhat of a mystery, as he neither captured nor killed any notorious desperados, although one of his men did achieve that honor in bringing John Wesley Hardin to justice. His career as a ranger was brief compared to some, enlisting in 1876 and resigning in early 1880. Why did he end his illustrious career at that point, after he had gained a statewide reputation for bravery and effective leadership?

The ranger ended that illustrious career for love. His activities frequently took him to the coastal area and on one occasion in Corpus Christi he met and was smitten with a young Pennsylvania girl, Bessie C. Weidman, who was then visiting her sister there. The young people quickly fell in love; Lee Hall wanted her. She wanted him but there was a string attached: if you wish to marry me, you have to resign from the rangers. She was driving a hard bargain. That was a romantic decision, perhaps, but as it turned out it was not the best decision Lee Hall ever made. He may never have said it aloud, but he was a man of action and the ranger service was the best career choice he could have made. Bessie C. Weidman Hall, as far as we can tell, never stated or admitted that the "choice" she gave her beloved was a wise one, but there is ample evidence that she should not have given him that choice, and he should never have resigned. During the years following his resignation there were long periods of separation and an increase in Hall's abuse of alcohol. There is no doubt her forcing him to resign from the rangers led to his descent. Bessie C. Weidman ought to have let him remain in the service; he ought not to have acquiesced to her demand.

Having resigned from the Texas Rangers, Hall was in a position to become a politician based on his experience as a Sergeant-at-Arms in the Texas House of Representatives, or he could have become a successful merchant or other type of businessman, or a successful rancher, which is perhaps what Bessie C. wanted all along: a safe and secure position similar to that of how she remembered her father's, a successful attorney, highly respected in the community. But Hall was never able to obtain that respected position in society that his wife yearned for. After his resignation his various ventures failed or never really got off the ground. Yet he found himself attracted to dangerous actions no different from those when he was a ranger. How else must we consider his efforts in early 1885 with La Salle County Sheriff Charles Brown McKinney meeting on an island in the Rio Grande with representatives from Mexico in an effort to reduce bloodshed and rustling? Or when he joined the pursuit of the murderers of U.S. Marshal Hal Gosling that same year? Or when he joined a Nueces County posse to hunt down some horse thieves? These were acts no different from actions he performed while being a ranger, actions that at any moment might result in violence with Lee Hall in the middle of a gun battle. He had been in gun battles and he was comfortable in such dangerous situations. Thrilling action was the place for Lee Hall; thrilling action was what he needed, but he abandoned that to have his Bessie C. But once the decision was made, happiness did not result; they remained together and they both suffered.

In 1883 he managed the Dull Brothers ranch in dangerous La Salle County. For one year he was postmaster for the huge ranch, but that position was not satisfactory. It was another job too tame for a man of action like Lee Hall.

In September 1885 he found a respectable position as agent of the Comanche-Kiowa tribe at Anadarko in the Indian Territory. While some agents may have spent much of their time behind a desk, safe and secure, Lee Hall did not. He rode amongst the Indians and improved their lot, dealing with issues of agriculture as well as reducing the amount of gambling and the reduction of thievery from white cattlemen. That position lasted less than two years as he had to endure the stress of being accused of illegally pocketing government funds for his personal use. The accusations proved to be false, but it ruined his career as Indian agent.

During the San Antonio & Aransas Pass Railway strike of 1892-93 Hall guarded the trains from "scab" violence in the DeWitt-Lavaca Counties area; his presence riding on a railroad car with heavily armed volunteer enforcers behind him prevented violence. Bessie C. Hall may have realized that work was no different than hunting an outlaw such as Sam Bass or King Fisher.

Disappointments continued throughout the life of Lee Hall. When the Spanish-American seemed imminent Hall volunteered himself and numerous former rangers and others to join Colonel Roosevelt's Rough Riders. That golden opportunity never materialized; thus he was not one of the men who ran up San Juan or Kettle Hill to become part of the famous group who contributed to Teddy Roosevelt's future success in world politics. Hall did, however, find some satisfaction in demonstrating his leadership during the Philippine Insurrection following the end of the Spanish-American War. He was again a commander of men, leading them into action, like he had been years before as a captain of Texas Rangers. But unlike his "safe years" of ranging, avoiding a desperado's bullet, he was severely injured during a battle in the Philippines, an injury that prevented him from continuing in the service. The injuries from which he suffered perhaps contributed to his finale from any and all action and to his early retreat from active life. His last service as captain of the Sultana Rangers guarding gold shipments in Mexico in 1906 proved to be so effective that the position was terminated.

His years with the Texas Rangers and his service as a soldier in the United States Army provided him honors at his death. He rests today in a well marked grave in the National Cemetery in San Antonio. He would not have objected of course, but if he had had his life to live over again he no doubt would have rejected Bessie C.'s demand to resign from the Texas Rangers. Perhaps she would have been the one to withdraw her demand, and would have advised him each morning as he left the ranger camp, "You do be careful today."

Appendix A

A Jesse Leigh Hall Family Tree

1. James King Hall (January 13, 1816–November 13, 1885) married Francis Mebane Rankin (November 19, 1826–August 5, 1913) on January 4, 1849. They had the following children, all sons: Jesse Leigh Hall (October 9, 1849); Richard Moore Hall (November 17, 1851); William Paisley Hall (December 13, 1853); James King Hall Jr. (April 5, 1856); Francis Rankin Hall (September 9, 1859); Charles Wharton Hall (August 15, 1864). All but Charles survived to adulthood.

2. (a) Jesse Leigh Hall married Elizabeth "Bessie" Cook Weidman (October 4, 1857–October 11,1926) on November 25, 1880.

(b) Richard Moore Hall married Elizabeth Hughes (July 20, 1854–December 24, 1924) on November 17, 1880; he died November 18, 1917.

(c) William Paisley Hall never married; he died in Denver, Colorado County, on September 19, 1917.

(d) James King Hall Jr. married Miriam Abigail Caldwell (January 31, 1856–Jauary 5, 1927) on April 25, 1883; he died March 18, 1891.

(e) Francis Rankin Hall married (1) Mary Josephine Kerr and (2) Ida M. Krause on July 22, 1901. He died on September 13, 1924.

(f) Charles Wharton Hall, died June 18, 1867.

3. Jesse Leigh Hall and Elizabeth "Bessie" Cook Weidman were married on November 25, 1880; they had the following children:

(a) Jessie Lee Hall was born on October 3, 1882; she married (1) Isham Keith on October 24, 1906; he died September 13, 1936; (2) Simon de Korsakoff, 1946; Jessie Lee de Korsakoff died on Aug. 29, 1958.

(b) Sarah Elizabeth Hall was born on December 23, 1883; she married Albert Couden Whitaker on April 28, 1928; Albert Whitaker died on October 7, 1951; Sarah Elizabeth Whitaker died on September 23, 1959.

(c) Martha Dorothy Hall was born on May 2, 1887; she married Frank Kerr Hall on August 9, 1911. Frank Hall died October 20, 1918, and Dorothy Hall died October 15, 1970.

(d) Mary Weidman Hall was born on September 13, 1889; she married Paul Gress Adams on April 12, 1913. Paul Adams died October 12, 1952, and Mary Hall Adams died April 23, 1963.

(e) Virginia Derr Hall was born on November 29, 1890; she married Siebert "Bert" Pearson on May 11, 1919. He died March 31, 1964, and Virginia died June 20, 1972.

Appendix B

Special State Troops

Muster Roll of Lt. J.L. Hall mustered in on January 25, 1877, prepared at Clinton, showing roll through March 31, 1877. Pay per month: the lieutenant received $125; sergeants received $50; corporals $40; privates $40; teamster $30.

J.L. Hall, Lieutenant—January 25, 1877

J.B. Armstrong, 1st Sergeant—"

O.S. Watson, 2nd Sergeant—"

A.L. Parrott, Corporal—"

N.R.J. Stegall, Corporal—"

Privates

G.H. Allen—"

C.T. Allen—"

C.W. Covington—March 1, 1877

W.T. Davis—January 25, 1877

T.W. Deggs—"

G.P. Durham—"

O.R. Erwin—March 1, 1877

W.H. Griffin—January 25, 1877

S.N. Hardy—"

C.W. Howery—"

D.W. Holden—February 17, 1877

E.R. Jensen—January 25, 1877

N.A. Jennings—"

Horace Maben—"

A.S. McKay—"

W.W. McKinney—"

C.B. McKinney—"

F.H. Miller—March 24, 1877

T.B. Menefee—"

S.A. McMurry—"

J.F. Pendleton—"

H.G. Rector—January 25, 1877

W.L. Rudd—"

G.W. Tally—"

L.L. Wright—February 15, 1877

H.C. Wilson—March 24, 1877

Alfred Walker, Teamster—[Not shown on muster]

Appendix C

First United States Volunteer Infantry, Field, and Staff

Colonel Charles S. Richie, Company M.

Officers

Captain Lee Hall

First Lieutenant T.N. Devine

Second Lieutenant, J.U. Rogers

Sergeants

First, C.W. Starck

Quartermaster, W.R. Langford

Second, D.N. Reid

Third, John Powers

Fourth, John Bracken

Fifth, W.G. Erwin

Corporals

First, Ed Metzner

Second, A.D. Radzinski

Fourth, Fred Schnell

Fifth, Aug. Schultz

Sixth, C.F. Jung

Seventh, John Boylan

Eighth, Fred Pitt

Privates

L. Addington

E. Addington

W. Addington

Charles Allen

W.S. Bennett

W.W. Blum

Al Bastion

George Brucker

Aug. Buchner

C.S. Bullock

W.W. Compton

Syd Coppard

J.J. Carker

A.C. Curtis

M.E. Camps

J.C. Carlisle

G.H. Downs

S.H. Davis

H.R. Donahoo

-- DuPree

W.L. Edwards

James P. Ealy

H.R. Forsyth

J.T. Gillespie

C. Goehmann

J.L. Guin

L.L. Guin

Thomas Gregory

J. Hart

Louis Hebberdier

G.H. Haynes

H.L. Hobbert

I.M. Johnson

A.R. Jurgens

Earnest Jones

H.F. Jackson

E. Kauffman

James Kavanaugh

Frank Kennedy

Van Kerr

H. A. Lowry

H.A. Lindle

Joseph Levy

Harry Liebrecht

George La Trace

Jeff J. Mapp

Ed. McPherson

John Morris

T. Maginnis

C.E. Mason

Aug. Murray

Aug. Nessie

F.S. Neely

E.D. Putaquat

Jul. Pfeiffer

H. Ross

H. Radke

Henry Rogers

W. Rees

F.S. Spurgeon

H. Schmidt

A.B. Simmons

James Sowells

Joseph Shely

George Spencer

C.A. Trexler

H.F. Thompson

-- Willis

Source: http://www.spanamwar.com/1stTexasroster.html Accessed December 28, 2018.

Endnotes

Notes to Chapter 1

1. The 1850 Iredell County census shows the J.K. Hall family with the head of household listed as a 33-year-old physician, his wife Francis M. ten years younger and their one child, son Jesse L. seven months of age. P.412B. The 1860 Guilford County census however lists the birth county of family members and shows Dr. James King Hall a native of Iredell, his wife a native of Guilford, and son Jesse L., now ten, as born in Davidson County. Younger siblings R.M., William P., James K., and Francis Rankin are listed as all born in Iredell County.

2. *The Greensboro Patriot*, Greensboro, North Carolina, October 21, 1859.

3. Vital information on the mother of Jesse L. Hall is from the *Official Certificate and Record of Death*, No. 5357, for Francis Mebane Rankin Hall. Her headstone shows her birth date as November 16, 1827, but the official death certificate shows her birth date as November 19. She died on August 5, 1913. This record shows she was born in Guilford County, North Carolina. Dr. Hall was born January 13, 1816, and died November 13, 1885. Both are buried in the Greensboro First Presbyterian Cemetery.

4. *Indexed Register of Marriages— Davidson County, North Carolina. North Carolina Marriage Records 1741-2011*, 124. No date. No place. An obituary for Dr. Hall states the marriage took place on January 4, 1849, to Miss Fannie Rankin.

5. Iredell County, North Carolina Census, enumerated July 27, 1850, by T.L. Tucker, 412B. In addition to the Hall family members a nineteen-year-old William Nash resided there, working as a laborer. Today the city is spelled Greensboro but as often as not in the nineteenth century it appeared as Greensborough, or Greensboro'.

6. Dora Neill Raymond, *Captain Lee Hall of Texas*, 12. Hall's daughter, Jessie L., died Aug. 29, 1958, in Warrenton, Fauquier County, Virginia. On her headstone this was engraved: "Jessie Hall Keith/ de Korsakoff/ daughter of/ Capt. Leigh Hall/ of the Texas Rangers/ Died 1958." Apparently the family continued to think of the famous son as Leigh. Of interest is that at least on two occasions Hall wrote to a friend from Cuero on February 11, 1878, and June 25, 1878, and signed the letters "Leigh Hall." The friend was Julia Maria Pease, daughter of Texas Governor E.M. Pease.

7. *Paris News* (Lamar County, Texas) June 8, 1943. Column "Lee Hall Was Man Who Filled Many Positions" by A.W. Neville. This was also printed in the edition of September 15, 1968.

8. John Adams Gilmer, Attorney-at-Law, was in his early fifties when the war broke out. He, like Dr. Hall, was a wealthy man according to the 1860 Guilford County, North Carolina, census, claiming $38,000 worth of real estate and $22,000 worth of personal estate. In addition he had a wife and five children. Guilford County, North Carolina Census, enumerated September 1860 by B.G. Graham, 209B. Active in promoting the causes of Greensboro and the state he was a Senator prior to the Civil War, and was opposed to secession. President Lincoln offered him a cabinet post, but when North Carolina seceded he turned down the offer. Carol Moore, *Greensboro's First Presbyterian Church Cemetery*, 39-41.

9. *The Greensboro Times*, Greensboro, North Carolina, May 8, 1861.

10. *The Fayetteville Observer*, Fayetteville, North Carolina, September 30, 1861, citing an undated issue of the *Greensboro Patriot.*

11. Slave holdings of J.K. Hall, Guilford County, North Carolina Slave Schedule, enumerated by B.G. Graham, 379B.

12. General James Johnston Pettigrew was born July 4, 1828, in North Carolina and proved to be a successful author as well as soldier. He was mortally wounded on July 17, 1863, and is buried at Bunker Hill, Virginia. www.civilwarhome.com/CMHpettigrewbio.html.

13. Newspaper column "Jim Bishop Reporter" appearing in *The High Point Enterprise*, High Point, North Carolina, April 21, 1966, 8A. Prolific writer, Bishop (1907-1987) is best known as the author of *The Day Christ Died.*

14. *Charlotte Observer*, July 8, 1879.

15. Per an advertisement in the *Greensboro Patriot*, July 15, 1869.

16. *Greensboro Patriot*, May 13, 1869.

17. *Greensboro Patriot*, July 1, 1869.

18. O.S. Glenn letters to J. L. Boardman dated April 22, April 29, and May 6, 1870, printed in the *Highland Weekly News* of Hillsborough, Ohio. Little is known of Glenn, but he appears to be primarily a newspaper correspondent. He was born in Ohio on March 10, 1840, and served in Company D of the 11th Regiment Ohio Cavalry during the Civil War. He was married to Miss Emma Marie DeLeon of Denver, Colorado, on March 10, 1870. The 1880 Alturas County, Idaho, census identifies him as the head of household living with his wife and children, occupation farming. In 1888 he was appointed Post Master of Bellevue, Idaho. He died October 18, 1895.

19. O.S. Glenn letter to J.L. Boardman dated May 6, 1870, printed in the *Highland Weekly News* of June 2, 1870.

20. *Galveston Daily News*, June 10, 1870, citing news from the *Harrison Flag* of Marshall.

21. Woolsey was the son of Nehemiah Cardinal and Elizabeth Woolsey. He was born in Caldwell County, Missouri, on June 27, 1849. He was married to Gertrude Isabella Woolsey and they had two children, Calvin Lee and Cardinal Boone. "Nap" Woolsey became a physician, graduating from the Ensworth Medical College in St. Joseph, Missouri, in 1893. Woolsey died on February 24, 1905, at Braymer, Missouri. He and his wife are both buried in the Evergreen Cemetery at Braymer; their graves are marked.

22. Grayson County, Texas Census, enumerated November 3, 1870, by William Montgomery, page 91. Somehow Montgomery spelled Hall's name as "D. Lee Hall," or the letter could be a "J." with extra swirls making it appear as an upper-case D. Another misspelling is the post office, spelled "McComb" but correctly spelled Macomb. Of interest is that Deputy U.S. Marshal Lou Burson arrested one N.B. Woolsey in early 1888 "charged with stealing hogs" in the Indian Territory. *Fort Worth Daily Gazette*, January 12, 1888. Presumably this is the same man who boarded with "D. Lee Hall."

23. *Dallas Daily Herald*, July 15, 1871, citing a report from the *Sherman Patriot*. A decade before Archer worked as a hostler for Henry Bates, District Superintendent of the Overland Mail Company. 1860 Grayson County census, 145B.

24. Ezekiel Pemberton Caywood was born on August 3, 1829, in Sullivan County, Tennessee, and lived until December 2, 1910. He announced as a candidate for sheriff in 1873 and again in 1895 but was not elected. After the death of his wife Mary Elizabeth (Snapp) Caywood he lived with his daughter and son-in-law, Charles B. and Sallie (Caywood) Banks. Although he died in Denver, Colorado, he is buried in the West Hill Memorial Cemetery of Sherman, Grayson County; he and his wife share a double headstone. Find A Grave.

25. *Dallas Daily Herald*, July 15, 1871.

26. Brady was commissioned and qualified as lieutenant on July 1, 1871, and resigned from the force on January 6, 1872, then was re-appointed March 1, 1873. See *The Governor's Hounds: The Texas State Police, 1870-1873*, by Barry A. Crouch and Donaly E. Brice.

27. State Police Lt. E.W. Brady to James Davidson, October 9, 1871.

28. Section 5 of the State Police Act, printed in the *Dallas Herald*, July 9, 1870. This was publicized in many Texas newspapers and the officials of Grayson County certainly were aware of its content. One is left to wonder why Lieutenant Brady did not call on the sheriff or Hall for assistance.

29. Sammy Tise, *Texas County Sheriffs.* Grayson County sheriffs are listed on 213-14. The forty-year-old Tuttle had been an assistant revenue assessor when the previous census was enumerated. He had a twenty-four-year-old wife, S.T. and they had six children. Thomas Taylor, occupation identified as "Sport" boarded with the Tuttles. 1870 Grayson County census, enumerated July 16 by H.H. Ribbs, 12.

30. *San Antonio Express,* March 18, 1911. This issue provides a fine sketch of Hall's life and career entitled "Capt. Lee Hall, Famous Texas Ranger, is Dead."

31. *Galveston Daily News,* July 17, 1872, citing a report from the *Texas Land Journal* of July 1, 1872. The community of Farmington was located about ten miles south of Sherman in south central Grayson County. The *Texas Land Journal* was published by the North Texas Land Company in Sherman and claimed to be "Devoted to Immigration and the Land Interests of Texas."

32. Grayson County Election Returns, 1872 at Texas State Library and Archives. Box 2-12/556.

33. "William Henry Trolinger" (1827-1895) in *Handbook of Texas Online,* by Aragorn Storm Miller and R. Matt Abigail, accessed July 27, 2018. http://www.tshaonline.org/handbook/online/articles/ftr40.

34. *Galveston Daily News* December 12, 1872 citing a report from an undated *Sherman Courier.*

35. Edward King, *The Great South: A Record of Journeys to Louisiana, Texas, The Indian Territory, Missouri, Arkansas, Mississippi, Alabama, Georgia, Florida, South Carolina, North Carolina, Kentucky, Tennessee, Virginia, West Virginia, and Maryland,* 177. This was published in 1875; King had been in Texas in late 1872 or very early 1873. We have used a facsimile version published in 1972.

36. Ibid., 178.

37. Ibid., 179. King obviously was impressed with Hall and his reputation; he obtained a likeness of the young man, perhaps a daguerreotype, which was included as an illustration in his book. The original has not yet been located. King was accompanied on his journeys by artist James Wells Champney whose name is listed on the title page.

38. *Dallas Daily Herald*, January 4, 1873.

39. *Dallas Daily Herald*, December 14, 1872, printing news from the *Sherman Patriot.*

40. *Dallas Daily Herald*, January 4, 1873, reprinting news from the *Sherman Patriot* of December 21, 1872.

41. *Denison News*, January 23, 1873.

42. News items from the *Sherman Patriot* printed in the *Dallas Daily Herald* of December 14, 1872.

43. *Junction City Union*, December 28, 1872, citing a report from Denison of the twenty-fourth. The *Union* was a Kansas newspaper. The Missouri-Kansas-Texas Railway was popularly known as "the Katy." Denison was the entry point for the first non-Texas railroad.

44. *Denison News*, February 20, 1873.

45. *Denison News*, February 20, 1873.

46. *Denison News*, May 8, 1873.

47. *Denison News*, May 15, 1873.

48. *North Texas Enterprise* (Bonham, Fannin County) May 31, 1873.

49. *Denison News*, July 24, 1873.

50. *Denison Daily News*, August 3, 1873.

51. *Denison Daily News*, August 3, 1873, citing article from an undated *Gainesville Gazette.*

52. *Denison Daily News*, August 19, 1873.

53. Information on William Andrew Jackson Posey from article by Bill Lehmann through www.ancestry.com/mediaui/tree and unpublished manuscript by David D. Johnson.

54. *Galveston Daily News*, July 1, 1873 citing a special telegram from Waco of June 30, 1873. Also from Austin's *Daily Democratic Statesman* of July 4, 1873, citing a report from an undated *Waco Examiner* and editorial in the *Dallas Weekly Herald* —"Lynch Law"— of July 12, 1873.

55. *Galveston Daily News*, October 10, 1873, citing a report from the *Sherman Patriot* of October 4, 1873.

56. *Greensboro Patriot*, Greensboro, North Carolina, September 17, 1873. The publishers of the *Patriot* were Duffy and Morehead. A "hop" was a popular term for a dance.

57. *Denison News*, September 4, 1873.

58. *Denison Daily News*, September 14, 1873.

59. Guilford County, North Carolina, census, July 4, 1870, 227. The Fetzer family were household number 26 while the Porter family was household number 27. *New North Star*, Greensboro, North Carolina, October 22, 1873.

60. *Denison Daily News*, December 2, 1873.

61. The account of Hall's duel with Wilkinson is from the *Charlotte Daily Observer*, January 28, 1900, which originally appeared in Philadelphia's *Saturday Evening Post*. It appeared in numerous other newspapers, including Hall's hometown *Greensboro Patriot* of January 24 as well as Asheville's *Daily Citizen* of January 12, 1900, headlined "Lee Hall, Fighting Man."

62. *Southern Argus*, Selma, Alabama, February 13, 1874, and March 13, 1874. Sammy Tise, *Texas County Sheriffs*, 213.

NOTES TO CHAPTER 2

1. Grayson County Census, enumerated September 1, 1870, by H.H. Ribbs, 78B. The head of household was the sixty-two-year-old James H. Vaden, born in Tennessee; he and his wife Elizabeth then had four children. In 1870 son James Williamson Vaden was shown to be twenty-nine-years-old and worked as a stock raiser. James W. Vaden was born March 17, 1842, in Smith County, Tennessee. After locating in Texas he became noteworthy to history as serving as county sheriff. He died on April 24, 1918, in Kingston, Marshall County, Oklahoma, but is buried in the West Hill Cemetery in Grayson County. His grave is marked.

2. *Southern Argus*, February 13 and March 13, 1874, and Tise, *Texas County Sheriffs*, 213.

3. *Charlotte Observer*, July 8, 1879, reprinting an article from an undated *Reidsville Times.*

4. Dora Neill Raymond, *Captain Lee Hall of Texas*, 22.

5. "Convict Record, Texas State Penitentiary," Huntsville, 101.

6. *Denison Daily News*, February 25, 1874, citing an undated report from the *Sherman Patriot.*

7. *Dallas Daily Herald*, April 25, 1874.

8. *Dallas Daily Herald*, May 13, 1874.

9. *Fugitives from Justice: The Notebook of Texas Ranger Sergeant James B. Gillett.* Facsimile of Gillett's copy published in 1997 by State House Press, Austin, 173.

10. The Civil War service records show a Jarrott (or Jarret) M. Hastings mustered in at Fort Washita, Cherokee Nation on December 28, 1861, in Company B of Taylor's Regiment of Texas Mounted Rifles, 22nd Cavalry.

11. *Denison Daily News*, February 28, 1874, citing reports from an undated *Sherman Courier.* The death of Hastings and the conviction of

E.V. Holder are reported in the *Marshall Weekly Herald*, April 12, 1877. At this time trials for the others were yet to be held.

12. *Denison Daily News*, March 14, 1874.

13. *Southern Argus*, Selma, Alabama, December 22, 1876.

14. *Denison Daily News*, March 14, 1874.

15. *Dallas Daily Herald*, January 25, 1874.

16. Betty Dooley Aubrey and Claude Dooley, *Why Stop? A Guide to Texas Historical Roadside Markers*, 375.

17. *Denison Daily News*, April 21, 1874.

18. *Sherman Register* of May 7, 1874 reprinted in the *Dallas Daily Herald* of May 12, 1874.

19. *Denison Daily News*, May 12, 1874.

20. *Denison Daily News*, May 10, 1874.

21. *Denison Daily News*, June 6, 1874, and the *Galveston Daily News*, June 10, 1874.

22. There were two Maupins who operated a mercantile in 1870 at this location. John Maupin was twenty-six and James Maupin was nineteen; a W. Centcher, age nineteen, worked as a clerk in the store. They were all natives of Kentucky. Grayson County census enumerated by H.H. Ribbs on August 10, 1870, 46. Their post office was given as Sherman.

23. William B. Morrison, ed., "Colbert's Ferry on Red River, Chickasaw Nation, Indian Territory: Recollections of John Malcolm," *Chronicles of Oklahoma*, September 1938, 16:3.

24. The most recent work on the murder family of Kansas is *Death for Dinner: The Benders of (Old) Kansas* by Phyllis de la Garza. Published in Honolulu by Talei Publishers, Inc., 2003.

25. *North Texas Enterprise*, Bonham, Fannin County, May 31, 1873.

26. *Denison Daily News*, June 6, 1874. The Denison newspaper gave Hall considerable attention in this issue, all on page one. The first article was "A Thief Arrested" followed by a smaller headline: "And a Dose of Morphine Fixes Him" while immediately following this was headlined "A Pitched Battle" and "Mike Gormly Down Again." This headline is an apparent reference to the fact that Hall earlier had Gormly in his custody but he had escaped, hence "down again."

27. *Denison Daily News*, June 6, 1874. The Wichita River eventually flows into the Red River, the northern border between Texas and Oklahoma.

28. Everheart was elected sheriff of Grayson County on February 15, 1876, re-elected November 5, 1878, and served until November 2, 1880. Sammy Tise, *Texas County Sheriffs*, 213.

29. *Denison Daily News*, July 3, 1874.

30. *Denison Daily News*, July 3, 1874; *Galveston Daily News*, July 9, 1874. A later account citing news from McLennan County identifies the four men arresting Posey as Hall, Everheart, Ball, and W.K. Rector assisted by "negro guides." *Galveston Daily News*, July 15, 1874. This issue states the reward was $700 as did the *Denison Daily News* of July 3, 1874.

31. Huntsville Convict Record Ledger, Archived in the Texas State Library and Archives.

32. *Galveston Daily News*, August 15, citing a special report from Sherman of August 14, 1874.

33. Austin's *Daily Democratic Statesman*, July 20, 1875, citing a report from Muskogee, Indian Territory. A lengthy article in the *St. Louis Dispatch* of August 3, 1875, identifies those killed who were against Ross.

34. The description of the murder of Journeycake by Calvin Coker appeared in the *Coffeyville Courier* of Kansas of June 17 and was reprinted in the *Atchison Daily Champion* of Atchison, Kansas, issue of June 20,

1875. Curiously this report also appeared in the *Los Angeles Daily Herald* of July 3, 1875.

35.*Galveston Daily News*, October 2, 1875.

36. *Leavenworth Daily Times*, Leavenworth, Kansas, September 9, 1876.

37. *Fort Worth Gazette*, September 28, 1891, citing a report from Denton County September 27, 1891.

38. *Denison Daily News*, September 19, 1874, citing news from the Sherman "Special Correspondent."

39. *Galveston Daily News*, September 29, 1874.

40. *Denison Daily News*, December 14, 1874, citing a report from the *Sherman Patriot.* Was this Edward W. Withers from Gonzales County? Efforts to learn conclusively have not confirmed but likely the Ed Withers arrested and then escaped was from Gonzales County. If so he managed to return to Gonzales County. He was the son of William E. Withers.

41. *Galveston Daily News*, April 11, 1876.

Notes to Chapter 3

1. *Dallas Weekly Herald* of Saturday, April 10, 1875, citing a report from an undated *Sherman Register.*

2. *The Kansas Tribune* (Lawrence), January 6, 1876. This is a reprint of an article that had appeared in an undated *Courier* of Independence, Kansas. This report may have been in error or else Coker was simply badly wounded. A later report indicates that Coker was alive and well as late as June 1876 when he and Deputy U.S. Marshal W.C. Ross arrested an unidentified desperado. Coker was perhaps acquainted with the man as at that point he shot and killed Deputy Ross. *Chetopa Herald*, Chetopa, Labette County, Kansas, June 17, 1876. To add to the uncertainty of this desperado's fate, another report from Kansas stated that Cal Coker, "a border desperado," was shot and killed by an unknown party at

Coffeyville, about midnight on September 4, 1876, adding "Coker is the man who murdered the Rev. Journeycake about a year and a half ago." The *Leavenworth Daily Times*, September 9, 1876.

3. John A. Purnell to Gov. E.J. Davis, June 31, 1872. Texas Governor Edmund Jackson Davis records, Archives and Information Services Division, Texas State library and Archives Commission, Box 2014/110-21 Folder 249.

4. Sammy Tise, *Texas County Sheriffs*, 258. Hereafter cited as Tise, *Texas County Sheriffs*. The Purnell household in 1870 consisted of head of household John A., a fifty-year-old "District" as the census identified him. His wife was Adelor R.W., forty-eight; they had seven children ranging in age from twenty-six-year-old Robert to the youngest, four-year-old Mary A. Hill County Census, enumerated July 15, 1870 by L.J. Sturgis, 369.

5. The reward notice appeared in several issues of the *Daily Democratic Statesman*, this quotation from the issue of June 28, 1873. The Legislature had "by a Concurrent Resolution" approved the amount of the reward in session on June 4, 1873.

6. *Minneapolis Daily Tribune* (Minnesota), July 25, 1872.

7. Efforts to learn more about this J.W. Holt have been unfruitful. He apparently made a career out of being a detective. In 1882 he was described as a detective from Pilot Point who had brought back a murderer from Tennessee. In 1885 after a gunbattle with outlaws, he was described as being "of the Indian Territory." Where he was from and what happened to Holt after the notice in 1885 is unknown. *Dallas Daily Herald*, June 6, 1882, and April 14, 1885.

8. John A. Purnell to Governor E.J. Davis, July 3, 1873. Governor E.J. Davis Papers, Box 2014/110-27, Folder 314. Purnell wrote that he learned of the $600 reward, but it was actually only $500.

9. *Galveston Daily News*, March 25, 1876, and *Tri-Weekly Herald* (Marshall), March 30, 1876.

10. *Dallas Daily Herald*, March 25, 1876, reprinting an article from an undated *Sherman Register.*

11. *Journal of the House of Representatives*, Fifteenth Legislature, April 1876, 5-7.

12. "Legislative Proceedings" reported in the *Daily Democratic Statesman*, August 2, 1876.

13. *Journal of the House of Representatives*, Fifteenth Legislature, August 1876, 582. W.I.C. Autry replaced Hall.

14. *Austin Weekly Statesman*, June 15, 1876.

15. Pendencia Creek, the Spanish word meaning "quarrel" or "brawl," flows from northwestern Dimmit County to southwestern Zavala County. Due to the frequency of Indian raiding parties it was not until after the Civil War had ended that settlers were able to establish and maintain ranches in this area. "Pendencia Creek" in *New Handbook of Texas*, V: 135.

16. George Durham, As Told to Clyde Wantland, "On the Trail of 5100 Outlaws: The Inside Story of McNelly's Texas Rangers," *West* Magazine, Part VI: "The Taking of King Fisher," 208.

17. *Daily Democratic Statesman*, June 7, 1876, citing a report to the Adjutant General. The arrested men were identified only as "noted desperadoes and outlaws."

18. N.A. Jennings, *A Texas Ranger.* I have used the 1960 facsimile edition of the original published by Charles Scribner's and Sons in 1899. The facsimile was published by the Frontier Book Company of Ruidoso, New Mexico, in 1960. The work was later published by the University of Oklahoma Press in 1997 with a foreword by J. Frank Dobie and an introduction by Dr. Stephen L. Hardin. Hereafter cited as *A Texas Ranger.*

19. Jennings, *A Texas Ranger*, 236-37.

20. Monthly Return of Lieutenant J.L. Hall dated August 31, 1876, at Oakville, Live Oak County.

21. *Weekly Democratic Statesman*, August 24, 1876.

22. *Galveston Daily News*, November 23, 1876. This was excerpted from the "State News" column printed from an undated *Frontiersman* newspaper of uncertain source.

23. *Galveston Daily News*, August 18, 1876, and the *New Orleans Republican* of August 23, which repeated the *News's* article with added editorial comments.

24. *Galveston Daily News*, September 7, 1876.

25. Ferguson left Texas and later became notorious during the Earp-Clanton feud of Tombstone, Arizona Territory, but was known then as Pete Spence. See *Pete Spence: "Audacious Artist in Crime"* by Roy A. Young.

26. *Galveston Daily News*, September 26, 1876. Upshur Brooking was a twenty-nine-year-old stock raiser at this time.

27. Monthly Return of J.L. Hall dated September 30, 1876.

28. *Tri-Weekly Herald* (Marshall, Texas), September 26, 1876.

29. *Galveston Daily News*, October 24, 1879. Rancher John McElroy was "the gentlemanly proprietor" who had "a fine lot of swine to eat them [the mast]" and he perhaps provided the description which appeared in a letter to the *Castroville Quill* and was printed in the Dimmit County news column.

30. John B. Armstrong's report is printed in the *Galveston Daily News* of October 3 in the form of a special telegram to the *News* from San Antonio dated October 2, 1876.

31. *Galveston Daily News*, October 4, 1876.

32. *Galveston Daily News*, October 20 and October 31, 1876.

33. Monthly Return of J.L. Hall dated October 31, 1876, prepared at San Antonio.

34. Monthly Return of J.L. Hall dated September 30, 1876.

35. Watson must have been an above average man. Only twenty-six in 1880, he was a corporal with the Special State Troops. An obituary states he died at his home in Kingsville the night of December 31, 1908, and was "for years a member of the Texas ranger service, and by his good works as a ranger in the old days, when this section was in need of such service, he became well known to the people of Southwest Texas." *Brownsville Daily Herald*, January 2, 1909.

36. *Galveston Daily News*, October 28, 1876, citing a special telegram to the *News* from Goliad on the twenty-third via Victoria of the twenty-seventh; and the *Galveston Daily News*, October 31, 1876, citing a special letter from a citizen of Refugio.

37. Monthly return of J.L. Hall, dated October 31, 1876.

38. *Galveston Daily News*, October 31, 1876.

39. Clifford R. Caldwell and Ron DeLord, *Texas Lawmen 1835-1899: The Good and the Bad*, 17-18.

40. *San Antonio Daily Express*, December 7, 1876.

41. *Galveston Daily News*, November 22, 1876.

42. *Galveston Daily News*, November 4, 1876.

43. *Galveston Daily News*, December 2, 1876.

44. Ibid., December 3, 1876.

45. Ibid.

The *News* wrote: "The sheriff of Goliad [C]ounty has been removed by petition of the citizens for incompetency. The county judge and district clerk resigned. All quiet in that section." *Galveston Daily News*, October 4, 1876.

47. Tise, *Texas County Sheriffs*, 207.

48. The surname of this family has had numerous spellings: Brazell, Brasell and so on; I have used the spelling for the doctor as well as his son George that is on their headstones in the Upper Yorktown Cemetery. One must assume that whoever paid for the stone cutting knew the correct spelling of their name.

49. The spelling of this man's surname has been problematical: Sitterlie, Sitterlee, Sitterly are the usual spellings. I have accepted that which appears on his headstone in the Catholic Cemetery in Victoria, Texas: *Sitterle*. Presumably the family selected the spelling and epitaph, a simple "Gone But Not Forgotten" giving his dates as 1844 born in Elauss and death date as February 10, 1887. Of interest is that four years after the 1876 Brassell killings he is listed as brother-in-law in the household of Perry Cox, a brother of William Cox. Perry Cox is shown to be twenty-one, brother Rufus Cox is eighteen, next listed is Joseph *Sitterly* [*sic*], twenty-five and his wife Malissa (Cox) *Sitterly*. Census taker Robert A. Pleasants was the son of Judge Henry Clay Pleasants. DeWitt County census, enumerated July 8, 1880, 402.

50. Jennings, *A Texas Ranger*, 282-86.

51. George Durham, *Taming the Nueces Strip: The Story of McNelly's Rangers*, 166-70. Durham first published his account of ranging under McNelly in a "pulp" Western magazine entitled simply *West* in 1937; the title then was "On the Trail of 5100 Outlaws." The University of Texas Press in 1962 published the account with a foreword by Walter Prescott Webb. Durham had related his experiences to Clyde Wantland, a freelance journalist. C.L. Sonnichsen reviewed the book for the *El Paso Herald-Post* and described it as "a fine piece of Texana which sheds some new light on a troublesome period in our history." Hall is not mentioned in the review, but Sonnichsen accurately noted that Durham pointed out that McNelly was "a beaten man more than once . . . and is beset by discouragements and frustrations." The review appeared in Laura Scott Meyers's column "The Bookshelf" in the *El Paso Herald-Post*, July

21, 1962. Durham was familiar with Jennings's autobiographical work and felt it was "pretty awful."

52. Monthly Return of J.L. Hall, dated December 31, 1876, prepared at Clinton.

53. Frederic Remington, *How the Law Got into the Chaparral: Conversations With Old Texas Rangers,* 25. Edited by John H. Jenkins.

54. *Galveston Daily News,* December 12, 1876.

55. *Austin Daily Democratic Statesman,* January 27, 1876.

56. *Austin Daily Democratic Statesman,* February 17, 1876.

57. 1880 Goliad County census: Jacobs, Fatheree, and Middleton families, 367A and 367B. John A. Middleton was buried in the "Buzzards Roost Cemetery" in rural Goliad County. He was born on February 6, 1841, and died on January 8, 1876. Once the various headstones were legible, but today the cemetery is in ruins due to various outside factors. Middleton's widow, née Mary Samantha Parker, later married R.A. Brown.

58. Little has been learned about Corporal Williams, identified on the muster rolls as simply "M.H. Williams." He began as a private under Captain McNelly and mustered in on April 1, 1875, and served until February 1, 1877. He rose to the rank of corporal. Another document reveals he was born in St. Helena Parish, Louisiana, but the man has not been found on census records there. Jennings recalled Williams as "a royal good fellow, was known always as 'Polly' Williams among the men." Muster Roll Index Cards; Muster Roll of J.L. Hall, prepared at Carrizo Springs, August 1, 1879; *A Texas Ranger,* 123.

59. Casper J. Wingate, the victim, was born July 22, 1854, to Edward Wingate and Elizabeth "Eliza" Steppe Wingate, one of nine children. Two of his siblings were James Franklin (September 30, 1845) and Edward Taylor Wingate (December 23, 1847). Casper J. married Leona Sapp at Stockdale on July 17, 1876. The widow Wingate later married John Riley

Fellers and this union lasted over fifty years. Correspondence from Jack Freyer to Parsons, August 5, 2010.

60. Horace Rowe was another literary ranger who, like McNelly, was active while suffering from consumption. Jennings recalled him as "a small, dark, delicately made man. He was a poet of no mean order and had published a book of verse." *A Texas Ranger*, 123. He was born April 15, 1852, in Travis County. While he was still a teenager his parents died and he and his siblings were placed under the guardianship of Rev. J.H. Wofford. He received further education under Dr. Burleson at Waco University. By the 1870s he had composed a book of verse that was entitled *The Years of Youth*, published by Lippincott & Co. of Philadelphia in 1873. He mustered into McNelly's company on September 10, 1876, and served until January 15, 1877. He then served under Hall. Unfortunately the poetic muse did not inspire Rowe to write of his ranger experiences. Horace Rowe died in Waco on September 15, 1883, and is buried in Oakwood Cemetery in Waco. *Galveston Daily News*, August 26, 1873; Samuel Houston Dixon, *The Poets and Poetry of Texas* (Austin: Sam H. Dixon & Co., 1885), 273-76.

61. Monthly Return of J.L. Hall, dated December 31, 1876, prepared at Clinton; *Austin Weekly Democratic Statesman*, December 28, 1876.

62. Monthly Return of J.L. Hall, dated December 31, 1876, prepared at Clinton.

NOTES TO CHAPTER 4

1. *Galveston Daily News*, January 6, 1877. The letter was written from Goliad on December 29, 1876.

2. *Daily Democratic Statesman*, January 10, 1877.

3. *Weekly Democratic Statesman*, April 6, 1876.

4. *Weekly Democratic Statesman*, August 31, 1876. To be fair the quartet were recaptured within hours by deputy sheriffs Moore and Carrington.

5. The complete order dated January 18, was published in the *Galveston Daily News* of January 23, 1877, as well as other publications.

6. Jennings, *A Texas Ranger*, 293.

7. Durham, *Taming the Nueces Strip*, 158. T.C. Robinson's career is best told in his own writings. See *"Pidge," Texas Ranger*, a collection of his writings and with annotations by Chuck Parsons. His letters (and some poems) were written while in Austin, then with McNelly during the Sutton-Taylor Feud, and then again with McNelly on the Rio Grande Frontier.

8. *Daily Democratic Statesman*, February 15, 1877.

9. Details of the Polecat fight and subsequent action from an unpublished biography of Alfred Y. Allee by Gary P. Fitterer and from Hall's Monthly Return for March 1877; and Austin's *Daily Democratic Statesman* February 15, 1877, and *Galveston Daily News*, February 21, 1877.

10. *Galveston Daily News*, December 21, 1876. Ajax was the pseudonym of the Goliad reporter, writing on December 15.

11. *Victoria Advocate*, March 17, 1877.

12. *Galveston Daily News*, March 3, 1877, from the Goliad correspondent letter dated February 27, 1877.

13. Monthly Return of J.L. Hall, dated February 28, 1877, prepared at Clinton, DeWitt County.

14. This refers to the noted Larkin Ferguson who was identified as one of the bank robbers. William Cavin here again appears as a desperado but in reality he was a ranger spy who was able to infiltrate various gangs, which aided in their capture. Rudd is William L. Rudd and Rector is Horace G. Rector who served under Captain McNelly from July 25, 1874, to October 31, 1876, and then under Hall.

15. "Statement of Arrests," report prepared by Lieutenant Hall, February 1877, signed "J.L. Hall Lt Comd'g Sp'e State Troops."

16. *Galveston Daily News*, March 13, 1877, reporting news from Travis County. Ranger Deggs has received little attention from historians. He was born in 1849 in Mississippi, the son of James and Olivia Deggs. He was mustered into McNelly's troop on August 6, 1876, and honorably discharged at Victoria on February 1, 1877. The record also shows he was mustered into Hall's Special State Troops on March 31, 1877, at Clinton and continued to serve with Hall through August 31, 1877. A brief item from Milam County and printed in the *Galveston Daily News* of January 25, 1876, identifies a Mr. Deggs as City Marshal at Rockdale, Texas. Possibly Deggs learned of McNelly's recruiting and contacted him at Burton, McNelly's hometown. Burton and Rockdale are less than seventy miles apart.

17. *Galveston Daily News*, March 13, 1877.

18. *The Texas Republican* (Marshall), January 19, 1867.

19. *Galveston Daily News*, March 28, 1877.

20. *Galveston Daily News*, March 28, 1877, in "Houston Local Items."

21. *Texas Republican* (Marshall, Texas), January 19, 1867. Family information on Wooten is from the 1860 Houston County Census, 240. Their post office was Prairie.

22. "Convict and Conduct Register, Huntsville State Penitentiary," 34.

23. Correspondence in the *Galveston Daily News*, March 9, 1877, reporting news from Goliad.

24. Lieutenant Hall's Monthly Return for March 1877; and "State News" from Gonzales County in *Galveston Daily News*, March 21, 1877.

25. *Dallas Daily Herald*, March 17, 1877.

26. Sheriff Columbus Lafayette Thurmond was born in Dreyer County, Tennessee, on November 13, 1833, and once he moved to Victoria County he remained there during his lifetime with only a few years spent elsewhere. His marriage to Margaret Alice McGrew produced seven

children. Thurmond was appointed sheriff on February 4, 1874, was elected February 24, and served until November 2, 1880. He was then elected again on November 2, 1886, was re-elected 1888, and served until November 8, 1890. Visit to Evergreen Cemetery; Tise, 511; 1880 Victoria County census, 144. Death claimed Thurmond after a brief illness on February 1, 1903. A lengthy obituary appeared in the *Daily Advocate*, February 2, 1903. Thurmond was popularly known as "Old Zip" but the *Advocate* offers no explanation as to how he was given that nickname.

27. *Victoria Advocate*, March 17, 1877.

28. *Tri-Weekly Herald*, Marshall, Texas, March 27, 1877; *Galveston Daily News*, April 4, 1877, and the *Tri-Weekly Herald*, April 10, 1877. For a superlative biography of Joe Horner see Robert K. DeArment's *Alias Frank Canton*, published by the University of Oklahoma Press, 1996.

29. *Galveston Daily News*, March 27, 1877.

30. N.A. Jennings, who should have known better, provided a version of the White incident for a Philadelphia newspaper, which was then picked up by the *San Antonio Express*. He wrote: "Hall personally arrested Ham White, the most dreaded and successful 'road agent' Texas ever knew, a man who invariably worked alone, and who, single-handed, robbed many a stagecoach. Hall trailed White from the scene of one of his exploits, caught him in a livery stable fifty miles away and arrested him. White was armed with two six shooters and showed fight, but Hall sprang at him, knocked him down and overpowered him after a desperate struggle." *San Antonio Express*, January 12, 1900.

31. The life and career of the stagecoach robber is thoroughly related in Mark Dugan's *Knight of the Road: The Life of Highwayman Ham White.*

32. *Galveston Daily News*, March 29, 1877. Hall may have also had with him Horace Rowe, according to the *Galveston Daily News* of March 30, 1877. The special telegram from Austin to the *News* stated that Rowe "recognized White as the person who murdered a Mr. Rowe, cousin of Horace, now in Bastrop [C]ounty."

33. *Galveston Daily News*, March 29, 1877, reported that Hall arrested the "lone highwayman" in Jackson's livery stable "where he was saddling his horse, preparatory to leaving." Caldwell County Tax rolls for 1877 do not list a Jackson owning a livery stable; perhaps the report merely indicated the stable was known by an employee named Jackson.

34. Much of the information on the discovery of the stage robber and then the arrest of White and Vaughn is from the *Austin Weekly Statesman* of April 5, 1877. The telegram is from Dugan's biography of White, and numerous newspaper articles are transcribed in *The Bad Boys of Caldwell County Texas Book Two: Murder and Mayhem in the 1880s* by Victoria Dunnahoo Daywood and Peggy White Engledow, 13-16.

35. Thomas Fassitt Purnell was born in Worcester County, Maryland, on March 3, 1820, the son of Marthena and Euphemia Purnell. Sometime during the next decades Thomas located to Indiana where he married Caroline Ariadne Porter. During the war he served as a quartermaster and rose to the rank of captain. By 1870 he was in Texas and was appointed United States Marshal of the Western District of Texas by President Grant. In 1877 he and Forbes Britton, the father-in-law of Gov. E. J. Davis, had an altercation on Congress Avenue in which Purnell was severely wounded which necessitated his right arm being amputated to save his life. Major Purnell died on December 3, 1894, in Austin and is buried in Oakwood Cemetery in Austin. His grave is marked. Find-A-Grave.com; 1850 Worcester County, Maryland, census, 300; 1880 Travis County census, 229B; *Daily Democratic Statesman*, August 11, 1877; *Austin Daily Statesman*, December 13, 1894. Carl H. Moneyhon, *Edmund J. Davis: Civil War General, Republican Leader, Reconstruction Governor.*

36. Dugan, 24, and *Galveston Daily News*, April 17, citing a special telegram from Austin dated April 16, 1877.

37. *Morning Star* (Wilmington, North Carolina) April 21, 1877, printing an item from the *Greensboro Patriot.*

38. David Alfred Theophalis Walton was born in Lawrence County, Alabama, on August 13, 1837; he served with the Confederacy, enlisting in 1861. In 1880 he was married to Amanda M. Lee and was listed as sheriff and farmer on the census with his seven children. He died in Alpine, Texas, on June 14, 1915, and is buried in the Elm Grove Cemetery. 1880 Bee County, Texas census and Find-A-Grave, accessed September 29, 2018.

39. The 1870 Victoria County census shows Edward J. Singleton as a seventeen-year-old white male, working as "Stock Laborer," son of William and Julia A. Singleton. The 1860 census, however, shows him as Edward, ten years old. The *Victoria Advocate* of May 5, 1877, wrote that "Singleton was born and reared in Victoria . . . and known personally to almost every one of our citizens" yet the same issue identified him as John E. Singleton. A letter supposedly written by Singleton to his mother, Mrs. J.A. Singleton from his cell, was signed as James Edward Singleton. 1860 Victoria County census, p. 80 and 1870 census, 296A; *Victoria Advocate* May 5, 1877 and May 12, 1877.

40. "State News" column in the *Galveston Daily News*, July 28, 1875.

41. *Galveston Daily News*, August 19, 1876.

42. *Galveston Daily News*, August 20, 1876.

43. *New Orleans Times-Picayune*, May 9, 1877.

44. *Galveston Daily News*, March 13, 1877.

45. "Statement of Arrests," J.L. Hall dated April 30, 1877.

46. *Galveston Daily News*, May 29, 1877, reporting news from San Antonio as printed in the *San Antonio News Reporter*.

47. *Galveston Daily News*, May 29, 1877. This was from a letter to the editors of the *News* dated May 24, from Cuero.

48. Monthly Return of J.L. Hall dated May 31, 1877, prepared at Clinton, DeWitt County.

49. "Statement of Arrests," May, 1877.

50. *Victoria Advocate*, May 25, 1877.

51. Monthly Return of J.L. Hall dated June 30, 1877, prepared at Clinton, DeWitt County.

52. "Statement of Arrests," July 1877.

53. Ibid., August 1877.

54. Ibid., August 1877.

55. *Victoria Advocate*, August 18, 1877. Citing a report from an undated *Corpus Christi Free Press.*

56. *Victoria Advocate*, August 25, 1877, citing an undated *Sutherland Springs Chronicle.*

57. *Austin Daily Democratic Statesman*, August 29, 1877.

58. *Galveston Daily News*, August 17, citing a special from Brownsville of August 16, 1877.

59. *Victoria Advocate*, August 25, 1877.

60. Ibid.

61. *Victoria Advocate*, August 25, 1877. Hall did not have his entire command ready to invade Mexico; several of his men remained in Goliad.

62. *Victoria Advocate*, September 1, 1877. The *Advocate* misidentified this man as Garcia but his name was Garza.

63. *Victoria Advocate*, September 8, 1877, citing an editorial from an undated *Dallas Daily Herald.*

64. J.L. Hall to Miss Julia Pease, September 7, 1877, written from Rio Grande City. The four Hall letters are at the Austin History Center, AR.A.001/RNGPC Incoming Correspondence, 1877, folder 82/3.

65. *Victoria Advocate*, September 22, 1877.

66. *Victoria Advocate*, September 22 and October 6, 1877.

67. *Victoria Advocate*, September 29, October 6, 1877, citing an article from an undated *Corpus Christi Free Press*; and *Advocate* of October 6, citing an article from an undated *Goliad Guard*.

68. *Victoria Advocate*, October 6, 1877 citing an article from an undated *Pleasanton Journal*.

69. *Victoria Advocate*, October 20, 1877.

70. *Victoria Advocate*, October 20, 1877.

71. "Statement of Arrests" November 1877. The next "Statement of Arrests" is for February 1 through March 31, 1878. All these are large documents in oversized Box 401-1238.

Notes to Chapter 5

1. Statement of Arrests, April 30, 1877.

2. The report from Flatonia misidentified the ranger with Deggs as "J. Jenson" but correctly E.J. Jenson. Jenson was born September 16, 1853, in Denmark; according to the 1910 Starr County census he immigrated to the U.S. in 1872 and was "naturalized." His wife, Mary Evans, was born in 1867. His work as a ranger began under McNelly, mustering in on August 1, 1876, and mustering out on February 1, 1877. He then joined Hall's command on January 25, 1877, and served until January 1, 1878. After his ranger career he became a manager of the Galveston Ranch and was later associated with the Jesus Maria Ranch in Jim Hogg County. In 1910 he was identified as "Stockman" of the Casa Verde Ranch in Starr County, Texas. Jenson died June 5, 1919, at Pasadena, California but is buried in St. Mary's Catholic Cemetery in San Antonio. Ranger Service Records, 1910 Starr County, Texas Census, and *San Antonio Evening News*, June 7, 1919.

3. *Galveston Daily News*, April 18, 1877, citing a special telegram from Flatonia dated April 17.

4. 1870 Natchitoches Parish, Louisiana, Census, 389.

5. "Convict Record, Texas State Penitentiary," Huntsville, Texas, 173. He entered as prisoner # 6341. The original prison records are in the Texas State Library but many of them are available online.

6. *Daily Democratic Statesman*, May 30, 1877.

7. A full treatment of this Thompson killing appears in *Ben Thompson: Portrait of a Gunfighter* by Thomas C. Bicknell and Chuck Parsons.

8. Statement of Arrests, Captain J.L Hall, May 1877.

9. Hall's Monthly Return for May 1877; *Daily Democratic Statesman*, May 30, 1877.

10. *Daily Democratic Statesman*, June 2, 1877.

11. Statement of Arrests, June 1877; Monthly Return, dated June 30, 1877.

12. Statement of Arrests, August 31, 1877.

13. Watson has received little attention among ranger historians of the Old West. He was born in Mississippi January 30, 1850, and died December 31, 1908, at his home in Kingsville, Texas. An obituary pointed out that "he came to Texas many years ago, and made this State his home ever since." He was a member of the ranger service and "and by his good works as a ranger in the old days, when this section was in need of such service, he became well known to the people of Southwest Texas." *Brownsville Daily Herald*, January 2, 1909. He was buried in the Chamberlain Cemetery in Kingsville, Kleburg County, Texas. After his ranger days Watson remained in Nueces County. In 1880 he worked as a dray keeper for hire. That year's census shows him as a resident of the widow Rachel Byington boarding house. There he met the widow's daughter; the two were married July 24, 1882, in Corpus Christi.

14. Further details on Armstrong's gunshot wound are in *John B. Armstrong: Texas Ranger and Pioneer Ranchman*, 47-48.

15. Hall to Adj. Gen. William Steele, May 31, 1877.

16. Hardin at the time of his capture had a $4,000 reward offered for him. The question has often been asked: did anyone receive the full reward? Jack Duncan in an 1895 interview claimed it, but an 1877 news item contradicts him. According to this the Comptroller had issued a warrant for $3,806 to Lieutenant Armstrong for the arrest of Hardin, "that being all the money left of the appropriation for this purpose. There is a balance of $194 due, which will be paid as soon as another appropriation is made." *Weekly Herald* (Marshall, Texas), September 8, 1877.

17. "Convict Record, Texas State penitentiaries at Huntsville, Walker County, Texas," 224.

18. The literature on Hardin is voluminous. Other than his autobiography, *The Life of John Wesley Hardin*, consult Rick Miller's biography of Duncan, *Bounty Hunter*, Richard C. Marohn's *The Last Gunfighter*, and Chuck Parsons and Norman Wayne Brown's *A Lawless Breed: John Wesley Hardin, Texas Reconstruction, and Violence in the Wild West.*

19. *Galveston Daily News*, October 25, 1877, citing news from Gonzales County.

20. Ibid. For details on the life of Bill Taylor and the feud that cost many lives, see this author's *The Sutton-Taylor Feud: The Deadliest Blood Feud in Texas.* It was Lieutenant Berch S. Foster and a squad of rangers from the Frontier Battalion who captured Taylor on April 15, 1877.

21. *Daily Democratic Statesman*, May 16, 1877.

22. Bracken was born about 1850. In 1870 he was living in Grimes County, with occupation listed as farm laborer. Grimes County Census, enumerated July 29, 1870, 331. This identical report was printed in the *Daily Democratic Statesman* of June 14, 1877, as well as in the *Weekly Democratic Statesman* of June 21, 1877.

23. "Convict Record, Texas State Penitentiaries at Huntsville, Walker County, Texas," 173.

24. *Galveston Daily News*, November 1, 1877, reporting "State News" from the *Victoria Advocate*, November 1, 1877. The "Convict Record, Texas State Penitentiary" identified the second convict as "Elsie Brown," a nineteen-year-old youth who used tobacco and was intemperate, who had no education and was a common laborer. He was born in Texas as was Callison. Brown was sentenced during the October term of Goliad County to a term of five years for "Theft of a gelding." He was received on October 26, 1877. A proclamation dated December 10, 1877, from Governor Hubbard reduced his term of prison to five months.

25. Monthly Return for June and July 1877.

26. The 1870 census shows the Trimble family residing in Medina County. Dorothy Trimble is listed as head of household number 338, a 62-year-old woman operating a farm. With her are the five children, Fredrich, Thomas, Robert and Madlie son and daughter both twenty years old suggesting they were twins, and Alice. Also in the household was Mary Trimble, age eighty-three years, perhaps the mother of the husband and father of the balance of the family. Next door, in household # 339 is the John Trimble family, that of the son who was now making his own way. The two households consisting of fifteen people listed heads of household from Kentucky, with others from Virginia, Ohio, and Texas. Medina County Census, post office Castroville, enumerated July 21, 1870, 206B.

27. *Galveston Daily News*, July 14, 1877, citing special correspondence to the *News* from San Antonio dated July 11, 1877.

28. Monthly Return of Lieutenant Pat Dolan, July 1877. Hall's Monthly Return also indicated the pursuers crossed over into Mexico.

29. *Daily Democratic Statesman*, July 29, 1877, citing a report from an undated *Atascosa Farmer*.

30. *Charlotte Daily Observer*, printing an article from the *New North State*, September 1, 1877.

31. *Victoria Advocate*, November 17, 1877, citing a news item from an undated *Cuero Bulletin.*

32. *Victoria Advocate*, November 17, 1877, citing a news item from an undated *Cuero Bulletin*; Monthly Return, November 1877.

33. *Austin Daily Democratic Statesman*, October 28 and November 10, 1877. See also *Texas Ranger N.O. Reynolds: The Intrepid* by Chuck Parsons and Donaly E. Brice, pp. 136-37, published by University of North Texas Press, 2014.

34. *Victoria Advocate*, December 8, 1877, citing news item from an undated *Goliad Guard*; Monthly Return, November 1877.

35. *Victoria Advocate*, December 15, 1877, citing a news item from an undated *Cuero Bulletin.*

36. *Victoria Advocate*, December 22, 1877, citing a news item from an undated *Cuero Bulletin.*

37. *Victoria Advocate*, December 29, 1877, citing a news item from an undated *Houston Telegram.*

38. *Victoria Advocate*, January 19, 1878, citing a news item from an undated *Cuero Bulletin.*

39. *Galveston Daily News*, February 19, 1878. The escape attempt occurred the night of February 17.

40. *Austin Daily Democratic Statesman*, January 18, 1878, headlined "A First Class Pummeling."

41. *Brenham Weekly Banner*, January 25, 1878. John Price remains an elusive figure. It is believed that he is the John Price who was the son of William and Frances Price, and was born in Louisiana about 1839. A lengthy article in the *San Antonio Light* reported him as a less than honorable figure. Before the war Price was a special officer for the New Orleans police "and was noted for his general crookedness and

cussedness." He had "killed his man" and was in the penitentiary when General Benjamin Butler occupied New Orleans "and was liberated by that doughty knight of the spoons." He arrived in Texas in 1869 and worked for the Houston & Texas Central Railroad but was dismissed for "dirty work and drunkenness." For a while "he lived the life of an adventurer of a low order" then attempted to establish a police department in Galveston but then moved to San Antonio. He "gave away some important detective work which was being done by Captain Lee Hall [who] flatly accused him of this treachery, when Price drew a pistol on the Captain." Hall's pummeling of Price was so unmerciful that Price was confined in his room for "several weeks." Was Price's title of "Captain" honorary or was it earned during the late war? He appears for the first and only time in the life of Lee Hall in this fistfight against Lee Hall on the streets of Austin in 1878. He later became a professional detective. In late November 1878 he was the object of an assassination attempt but he received only head wounds and survived. The Austin report sarcastically stated that "He only got shot in the head and was very bloody, and such things are too common to be seriously joked about. It was all done in the dark at the very sweet town of Hempstead." He at one time worked with the more famous detective Jim Courtright in Fort Worth. His final fate remains unknown. *Austin Daily Democratic Statesman*, January 18, 1878; *Weekly Democraic Statesman*, December 5, 1878; *San Antonio Light*, January 23, 1883; February 13, 1883; and *Galveston Daily News*, October 2, 1883.

42. *Daily Democratic Statesman*, December 12, 1877.

43. *Victoria Advocate*, February 2 and 16, 1878.

44. Pattie Townes, born March 15, 1856, would marry Eldridge Lee Rector and eventually locate in San Saba County, Texas. By 1930 Mr. Rector had passed and she lived with her daughter Lucy Rector, forty years of age and a public school teacher, and her brother-in-law H.J. King, eighty years of age yet a lawyer, practicing "General Law." San Saba 1930 Census, 116A. She died December 5, 1935, at the age of seventy-nine.

45. *Austin Daily Democratic Statesman*, February 21, 1878. The wedding is further described in *John B. Armstrong: Texas Ranger and Pioneer Ranchman.*

46. Rick Miller, *Sam Bass and Gang*, 125-30. The four robbers were identified as Sam Bass, Frank Jackson, Seaborn Barnes, and Tom Spotswood. Miller's biography of Bass and his outlaw career remains the near-definitive work on this outlaw who became a Texas folk hero.

47. *Tri-Weekly Herald* (Marshall, Texas), February 26, 1878.

48. *Galveston Daily News*, February 26, 1878.

49. Monthly Return, March 1878.

50. Charles M. Holden was a Kentuckian who in 1870 had a wife, Hatty S., and a two-month-old son George W. residing in Refugio County. Aransas County was created in September 1872 and his residence then was in the newly created county without his having relocated. Hattie S. Holden was the daughter of G.M. Fulton, the civil engineer who constructed the famous Fulton Mansion that still stands in spite of numerous hurricanes, which have inflicted some damage.

51. *Victoria Advocate*, March 9, 1878, citing a report from an undated *Rockport Transcript.*

52. *Galveston Daily News*, February 26, 1878, citing a special telegram from Rockport to the *News* dated February 25.

53. Alexander Shaw McKay, a native of Scotland, served first under McNelly from July 26, 1876, to February 1, 1877; and served under Hall from January 26, 1877, through December 1, 1878. Honorably discharged he soon developed a relationship with Miss Alice White, a Louisiana native, of Galveston. They were "joined in the holy bond of matrimony" on January 27, 1879, prior to leaving for Houston. Alice White McKay (frequently Mackay) was born November 15, 1851, and survived her husband many years before passing on April 29, 1930. She is buried in Galveston. The McKays had four children, Jeannette, Gloria, Katherine,

and Ella Alexandria. Ranger A.S. McKay (as he signed his papers) died relatively young, passing on June 8, 1886, in Galveston, from what was then described as "nervous exhaustion." As yet no headstone has been discovered although it is presumed he was buried in the same plot as his wife. *Galveston Daily News*, January 28, 1879; June 9, 1886; "Mortuary Report," June 13, 1886; 1910 Galveston County Census, Alice Mackay.

54. *Tri-Weekly Herald*, Marshall, Texas, March 5, 1878, citing a news item from Rockport dated February 26.

55. The spelling of this man's surname posed a problem for reporters and later historians. The 1850 Calhoun County census shows a Hans Witnabed, twenty-nine, with wife Louisa, thirty, and her child Fred Halshoffer, nine years of age. In addition there is a Charles Witnabed, age two years, and a daughter Martha, three years of age. This census shows Louisa as the head of household; she and her son were born in Germany with Charles and Martha born in Tennessee. Their post office was Indianola. In the Elgin, Bastrop County, cemetery there is a grave marker for a Charles E. Wittnebirt which is believed to be the same man.

56. *Galveston Daily News*, March 13, 1878, reporting news from Nueces County. A news item in the *Dallas Daily Herald* of March 15, 1878, cited a report from Aransas County to the effect that Charles Franks Lebree, *alias* Frank Richmond, *alias* Coloma Franks, was the wounded robber and was "improving rapidly." The *Victoria Advocate* of May 18, 1878, identifies the four men as Frank LeBrecht, Gordon Franks, Charles Willinbert and Frank Hartman. They plead guilty to the indictment and were each sentenced to four years imprisonment in the penitentiary.

57. The prison record showing escape attempts and punishments is in the large ledger "Office Sup't. of Public Instruction State of Texas," pages 698-99. Of interest is that Charles Franks was a native of Germany while Frank Hartman was a native of New York.

58. *Galveston Daily News*, March 2, 1878, citing a special telegram from Indianola dated March 1 to the *News*.

59. Cavin's name is sometimes seen as William P. although his Ranger Service Record clearly shows he signed his documents as W.T. Cavin. His surviving service records show he served under Hall from June 1 to August 31, 1878; October 1, 1879, to August 31, 1879, and then after reorganization September 1, 1879, and was discharged February 29, 1880. He was born May 18, 1857, the son of William T. and Mary Lamar Cavin. By the time of the 1880 Burnet County Census he was a resident of that county, age 23, with his wife Sarah Elizabeth, 21, and a three-month-old son named William H. Cavin. The ranger-spy died on July 4, 1936, in Ballinger but is buried in Brady, Texas. He and his wife, who predeceased him, share a double headstone in the Live Oak Cemetery in McCulloch County. 1880 Burnet County Census, 156, and death certificate # 37755. Henry C. Cavin, a younger brother by six years of William Thomas, also entered the Texas Ranger service on December 1, 1879, under Captain Hall, and served under Oglesby and then McMurry until he was discharged on March 31, 1884. Ranger Service Records.

60. The newspapers spell this man's surname in a variety of ways. The Huntsville prison record spells his name Withenbirt. There is a headstone in the Elgin, Texas, cemetery which is probably his and the name is Wittnebirt. Presumably the stone cutter erred in switching the "ne" rather than "en" but that is not certain. That Charles Wittnebirt died February 14, 1891, at the age of forty years, four months, and one day.

61. *Victoria Advocate*, February 15, 1878, citing a report from an undated *Goliad Guard.*

62. *Galveston Daily News*, January 3, 1878; January 30, 1878. *Victoria Advocate*, March 2, 1878, citing a news item from an undated *Pleasanton Stock Journal* (Atascosa County), March 2, 1878.

63. *Austin Daily Democratic Statesman*, July 4, 1879. Family information on Ben or Warren Goodwin has not been located. His Wilson County victim, William Volrath, was the son of Louis and Auguste Volrath, and was born about 1855 in Texas. His parents, father a blacksmith, were both natives of Saxony. The 1870 Wilson County census shows Louis and

Auguste (46 and 35 years old respectively) and children Louisa, William, age fourteen, Adolphe, Fredrick, Emilie, Louis, and Edward. 1870 Wilson County Census, post office Lodi, 470B.

64. *Victoria Advocate*, April 13, 1878.

65. Monthly Return of Capt. J.L. Hall, October 31, 1878; *Victoria Advocate*, November 16, 1878.

66. *Victoria Advocate*, April 20, 1878, citing a report from an undated *Wilson County Chronicle*; "Results of Operations of State Troops," Adjutant General Records, Texas State Library, RG 401-1082.

67. *Dallas Weekly Herald*, reporting news from Grayson County, May 4, 1878.

68. William L. Rudd, born in England, August 10, 1845, served a lengthy term as a Ranger, beginning his career under Captain L.H. McNelly on October 1, 1874, until January 1, 1877, then under J.L. Hall, and then serving under Thomas L. Oglesby, Charles B. McKinney when acting lieutenant of Company F, and then Joseph Shely. His ranger service ended on February 29, 1880. Rudd was appointed sheriff of Karnes County September 9, 1886, elected November 1886 and served until November 6, 1888. He died in Karnes City on January 9, 1945, but is buried in Westside Cemetery in Yorktown, DeWitt County. His death certificate identifies him as "Captain" Rudd, an honorary title. Texas Ranger Service Records; Tise, *Texas County Sheriffs*, 296 and author's visit to gravesite.

69. Theodore Storey Hillyer, the son of famed Austin photographer Hamilton B. Hillyer, served first under Captain John C. Sparks of Company C, Frontier Battalion from September 27, 1876, to November 30, 1876, and then under Hall, June 1, 1877 until honorably discharged July 20, 1878. He died in Houston August 17, 1913. He is buried in Austin's historic Oakwood Cemetery. Ranger Service records and *Austin Daily Statesman*, August 19, 1913.

70. *Galveston Daily News*, May 18, 1878.

71. *National Police Gazette,* June 1, 1878, page 9.

72. *Victoria Advocate,* May 25, citing a lengthy report from the *Gonzales Inquirer* of May 18, 1878.

73. Monthly Return of J.L. Hall, May 31, 1878, prepared at Corpus Christi.

74. The most complete biography of this Texas folk-hero is *Sam Bass & Gang* by Rick Miller, published by State House Press of Austin in 1999.

75. Monthly Return of J.L. Hall, May 31, 1878, prepared at Corpus Christi.

76. Rick Miller, "Ex-Ranger Maurice Moore: Quick to Quarrel," *Journal* of the Wild West History Association 10, no.2 (June 2017).

77. *Galveston Daily News,* July 25, 1878.

78. The summary of the last fight of Bass is from the *Galveston Daily News,* July 23-25, 1878, and from Rick Miller, *Sam Bass and Gang.*

79. *Victoria Advocate,* July 27, 1878.

80. *Victoria Advocate,* August 17, 1878.

81. The notorious Brack Cornett was finally run down by Deputy Sheriff Alfred Y. Allee on Sunday February 12, 1888. The amount of rewards offered for Cornett had reached nearly $5000. Allee's version of the killing appeared in the *Galveston Daily News* of February 15, 1888. See also the *Austin Daily Statesman,* February 14, 1888. For a complete study of the gang see *The Cornett-Whitley Gang: Violence Unleased in Texas* by Dave Johnson.

82. *Victoria Advocate,* September 21, 1878.

83. *Victoria Advocate,* October 19, 1878, posting news from Goliad "from our regular correspondent."

84. *Victoria Advocate,* November 2, 1878.

85. The 1870 Cameron County Census shows the Vicente Rodriguez family, consisting of Vicente and his wife Pablo and their two sons, Gil, seventeen, and Martin, fifteen. The males are all listed as "Farm Laborers" and all were Mexico-born. Cameron County Census, August 17, 1870, 64.

86. Monthly Return of J.L. Hall, December 31, 1878, prepared at Corpus Christi.

87. Scanlon was first elected Cameron County sheriff on December 3, 1869, and served until December 2, 1873; he was then elected a second time February 15, 1876, and served until November 2, 1880. Tise, *Texas County Sheriffs*, 86.

88. *Galveston Daily News*, December 10, 1878, quoting an undated *Rio Grande Democrat*.

89. Monthly Return of J.L. Hall, December 31, 1878, prepared at Corpus Christi.

NOTES TO CHAPTER 6

1. Joshua E. Peters was the son of Stephen and Margaret Peters and was born in Mason, Mason County, Texas, January 14, 1854. By the time of the 1870 census the Peters family resided in Refugio County, where the father and three eldest sons were identified as "Sailor." Joshua was then seventeen. What work he did until his marriage to Ida L. Williams in 1877 in Live Oak County is unknown. Also uncertain is whether his wife and child were with him that day of August 1 when the tragedy took place. Peters was buried in the Banquette Cemetery. His grave is marked.

2. The spelling of this ranger's family name varies as "Tally" and "Talley." He was born in Jackson County, Missouri, the son of B.C. and Martha Tally, per the 1850 census. Through the years his name appears as both Tally and Talley. In fact on the Texas Ranger service records his own signature appears as both Tally and Talley. For consistency I have used the Talley spelling, as that is the spelling on his official death

certificate (# 21691) as well as how his name appears in the report of his death. *Falfurrias Facts* (Brooks County, Texas), May 13, 1938. Talley is buried in the Falfurrias Burial Park, Plot D/3/19, although his grave has no marker. The death certificate gives his date of birth as October 16, 1848, and date of death as May 10, 1938.

3. *Marshall Messenger*, August 16, 1878, citing reports from Corpus Christi dated August 1.

4. *Galveston Daily News*, August 16, 1878, citing a special telegram dated August 15 from Corpus Christi.

5. George Durham, *Taming the Nueces Strip: The Story of McNelly's Rangers*, 175-76.

6. *The Missouri Sharp Shooter*, Rolla, Missouri, December 22, 1905.

7. Mike B. Wright was elected sheriff of Nueces County November 4, 1902 and was reelected six times and served until November 7, 1918. Tise, *Texas County Sheriffs*, 395.

8. *El Paso Daily Times*, March 18, 1905; *Corpus Christi Caller*, May 9, May 10, 1905; *Houston Post*, December 16, 1905, May 19, 1906, December 4, 1906; *San Antonio Daily Express*, December 18, 1906.

9. George Washington Talley was born in Jackson County, Missouri, on October 16, 1848, and died May 10, 1938, at the age of eighty-nine in Falfurrias, Brooks County, Texas. His death certificate states he died of "Natural Causes" and "Old Age." Nueces County Death Certificate # 21691. One obituary reported that for many years he had been an employee of the King Ranch. Ignoring the Peters killing and the decades of being a fugitive from Texas justice, the obituary identified him as "an early Ranger and pioneer in the South Texas region. . . . Coming to Texas from Missouri, he was closely associated with the development of the territory south of the Nueces River." *Falfurrias Facts*, May 13, 1938.

10. Hall's Monthly Return for September 1878.

11. *Galveston Daily News*, October 4, 1878.

12. Monthly Return of Captain Hall, October 1878; *Galveston Daily News*, November 29, 1878, citing "State News" from the *Corpus Christi Gazette* of November 21. Articles describing the hanging were reported nationally, including reports from Galveston of July 11 and reprinted in Massachusetts's *Boston Post* and *Boston Daily Globe* of July 12, 1879, and in the *Brenham Weekly Banner*, July 18, 1879. "He was defiant to the last" it from a dispatch from Corpus Christi appearing in the *News* and reprinted in the *Boston Post* of July 12. Lengthy articles on the execution and a summary of the trial and appeal appear in the *Galveston Daily News* of July 12, 1879 and January 16, 1879.

13. *Galveston Daily News*, January 23, 1879, citing a report from Eagle Pass of January 18, 1879.

14. David Johnson, *The Mason County "Hoo Doo" War, 1874-1902*, 5.

15. C.L. Sonnichsen, *Ten Texas Feuds*. Hoodoos "were members of a vigilance committee which attempted, by ambushes and midnight hangings, to get rid of the thieves and outlaws who had been holding a carnival of lawlessness in Mason County, as in other parts of Texas," 88.

16. John Wesley Hardin to Mannen Clements, May 11, 1879. The bulk of the Hardin letters are preserved in the Special Collections at the Texas State University in San Marcos, Texas. They have been published in the *Letters of John Wesley Hardin* transcribed and compiled by Roy and Jo Ann Stamps. The May 11 letter appears on pages 119-20.

17. *San Antonio Express*, January 12, 1900. This is a lengthy article, "Capt. Lee Hall Written Up," composed by Jennings, which apparently had appeared in the *Saturday Evening Post*. The description of Hall running from Hardin is doubted by this writer. If Hall wanted the $4000 reward the incident would have had to happen after June 1874; there was little time for the attempted arrest to happen in Texas as Hardin had left the state in late June or July.

18. *The Union Republican* (Winston, North Carolina), June 12, 1879.

19. *Daily Democratic Statesman*, June 17, 1879 and also in the *Tri-Weekly Herald* (Marshall) of June 21, 1879.

20. George Durham, "On the Trail of 5100 Outlaws," *West* magazine, 108.

21. *Brenham Weekly Banner*, August 15, 1879, printing an item from an undated *San Antonio Herald.*

22. *Victoria Advocate*, September 13, 1879.

23. *Victoria Advocate*, September 27, 1879.

24. *Victoria Advocate*, September 17, 1879; Lee Hall's Monthly Return gives the date of the arrest as September 18, 1879.

25. *Daily Democratic Statesman*, July 13, 1876.

26. Hall's Monthly Return, October 31, 1879. The *Helena Record* reported that the October 1 escort was composed of Karnes County Sheriff Walter Napier and three men of Hall's company, but not Hall himself. The prisoner was brought into open court and the judge "very solemnly proceeded to pronounce the sentence of imprisonment in the state penitentiary for life. It was quite an affecting scene; some who were present were even moved to tears. Sharp protested his innocence of the crime for which he is sentenced." *Helena Record* item cited in the *Galveston Daily News*, October 10, 1879. If four men had been together when Sharp killed Cone then the prisoner perhaps believed the other three should be punished as well; or perhaps Sharp did not believe he was being treated fairly.

27. "Texas, Convict and Conduct Register, 1875-1945," 20. The originals of these ledgers are housed in the Texas State Archives; they are also on line.

28. Lieutenant T.L. Oglesby's Semi-monthly Report, dated September 30, 1879, Special Forces Correspondence, RG 401-1157-19.

29. *Galveston Daily News*, October 16, 1879.

30. *Gonzales Inquirer*, November 1, 1879.

31. *Daily Democratic Statesman*, April 15, 1881, and *Weekly Democratic Statesman*, April 21, 1881.

32. Captain Hall's Monthly Return for September 1879.

33. *Galveston Daily News*, September 26, 1879, printing news from Uvalde County.

34. *Galveston Daily News*, October 16, 1879, citing a special telegram of October 15 from Uvalde County.

35. Durham, "On the Trail of 5100 Outlaws," 114.

36. Texas Ranger Service Record, Texas State Archives. An item in Austin's *Daily Democratic Statesman* on August 3, 1879, provides a glimpse into Allen's career. Allen, "an applicant for the position of lieutenant in Capt. Hall's company, is a gentleman of high moral worth and of exceptional character. Having had an experience of four years, holding different positions in the rangers, and being thoroughly acquainted with the habits of the frontiersmen, is well fitted to the position, and should receive the appointment in the lieutenancy." He did not receive that appointment, as Thomas L. Oglesby did. The force was reduced to seven men by 1880 when he and his company were enumerated on the1880 Duval County census, "encamped near San Diego." Oglesby was identified as "Commander of Company" with Samuel A. McMurry as lieutenant. The six privates —William Wilder, William E. Blackshear, Samuel M. Platt, John McNelly (the nephew of the late Captain McNelly), William Scott, and Pablino S. Coy— were simply listed as "Ranger" with Jack Robinson, the sole black, listed as teamster. Oglesby on November 7, 1882, was elected sheriff of Maverick County, Texas, and served until his resignation on January 17, 1887. 1880 Duval County Census, 241; Tise, *Texas County Sheriffs*, 363.

37. *Weimar Mercury*, December 23, 1893, reported George Henry Allen's death as happening in Coleman, Coleman County, Texas, on December 15

of pneumonia, at the age of forty. He was married to Miss Allee Jackson, "about the year '82." He left his widow and five children to mourn the loss. Allen was buried in the Odd Fellows' Cemetery of Weimar. His grave is marked.

38. Burns Station began in 1826 when Arthur Burns built a two-story house on the east bank of the Guadalupe River, south of Irish Creek in (today) DeWitt County. When other settlers moved to the area the settlement became known as Burns Station, as it was also a stagecoach stop on the Victoria-Gonzales road, located there to change horses. Willie S. Sutton, daughter of feud victim William M. Sutton, described the settlement as the "beautiful, flourishing town of Burns Station, situated in a very romantic district of country on the Southern Pacific R.R." *The History of DeWitt County*, 81. Today all that marks its location is the cemetery and a state historical marker.

39. *Victoria Advocate*, October 25, 1879, printing a news item from the *Cuero Bulletin* of October 16.

40. Dowlearn, identified by Hall in his report as "Doolan," was born July 24, 1854, and died January 10, 1924. He married Mary Goodson on November 6, 1871. Dowlearn is buried in County Line Cemetery at Yoakum, DeWitt County. See *Dowlearn-Lowe* by Rosalie Key Myers, 6. This is a 22-page self-published pamphlet, 1992.

41. *Victoria Advocate*, October 25, 1879, printing a news item from the *Cuero Bulletin* of October 16, 1879; Monthly Return, October 31, 1879, prepared at San Diego, Texas.

42. *Galveston Daily News*, November 9, 1879, citing a report from an undated *Goliad Guard*.

43. 1880 Goliad County Census shows Dr. L.S. Lipscomb age 52 with a wife, M.L., as Alabama natives. Goliad County Census, 312. Leonidas Star Lipscomb was born November 29, 1827, and died April 2, 1913, at Runge. Mrs. M.L. Libscomb was born June 10, 1825, in Mississippi and died July 28, 1898; she and her husband are both buried in the Runge

Cemetery in Karnes County. Their graves are marked. Also buried in the Runge Cemetery are the Allee brothers, Alfred Y. and Alonzo R., as well as John Wesley Hardin Jr.

44. The 1880 Duval County Census shows Rafael Salinas as a 22-year-old white male, "Herding Stock" with wife Jesusa, 18, both born in Mexico.

45. *Galveston Daily News*, October 24 and November 8, 1879, reporting news from Duval County.

46. Monthly Return of J.L. Hall, October 31, 1879, prepared at San Diego, Duval County. Johnson had experience before serving with Hall; he was mustered into Hall's Special State Troops on August 1, 1879, and was honorably discharged February 1, 1880. Service Records.

47. Norman F. Porter, Sr., *Atascosa County History Through 1912*, 133; 1880 Atascosa County Census, 332; *Galveston Daily News*, April 10, 1911, providing a brief obituary of John Campbell.

48. Captain Hall's Monthly Return for November 1879.

49. This is Private W.D. Martin who Graham remembers, although the service record shows he was not mustered into the Special Forces State Troops until December 1, 1879. Graham perhaps here remembers incorrectly, as Martin and he both continued under Thomas L. Oglesby.

50. Sam Graham was born in Paterson, New Jersey, on April 3, 1858, and served under Neal Coldwell, Guy B. Broadwater, Hall, Thomas L. Oglesby, and Charles L. Nevill. He served for four years almost continually from July 8, 1878, until his honorable discharge on August 31, 1882. He died December 19, 1951, in the Robert B. Green Memorial Hospital in San Antonio. He is buried in Sunset Memorial Park Cemetery located at 1701 Austin Highway in San Antonio. The complete autobiography is printed in the English Westerners Society *Brand Book* 49, no. 1 (Winter 2015): 1-39.

51. *Galveston Daily News*, November 8, 1879; November 11; November 28 citing a report from the *Pleasanton Journal* of November 22. The *New*

Orleans Daily Picayune of November 13 reported the robbery attempt had taken place the night of November 6, not on the fourth.

52. Monthly Return December 1879 and January 1880. Caffall was born September 16, 1842, in England and died April 6, 1923. The 1880 Karnes County Census shows him with his wife Louisa Asher Caffall and their four children. He is there listed as a stockman. Dr. James M. Bockius, whom the enumerator spelled as "Brockus," is listed as a boarder. This is the 45-year-old Prussia-born man who in 1874 was arrested with other cowboys working for John Wesley Hardin and then narrowly avoided being lynched at Clinton. Three other cowboys were lynched but Bockius escaped. 1880 Karnes County Census, 26; Thomas Caffall and his wife share a double headstone in the Asher Cemetery; Jane Bowen Hardin, the wife of J.W. Hardin, is also buried in Asher Cemetery.

53. *Austin Daily Democratic Statesman*, December 24, 1879. Monthly Return, prepared December 1, 1879 at San Diego.

54. *Reading Gazette and Democrat*, Berks County, Pennsylvania, May 2, 1863.

55. "Office of Coast Survey" in Wickipedia.org, accessed August 19, 2018.

56. *Lebanon Daily News*, Lebanon, Pennsylvania, September 13, 1876.

57. "Lebanon Notes" column in the *Reading Times and Dispatch*, July 18, 1880.

58. *Reading Times and Dispatch*, October 12, 1877.

59. *Reading Times and Dispatch*, July 25, 1878.

60. *Reading Times and Dispatch*, December 18, 1879.

61. Captain Hall's Monthly Return for December 1879 and additional page dated January 1, 1880, prepared at San Diego.

62. Lou Conway Roberts (Mrs. D.W. Roberts) *A Woman's Reminiscences of Six Years in Camp with the Texas Rangers.*

63. 1880 San Patricio County Mortality Schedule, prepared by U.R. Wallace, 1.

64. *Galveston Daily News*, January 20, 1880.

65. 1880 San Patricio County Census, 383. Clifford R. Caldwell and Ron DeLord, *Texas Lawmen, 1835-1899: The Good and the Bad*, 200-01.

66. *Galveston Daily News*, May 15, 1880.

67. The rangers found twenty-one head of horses belonging to Mariano Trevino of Cameron County. Hall and Sergeant McMurry delivered the three McCampbell men to Brownsville where they were charged with theft.

68. "Short" Day remains elusive, although apparently it was accepted his name was the genuine article. He was the son of John and Francis Ann Day, and was born about 1863. His older brothers, at the time of his birth fifteen-year-old Alfred and thirteen-year-old Jackson, who would write under the full name of Jack Hays Day, were active in the Sutton-Taylor Feud but apparently Short was considered too young. The family appears as household # 284 with the household of J.M. Dowlearn # 283 and the household of B.F. Lowe. 1870 DeWitt County Census enumerated by Willis Fawcett, 250.

69. This was Edward Davis Grumbles who was charged with the murder of T.J. Thaxton at Sour Springs in Gonzales County eleven years before. The *Gonzales Inquirer* of February 6, 1880, expected him to be delivered to Gonzales "soon." An item in the *Statesman* of Austin reported he had been tried for the Thaxton killing, which occurred in 1869, and he was acquitted on the grounds of self-defense. *Austin Daily Democratic Statesman*, April 18, 1880. By the time of the Federal Census in 1880 Grumbles was living in Frio County, 34 years of age, with wife Mary A., 27, raising two children of his own both under the age of five, and two stepchildren. 1880 Frio County Census, 614. An unconfirmed statement suggests he was killed in La Salle County in 1881.

70. *Victoria Advocate*, February 28, 1880.

71. *Victoria Advocate*, February 14, March 6, and April 10, 1880.

72. *Victoria Advocate*, March 20, 1880.

73. *Daily Democratic Statesman*, March 7, 1880.

74. *Dallas Daily Herald*, March 9, 1880.

75. *Daily Democratic Statesman*, March 27, 1880.

76. Adjutant General Steele's service ended on January 25, 1879, due to health issues; John B. Jones, former Major of the Frontier Battalion, replaced him on January 25, 1879, and continued until his death on July 19, 1881.

77. *Belton Journal*, April 15, 1880, reprinting the article from the *San Antonio Express* of March 29, 1880.

78. *Daily Democratic Statesman*, April 8, 1880.

Notes to Chapter 7

1. Claude Elliott's review of *Captain Lee Hall of Texas* book review published in the *South Western Historical Quarterly*.

2. *Austin Daily Democratic Statesman*, February 3, 1880.

3. *Victoria Advocate*, March 27, 1880.

4. From Victoria, Texas, to the Sierra Mojada municipality was a little over 500 miles, going through Laredo, Texas.

5. *Victoria Advocate*, citing an item from an undated *Rockport Transcript*.

6. *Victoria Advocate*, May 22, 1880.

7. Curiously neither Raymond in *Captain Lee Hall of Texas* nor Darren L. Ivey in *The Ranger Ideal: Texas Rangers in the Hall of Fame* make

mention of the possibility of this venture. We suspect it was an intended career move but for some reason did not materialize.

8. *Austin Daily Democratic Statesman*, May 26, 1880.

9. *Texas Republican* (Marshall) August 26, 1858, citing a report from an undated *San Antonio Ledger*; *Galveston Daily News*, April 15, 1880; *Weekly Democratic Statesman*, April 22, *Weekly Democratic Statesman*, December 23, 1880.

10. 1880 Nueces County Census, enumerated by Joseph FitzSimmons, 2.

11. *Austin Weekly Statesman*, August 12, 1880.

12. *Austin Weekly Statesman*, August 26, 1880.

13. *Philadelphia Times*, October 1, 1880, from the *Kinney News*.

14. *Victoria Advocate*, January 17, 1880.

15. *Victoria Advocate*, February 4, 1899.

16. *Victoria Advocate*, January 17, 1880.

17. For a superior biography of Jones see Rick Miller's *Texas Ranger John B. Jones and the Frontier Battalion, 1874-1881*. Neither Oglesby nor McMurry have yet received a biography.

18. *Brenham Weekly Banner*, May 28, 1880.

19. *Raleigh Daily News* (North Carolina), June 11; *Morning Star* (Wilmington), June 13 and *Weekly Star* of Wilmington, North Carolina, June 18, 1880.

20. *Greensboro North Star*, July 8, 1880.

21. "Our Lebanon Letter" in the *Reading Times and Dispatch*, September 29, 1880.

22. *Austin Daily Statesman*, November 20, 1880.

23. *Reading Times and Dispatch*, Reading, Pennsylvania, November 27, 1880. An identical report of the wedding appeared in the *North State*, of Greensboro, North Carolina, Thursday, December 2, 1880.

24. *Reading Times and Dispatch*, November 27, 1880.

25. Captain Halter died December 10, 1895, in San Antonio. An obituary noted the deceased "was prominent in the U.S. coast and geodetical survey, and his services were marked by superior knowledge and experience." His wife, Sarah Weidman Halter, and three children survived him. *Lebanon Semi-Weekly News*, December 12, 1895.

26. *The North Star*, Greensboro, June 30, 1881.

27. *Greensboro Patriot*, November 2, 1881. The full identity of Bella has not been determined. In the issue of November 9, 1881, appears this line: "'Who is Bella?' That's the question. 'Bella' is a young lady, who, some day, will make a reputation with her pen." The available issues of the *Greensboro Patriot* skip from December 21, 1881, until the issue of September 9, 1882.

28. *Montgomery Weekly Advertiser*, November 1, 1881.

29. "International Cotton Exposition" in *Wikipedia, the Free Encyclopedia*, accessed December 10, 2018.

30. At this time the community of La Salle was the temporary county seat of the county of the same name, adjacent to what would become Cotulla, the present county seat. See *La Salle County: South Texas Brush Country 1856-1975* by Annette Martin Ludeman, 8.

31. C. Alphonso Smith, *Selected Stories from O. Henry* (New York: The Odyssey Press, 1906), xiii.

32. Arthur W. Page, *O. Henry Papers* (New York: Doubleday, Doran & Company, Inc., No date). Page records that Dr. and Mrs. Hall came to Texas to visit their sons and brought young Porter in 1881, the reason being ". . . Will Porter was sent with them, because it was thought that the close confinement in the drugstore was undermining his health," 29.

33. The 1880 Travis County Census shows Richard Hall as a single 28-year-old male. See page 100. Younger brother Frank Hall is shown in the 1880 LaSalle County Census as a 20-year-old sheep raiser. He was listed as head of household with six workers. Identified by enumerator Ebenezer B. Nelson as servants were Victor Hendriguez, age fifty; Simon Sanchez, eighteen; Albert Johns, twenty-eight; Jose Flores, twenty-five; Belladonna Florez, twenty; and Francisco Flores, twenty-eight. The occupation of all the servants —who were all natives of Mexico—was given as sheepherders. 1880 La Salle County Census, 339.

34. Grave Miller White, "A Texas Troubadour," *Frontier Times* 18, no. 6 (March 1941): 253-58. J.S. Gallegly, "Background and Patterns of O. Henry's Texas Badman Stories," Rice University Pamphlet, 42:3, 1955.

35. *La Salle County,* 126. Annette Martin Ludeman was born January 8, 1921, and died August 13, 1987. She is buried in the Cotulla West Cemetery, Cotulla, La Salle County.

NOTES TO CHAPTER 8

1. *Victoria Advocate,* August 26, 1882.

2. Annette Martin Ludeman, *La Salle County: South Texas Brush Country, 1856-1975,* 64.

3. *Weekly Democratic Statesman,* May 10, 1883.

4. James A. Paulauskas, Introductory Remarks, *Record of Appointments of Postmasters 1832-September 30, 1971.* National Archives Microfilm Publications, M841, 494-95. My special thanks go to Rick Miller for alerting me to this publication.

5. *Gonzales Inquirer,* June 4, 1881. The Buck family had a total of ten children, all of whom survived their parents; Martha Ann Rowland Buck died in 1898 and James Madison died on January 18, 1911. J.M. Buck is buried in South Park Cemetery in Roswell, Chaves County, New Mexico. A lengthy obituary appeared in the *Carlsbad Current* on January 20, 1911.

6. Service record of William O. Tompkins, Texas State Library and Archives.

7. *Texas County Sheriffs*, 321.

8. Robert M. Utley, *Lone Star Justice: The First Century of the Texas Rangers*, 239-41.

9. Special telegram from San Antonio to the *Statesman. Daily Democratic Statesman*, June 6 and *Weekly Democratic Statesman*, June 7, 1883.

10. *Austin Daily Statesman*, January 10, 1884.

11. According to the *1885-86 Austin City Directory* published by C.D. Morrison & J.V. Fourmy, the restaurant was operated by Isaac S. Simon and John B. Billeisen and was at 609 Congress Avenue, 195. The *Austin Daily Statesman* frequently ran one-line advertisements for Simon's in its columns. The restaurant may have actually included two locations as the advertisement in the issue of December 28, 1884, gave the address as 610 Congress Avenue. What eventually happened to Isaac S. Simon is unknown.

12. *Austin Daily Statesman*, January 12, 1884.

13. Lucy's interview appeared in the *Austin American*, March 15, 1927. We are fortunate that Fitzgerald interviewed Captain Lucy when he did. The noted ranger and city marshal died four months later on July 10, 1927. James E. Lucy, born May 1, 1854, began his ranging career in September 1879 as a private serving under Charles L. Nevill, commander of Company E of the Frontier Battalion. He also served under J. L. Hall, Dan W. Roberts, and George W. Arrington. He is buried in Oakwood Cemetery in Austin. His grave is marked.

14. *Austin Daily Statesman*, January 12, 1884.

15. *Austin Daily Statesman*, January 16, 1884.

16. For a full and complete biography of the gambler-gunfighter see *Ben Thompson: Portrait of a Gunfighter* by Thomas C. Bicknell and Chuck Parsons.

17. *Galveston Daily News*, May 22, 1883.

18. *Galveston Daily News*, September 4, 1884, printing news from the "San Antonio Siftings" column.

19. Hickey, born February 19, 1850, in Ireland, was a clerk in his brother's mercantile in Nueces County before locating in La Salle County where he became the district and county clerk. The 1880 census shows his brother Thomas as head of household; others include Thomas's wife and children, mother Eliza now a widow, P.D. Hickey, siblings, and a cousin named Dargan Hickey. Three others listed are the domestic servant and her two children. 1880 Nueces County census, 4. P.D. Hickey died on August 16, 1896, in Laredo but is buried in Cotulla. His grave is not marked.

20 *Galveston Daily News*, November 13, 1884.

21. These were the posse members so identified in the "Bayou Locals" although efforts to learn more about the men have not been successful; even their proper names are elusive. Nothing definite has been learned of Deputy Sheriff H.R. Glasscock or Ben Keggans. Dave Lubbock is certainly the 30-year-old bookkeeper living in Harris County in 1880, p. 18; G. Harris remains unknown; Daly is perhaps the 25-year-old John B. Daly, a plasterer in Harris County, 145B. Perhaps the deputy sheriff Coy is Cristoval Coy, a 25-year-old laborer living in Bexar County in 1880, born in Coahulia, Mexico, 46B.

22. *Galveston Daily News*, November 28, printing "Bayou City Locals" of Houston dated November 27, 1884.

23. *Dallas Weekly Herald*, February 12, 1885.

24. *Dallas Weekly Herald*, February 12. This lengthy article, "Slaying Mexican Bandits," is a gathering of telegrams from Eagle Pass, Cotulla, San Antonio, Uvalde, and Del Rio dated February 5 and 6, 1885.

25. *Galveston Daily News*, February 12, 1885; *Fort Worth Daily Gazette*, June 29, 1885; *San Antonio Light*, June 29, 1885; *Dallas Daily Herald*, June 30, 1885; *Galveston Daily News*, October 4, 1885. Senator Hall took "a thorn out of the side of the state troops" when he resigned to enter into partnership with one of the large law firms of El Paso. The senator died in Laredo April 28, 1886, leaving his wife and six children to mourn. *Galveston Daily News*, April 30, 1886.

26. Dr. Pope, as he was identified in various news sources of the day, was a highly successful Baptist minister who established many churches from Fort Worth to El Paso and into Mexico as well. He was elected the third president of Simmons College in 1898. His later years were spent saving the college, which today is known as Hardin-Simmons University. Dr. Pope died November 20, 1901, after a lingering illness.

27. Paso de Las Islas is in the Rio Grande about one mile below the more famous Paso de Francis. Robert S. Weddle, "Paso de Las Islas," *Handbook of Texas Online*. Paso de Las Islas is approximately opposite the village of Guerrero, Coahuila, Mexico.

28. Raymond, in her chapter "At Las Islas Crossing," claims that there was a signal to open fire, "the drop of a handkerchief," 220. No contemporary account suggests this was the signal, or that there was a signal at all, however.

29. *Dallas Daily Herald*, February 12, 1885.

30. *Wise County Messenger*, February 28, 1885.

31. *Galveston Daily News*, February 12, 1885. The contemporary newspapers frequently spelled this ranger's name as "Sheely" or "Sheley" but he consistently spelled his name as "Shely" on his service records.

32. *Galveston Daily News*, February 10, 1885.

33. "Memoirs," from an unpublished autobiographical manuscript, included in *Captain J.A. Brooks, Texas Ranger* by Paul N. Spellman, 35. See also *Rawhide Ranger, Ira Aten: Enforcing Law on the Texas Frontier* by Bob Alexander.

34. Monthly Return of Capt. Joseph Shely, February and March 1885, prepared at Cotulla, La Salle County.

35. Ira Aten, "Six and One Half Years in the Ranger Service Fifty Years Ago," Unpublished typed manuscript archived in the Collections in the Center for American History, The University of Texas, Austin, 18-19.

36. Prolific historian of the Texas Rangers Bob Alexander provides the final acceptable explanation for the discrepancies of the various accounts: it was the "understandable fogginess due to age." The same could be said for James A. Brooks's memoir and others. Bob Alexander, *Rawhide Ranger Ira Aten: Enforcing Law on the Texas Frontier*, 349.

37. *Charlotte Observer*, February 15, 1885.

38. For additional information on Manning, see *Dallas Stoudenmire: El Paso Marshal* by Leon Claire Metz.

39. *San Antonio Light*, February 23, 1885.

40. Robert W. Stephens, *Bullets and Buckshot in Texas*, 9.

41. *Lenoir Topic*, July 8, 1885.

42. *Indian Journal* (Muskogee, I.T.), July 30, 1885.

43. *Lenoir Topic*, August 5, 1885.

44. *Lenoir Topic*, August 5, 1885.

45. *Fort Worth Daily Gazette*, July 28, 1885.

NOTES TO CHAPTER 9

1. *Galveston Daily News*, August 23, 1885.

2. *Cheyenne Transporter*, October 3, 1885. Published at Darlington, near El Reno, Oklahoma.

3. James Q. Chenoweth (1841-June 20, 1909) was born in Kentucky and studied law in Montgomery, Alabama, but the Civil War interrupted his studies. After four years in the Confederate Army he was discharged as a colonel. He then returned to his studies and was admitted to the bar in 1865. After the death of his wife he moved to Bonham, Fannin County, Texas, where he impressed Gov. Richard Coke who appointed him special district judge of the criminal courts of Fannin, Lamar, and Red River Counties. He served two consecutive terms in the Texas Legislature and then Grover Cleveland appointed him Auditor of the United States Treasury. After Cleveland was defeated he returned to Texas where he continued as judge. He worked in the judicial circle and also edited the Bonham newspaper, the *Daily Favorite*. He later was appointed superintendent for the Confederate Home for Men. Illness forced him to resign and he died in Virginia in 1909. David Minor, *The New Handbook of Texas,* II, 57-58.

4. *Dallas Daily Herald*, August 26, 1885.

5. *Dallas Daily Herald*, August 26, 1885.

6. *Galveston Daily News*, September 27, 1885.

7. *Galveston Daily News*, September 27, 1885.

8. *Our Brother in Red* 4, no. 1, September 1885, a monthly newspaper published in Muskogee, Indian Territory. Captain Lee had seen military service and was recommended by General P.H. Sheridan, *Weekly Chieftain* (Vinita, Indian Territory), July 30, 1885.

9. *Cheyenne Transporter*, November 12, 1885.

10. *Cheyenne Transporter*, November 30, 1885.

11. *Lenoir Topic*, Lenoir, North Carolina, November 18, 1885. G.W.F. Harper was a fifty-five-year-old dry goods merchant in Lenoir; his wife

Ella was forty-four and at the time of the 1880 census his sister-in-law Emma Rankin, forty-one, was living with the Harpers. Emma Rankin was teaching school at the time. 1880 Caldwell County, North Carolina Census, 543. Of Dr. Hall's immediate family, only his wife and her sister were noted as being present at the funeral.

12. *The Morning Star*, Wilmington, North Carolina, November 19, 1885, printing an article from the *Greensboro Workman.*

13. *The North Star*, Greensboro, North Carolina, Thursday, November 19, 1885.

14. The image appears in the Lawrence T. Jones, III, pictorial book, *Lens on the Texas Frontier*, 109-10.

15. *Fort Worth Daily Gazette*, December 22, 1885.

16. *Fort Worth Gazette*, December 21, 22, 23, 1885; *Austin Weekly Statesman*, December 24, 1885; *Galveston Daily News*, December 24,1885; *New York Times*, December 25, 1885.

17. *Fort Worth Daily Gazette*, December 22, 1885. Burnett was in charge of the massive Four Sixes Ranch whose headquarters was near Wichita Falls. Through the years Burnett leased lands in Indian Territory for little lease money. The friendship between Quanah Parker and S.B. Burnett was mutually beneficial to both. David Minor, "Samuel Burk Burnett," *The New Handbook of Texas*, 1:854-55.

18. *Fort Worth Daily Gazette*, December 23, 1885.

19. *Galveston Daily News*, December 24, 1885.

20. A December 30 Dallas special printed in the *Fort Worth Daily Gazette*, December 31, 1885.

21. This interview on January 2, 1886, appeared on the same day in the *Plainfield Evening News* of Plainfield, New Jersey, as well as the *Courier Evening News* of Bridgewater, New Jersey, and *Chester Times* (Pennsylvania) of the same date and perhaps other newspapers as well.

The recognition of Hall's name as well as the idea of Indians becoming educated farmers was considered a matter of great interest.

22. *Cheyenne Transporter*, February 20, 1886.

23. *Galveston Daily News*, May 11, citing a special from Wichita Falls dated April 10, 1886.

24. *Galveston Daily News*, May 4, 1886.

25. *Austin Daily Statesman*, May 15, 1886.

26. *Baxter Springs News*, Baxter Springs, Kansas, May 29, 1886.

27. *Cheyenne Transporter*, July 12, 1886.

28. *Cheyenne Transporter*, August 12, 1886, citing an article from an undated *Mobeetie Texas Panhandle.*

29. *Reading Times* (Pennsylvania), September 28, 1886.

30. *Galveston Daily News*, November 7, 1886.

31. *Annual Report of the Commissioners of Indian Affairs, for the Year 1886*, 127. Hall's report is pages 127-32.

32. Ibid., 128.

33. Ibid., 127.

34. Ibid., 128.

35. Ibid., 128.

36. Ibid., 128.

37. Ibid., 128-31.

38. Reports on the assassination of Sheriff McKinney and its follow-up are numerous. In addition to the biography of McKinney by this author and research by Gary P. Fitterer, see reports from Cotulla published in the *St. Louis Post-Dispatch* of December 27, 1886, the *Fort Worth Daily Gazette* of January 4, 1887, from San Antonio published in the *Fort Worth*

Daily Gazette and the *Austin Daily Statesman* of January 14, and the *Fort Worth Daily Gazette* of January 26, 1887. Parsons and Fitterer, *Captain C.B. McKinney: The Law in South Texas*, 97-120.

39. C.C.C. Painter, *The Condition of Affairs in Indian Territory and California*, 34.

40. Ibid., 44.

41. J.J. Methvin, *In the Limelight, or History of Anadarko [Caddo County] and Vicinity from the Earliest Days*, 50.

42. Dianna Everett, Biographical sketch of Methvin in *The Encyclopedia of Oklahoma History and Culture*. https://www.okhistory.org/publications/enc/entry.php?entry=ME022 accessed January 1, 2019. John Jasper Methvin died at the age of 94 on January 17, 1941, at Anadarko after devoting more than fifty years of his life to teaching and missionary work among Oklahoma Indians. Obituary in *The Daily Oklahoman*, January 18, 1941.

43. The 1880 Grayson County census shows Morrill as a thirty-six-year-old white male born in Illinois, his profession listed as "City Policeman." His family consisted of his thirty-year-old wife Emma born in Texas, and ten-year-old son Clifford, born in Missouri. They resided in Denison. Grayson County census, 184B. By 1900 he was residing in Austin, his profession listed as "Clerk."

44. *Fort Worth Daily Gazette*, April 25, 1887. The headlines revealed there was not a real problem: "Rude Redskins" and "A Few Kicking Kiowas Raise a Racket in the Territory that is all Bluster."

45. J.J. Methvin, *In the Limelight*, 65-66.

46. *Denison Gazetteer*, October 23, 1887, citing an item from an undated *Sherman Courier*.

47. *Fort Worth Daily Gazette*, October 16, 1887.

48. Ibid., October 17, 1887.

49. *Dallas Daily Herald*, October 25, 1887.

50. *Fort Worth Daily Gazette*, December 9, 1887.

51. *Galveston Daily News*, February 24, citing special report from Waco, February 23, 1888.

52. *Fort Worth Daily Gazette*, April 22, printing a special report from Waco, April 21, 1888. The four bondsmen "among our best citizens" were Colonel Van Hall, Smith Parr, William Edwards, and J.V. Smith.

53. *Fort Worth Daily Gazette*, February 2, 1888.

54. *El Paso Times*, February 14, 1888, printing "Washington Notes" from Washington, February 9, 1888.

55. *Fort Worth Daily Gazette*, April 24, citing a special report from Austin, dated April 23, 1888. This article was headlined "Border Troubles."

56. *Austin Daily Statesman*, March 6, 1889.

57. George Durham, *Taming the Nueces Strip: The Story of McNelly's Rangers*, 177.

58. The descriptive list document is from the Heritage Auctions of Dallas, lot # 44206; the oath is from the Texas Adjutant General Service Records, archives in the Texas State Library and Auctions.

Notes to Chapter 10

1. *Galveston Daily News*, October 21, citing a report from Graham, October 20, 1891.

2. *The Daily Messenger* (Marshall, Texas), November 16, 1891.

3. A December 30 special from San Antonio to the *Austin Daily Statesman*, December 31, 1891.

4. *Austin Daily Statesman*, January 5, citing a report from Cuero, January 4, 1892.

5. *Galveston Daily News*, January 5, citing a report from Yoakum, January 4, 1892.

6. *Austin Daily Statesman*, January 7, 1892, citing reports from San Antonio of January 6, 1892.

7. *Galveston Daily News*, January 7, citing reports from Yoakum dated January 6, 1892.

8. *Austin Daily Statesman*, January 6, citing reports from San Antonio and Corpus Christi dated January 5, 1892.

9. *Austin Daily Statesman*, January 7, citing a report from San Antonio dated January 6,1892.

10. *Austin Daily Statesman*, January 20, citing a report from San Antonio dated January 19,1892.

11. *Austin Daily Statesman*, July 5, 1892.

12. *Abilene Reporter*, August 19, 1892.

13. Robert C. Cotner, "James Stephen Hogg," *New Handbook of Texas*, 3: 652-53.

14. Doug Johnson, "George W. Clark," *New Handbook of Texas*, 2:132-33.

15. "A Good Appointment," special from San Antonio of August 25, appearing in the *Austin Daily Statesman* August 26, 1892.

16. *Galveston Daily News*, December 28, 1892.

17. Dora Neill Raymond, *Captain Lee Hall of Texas*, 364.

18. *Evening Messenger* (Marshall, Texas) February 20, 1894.

19. *Galveston Daily News*, June 27, 1894, citing news from an undated *Karnes County News*.

20. *Austin Daily Statesman*, July 15, 1894.

21. *Daily Ardmoreite* (Ardmore, Oklahoma), January 15, 1894 and April 19, 1894.

22. *Fort Worth Gazette*, July 22, 1894.

23. Darren L. Ivey, *The Ranger Ideal*, vol. 2, 263-64.

24. *Galveston Daily News*, August 3, 1895.

25. Besides the *Saturday Evening Post*, the fanciful story appeared in the *Saturday Bee* of Hutchinson, Kansas, of February 10, 1900; the *Richmond Planet*, Richmond, Virginia, of February 10, 1900 and perhaps many other publications.

26. *Galveston Daily News*, April 19, May 15, July 4, July 10, July 22, July 30, August 30, September 1, 1895; *Houston Daily Post*, December 12, 1895. During his time in Houston Hall stayed at the Grand Central at least on one occasion, but on all others he is described as staying at the Lawlor; when Mrs. Hall and daughters visited they stayed in the "apartments" meaning suites. The proprietor, James Lawlor, was a native of Ireland, born November 1, 1855. The Lawlor, located at 701-707 Washington, was one of the top hotels of Houston in the 1890s. One advertisement described it as a "New and Elegant Hotel./ Convenient to all Trains./ Best Meals in the City./ Rooms Cool and Pleasant./ Rates Reasonable." It was located opposite the Central Depot and electric cars passed the hotel to the business center every five minutes. A final note in the advertisement pointed out that "We Cater to the Traveling Public." Lee Hall during this period of life certainly was part of the "traveling public." No doubt Hall missed the action of being a Texas Ranger, but he certainly preferred the soft beds of the Lawlor over the hard Texas ground.

27. *Harrisburg Telegraph* (Harrisburg, Pennsylvania), January 2, 1896.

28. *Daily Picayune* (New Orleans), January 17, 1896.

29.Frederic Remington "How the Law Got into the Chaparral," 26. In the original *Harper's* this quotation appears on page 69.

30. 1900 Arapahoe County, Colorado, census. The 1910 census of the same county shows him as a laborer, working at odd jobs. At his death W.P. Hall's estate was but $145. His casket cost $60, the hearse $10, and

the opening of the grave $6.00. Whatever ceremony was performed at his grave was thanks to Rev. Burlington, at a cost of $5.00. 1900 and 1910 census; probate record of William P. Hall.

31. *Salt Lake Tribune*, April 1, 1898.

32. This is from a communication from John Hay, the United States Ambassador to England, writing Colonel Theodore Roosevelt of the "Rough Riders" in 1898, that "It has been a splendid little war, begun with the highest motives, carried on with magnificent intelligence and spirit, favored by that fortune which loves the brave." Needless to say the further from the battlefields the more splendid the little war became. Cited in Frank Freidel's *The Splendid Little War*, 1.

33. *Austin Daily Statesman*, June 11, 1898, from Galveston, June 10.

34. James M. McCaffrey, "The Texas Immunes in the Spanish-American War," chapter 10 in *Texans and War: New Interpretations of the State's Military History*. Edited by Alexander Mendoza and Charles David Grear, 214.

35. *Times-Democrat* (New Orleans, Louisiana), June 14, 1898.

36. *Times-Picayune* (New Orleans, Louisiana), June 16, 1898; *Houston Post*, June 14 and June 18, 1898; *Times-Democrat* (New Orleans) June 16, 1898.

37. James M. McCaffrey, "The Texas Immunes in the Spanish-American War," 217.

38. *Evening Report* (Lebanon, Pennsylvania), July 21, 1898.

39. *Lebanon Courier*, July 27, 1898.

40. Hall served as captain of Company M in the First U.S. Volunteer Infantry from May 25–October 28, 1898.

41. *Times-Democrat* (New Orleans), August 3, 1898.

42. *Greensboro Patriot*, August 31, 1898.

43. *Greensboro Patriot*, October 5, 1898.

Notes to Chapter 11

1. *Chicago Tribune*, May 15, citing a report from San Antonio of May 14, 1898.

2. Jack DeMattos, "Gunfighters of the Real West: Lee Hall," *Real West* 27, no. 198 (August, 1984).

3. *Yazoo City Herald* (Mississippi), July 22, 1898.

4. *The Daily Picayune*, July 24, 1898.

5. Ibid., July 26, 1898.

6. Ibid., July 28, 1898.

7. Ibid.

8. Ibid.

9. Ibid., August 1, 1898.

10. Ibid., August 3, 1898.

11. Ibid., August 4, 1898.

12. Ibid., August 5, 1898.

13. Ibid., August 6, 1898.

14. Ibid., August 8, 1898.

15. Ibid., August 10, 1898.

16. Ibid., August 11, 1898.

17. *Times-Democrat* (New Orleans), August 11, 1898.

18. *Times-Democrat* (New Orleans), August 12, 1898.

19. *The Daily Picayune*, August 12, 1898.

20. Ibid., August 14, 1898.

21. Ibid., August 16, 1898.

22. Ibid., August 18, 1898.

23. Special from Galveston dated August 25 and published in the *Daily Picayune*, August 26, 1898.

24. Special from Galveston dated October 27 and published in the *Daily Picayune*, October 29, 1898.

25. *Washington Times*, District of Columbia, December 20, 1898.

26. Biographical sketch of Aguinaldo from *The World of 1898: The Spanish-American War*; *Philippine Independence Declared: This Day in History* and other internet sources.

27. Hall's service record as well as a San Antonio special printed in the *Austin Daily Statesman*, August 18, 1899.

28. Official Roster of 1st Texas Volunteer Infantry, *The Spanish-American Centennial War* website, contributed by Peggy Miller Trevathan.

29. *Lebanon Semi-Weekly News*, July 31 and *Lebanon Daily News*, July 31, 1899.

30. Laurie E. Jasinski and Casey J. Monahan, eds., *Handbook of Texas Music.*

31. *Evening Ledger*, Mexia, Limestone County, Texas, August 23, 1899. Gilder Howard Fields has not been located on any U.S. census. His World War I draft registration card shows he was then a resident of San Francisco; was then forty years of age and was born February 11, 1878. Then his occupation was "Mechanical Superintendent" for the *San Francisco Daily News.*

32. *San Francisco Examiner*, September 30, 1899; *San Francisco Call*, October 1, 1899.

33. *Arkansas Democrat* (Little Rock), October 30, 1899, citing a lengthy article from the *Pacific Commercial Advertiser* published in Honolulu on

October 9. Hall was indeed a captain although in the same article he is referred to as a First Lieutenant.

34. *Greensboro Telegram*, September 11, 1900, printing the report from the *Lebanon Daily Times*.

Notes to Chapter 12

1. *Annual Reports of the War Department for the Fiscal Year Ended June 30, 1900*, House of Representatives, 56th Congress, 2d Session. Document No. 2. (Washington, D.C.: Government Printing Office, 1900). Report of Col. Cornelius Gardener, prepared at Tayabas, Luzon, Philippine Islands, February 8, 1900, 509.

2. Ibid., Report of William C. Geiger, First Lieutenant, Fourteenth Infantry to Theodore Schwan, 546-47.

3. Ibid., Report of Action prepared at Atimonan, Luzon, February 21, 1900, by Thomas L. Hartigan, Major Thirtieth Infantry, United States Volunteers, 512.

4. Ibid., Lieutenant Hall's report to First Lieutenant William C. Geiger, Commanding Macabebe Scouts, 547.

5. Although she signed her articles with the penname of Nan Byxbee her real name was Miss Ernestine Coughran. She was connected with newspapers in Seattle, Butte, San Francisco, and Honolulu and was "considered one of the best women writers on the Pacific Coast." She was married to W.P. Strandberg in early February 1907. "Miss Coughran Maried [*sic*] " in the *Honolulu Star*, of Honolulu, February 8, 1907.

6. Hall uses the term "Macabees" in this conversational setting with Byxbee, but in official correspondence as well as in most general correspondence the term " Macabebes " is used.

7. Hall refers to the year 1870 here but in that year he was teaching school in Grayson County, Texas. One gets the impression that Hall

is making his past sound more exciting than it actually was. He will also refer to fighting Indians in the Territory, but other than the Indian Territory of Oklahoma it is doubtful if he had any conflict with Indians.

8. The Texas regiment in which Hall was enrolled wore khaki uniforms, "which set them apart from soldiers of the other regiments . . . who sported the standard blue uniforms." McCaffrey, "The Texas Immunes in the Spanish-American War," 221.

9. *San Francisco Call*, Sunday, October 14, 1900.

10. *Lebanon Courier*, October 10, 1900.

11. *El Paso Daily Herald*, October 5, 1900 citing a report from an undated *San Antonio Express.*

12. Brian McAllister Linn, "The Thirty-third Infantry, United States Volunteers: An American Regiment in the Philippine Insurrection, 1899-1901," 101.

13. *Reading Times*, Reading, Pennsylvania, October 27, 1900.

14. *Lebanon Courier*, November 14, 1900.

15. *Lebanon Daily News*, November 10, 1900.

16. Henry Cabot Lodge of Massachusetts was the first chair of this committee. https://en.wikipedia.org/wiki/United_States_Senate_Committee_on_the_Philippines

17. *Boston Globe*, May 16, 1902, headlined "Enemies of the Tagalogs."

18. *The Commoner* (Lincoln, Nebraska), February 21, 1902.

19. *Boston Globe*, May 16, 1902.

20. *Lawrence Daily World* (Lawrence, Kansas) May 16, 1902.

21. *Weekly Advocate* (Victoria) October 31, 1903.

22. *Daily Advocate* (Victoria) December 7, 1903.

23. *Arizona Republican* (Phoenix), April 25, 1906. Reports of this action appeared in many newspapers throughout the country, especially in those that represented a mining community. *The Copper Era* of Clifton, Arizona of April 26; the *Washington Post* of April 20, which emphasized the fact that the Yaquis mutilated the body of Samuel Williams; the *Mining Review* of Salt Lake City, Utah, of May 15; the *Butte Daily Post* (Montana) of April 19 and the *Natchitoches Times* (Louisiana) of April 20, 1906, also reported the action. One of the more important articles on this Giroux-Cunningham raid appeared in the *Los Angeles Daily Times* of May 14 in an article "Red Raiders of Sonora's Hills / Guerrilla Operations of Bronco Yaquis in the Mining District" by Allen Kelly. This article filled nearly a page and included two photographic illustrations, one showing bronco Yaquis after execution by Mexican soldiers and one showing two Yaquis hanging from a tree limb.

24. *Daily Ardmorite* (Ardmore, Oklahoma), May 23, 1906. This article was headlined "This Smacks of Old Times/ Captain Lee Hall and Old Rangers to Fight Indians/ Or Rather to Protect Transportation of Bullion Through the Yaqui Indian Country in Old Mexico. Dangerous Work."

25. *El Paso Morning Times*, June 2, 1906. Various newspapers reported Hall gathering six men to be the guard but only five were named, suggesting he never actually had the half-dozen. However, Raymond, in her biography of Captain Hall, writes that former Texas Ranger George W. Talley "added himself immediately to Hall's force" citing an interview with Talley by Kleber Miller in Falfurrias, Texas, in April 1935. This remains somewhat suspect as at the time Talley was in the legal system in Corpus Christi facing the charge of murdering Joshua Peters in 1878, twenty-eight years before. In December 1906 Talley was found not guilty. Raymond, *Captain Lee Hall of Texas*, 335 and *Houston Post*, May 19 and December 18, 1906.

26. *El Paso Morning Times*, June 5, 1906.

27. *Austin Statesman*, June 5, citing a report from San Antonio dated June 4, 1906.

28. *El Paso Herald*, June 30, 1906, citing a report from San Antonio.

29. *Houston Post*, September 9, 1906.

30. Raymond, 335. Raymond cites a letter from Hall's daughter Francis Weir Hall with nothing to confirm said claim.

31. The mines are occasionally referred to as "Las Sultanas" as well as La Sultana. Since the name in the singular is most often seen I have retained it as La Sultana, and La Sultana Rangers.

32. *Austin Statesman*, April 16, citing a report from San Antonio dated April 15, 1907.

33. Ibid.

NOTES TO CHAPTER 13

1. Charles H. Harris III and Louis R. Sadler, *The Texas Rangers and the Mexican Revolution: The Bloodiest Decade, 1910-1920*, 67.

2. *Yorkville Enquirer* (York, South Carolina), November 4, 1910.

3. Did Lee Hall ever work for the famous Wells Fargo Company? We contacted John Boessenecker, highly acclaimed historian of the Wild West era and author of the award-winning *Shotguns and Stagecoaches: The Brave Men Who Rode for Wells Fargo in the Wild West*. He answered: "Unfortunately there are no Wells Fargo employment records as they were all destroyed in the 1906 earthquake and fire. Everything the company has today was gathered by its staff in about 1920 as they tried to reconstruct their history. I have never run across Lee Hall working for WF. Because his name is so well known to all us western nuts, it would have jumped out at me if I ever found him mentioned." Boessenecker, e-mail to Parsons, December 8, 2018.

4. *El Paso Herald-Post*, March 18, 1911.

5. *Greensboro Patriot* (Greensboro, North Carolina), March 23, 1911.

6. *San Antonio Light*, March 18, 1911.

7. *Beaumont Enterprise* (Beaumont, Texas), March 17, 1911.

8. "Record Book of Interments. National Cemetery at San Antonio, Texas," 73.

9. *El Paso Morning Times*, June 12, 1912.

10. *Austin Daily Statesman*, June 17, 1912.

11. *El Paso Morning Times*, June 12, citing a San Antonio Special of June 11, 1912.

12. *Houston Post*, June 16, 1912, "A Monument for Lee Hall" from an undated *Texas Republic* of San Antonio.

13. *El Paso Morning Times*, June 12, 1912.

14. *Lebanon Daily News*, October 14, 1926.

Selected Bibliography

UNITED STATES CENSUS

Colorado

Arapahoe County, 1900, 1910

Idaho

Alturas County

Louisiana

Natchitoches Parish, 1870

Maryland

Worcester County, 1850

Missouri

Jackson County, 1850

North Carolina

Caldwell County, 1880

Davidson County, 1860

Guilford County, 1860

Guilford County, Slave

Iredell County, 1850

Texas

Atascosa County, 1880

Burnet County, 1880

Calhoun County, 1850

Cameron County, 1870

DeWitt County, 1870, 1880

Duval County, 1880

Frio County, 1880

Galveston County, 1910

Goliad County, 1870, 1880

Grayson County, 1870, 1880, 1900

Grimes County, 1870

Harris County, 1880

Hill County, 1870

Houston County, 1860

Karnes County, 1880

La Salle County, 1880

Medina County, 1870

Nueces County, 1880

San Saba County, 1930

Starr County, 1910

Travis County, 1880

Victoria County, 1870, 1880

Wilson County, 1870

BOOKS AND PERIODICALS

Alexander, Bob. *Rawhide Ranger, Ira Aten: Enforcing Law on the Texas Frontier.* Denton: University of North Texas Press, 2011.

Anonymous. *The World of 1898: The Spanish-American War: Philippine Independence Declared: This Day in History.* Internet source.

Aten, Ira. "Six and One Half Years in the Ranger Service Fifty Years Ago." Unpublished manuscript archived in the Collections in the Center for American History— University of Texas, Austin.

Awbrey, Betty Dooley, and Claude Dooley. *Why Stop? A Guide to Texas Historical Roadside Markers.* Lone Star Books: Lanham, MD. 1999.

Bicknell, Thomas C., and Chuck Parsons. *Ben Thompson: Portrait of a Gunfighter.* Denton: University of North Texas Press, 2018.

Boessenecker, John. *Shotguns and Stagecoaches: The Brave Men Who Rode for Wells Fargo in the Wild West.* New York: St. Martin's Press, 2018.

Caldwell, Clifford R., and Ron DeLord. *Texas Lawmen 1835-1899. The Good and the Bad.* Charleston, SC: The History Press, 2011.

Crouch, Barry A., and Donaly E. Brice. *The Governor's Hounds: The Texas State Police, 1870-1873.* Austin: University of Texas Press, 2011.

Davis, Samuel Houston. *The Poet and Poetry of Texas,* Austin: Sam H. Dixon & Co., 1885.

De la Garza, Phyllis. *Death for Dinner: The Benders of (Old) Kansas.* Honolulu, HI: Talei Publishers, Inc., 2003.

DeMattos, Jack. "Gunfighters of the Real West: Lee Hall." *Real West* 27 (August, 1984): 198.

DeWitt County Historical Commission. *The History of DeWitt County, Texas.* Dallas: Curtis Media Corporation, 1991.

Dugan, Mark. *Knight of the Road: The Life of Highwayman Ham White.* Athens, OH: Swallow/University Press, 1990.

Daywood, Victoria Donnahoo, and Peggy White Engledow. *The Bad Boys of Caldwell County Texas Book Two: Murder and Mayhem in the 1880s.* Luling, TX. Privately printed, 2011.

Durham, George. "On the Trail of 5100 Outlaws: The Inside Story of McNelly's Texas Rangers," as told to Clyde Wantland. Ed. Harry E. Maule. *West* magazine serial. N.P.: Doubleday, Doran & Co., 1934-35.

Durham, George. *Taming the Nueces Strip: The Story of McNelly's Rangers.* Austin: University of Texas Press, 1962.

Elliott, Claude. Book review of Dora Neill Raymond's *Captain Lee Hall of Texas.* Austin: *Southwestern Historical Quarterly* 44, no. 3 (January 1941).

Fitterer, Gary P. "Life of Alfred Y. Allee" (unpublished manuscript)

Freidel, Frank. *The Splendid Little War.* Short Hills, NJ: Burford Books, Inc., 1958.

Gallegly, J.S. *Background and Patterns of O. Henry's Badman Stories.* Houston, TX: Rice University Pamphlet, 1955.

Gillett, James B. *Fugitives from Justice: The Notebook of Texas Ranger Sergeant James B. Gillett.* Facsimile of 1878 publication. Austin: State House Press, 1997.

Graham, Sam. "Reminiscences of Sam Graham." Edited and annotated by Chuck Parsons. *Brand Book* of the English Westerners Society. London: English Westerners Society, 2015.

Guthrie, Diana, Chair. *Atascosa County, Texas Pioneer Family Histories Compiled during Atascosa County's Sesquicentennial Anniversary 2006.* No place, 2007.

Harris III, Charles H., and Louis R. Sadler. *The Texas Rangers and the Mexican Revolution: The Bloodiest Decade, 1910-1920.* Albuquerque: University of New Mexico Press, 2004.

Haynes, David. *Catching Shadows: A Directory of Nineteenth-Century Texas Photographers.* Austin: Texas State Historical Association, 1993.

Ivey, Darren L. *The Ranger Ideal: Texas Rangers in the Hall of Fame, 1874-1930.* Denton: University of North Texas Press, 2018.

Jasinski, Laurie E., and Casey J. Monahan, eds. *Handbook of Texas Music.* Austin: Texas State Historical Association, 2012.

Jennings, N.A. *A Texas Ranger.* New York: Charles Scribner's Sons, 1899; facsimile edition by Frontier Book Company, Ruidoso, NM, 1960 and reprint Norman: University of Oklahoma Press, 1997.

Johnson, Dave. *The Mason County "Hoo Doo" War, 1874-1902.* Denton: University of North Texas Press, 2006.

Johnson, David. *The Cornett-Whitley Gang: Violence Unleashed in Texas.* Denton: University of North Texas Press, 2019.

Jones, Lawrence T. III. *Lens on the Texas Frontier.* College Station: Texas A&M University Press, 2014.

King, Edward. *The Great South: A Record of Journeys to Louisiana, Texas, The Indian Territory, Missouri, Arkansas, Mississippi, Alabama, Georgia, Florida, South Carolina, North Carolina, Kentucky, Tennessee, Virginia, West Virginia and Maryland.* Hartford, CT: American Publishing Company, 1875.

King, Edward. *The Great South.* Edited by W. Magruder Drake and Robert R. Jones. Baton Rouge: Louisiana State University Press, 1972.

La Salle County Historical Commission. *La Salle County.* Charleston, SC: NP, 2010.

Ludeman, Annette Martin. *A History of La Salle County: South Texas Brush Country 1856-1975.* Quanah, TX: Nortex Press, 1975.

Marohn, Richard C. *The Last Gunfighter: John Wesley Hardin.* College Station: The Early West, 1995.

Mendoza, Alexander, and Charles David Grear, eds. *Texans and War: New Interpretations of the State's Military History.* College Station: Texas A&M University Press, 2012.

Methvin, Rev. J.J. [John Jasper] *In the Limelight: History of Anadarko [Caddo County] and Vicinity from the Earliest Days.* Anadarko, OK: Self published, 1928.

Metz, Leon Claire. *Dallas Stoudenmire: El Paso Marshal.* Austin, TX: Pemberton Press, 1969.

Meyers, Rosalie Key. *Dowlearn Lowe.* No Place: Privately printed, 1992.

Miller, Rick. *Bounty Hunter.* College Station: The Early West, 1988.

Miller, Rick. *Sam Bass and Gang.* Austin: State House Press, 1999.

Miller, Rick. *Texas Ranger John B. Jones and the Frontier Battalion, 1874-1881.* Denton: University of North Texas Press, 2012.

Miller, Rick. "Ex-Ranger Maurice Moore: Quick to Quarrel." *Journal* of the Wild West History Association 10, no. 2 (June 2017).

Moneyhon, Carl. *Edmund J. Davis: Civil War General, Republican Leader, Reconstruction Governor.* Fort Worth: Texas Christian University Press, 2010.

Moore, Carol. *Greensboro's First Presbyterian Church Cemetery.* Charleston, SC: No publisher, 2006.

Morrison, C.D., and J.V. Fourmy. *Austin City Directory 1885-86.* Galveston, Texas: Morrison & Fourmy, 1886.

Morrison, William B., ed. "Colbert's Ferry on Red River, Chickasaw Nation, Indian Territory: Recollections of John Malcolm." *Chronicles of Oklahoma*, September 1938.

Page, Arthur W. *O. Henry Papers.* New York: Doubleday, Doran & Company, Inc., No date.

Painter, C.C. "The Condition of Affairs in Indian Territory and California. Philadelphia," Office of the Indian Rights Association, 1888.

Parsons, Chuck, and Gary P. Fitterer. *Captain C.B. McKinney: The Law in South Texas.* Wolfe City, TX: Henington Publishing Company, 1993.

Parsons, Chuck, and Marjorie Parsons. *Bowen and Hardin.* College Station: The Early West, 1991.

Parsons, Chuck. *John B. Armstrong: Texas Ranger and Pioneer Rancher.* College Station: Texas A&M University Press, 2007.

Parsons, Chuck, and Donaly E. Brice. *Texas Ranger N.O. Reynolds: The Intrepid.* Denton: University of North Texas Press, 2011. First edition Honolulu, Hawaii, 2005.

Parsons, Chuck, and Norman Wayne Brown. *A Lawless Breed: John Wesley Hardin, Texas Reconstruction, and Violence in the Wild West.* Denton: University of North Texas Press, 2013.

Paulauskos, James A. "Introduction," *Record of Appointments of Postmasters 1832-September 30, 1971.* National Archives Microfilm Publication M841.

Porter, Norman F. *Atascosa County History Through 1912.* Pleasanton, TX: Galvan Creek Publishers, 2007.

Raymond, Dora Neill. *Captain Lee Hall of Texas.* Norman: University of Oklahoma Press, 1940, reprint 1982.

Remington, Frederic. *How the Law Got into the Chaparral: Conversations with Old Texas Rangers.* Edited by John H. Jenkins. Austin: Jenkins Publishing Company, 1987.

Roberts, Lou Conway. *A Woman's Reminiscences of Six Years in Camp with the Texas Rangers.* Austin: Von Boeckmann-Jones, 1928.

Smith, C. Alphonso. *Selected Stories from O. Henry.* New York: The Odyssey Press, 1906.

Sonnichsen, C.L. *Ten Texas Feuds.* Albuquerque: University of New Mexico Press, 1957, 1971.

Spellman, Paul N. *Captain J.A. Brooks, Texas Ranger.* Denton: University of North Texas Press, 2007.

Stamps, Roy, and Jo Ann Stamps. *The Letters of John Wesley Hardin.* Austin: Eakin Press, 2001.

Stephens, Robert. W. *Bullets and Buckshot in Texas.* Privately printed, 2002.

Tise, Sammy. *Texas County Sheriffs.* Albuquerque, NM: Oakwood Printing, 1989.

Utley, Robert M. *Lone Star Justice: The First Century of the Texas Rangers.* New York: Oxford University Press, 2002.

White, Grave Miller. "A Texas Troubadore," *Frontier Times*. March, 1941.

Young, Roy B. *Pete Spence: "Audacious Artist in Crime."* Apache, OK: Young & Sons Enterprises, 2000.

OFFICIAL DOCUMENTS

Annual Report of the War Department for the Fiscal Year Ended June 30, 1900. House of Representatives, 56th Congress, 2d Session Doc. No. 2. Washington, D.C. Government Printing Office.

Death Certificate of Francis Mebane Rankin Hall, Guilford County, North Carolina.

Death Certificate of William Thomas Cavin, No. 37755, Burnet County, Texas.

Death Certificate of George Washington Talley, No. 21691, Nueces County, Texas.

Grayson County, Texas Election Returns, 1870.

Hall, Jesse L. *Annual Report of the Commissioners of Indian Affairs, for the Year 1886*.

Convict and Conduct Register, Huntsville, Texas Penitentiary.

Indexed Register of Marriages— Davidson County, North Carolina.

Journal of the House of Representatives, Fifteenth Legislature, Austin, Texas.

Mortality Schedule, San Patricio County, Texas 1880.

Muster Rolls, J.L. Hall 1879.

Monthly Returns. Lieutenant J.L. Hall, 1876, 1877, 1879, 1880; and Monthly Return, Lieutenant Pat Dolan, 1877; Lieutenant T.L. Oglesby Semi-monthly Return August 1880.

"Record Book of Interments, National Cemetery at San Antonio, Texas."

Statement of Arrests, Lieutenant J.L. Hall, 1877.

Texas Ranger Service Records.

CORRESPONDENCE

Leigh Hall to Julia Maria Pease, September 7, 1877, Austin History Center. AR.A.001/RNG PC Incoming Correspondence, 1877.

Jack Freyer to Chuck Parsons, August 5, 2010.

John A. Purnell to Gov. E.J. Davis, June 31, 1872 and July 3, 1873.Texas State Archives.

John Boessenecker to Chuck Parsons, December 8, 2018.

John Luckey to Chuck Parsons, September 23, 2019.

Richard E. Lucy to Chuck Parsons, March 9 and 10, 2019.

NEWSPAPERS

Abilene Reporter, Abilene, Texas

Arizona Republican, Phoenix, Arizona

Arkansas Democrat, Little Rock, Arkansas

Atchison Daily Champion, Atchison, Kansas

Austin American, Austin, Texas

Austin Weekly Statesman, Austin, Texas

Baxter Springs News, Baxter Springs, Kansas

Beaumont Enterprise, Beaumont, Texas

Belton Journal, Belton, Texas

Boston Globe, Boston, Massachusetts

Boston Post, Boston, Massachusetts

Brenham Weekly Banner, Brenham, Texas

Brownsville Daily Herald, Brownsville, Texas

Butte Daily Post, Butte, Montana

Carlsbad Current, Carlsbad, New Mexico

Charlotte Observer, Charlotte, North Carolina

Chester Times, Chester, Pennsylvania

Chetopa Herald, Chetopa, Kansas

Cheyenne Transporter, Darlington, Oklahoma

Chicago Tribune, Chicago, Illinois

Coffeyville Courier, Coffeyville, Kansas

The Commoner, Lincoln, Nebraska

The Copper Era, Clifton, Arizona

Corpus Christi Caller, Corpus Christi, Texas

Corpus Christi Gazette, Corpus Christi, Texas

Courier-News, Bridgewater, New Jersey

Daily Advocate, Victoria, Texas

Daily Ardmoreite, Ardmore, Oklahoma

Daily Citizen, Asheville, North Carolina

Daily Democratic Statesman, Austin, Texas

Daily Messenger, Marshall, Texas

Daily Oklahoman, Oklahoma City, Oklahoma

Dallas Daily Herald, Dallas, Texas

Dallas Weekly Herald, Dallas, Texas

Denison Gazetteer, Denison, Texas

Denison News, Denison, Texas

El Paso Daily Herald, El Paso, Texas

El Paso Daily Times, El Paso, Texas

El Paso Herald-Post, El Paso, Texas

El Paso Morning Times, El Paso, Texas

El Paso Times, El Paso, Texas

Evening Ledger, Mexia, Texas

Falfurrias Facts, Falfurrias, Texas

Fayetteville Observer, Fayetteville, North Carolina

Fort Worth Daily Gazette, Fort Worth, Texas

Galveston Daily News, Galveston, Texas

Gonzales Inquirer, Gonzales, Texas

Greensboro North Star, Greensboro, North Carolina

Greensboro Patriot, Greensboro, North Carolina

Greensboro Telegram, Greensboro, North Carolina

Greensboro Times, Greensboro, North Carolina

Harrisburg Telegraph, Harrisburg, Pennsylvania

High Point Enterprise, High Point, North Carolina

Highland Weekly News, Hillsborough, Ohio

Honolulu Star, Honolulu, Hawaii

Houston Daily Post, Houston, Texas

Houston Post, Houston, Texas

Indian Journal (Muskogee, Indian Territory)

Junction City Union, Junction, Kansas

Lawrence Daily World, Lawrence, Kansas

Kansas Tribune, Lawrence, Kansas

Leavenworth Daily Times, Leavenworth, Kansas

Lebanon Courier, Lebanon, Pennsylvania

Lebanon Daily News, Lebanon, Pennsylvania

Lebanon Semi-Weekly News, Lebanon, Pennsylvania

Lenoir Topic, Lenoir, North Carolina

Los Angeles Daily Herald, Los Angeles, California

Los Angeles Daily Times, Los Angeles, California

Morning Star, Wilmington, North Carolina

Morning Weekly Star, Wilmington, North Carolina

Marshall Messenger, Marshall, Texas

Marshall Weekly Herald, Marshall, Texas

Minneapolis Daily Tribune, Minneapolis, Minnesota

Mining Review, Salt Lake City, Utah
Missouri Sharp Shooter, Rolla, Missouri
Montgomery Weekly Advertiser, Montgomery, Alabama
Morning Star, Wilmington, South Carolina
Natchitoches Times, Natchitoches, Louisiana
National Police Gazette, New York, New York
New North Star, Greensboro, North Carolina
New Orleans Daily Picayune, New Orleans, Louisiana
New Orleans Republican, New Orleans, Louisiana
New Orleans Times-Democrat, New Orleans, Louisiana
New Orleans Times-Picayune, New Orleans, Louisiana
New York Times, New York
North Star, Greensboro, North Carolina
North Texas Enterprise, Bonham, Texas
Our Brother in Red, Muskogee, I.T.
Paris News, Paris, Texas
Plainfield Evening News, Plainfield, Pennsylvania
Philadelphia Times, Philadelphia, Pennsylvania
Raleigh Daily News, Raleigh North Carolina
Reading Gazette and Democrat, Reading, Pennsylvania
Reading Times, Reading, Pennsylvania
Reading Times and Dispatch, Reading, Pennsylvania
Richmond Planet, Richmond, Virginia
San Antonio Evening News, San Antonio, Texas
San Antonio Express, San Antonio, Texas
San Antonio Light, San Antonio, Texas
San Francisco Call, San Francisco, California
San Francisco Examiner, San Francisco, California

Saturday Bee, Hutchinson, Kansas

Sherman Register, Sherman, Texas

Southern Argus, Selma, Alabama

St. Louis Dispatch, St. Louis, Missouri

St. Louis Post-Dispatch, St. Louis, Missouri

Texas Republican, Marshall, Texas

Tri-Weekly Herald, Marshall, Texas

Union Republican, Winston, North Carolina

Victoria Advocate, Victoria, Texas

Washington Times, Washington, D.C.

Washington Post, Washington, D.C.

Weekly Advocate, Victoria, Texas

Weekly Advocate, Victoria, Texas

Weekly Chieftain, Vinita, I.T.

Weekly Herald, Marshall, Texas

Weimer Mercury, Weimer, Texas

Wise County Messenger, Decatur, Texas

Yazoo City Herald, Yazoo, Mississippi

Yorkville Enquirer, York, South Carolina

THE NEW HANDBOOK OF TEXAS 1996

published by Texas State Historical Association

"Hogg, James Stephen," by Robert C. Cotner

"Chenowith, James Q.," by David Minor

"Clark, George W.," by Doug Johnson

"Paso de Las Islas," by Robert S. Weddle

"Pendencia Creek," by Anonymous

"Burnett, Samuel Burk," by David Minor

UNPUBLISHED SOURCES

Linn, Brian McAllister. "The Thirty-third Infantry, United States Volunteers: An American Regiment in the Philippine Insurrection, 1899-1901." A Thesis Presented in Partial Fulfillment of the Requirements for the Degree Master of Arts. Ohio State University, 1981.

Index